BESTSELLING BOOK SERIES

Buying a Property Eastern Europe For Dum

NORWAY
SWEDEN
Tallinn
ESTONIA
RUSSIA
Riga
LATVIA
DENMARK
Baltic Sea
LITHUANIA
Vilnius
RUSSIA
Gdansk
BELARUS
Poznan
Warsaw
GERMANY
POLAND
Kiev
Karlovy Vary (Carlsbad)
Prague
Krakow
Lvov
UKRAINE
CZECH REPUBLIC
SLOVAKIA
Bratislava
Danube
DANUBE VALLEY
Budapest
MOLDOVA
Odessa
AUSTRIA
HUNGARY
Maribor
Lake Balaton
Ljubljana
SLOVENIA
Zagreb
CROATIA
ROMANIA
Sevastopol
Belgrade
Bucharest
Constanta
Black Sea
BOSNIA AND HERZEGOVINA
Varna
Samsun
Split
YUGOSLAVIA
BULGARIA
Sofiya
Plovdiv
ITALY
Adriatic Sea
Dubrovnik
Bansko
Istanbul
MACEDONIA
ALBANIA
TURKEY
Tyrrhenian Sea
GREECE
Aegean Sea
Ionian Sea
Bodrum
Antalya
SICILY
Nicosia
CYPRUS
Mediterranean Sea
CRETE
MALTA

For Dummies: Bestselling Book Series for Beginners

Buying a Property in Eastern Europe For Dummies® Cheat Sheet

Researching the Market

- **Research pays dividends.** Save days of time and hundreds if not thousands of pounds by narrowing down your choice of desirable countries and areas within those countries to a short list of two or three before dusting down your passport. Start your research by reading this book!
- **Decide your budget.** Build in costs of around ten per cent above the cost of the property itself to pay for legal fees, local property taxes, and surveys.
- **Consider your appetite for risk.** Some overseas property markets are riskier than others; if investing a smaller proportion of your wealth, you may decide on a riskier country to buy in, or plump for a safer country if you're investing a heftier sum.
- **Check out the tax position if escaping taxes is a primary goal.** It *is* possible to pay lower taxes on your income abroad than in your home country, and it may even be possible to legally avoid paying tax on the gain you make when selling a second property, but an awful lot of misinformation surrounds the possible tax benefits of owning a property overseas. Check your options at an early stage.

Deciding on a Country

- **Climate matters.** Or at least it does to some buyers. You need to decide what you want in terms of climate, sun, and snow, which depends on your own personal reasons for buying abroad.
- **Living costs and living standards.** No country in this book is as expensive to live in as the UK, but you won't necessarily find a museum, a cinema with English films, a reasonable choice of restaurants, pleasing buildings, good roads, street lighting, or perhaps even regular refuse collection. If you are self contained this may not matter to you, but if you're more socially minded you may find it worth trading up to a higher cost and higher quality of living.
- **Cultural fit.** You need to decide to what extent you want, need, or indeed can integrate. If you are principally interested in an investment overseen by a property manager, this factor is not as important as if you hope to live in or retire to your new property.

Finding the Right Property

- **Value.** If you intend to live in the property, buy the one you like the most. If you plan to rent or resell, buy something that appeals to local as well as international buyers.
- **Neighbourhood.** Never buy a property without spending at least a few days living in the immediate neighbourhood. Ideally you should go back to the area in each of the seasons that are of importance to you.
- **Check out the property, its access, and grounds.** Where surveys are required, they are often only valuation surveys for the mortgage lender. But always get a full survey carried out before you buy, ensuring any defects are put right before completing the purchase.

Buying a Property in Eastern Europe FOR DUMMIES®

Buying a Property in Eastern Europe FOR DUMMIES®

by Colin Barrow

JOHN WILEY & SONS, LTD

Buying a Property in Eastern Europe For Dummies®

Published by
John Wiley & Sons, Ltd
The Atrium
Southern Gate
Chichester
West Sussex
PO19 8SQ
England

E-mail (for orders and customer service enquires): cs-books@wiley.co.uk

Visit our Home Page on www.wileyeurope.com

Published by John Wiley & Sons, Ltd, Chichester, West Sussex

British Library Cataloguing in Publication Data: A catalogue record for this book is available from the British Library.

ISBN-13: 978-0-7645-7047-6

ISBN-10: 0-7645-7047-1

Printed and bound in Great Britain by Bell and Bain Ltd, Glasgow

10 9 8 7 6 5 4 3 2 1

About the Author

Colin Barrow has an extensive background in European property and works across a diverse range of related industries. He has researched most international property markets and has first hand experience of buying, building, developing, and selling over two hundred properties in overseas markets. He has written a score of books on property and other wealth creation matters including the bestselling *Starting a Business For Dummies*.

Author's Acknowledgements

I would like to thank Jason Dunne, Samantha Clapp, and Martin Tribe for the opportunity to write this book – as well as their help, encouragement, guidance, and sound advice on what to omit as much as what to include; an inevitable problem when such a wide landscape as the European property market has to be distilled to its essence. Their tireless work, and that of everyone else who works behind the scenes at Wiley, have both my gratitude and admiration for their efforts in making this book possible as well as punctual.

Outside of the team at Wiley, Jane Hoskyn helped with the structure for the country chapters and Brian Kramer did the rewriting and development that contributed much to bringing some dry facts to life. The technical reviewer kept me up to the mark and added greatly to my knowledge as the book developed. He has my thanks and ultimately yours too for ensuring the accuracy of the thousands of facts that go to making up and appreciation of these markets.

Not withstanding the many people who deserve and have my gratitude any faults or failings in the text remain mine and mine alone. I would certainly appreciate your feedback as you travel the path that I have taken around what has become known as 'New Europe'. Any tips, pointers and advice that can be incorporated into future editions would be a service to future readers. [e-mail: colin_barrow@msn.com]

Publisher's Acknowledgements

We're proud of this book; please send us your comments through our Dummies online registration form located at www.dummies.com/register/.

Some of the people who helped bring this book to market include the following:

Acquisitions, Editorial, and Media Development

Executive Project Editor: Martin Tribe

Content Editor: Steve Edwards

Commissioning Editor: Samantha Clapp

Development Editor: Brian Kramer

Copy Editor: Sally Lansdell

Proofreader: Colette Holden

Technical Editor: Dr Andrew Cartwright, Central European University, Budapest

Executive Editor: Jason Dunne

Cover Photo: © Nik Wheeler/CORBIS

Cartoons: Ed McLachlan

Composition Services

Project Coordinator: Jennifer Theriot

Layout and Graphics: Carl Byers, Stephanie D. Jumper, Julie Trippetti

Proofreaders: Laura Albert, Susan Moritz, Charles Spencer

Indexer: Techbooks

Publishing and Editorial for Consumer Dummies

Diane Graves Steele, Vice President and Publisher, Consumer Dummies

Joyce Pepple, Acquisitions Director, Consumer Dummies

Kristin A. Cocks, Product Development Director, Consumer Dummies

Michael Spring, Vice President and Publisher, Travel

Kelly Regan, Editorial Director, Travel

Publishing for Technology Dummies

Andy Cummings, Vice President and Publisher, Dummies Technology/General User

Composition Services

Gerry Fahey, Vice President of Production Services

Debbie Stailey, Director of Composition Services

Contents at a Glance

Table of Contents

Introduction

Welcome to *Buying a Property in Eastern Europe For Dummies*! You can certainly find gold in them there hills of Central and Eastern Europe. In addition to gold, early investors in the market have located comfortable seaside villas, ski chalets, and city-centre apartments – at prices not seen in the UK, France, or Spain for more than a generation.

Rather than getting to know Central and Eastern Europe through this book, you could just look on a few Web sites, call a couple of brokers, hop on a budget flight, inspect a handful of properties, and be home for dinner – all in the same day. But anyone following this strategy is behaving as one broker I interviewed predicts. He claims that two-thirds of people buying property in Eastern Europe make two mistakes: They take their credit cards with them, and they leave their brains at home.

Buying a property in this market has never been easier – a fact that has both positive and negative aspects. For a deposit of €500 (£343), you can be fully committed to a very large purchase. If you don't completely research an investment, you have a better than even chance of purchasing a property that ends up giving you little pleasure or value and plenty of pain and problems.

Buying a Property in Eastern Europe For Dummies maps out a path through the dangers and pitfalls that can ensnare the unwary. Reading this book puts you on track to find a fantastic-value home for as little as €5000 (£3430) and helps you set a course to build a property portfolio involving less cash than you probably have tied up in your home right now.

About This Book

Buying a property in any market requires you to have at least an appreciation of the legal matters concerning ownership, be able to appraise a property's physical condition, know something of financing options, and have an informed view about value.

Much of Eastern Europe is in the early stages of shifting from a black-market economy to a market economy, so getting a handle on value is difficult. This book considers many factors relevant to value, including each nation's economy, currency, government, tourism industry, multinational inward investment, and even budget airline options. These are all factors that influence whether a country is a pleasure to visit and has a well-founded property market, something that few of the countries covered in this book have at present. The book also explains how to make sense of all these economic factors as well as giving an appreciation of the culture, climate, and leisure opportunities in each country.

The information comes in a light, easy-to-access format. Anything to do with money is always a serious matter, but this book can help you keep a sense of humour – and your sanity – as you unravel the mysteries of these new property markets.

Please be advised that travel information, prices and exchange rates are subject to change at any time. Write or call ahead for confirmation when making your travel plans.

Conventions Used in This Book

To help you navigate through this book, I follow a few conventions:

- *Italic* is used for foreign words and whenever I introduce a new term.
- `Monofont` is used for Web addresses.

What You're Not to Read

I have written this book in a way that helps you find the facts easily and understand what you find. You may discover more information than you need to digest all at one sitting. Some information, although interesting and related to the topic at hand, may not be essential for you to know from the outset. You can scoop the following bits of text on to a plate for later:

- **Text in sidebars.** Sidebars are shaded boxes that appear here and there throughout the chapters. Some share personal stories and observations; others give another slant on the topic. All are interesting (of course!), but they aren't necessary reading.
- **Anything with a Technical Stuff icon attached.** Again, this information is interesting but not critical to your understanding of the subject. You can return to any of this material later, after you decide, for example, that a particular country is worthy of closer scrutiny.

Foolish Assumptions

In this book I make some general assumptions about who you are. If none of these strikes a chord with you, take care not to mark any pages or damage the cover in any way and put the book aside in your drawer for next year's Christmas presents.

- **You are aspiring to get on to the property ladder in the UK but are finding that the first rung is still out of reach.** In which case, you may find this book helpful in finding a way to start building up property equity elsewhere, returning later with enough of a war chest to get into the UK market.
- **You've read in the press, seen on television, or heard from friends and colleagues about the 'hot' Eastern European property market.** This book helps you pick through the market and find the places that, while hot, are not too hot to handle.
- **You are looking ahead to retiring and want to find somewhere where your pension goes a little further.** This book helps you find places where a standard British pension is still more than double the average wage, rather than a quarter as it is in the UK.
- **You are considering entering or are already in the buy-to-let or holiday cottage market.** This book helps you identify markets where the rental yields are at least twice that being achieved in the UK.
- **You already have some expertise in the property field and want easy-to-find information that can help you apply that to the Eastern European market.** This book shows you how to turn knowledge about property into income.

How This Book Is Organised

Buying a Property in Eastern Europe For Dummies is organised in five parts. The chapters within each part cover specific topic areas in more detail, so you can easily and quickly scan a topic that interests you – or troubleshoot an area that is of current concern.

Part I: Getting Prepared

Property is perhaps the only investment where you can borrow other people's money to make money of your own. As long as you make sound financial decisions, the more money you borrow the more money you can potentially make. But the sting in that sentence is in the word 'potentially'. Buying property in Eastern Europe is more risky than buying in more established overseas markets. This part helps you figure out what those risks are, if you are willing to take them, and what the rewards may be.

Part II: Examining the New Europeans

Back in May 2004, the European Union (EU) acquired a whole new raft of members. In the lead-up to membership, all these countries were encouraged and cajoled to lick their economies into shape, encourage democracy, strengthen their judiciary, and open up their hitherto introspective countries to investment from more developed economies. Since joining the EU, all the new additions have seen stunning economic growth and meteoric interest from multinational companies, tourists, and foreigners coming to look at and buy property. One of the pre-conditions for membership of the EU is that restrictions on foreigners buying property are lifted, and now EU citizens by and large have equal ownership rights with nationals of these countries.

In this part, I examine each of the new EU members, probing the nature of their economies, their prospects for development, and the likely impact of these and other factors on local property markets, for growth in both value and rental yields. I also look at everyday life, culture, travel, and healthcare, as well as identifying key professionals who can help you find, buy, and, if needed, renovate your property.

Part III: Reviewing the Hopefuls

The magic wand that waved over the new Europeans has already begun to work wonders for its property market. Thousands of foreigners, mainly from the UK, Ireland, the Netherlands, and Germany, have already bought properties in the first group of EU entrants and have had rewarding experiences. Now they and others are casting an eye further afield in the hope of getting in earlier and seeing even greater value.

The countries that are 'hopeful' are in varying degrees of readiness for EU membership, but each already has the first green shoots of economic wellbeing. These countries are experiencing rapid growth in the wealth of their citizens and thriving mortgage markets, which although only a couple of years old mean that the locals can afford to buy new properties. (Any property market that is not underpinned by a strong demand from its citizens is unlikely to be anything better than a speculative risk rather than a calculated investment.)

In this part, I examine each of the hopefuls, evaluating them in all the ways in which I explore the recently established EU member countries in the preceding part.

Part IV: Getting Comfortable

Finding a property is just part of the process. You have a whole host of other factors to consider. How should you pay for the property? Who should own it – you personally, or should you set up a company? Should you move your tax affairs to your new country, and what happens if and when you come back to the UK? And how should you go about learning the language, setting up a bank account, drawing your British pension, and educating your kids? In this part, I cover all these important questions.

I also explore your prospects of getting rental income from your properties at home and abroad, how to find tenants, and how much money you can realistically make if you do decide to go into the rental business.

Part V: The Part of Tens

In two concise chapters I give some of my best tips, the little jewels that can make the difference between merely surviving and prospering in the Eastern European property market. One chapter covers the ten people you must talk to before making a property purchase. and the other chapter offers some practical ideas for making some additional income by using your skills and experience.

Icons Used in This Book

Like all *For Dummies* books, this one includes helpful icons sprinkled throughout the text. The following interprets the icons I use in this book:

This icon calls your attention to particularly important points and offers useful advice on practical topics.

This icon serves as a friendly reminder that the topic in hand is important enough for you to make a note of it.

This icon tells you that I'm using a practical, real-world example showing how another investor has tackled a particular topic. You can apply the example to your own property-purchasing process.

This icon alerts you to a potential danger. Proceed with caution – look left and right before crossing. In fact, think carefully about crossing at all when you see this icon.

This icon refers to specialised business facts and data, which are interesting as background data and can help you build your understanding of Eastern and Central European property markets.

Where to Go from Here

This book is organised so you can go wherever you want. If you have found a property you want to buy and just want to see how you can finance it, go straight to Chapter 17. If you have only thought of property as your home and want to see why you should consider property as an investment, head for Chapter 1. If you are already convinced that property is a great investment but are not sure whether right now is the time to buy, check out Chapter 2, where I look at property cycles. If you have a particular country in mind or want to begin exploring your options in Eastern and Central Europe, skip forward to Parts II and III.

The table of contents shows you where to find broad categories of information, and the index helps you put your finger on more specific topics. If you're not sure where to start, turn the page and jump into Part I, where you find everything you need to give you a flavour of the property markets in general and Eastern Europe in particular.

Part I
Getting Prepared

"Jeffrey — I've got something to tell you . . ."

In this part . . .

Before you can think seriously about buying a home abroad you need to make sure you are ready for the big step. This part will let you see how the property market really works and help you be confident about timing. You can also check out your attitude to risk and see how going into the property market in one of these countries stacks up against the financial resources you want to commit to the project and the potential gain, both in enjoyment and cash that you could get in return. You will be able to get a good idea about the country, its property market and the people who can help you make the best possible decision. Once the groundwork is done you can start turning your intangible ideas into a more concrete plan and make a shortlist of the countries and areas within those countries that appeal to you the most.

Chapter 1

Taking the Plunge: Choosing to Buy Property

In This Chapter

- Exploring the returns that property really makes
- Developing a diverse investment portfolio
- Appreciating the European Union's ability to spur the property market
- Identifying bargain property markets of the near future
- Getting to your chosen country by plane, train, and coach

Property has been a worthwhile source of wealth for generations. More private individuals have become millionaires by investing in property than by any other route to wealth. Research shows that most people who achieve a comfortable retirement make property – often both in their home country and overseas – a large element within their financial portfolios.

Property is an appealing investment for private investors as well as financial institutions. Banks and other lending organisations back a property investment as a matter of course rather than requiring extensive persuasion to extend funds, as for other wealth-creating activities, such as starting your own business. And with that borrowed money, you can acquire an asset 10 or even 20 times the value of the ready cash you have to hand (see the section 'Understanding the gearing effect' later in this chapter for more information). So as a property investor, you enjoy a growth in value of the whole asset for just a fractional downpayment.

The spur to the next wave of property millionaires is undoubtedly the extension of the European Union (EU), which is opening up vast new tracts of Europe. Countries that until recently placed restrictions on foreigners owning property or staying for extended periods have removed these limits in order to gain EU membership. As a consequence, for the first time in several generations, citizens of one EU country can buy property in a score of other countries that were previously off limits.

Not only can you buy property, but also this property is available at prices a fraction of those currently available in the British market. Investors who, until now, have found getting a foot on the property ladder or building a property portfolio near impossible now find an escalator in front of them.

This chapter explores the power and possibilities of investing in property in general, as well as some of the specific rewards – and, yes, risks – of buying in Eastern and Central Europe.

Exchange rates vary daily, sometimes even hourly. Many websites offer up-to-date exchange rates. Try `www.xe.com`, `www.oanda.com/convert/classic` or `www.onlinefx.co.uk`.

Buying More Property

You probably already own a property, most likely in the UK. Like around three-quarters of a million Brits, you may even own a second home in the UK or abroad. If you bought your property three or more years ago, you may already be sitting on a sizeable profit. This success in itself may be enough of a spur for you to look carefully at buying one or two more properties.

Property is not only a good investment; it is also potentially the best investment pound for pound you can make. Plus, if you add in the fun factor, the chance to see pastures new, and the fact that more people become millionaires in this way than any other, you have every reason to look carefully at adding more properties to your financial portfolio.

The following sections explore the multifaceted appeal of owning property.

Appreciating property as an investment

Any sound investment meets four criteria:

- **The investment has the capacity for being profitable.** This doesn't mean an investment *has* to be profitable – just that it *can* be. Of course, anything to do with making money involves risk – events sometimes just don't pan out as expected. Still, an investment always has the potential to be profitable. For a vivid example of a purchase that has little to no capacity for being profitable, consider what happens to your money when you buy a new car. The day you drive your car from the showroom, its value drops by up to 20 per cent and within a year it may be worth as little as half its cost. This fact doesn't seem to deter nearly 2.5 million people a year buying new cars in the UK, but almost no car purchase even remotely qualifies as an investment.

- **The investment is reasonably secure.** In other words, the money you put into an investment should generate value for you, a customer, and/or a market. Pyramid sales schemes are a good example of 'investments' that fail this test, because most of the money people can potentially make comes from recruiting more salespeople rather than selling any real product.
- **The investment has a ready second-hand market.** You need to be able to get out of – as well as get into – investments, because you may need your money for some other purpose. You also may have spotted an even better investment.
- **The investment has the capacity to produce cash flow during its life as well as grow in value.** Wine, art, and jewellery don't meet this criterion, but that's not to say you shouldn't buy them – just as buying a new car isn't wrong if that is how you want to spend your money. By contrast, stocks, bonds, bank deposits, and property are all able to produce a stream of cash during the time you own them.

Understanding the gearing effect

If you were a high-flying sales executive who had pocketed a £20,000 bonus in 2002 and put it in the stock market across a spread of shares to track the market average, you would have made a hefty 74.5 per cent return by 2005. Your realised investment would be a cash pile of £34,900. According to the Nationwide Building Society, if you had invested in property over the same period, you would have made just 36.92 per cent. In fact, if you go back as far as 1973, stock-market returns average 11 per cent while property delivered 9 per cent.

Looks like the stock market is a better investment, at least in recent years, you may be saying. But before you toss this book aside and back out of the property market, consider how the deals work out in reality.

In 2002, no properties were on the market for £20,000, and the average house price was around £150,000. Of course, you could have bought an average property using the £20,000 as a deposit and got a loan or mortgage for the balance of £130,000. (Incidently, property is the *only* type of investment where you can borrow to buy without offering any other collateral.) According to the Nationwide records, the £150,000 house you purchased in 2002 would be worth £205,380 in 2005. You would have paid out £7,800 a year in interest at 6 per cent to whoever lent you the £130,000, a total of £23,400. So you are a net £181,980 (£205,380 – £23,400) better off than you were back in 2002. You are also more than five times better off in buying a property (£181,980 divided by £34,900) than you would have been if you'd gone into the stock market.

The magic that turns a seemingly lower total return over three years (36.92 per cent for property versus 74.5 per cent in the stock markets) into a much higher return of 108.77 per cent a year is known as *gearing*. Gearing works in much the same way as the gears on your car. Changing up the gears enables you to go faster for any given amount of power. When you buy a property using borrowed money, you enjoy all the increase in value but have to put down only a fraction of the cost at the outset. Simply put, over a three-year period, you get a return of 36.92 per cent on money that cost only 6 per cent (the average mortgage rate).

To work out an investment return yourself, use a compound interest calculator. Simply supply a property value, time period, and interest rate. A free calculator is available online at 1278 Software Systems (`www.1728.com/compint.htm`).

Getting pleasure from your property investment

One thing is for sure: Even if you believe in holding stocks and shares, and I certainly do, you can't sleep in these investments like you can with property. Nor can you invite people round or have family and friends to stop over. If you are a do-it-yourself expert or gardener, you can even add value to your property while getting a kick out of doing some of your favourite activities.

In fact, you can do absolutely nothing with stocks and shares – except file the paperwork. Today, most stock-market investors buy into mutual funds that hold hundreds, perhaps even thousands, of shares in an anoymous bundle, so you can't even get the satisfaction of claiming to own a bit of this or that company and take pleasure in its progress.

A caveat is necessary here, in case this sounds too much like a sales pitch for property at the expense of shares and other forms of investment. You can have too much of a good thing. With investments, the key to success is to have a *balanced portfolio.* Smart people spread their money round a number of different types of assets, which reduces the consequences if one area goes down sharply. You need to be more than unlucky to see every type of investment fall out of the sky at the same time.

Choosing to Buy Abroad

The two most compelling arguments for owning property outside of the UK are diversification and reward.

The foreign markets I cover in this book are, without a doubt, more risky than investing in property in the British market. I would go further and say that these markets are definitely not 'widows and orphans' investments, a term that financial advisers use to describe an extremely safe investment.

While risk is not in itself a guarantor of profits, it is one of the conditions that helps create a climate in which profits can be made. Think of risk this way: No one will take your bet on a horse race after the race begins. Instead, you need to assess the uncertainties *beforehand* – What are the conditions? Will all the horses show up? How well trained are the horses? Who are the jockeys – and make your best bet.

Having all your eggs in one basket is never a good idea. Even if you decide after reading this book to keep your property investments in the UK, you are safer if you spread your bets by having property in different parts of Britain – and perhaps even different types of property such as shops, offices, and warehouses.

Higher potential rewards

According to *The Economist* magazine's Global House Price Index, the British property market has given the world a good run for its money. From 1997 to 2005, it stacked up a 155 per cent gain, more than all but three of the 20 countries in the index and much better than the average of 80 per cent clocked up by the whole of the market under study.

This fact may sound like a compelling reason for staying at home, until you look a little more closely at the figures. If you consider 2005 figures, growth in property prices in the UK is the fifth slowest in the developed world, and the average growth rate of all nations in the index is four times that achieved by British properties. In fact, the fastest-growing markets have been those overseas markets that the Brits have been buying into strongly.

Of course, as the fine print for all good investments notes, the past is not always a guide to future performance. But it does seem highly unlikely that mature markets such as the UK, France, and Spain, which foreigners have already researched and bought into for decades, can deliver the growth in value that the hidden gems of Eastern and Central Europe have to offer. For example, properties in some areas of Croatia, Lithuania, and Poland at the time of writing are increasing in value by between 15 and 50 per cent a year, whilst in the UK prices are increasing by 2 or 3 per cent – and in some areas of the country they are static. The price trends for each market and key areas within each country are given in the country chapters of this book.

Higher and different risks

If one side of the coin is the potential for higher profits from investing in Eastern and Central Europe, the other side has a warning of danger ahead. Overseas property markets carry all the usual risks of property investments – plus the adverse effects of rises in interest rates, growth in unemployement, and a decline in the economic wellbeing of the population.

And Central and Eastern European nations carry a few more risks:

- **None of the countries in this book uses sterling as its currency.** That means that changes in exchange rates can reduce, eliminate, or (possibly) enhance your profit in terms of pounds returned. Currency changes can be violent and are rarely predictable. I cover this topic in Chapter 4.
- **Many of the countries in this book have only the most limited experience of being functioning market economies.** A *functioning market economy* is the EU's term for nations that use market forces, rather than a centralised command system such as those favoured by the Soviets, to determine economic conditions.
- **Few countries featured in the book have had more than a handful of elected governments in their entire history.** In many cases, land ownership is at best in dispute and at worst still mired in conflicts barely a decade in the past. Even in countries where land titles are reasonably certain, buyers and sellers are often pressured to declare illegally low purchase prices. (I cover this in Chapter 4.)

I cover other very real risks in each of the country chapters throughout Parts II and III in order to give you some idea of the size and scope of specific risks. I also offer suggestions for how you can counter these risks.

Deciding to Invest inside – or outside – the European Union

Europe had been in turmoil for centuries before the Romans had a first shot at installing the rule of law and something approaching peace across its borders. The fall of the Roman Empire put an end to a tenuous peace, and in the coming centuries Britain, France, Germany, Austria, and assorted allies slugged it out in battles for territory.

Along the way, some war-weary souls offered tentative solutions to foster peace. In 1728, Abbot Charles de Saint-Pierre, a French social philosopher, proposed creating a European league of 18 counties, with a common treasury, no borders, and an economic union. In the 1800s, Napoleon took a slightly different approach to unifying Europe with his ideas for a 'Customs Union', as did Hitler a century or so later with plans for a European Confederation, both to be imposed by force.

After the disasters of two world wars in barely a generation, politicians finally set themselves the goal of ensuring that Europeans never fought each other again. Winston Churchill, in a speech in Zurich in 1946, called for the establishment of a 'United States of Europe', but the responsibility of taking the idea further fell to French and German leaders. Starting with six members in 1951 and the limited goal of pooling the steel and coal resources of the member states, the European Union, as it eventually became known, expanded by stages to its current membership of 25 countries. The EU has extended its role from cooperation in a handful of natural resources to the management of the day-to-day lives of 350 million people.

Creating the EU has given Europe the longest period of peace and prosperity in its history. From the perspective of property ownership, the EU has had an absolutely profound effect. By allowing the free movement of European citizens and their right to live, work, and retire anywhere, the EU has opened up a property market that was until recently largely restricted to the nationals of each country. Member countries must grant the citizens of other member states the same property rights as for their own citizens. This requirement is gradually sweeping away restrictions on foreigners not being allowed to own certain types or amounts of land.

Exploring the new Europe

The EU began in 1951, and the UK, Ireland, and Demark joined in 1973. Over the next two decades, Spain, Portugal, Austria, Sweden, Finland, and Greece signed up, leaving only Iceland, Liechtenstein, Norway, and Switzerland of the European countries not kept behind the Soviet Iron Curtain outside the EU.

But in May 2004, Estonia, Latvia, Lithuania, Poland, the Czech Republic, Hungary, Slovakia, Slovenia, Malta, and Cyprus became members. (See Part II for coverage of all of these countries.) The significance of this expansion is profound, as it swept away the last vestiges of Soviet influence in Europe. The May 2004 expansion was the largest in terms of numbers of countries and their combined population of 75 million, adding roughly a quarter to the total population of the EU.

But for property buyers, the significance of Central and Eastern European nations joining the EU lies in a different set of numbers.

- The 10 new countries had a combined wealth roughly equal to that of Spain, itself far from being one of the most affluent members.
- The average wages in the new countries were less than a fifth of those in *old Europe*, as earlier EU members have become known.
- Average property prices were similarly low, thus creating an unprecedented opportunity for people in the more wealthy European countries to buy houses at prices not seen in their own markets for, in many cases, several decades.

Anticipating the next wave

The EU, having barely digested the 10 newest members, is set on expanding still further. Romania and Bulgaria have been given a date of 1 January 2007 for full membership, though at the time of writing there is some discussion about putting the date out by a year to bring their political and economic structures more in line with mainstream Europe. Romania and Bulgaria are much poorer than even the poorest member states that joined in 2004. Questions linger over their legal systems, border security, and food safety. For information on Bulgaria, turn to Chapter 12.

Beyond 2007, Croatia, Turkey, and Ukraine have also begun discussions on EU membership. Any of these, in principle, may become a member at some indeterminate date in the future, provided that it meets criteria.

- Croatia, already geographically at the heart of Europe, seems to be moving quickly towards EU membership. Its coastline, long a holiday destination for affluent Europeans, has one of the strongest economies in the region, and interest in property is already strong from near neighbours such as Italy and Austria. Significant problems remain, as the title to some properties is far from secure due to the legacy of ethnic cleansing during the Yugoslav break-up. I cover Croatia in greater detail in Chapter 13.
- Turkey's membership prospects are being debated at great length, and membership may be decades rather than a year or two away. This fact should not deter Turkey from enjoying many of the benefits of prospective EU membership, particularly growth in inward investment by businesses. It is has a strong economy, and its trading relationships with potential new members such as Bulgaria and Romania are strong. I explore investment options in Turkey in Chapter 15.

- Ukraine is a very different proposition. It has not begun formal talks on joining the EU. However, Ukrainian president Viktor Yushchenko claims that his strategic goal is to join the EU while improving relations with neighbouring Russia. So far the EU has been offering the carrot of membership to pry Ukraine away from the Russian camp. Some big players are backing Ukraine's chances of becoming a successful member one day. For example, in 2006 Mittal Steel Co., the world's biggest steel company, bought Ukraine's VAT Kryvorizhstal for $4.8 billion and Vienna-based Raiffeisen International Bank-Holding AG bought Ukrainian Bank Aval for $1 billion. Ukraine (see Chapter 16) is perhaps the riskiest property market that I cover in this book, but Odessa, Yalta, and its Black Sea coast resorts have much to offer.

Getting There

There are many ways to get to your chosen country. Here's a list of a few to get you started.

Airlines that fly between the UK and many of the countries described in this book include the following:

- British Airways (0870-850-9850; www.ba.com)
- easyJet (0905-821-0905; www.easyjet.com)
- Jet 2 (0871-226-1737; www.jet2.com)
- Ryanair (0906-270-5656; www.ryanair.com)
- Sky Europe (0905-7222-747; www.skyeurope.com)
- Thomsonfly (0870-165-0079; www.thomsonfly.com).
- Wizzair (+48-22-351-9499; www.wizzair.com)

The Man in Seat Sixty-One Web site (www.seat61.com) has stacks of info on rail travel, both to and within the countries I describe in this book. Deutsche Bahn's UK office (0870-243-5363) and European Rail (020-7387-0444) can issue tickets for rail travel to most the countries in this book.

Eurolines (0870-514-3219; www.nationalexpress.com/eurolines) runs coach services between the UK and most of the countries I discuss in this book.

Chapter 2

Deciding to Buy in Eastern and Central Europe

In This Chapter

- Getting to grips with the property market
- Seeing what is different about Eastern and Central Europe
- Spotting economic trends
- Appreciating property value

The property market moves in a different way from the stock market. In the last couple of major stock-market busts, property prices hardly moved. The reasons for property's solidity include negatives such as the fact that a property is harder to sell than a share, and positives such as people's greater confidence in physical assets than in concepts and ideas such as those being floated around during the high-tech bubble of 1999.

The reasons for property being less volatile than shares don't matter half as much as whether you understand how the property market itself works. The property market is certainly cyclical, and it provides a few clear warning signs for peaks and troughs. This chapter helps you identify these signs – hopefully well in advance of any downfalls.

Over the next decade or so, the factors driving up property prices and rental incomes in the new European economies look strong. In the following sections I explore the most compelling reasons to consider investing in the property markets of Eastern and Central Europe.

Understanding Property Markets: A Beginner's Guide

Generally the *property market* is split into two main sub-groups – residential property and commercial property (which includes retail outlets, factories, warehouses, offices, and the like). Economic theory suggests that these two markets behave differently and are driven by different factors.

Residential property is largely owner occupied. Even in the UK after a decade of buy-to-let activity, only 10 per cent of the housing stock is in the hands of landlords, whose prime interest is renting out their properties and hoping for capital growth. Of the remainder, 20 per cent is in the hands of councils and 70 per cent owner-occupiers.

The factors that cause house prices to rise in this market include the usual suspects, in somewhat simplified form:

- **Supply:** Prices tend to go up when too few new properties are being built, perhaps because of planning constraints.
- **Demand:** Prices tend to rise when employment is reasonably full, wages are rising, interest rates are low, and the population is expanding (from an increase in the birth rate, more immigrants arriving, or households fragmenting through divorce). The key ratio here is affordability. When mortgage repayments exceed five times salary, house prices may be constrained; below three times salary, and people feel they can afford to splash out a bit more.

In many ways, commercial property is the mirror image of residential property. Only 10 per cent of commercial property is in family ownership (a boss or his or her family owning a shop, factory, or office, for example). The remaining 90 per cent is owned by institutional investors whose primary goals are to diversify their portfolios so that they are not over-dependent on the stock market and to get a satisfactory and rising rental yield.

Institutional investors have deep pockets and hold their property portfolios for decades. What drives up property prices in the commercial sector is rental yield – and that has more to do with the general health of the economy, including strong economic growth, plenty of inward investment from overseas companies eager to set up in the country, and a healthy balance of trade. When the economy is expanding, consumers are spending plenty of money and businesses are buoyant, the rental yield, expressed as a percentage of the value of the property starts to rise (£5000 rent for a property that cost £100,000 is a 5 per cent yield).

- **Supply:** Prices tend to go up when too few new offices, shops, and warehouses are being built, perhaps because of planning constraints.
- **Demand:** Prices tend to rise when the economy is expanding, consumers are spending rather than saving, and new businesses are being set up at a faster rate than before. The key factor for businesses is to get their facilities set up as quickly as possible to take advantage of an expanding market. Rather than get left behind, or leave room for a competitor to expand, a business is likely to pay a bit more to get a property *now*, rather than wait for prices to stabilise or decline.

You can track British commercial property yield and growth on the Investment Property Web site (`www.ipdindex.co.uk`). You can track British residential property on the Nationwide Building Society House Price Index Web site (`www.nationwide.co.uk/hpi`).

Overseas property, such as apartments and houses, is a hybrid of residential and commercial property markets. On the one hand, overseas property is a residential product bought for, at least in part, a commercial purpose – to rent and eventually sell for a profit. As a buyer of overseas property for your own use, you are mostly concerned with the set of factors that apply to residential property. But if your interest is primarily in getting a good rental yield while your property's value steadily rises over the long term, then the factors related to commercial property matter more.

While all these factors do affect property markets, they are not easily distilled into advice that you can use yourself. In the following sections, I set out some practical ways for you to begin to get a handle on the markets you are looking at.

Watching the cycles

Any economy follows a cyclical pattern that moves from *boom*, when demand is strong, to *slump* – economists' shorthand for a downturn. This is the theoretical *textbook cycle*.

Four phases typically occur in each textbook cycle:

- **U1**, where demand is picking up and toeing the line of the long-term trend.
- **U2**, where demand exceeds the long-term trend.
- **D1**, where demand dips down to hit the long-term trend.
- **D2**, where demand slumps below the long-term trend.

Spotting a turning point

To make sound property investments, avoid buying in at the top of a cycle. Of course, this advice is easier said than done. No economic model exists that can work out the *exact* turning point for a market.

While property markets as a whole experience cycles, parts of the market lead and lag in the cycle, often by many years. For example, between December 2004 and December 2005 house prices in the north of England fell back by 2.07 per cent, while those in Northern Ireland powered ahead by 13.22 per cent, a difference of more than 15 per cent in the behaviour of one market compared with the other. For individual postcodes within the UK the differences were more marked still.

In the final analysis, all property markets are local. It doesn't matter a jot where you buy a share in a public company, in Wales or Belfast or wherever. But in terms of property, where you buy is nearly everything: Location, location, location!

Still, you can get a feel for when a local property market is becoming overheated. If prices in a particular area rise by 20 per cent a year for several years, it is hard to see how they can go on rising at that rate for several more years and still represent good value. Buyers are more likely to search out better value elsewhere, causing price rises in the area to slow down or even drop back.

The 'dinner-party test', also known as the 'taxi-driver test', is another pointer to excessive euphoria. Back in 1999, all anyone talked about was shares in Internet companies – dinner guests and taxi drivers alike. Then the Internet share-price bubble burst.

In the next section, I look at the general factors that influence the property markets in Eastern and Central Europe. Chapter 4 includes a table that helps you assess a particular country or market's potential for capital growth and yield.

Identifying factors that drive property yields and returns

The imperative that made the timing of this book so crucial is the recent enlargement of the EU – a factor that, to a greater or lesser extent, will affect all the countries in this book in the decades to come. (I review this topic in detail in the section 'Estimating the benefits of European Union membership' later in this chapter.)

Consider EU membership as a *special factor* in favour of investing in the markets I cover in this book. Special factors can be specific to a country, but they can also relate to a single area within a country. For example, Bansko in Bulgaria has come to prominence as a ski resort for a number of special reasons, including a major investment in ski infrastructure, a new highway, and a major airport. Even very local factors can have a strong positive effect on property prices in a particular area. For example, a new metro station, international school, or five-star hotel can give a spur to the property prices because these additions all increase the desirability of a location.

Aside from special factors, the following are the key *rational factors* that affect the performance of an investment in property. In each country chapter I give information on these factors and how to monitor them.

- **A growing and functioning economy:** Over the long term, the rate of growth in the economy is a measure of a country's wealth-creating ability and eventually of the wealth of the local people. The economy needs to be able to provide jobs, increased wages, and an effective banking and mortgage market to allow the local population to buy property. Locals buy more than 90 per cent of the residential property in any market, so they ultimately underpin the real prices rather than the froth. If locals can't afford their own market, prices may be getting too high.
- **Inward investment:** A country with cheap resources such as labour, land, and materials is attractive to companies based in high-cost economies, often leading these companies to relocate part of their operations. Inward investment in turn helps to make the economy prosper and provides a pool of executives from the parent company in need of good-quality accommodation.
- **Tourism:** Tourists, like inward-investing companies, bring piles of money into a country and create jobs in restaurants and hotels, among other trades. But a country must have something worth seeing or doing in order to draw in the crowds. Whatever that is, it needs to have uniqueness of some sort, because the world tourism market is highly competitive. The cost of living and availability of amenities such as theatres, museums, cinemas, golf courses, and the like are all factors to consider, as is the ability to get to and from the country easily by air, land, or sea.

  Moneycorp, a foreign exchange company, has done some research into the impact of budget airline routes on local housing prices. Its research indicates that the presence of budget airlines can lead to a huge increase in property prices – up to 60 per cent in some cases. Find budget airline routes between any two European countries or airports by using the search tool at CheapO.com (`www.cheapo.com`). For a map of many of the budget airline flights within Europe, see Flight Site (`www.flitesite.co.uk`).
- **Political stability:** There needs to be a democratically elected government and an independent and effective judiciary. Without the rule of law, property ownership is insecure and values are held in check.

- **Taxes:** When taxes are too high overall, the economy ends up moving away from being market driven to being run by bureaucrats. Property taxes in particular need to be simple to understand and aimed at making entry to and exit from the market easy.

Measuring the downside

While investors are undoubtably making fortunes in Eastern and Central Europe, a number of factors may spoil the party for you. Some of the following factors are common to every property market, but they are all more in evidence in the countries covered in this book.

- **Lack of liquidity:** By its very nature, property is not easily turned into cash – unlike shares in a public company that you can trade in seconds. In most of the markets I cover in this book, the only buyers for the types of properties that foreigners buy are other foreigners. That is because many of the developments on the market are in holiday areas rather than major centres of employment. In addition, very few of the locals have sufficient income to finance properties that are often greatly superior to those generally available in the market. You may wait months or even years to find a suitable buyer. Also, in many cases first-time buyers prefer to go for new properties because often these properties are marketed with a mortgage thrown in, making them easier to buy.
- **A rash of rogues:** In any new investment area, a number of rogues operate until sound information and professional firms get into the market. The overseas property market has its fair share of rogues, and in each country chapter I give you contact details of relevant professional bodies that can help you find experts.
- **Depressed yields:** The rental and holiday let markets in all the countries covered in this book are still in their infancy. The more successful brokers are at selling property in an area, the less likely you are to see the forecasted rental yields. In fact, take any broker's forecast of likely rental yields for properties that they are selling with a big pinch of salt. Check out a dozen properties in the area with a view to renting them yourself and see exactly which rents seem realistic. A lot of new property is coming on to these markets, and finding good tenants and maintaining high occupancy rates is a tough task. Many developers have absolutely no idea how to advise their clients to go about renting out their properties. I cover the ins and outs of renting in Chapter 19.

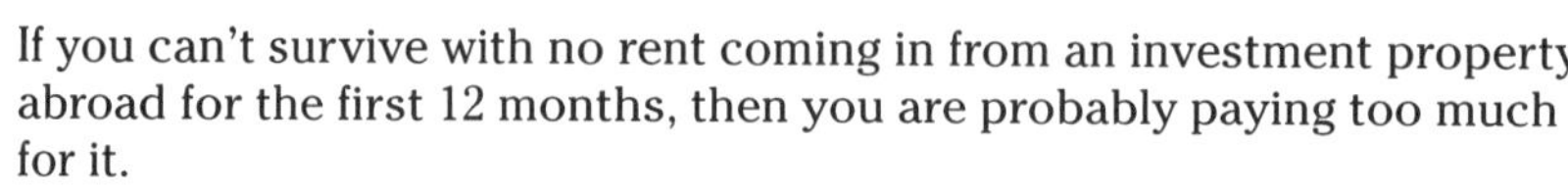

If you can't survive with no rent coming in from an investment property abroad for the first 12 months, then you are probably paying too much for it.

Beware of property investment seminars

Before you even reach the airport, you may be tempted by one breed of rogues: property investment seminars and clubs. Organisations offering seminars and clubs have sprung up claiming in their literature that they can show people how to get rich investing in properties. These schemes often offer the near certainty of building a £1 million property portfolio by signing up for a seminar that costs between £2500 and £6000. (Don't confuse these seminars with the wholly worthwhile property exhibitions and seminars that I list in Chapter 3, which can provide a valuable role in linking buyers and sellers.)

What you get for your money from the rogue seminars, according to one industry professional, is less than what you can glean in an hour on the Internet yourself visiting a few competent estate agent Web sites.

The Department of Industry took High Court action recently to close down six such schemes following an avalanche of complaints from dissatisfied clients who felt that they had been duped. The more reputable players have called on the Financial Services Authority to regulate the sector. Wait until they do!

Exploring the Appeal of Eastern and Central Europe

The world offers plenty of exciting property opportunities, so there has to be a compelling reason for narrowing down your choice to this single continent and then a relatively small part of it.

Well, the compelling case for investing in the Eastern and Central European property market lies in appreciating the impact of pent-up growth. For half a century, some of the most enterprising and talented nations in the world were held in check by an iron grip. Communism, the guiding philosophy for much of this region, marched millions of people in the wrong direction, stiffled their aspirations, and misused their abilities and resources.

Today, that is all changing with membership of the EU, the spread of democracy, and the creation of flourishing market economies. Already the signs are encouraging: Ecomonies are growing fast, and citizens who left their homes in search of opportunities abroad are returning with valuable skills and contacts. These positive trends are already being translated into a property market that is growing and profitable.

Sure, there are dangers ahead. But these dangers don't look more serious than those in any market. With care and research, you can avoid the worst pitfalls. The following sections cover the key appeal of property markets throughout Eastern and Central Europe.

A brave new world

Marco Polo, Christopher Columbus, and Sir Walter Raleigh all had one thing in common with Captain Kirk of starship *Enterprise* fame: They all boldly went where no one had been before. The first three, however, went to make their fortunes and – to varying degrees – were successful.

Individuals going early into a market have the potential to make the greatest profits. After a market becomes mature – when thousands of competitors (others in search of bargain properties) and suppliers (property developers and brokers with property to sell) exist – prices tend to stabilise. Prices that once grew at between 20 and 50 per cent a year settle back to less stratospheric levels.

Estimating the benefits of European Union membership

One way of seeing how being in the EU may benefit both the new members and those aspiring to join is to see how it has worked out for the others.

No disrespect to Ireland, but back in the 1970s the nation was an economic basket case with a stagnant economy, its biggest export being young university graduates leaving for lives abroad. Its biggest trading partner was the neighbouring UK, whose population was among the wealthiest in the world, while the Irish barely scratched a living. Yet by 2005 in terms of wealth per head, the 'Celtic Tiger', as the Irish economy had become known, was alongside that of the UK and even ahead by some measures.

The transformation came about in good measure as a result of Ireland joining the EU, which, in addition to pumping in billions of 'transitional funds', helped the Irish ecomony become more efficient and opened up a market of millions more customers to its goods. Of coure, the EU was not Ireland's only asset, but membership was one of a number of triggers that set the economy on its new and more prosperous direction. For example, its geographical position made it an ideal stepping stone for US companies into Europe.

In contrast, Bulgaria saw its population dip by a million between 1989 and 2003. The nation, not unlike Ireland's pre-EU days, is still somewhat economically backward. But therein lies the opportunity for the property investor. Table 2-1 contrasts the economies of Ireland and Bulgaria. For Ireland, you can see serious economic progress. Income per head has nearly trebled over the past 15 years, foreign companies have piled in, jobs have been created, and Irish nationals have returned. At the same time property prices soared by 196 per cent between 1997 and 2005, the highest growth rate in the developed world.

Bulgaria in contrast is only just beginning to get a whiff of the benefits of joining the EU. It has received only a fraction of the inward investment that Ireland has had, but it is early days yet. Wages are low and unemployment is high but falling, but the Bulgarian economy is now growing fast. Look at the percentage of the population in secondary education and you can see that Bulgaria's workforce is in good shape, which bodes well as intellectual capital continues to become more valuable. If Bulgaria mirrors Ireland's transformation, the coming decade may be amazing.

Table 2-1 Ireland and Bulgaria Compared, the European Union Effect Revealed

Factor	*Ireland*	*Bulgaria*
National income per head, 1990	$13,329	$2,360
National income per head, 2005	$34,280	$2,740
Unemployment, 1990	16%	25%
Unemployment, 2005	5%	18%
Average inflation, 1990–2005	4%	68%
Foreign direct investment, 1990–2005	$139 billion	$6 billion
Proportion of population in secondary education	87.5%	92.5%
Increase in house prices, 1997–2005	196%	62%

Were Ireland the only country in which the EU's magic wand had worked miracles, this argument would be less convincing. But for Portugal, Spain, and to a lesser extent Greece, the benefits have been equally convincing. And all three have acquired thriving property markets that are driven forward by enterprising foreign buyers, most of whom have come from the UK.

Enterprising Traveller

So which Brits are buying property overseas? According to *Social Trends 2005*, the British government's snapshot of what Brits are up to, more than 300,000 British citizens now own homes abroad. That figure only records individuals who chose to tell the survey that information. As no law requires you to inform anyone that you have bought a property abroad, this figure is likely to be a serious understatement. Most surveys by banks, building societies, foreign exchange specialists, and the like put the figure at around three-quarters of a million.

One thing that everyone seems to agree on is that the figure is rising fast. *Social Trends* puts the numbers buying overseas as 84 per cent up over the past decade.

Buying property in groups

The small initial outlay and easy access to low-interest finance – in the Baltic states, for example, you can find mortgage finance at 3 per cent – has meant that a new generation of budding property magnates are getting their acts together. Either singly or much more frequently in syndicates of three to five, these entrepreneurs are putting together portfolios of properties across several regions within a country and in some cases across a number of different countries.

The leverage that these groups get in buying multiple properties means that they can use their buying muscle to negotiate 10–20 per cent off the cost of any purchase. This discount is made up of a combination of a cut in the selling price from developers, reduced professional fees by sharing lawyers and surveyors, and by having more people to do the basic research and hunt out bargains.

Paying Attention to Rises in the Cost of Living

The old European economies are growing at less than 2 per cent a year. The newer economies, growing at 6 per cent, will require between 15 and 30 years for the standards and costs of living to equal out. So theoretically at least, anyone aged between 50 and 60 from the UK can expect to enjoy a lower cost of living on average in more or less any of the countries featured in this book. Additionally, these countries have the benefit of low tax strategies.

There are a couple of problems with these averages:

- If lots of foreigners move into a country, prices of certain goods and services tend to rise very quickly. Hotels, cleaners, babysitters, and restaurants are among the first sectors to see price hikes.
- International commodities such as oil and gas are priced independently of the cost structure of the country. Few of the countries covered in this book have such natural resources, so the vagaries of world markets hit hard and fast, as the Ukraine felt when the Russians imposed a 400 per cent price rise on gas in 2005.

Having said all that, it is hard to see how any of the Eastern or Central European countries in the book could become *more* expensive a place to live than the UK.

Chapter 3

Researching the Market

In This Chapter

- Planning your background research
- Exploring potential properties abroad
- Establishing what you're willing to pay for – and what you're not
- Extending and using your network of contacts
- Getting estate agents and others to do the legwork for you

Eastern and Central Europe is too big and varied a region to start looking for a property without setting some boundaries to your search.

Early on in the process, ask yourself (and your partner) probing questions to figure out exactly what you want from your new property. Your answers can save you a lot of wasted time and effort. Your responses can lead you to:

- Research specific areas to find out what they're like in different seasons, what facilities are available, and travel times to and from the UK.
- Look for estate agents in a specific region and find out property prices.
- Consider how difficult an area is to get to and from. (In the early months and years, you are likely to spend a lot of time travelling to and fro.)

All these factors and more are important parts of your research of the area. This chapter gives you strategies for conducting your research and locating houses that you can afford and that you find appealing.

Researching from Home

You will find no shortage of different types of property on the Eastern European market – from ruined farms in Bulgaria at one end of the spectrum to posh palaces in Poland at the other. Fortunately, you can discover properties by conducting research at home before ever setting foot abroad.

Unless you have a clear idea of what type of house you want and where you want it, start with wide search criteria. After you do a broad sweep, perhaps by attending an overseas property exhibition and spending a few evenings visiting Web sites, you can begin to narrow your search to a particular area and property type. Then you can head for the airport!

This section guides you through some excellent research options that you can utilise without ever leaving the comforts of home – or at least the comforts of the UK.

Attending exhibitions

You can now attend literally hundreds of exhibitions all over the UK – and indeed the world – that focus on various aspects of overseas house and property buying, including in countries in Eastern and Central Europe.

Some exhibitions focus on a particular country, such as Bulgaria, while others group together a clutch of neighbouring or similar (at least in the eye of the organiser) countries. So Hungary, the Czech Republic, Slovenia, and Croatia are often bundled together, as are Malta, Cyprus, and Turkey. Though administratively convenient, from a property buyer's perspective these countries have as much in common as chalk and cheese.

Other exhibitions, such as EMIGRATE, the Emigration Show run by Outbound Publishing, start from the supposition that attendees are planning a new life in a new country. These exhibitions typically have immigration officials on hand from a number of countries to explain the relocation procedures and to actually process applications.

At many exhibitions, you see firms specialising in building and renovation, removals, insurance, overseas mortgages, medical and health services, pet passports, and transportation. You may even be able to enjoy food and wine from the region, which adds to the overall experience of the event.

Although a useful starting point for research, exhibitions run by a single selling agent or by a particular developer showing its portfolio of properties should never be seen as the only research you need to do.

Following are some of the major overseas property exhibitions throughout the UK. In addition to these, look in the press for details of other exhibitions – more are being launched every year and many national exhibitions now run regional road shows.

- **Daily Mail Ideal Home Show** (020-8515-2000; `www.idealhomeshow.co.uk`) usually runs at Earls Court, London, in March.
- **Evening Standard Homebuyer Show** (020-8877-3636; `www.homebuyer.co.uk`) runs at ExCel, London, usually in March.

- **Homes Overseas Exhibition** (020-7939-9888; www.homesoverseas.co.uk) runs at Olympia, London, usually in March.
- **International Property Show** (01962-736-712; www.internationalpropertyshow.com) runs several times a year in London and Manchester.
- **Property Investor Show North** (020-8877-3636; www.propertyinvestor.co.uk) runs at the G-MEX Centre, Manchester, in June.
- **World Class Homes** (0800-731-4713; www.worldclasshomes.co.uk) runs local exhibitions monthly around the UK.
- **World of Property Show** (01323-745-130; www.outboundpublishing.com) is held three times a year, once in the north of England and twice in the south.
- **EMIGRATE: Emigration Show** (01323-726-040; www.outboundpublishing.com) runs at Sandown Exhibition Centre, Esher.

Aside from these major exhibitions, you can attend hundreds of smaller property shows, usually run in hotels, taking place throughout the year. Look for advertisements in local newspapers.

Using the Internet

The Internet can be a great way to find out a little about the property market in a particular area relatively quickly from the comfort of your own home. Hundreds of Web sites offer (or claim to offer) comprehensive details on property in Eastern and Central Europe.

While the Internet is a useful starting point for your research, do not consider it the end of your process.

As you search online, you're sure to encounter many sites promoting properties *off plan*, which means that building work may well not even have started and a completed apartment or villa may be years away. Often off-plan Internet sites show a convincing computer image of the property on offer and invite you to 'reserve' your villa or apartment for a mere £500, usually payable online using your credit card. You must understand that you are getting *absolutely nothing concrete* for your money and that you have little chance of recovering any investment if the property is not completed for years or – worse – never completed. (I cover the legal position on deposits in Chapter 4.)

The following Internet property sites cover most of the countries I include in this guide. However, this is not an exhaustive list; sites come and go all the time.

- **www.europerealestatedirectory.net** is a portal with links to about 60 brokers selling property throughout Europe.
- **www.oliproperties.com/oliproperties** accepts registration from any individual or agent who has property to sell or let, both residential and commercial. The site lists more then 9,000 properties in countries including Bulgaria, Croatia, Cyprus, Czech Republic, Hungary, Malta, and Turkey.
- **www.primelocation.com/international-property** was launched in 2001 by a consortium of more than 200 leading independent estate agents across the UK who wanted to be in the vanguard of online property marketing. In 2006, the company was bought by Daily Mail & General Holdings Limited as part of its further expansion into the online business sector. The site's international section carries more than 50,000 properties from estate agents in more than 40 countries, including Cyprus, Croatia, and Bulgaria. The site has a search engine for filtering property by country, price, and for sale or for rent.
- **www.propertyfinder.com/property/international** has links to 270,000 properties for sale or rent, covering all the countries in this book.
- **www.propertiesabroad.com** (which is not to be confused with the less helpful www.property-abroad.com) offers strong listings, primarily in Turkey and Cyprus, but its scope is extending fast.
- **www.property-abroad.com** is a family-run business set up by Les Calvert and features more than 28,000 properties in more than 42 countries, including Bulgaria, Croatia, Cyprus, Czech Republic, Hungary, Malta, Poland, and Turkey.
- **www.themovechannel.com** was founded in 1999 by Dan Johnson. The site started life as a simple guide to the buying procedures for residential properties in the UK, but with 200 partners it now covers buying guides and property listings for nearly 100 countries, including all the countries this book talks about. The site has an amazing filter allowing you to pre-select properties to view by a host of specialised criteria, including ski property, golf property, renovation projects, and commercial property.
- **www.remax.com** is a franchised estate agent network with 5,400 offices in more than 50 countries, including all the nations covered in this book.
- **www.viviun.com/Real_Estate/Central_and_Eastern_Europe** currently has more than 6,300 listings in countries that include Bulgaria, Croatia, Czech Republic, Estonia, Hungary, Lithuania, Poland, Slovenia, Turkey, and Ukraine.
- **www.worldrealtynews.com** carries 700 properties including those from Bulgaria, Croatia, Cyprus, Czech Republic Hungary, Malta, and Turkey.

Talking to international property agents

Almost certainly one of the first people you will come across in your property quest is an estate agent. Estate agents play a pivotal role in matching supply and demand. Despite appearing to sit between buyers and sellers in the housing supply chain, estate agents are in fact appointed by the sellers to look after their interests. Not only do sellers choose the estate agents, but also the sellers pay them, by way of a percentage of the price realised on the property.

Estate agents in Eastern European countries are usually called *brokers* and occasionally *international realtors* in countries where they think sounding American is cool.

Agents have hundreds of villas, apartments, and plots of land on their books. They also have links with dozens of other estate agents, who in turn have hundreds more properties for sale.

Getting agents to work for you

The really neat aspect of working with an estate agent is that, if you handle the process right, the agent can be working for you in your team, while being on the payroll of someone else. In other words you have a free resource. If you handle the agent right, they can take much of the sweat out of the job.

To get an estate agent on your side, utilise the following strategies:

- Only contact an estate agent after you do some initial spadework and establish a firm idea for yourself of the sort of property you're looking for. You need to appear serious in order for an agent to take you seriously.
- Keep in regular contact with the agent so you stay at the forefront of their mind. The more contact you have with the agent, the more likely he or she is to think of you first if something suitable comes on the market.
- Keep a record of your dealings with the estate agent. Record details of any telephone conversations you have with them, including who you spoke to, on what date, and what was said. This record demonstrates your professionalism and keeps the agent on his or her toes. A record can also help to avoid any disputes further down the line if something that you thought was agreed is later denied.
- Try to have the money in place *before* you start to look. Estate agents take you more seriously if they know that you are a cash buyer or at least have a 'decision in principle' from your lender that indicates you can borrow a specific sum. Also, having your money in place before working with an agent may give you the edge over other potential buyers.

- Ask lots of questions. Far from being an irritation, questions serve only to reinforce your interest in doing the deal. The questions closest to an estate agent's heart are those related to how quickly the sale can wrap up. So ask at the outset how quickly the seller wants to sell or how soon the seller can vacate the place. Make sure that this schedule fits in with your timing, but generally anything that speeds up the process and moves money into the agent's coffers more quickly endears you to him or her.

Assessing an agent's qualifications

Not every country has its own regulations, code of conduct, or professional association for estate agents and brokers. But for nations that do have such associations, stick with their members. The advantage of dealing with licensed agents is that they, like lawyers and other professionals, are regulated and you can claim against the governing body if you are dissatisfied in any way. Working with an unlicensed estate agent is more risky.

Many UK-based international estate agents have jumped on the overseas property bandwagon, some with little or no previous experience dealing in international property. Try to deal only with *established* estate agents with a strong track record in the country or countries you are most interested in.

The international professional association connected with British professionals is the Federation of Overseas Property Developers, Agents and Consultants (0870-350-1223; www.fopdac.com). Other useful resources include the Confederation of European Real Estate Agents (+31-70-345-8703; www.webcei.com) and the International Real Estate Federation (www.fiabci.com), which offers a full A–Z listing of members.

Working with a house hunter

If you can't spend much time travelling around Europe, you may consider employing the services of a person or organisation to do some of the legwork for you. *House hunter* seems to be the common descriptive term for this sort of service. They don't replace the estate agent; rather, their work is complementary. House hunters may or may not be affiliated with a specific estate agent. You want a house hunter who works with *every* estate agent so that you can be sure of getting unbiased help.

Usually house hunters ask you to fill in detailed questionnaires designed to capture your needs precisely. They then set to the task of finding properties in the area you want, at your price, and that they believe correspond to your needs. They personally visit properties, take detailed notes and photos, and send information to you for viewing before you make the trip to visit their selections.

After you're in the country, they set up viewing appointments and even accompany you on visits. If you decide to buy one of the properties, you deal directly with the estate agent. The fee structure depends on the type and level of service you decide on, but the following gives you an approximate idea of the cost range of house-hunting services:

- **Retainer fee:** €1,500–2,000 (£1,030–1,370) to search for a property to purchase or rent. You can deduct this fee from the final completion fee if your search is successful. This fee retains services for a period of usually 13 weeks.
- **Completion/success fee:** Between 1 and 2 per cent of the final purchase price, with a minimum fee payable of €7,000–10,000 (£4,800–6,800).
- **Search for rented accommodation:** Typically one month's rental fee.
- **Orientation tour:** Beginning at €1,000 (£860), this service involves taking you around a chosen region, highlighting important factors such as roads, schools, building projects, and anything that may make an area more or less attractive.
- **Area review report:** Around €400 (£275). If you can't visit an area or want an overview of several areas, house hunters can write you a report that covers much the same ground that an orientation tour provides.

Useful Web sites for locating house hunters include WNM International Property Search (07786-081-027; www.wnm-int.com), Elite and VIP (01737-366-986; www.eliteandvip.com), and Second Home (01937-590-574; www.secondhome.uk.com).

Reading papers and magazines

Almost all the British Sunday newspapers and many of the dailies have overseas property sections. The newspapers also carry articles on most aspects of living abroad, ranging from getting medical cover to pension rights and finding a mortgage. From time to time, you can also find detailed coverage of particular regions in a country. On a recent count, more than 30 Eastern and Central European properties were for sale in British newspapers in most months. You can also find a number of glossy magazines that tend to feature new resorts, often adjacent to ski resorts, golf courses, or marinas.

Make the following papers and magazines part of your regular reading list while researching the property market:

- *Dalton's Weekly* is available as a hard-copy version as well as a new Web site (www.daltonsholidays.com). Both carry advertisements for properties in Eastern and Central Europe.
- *Homes Overseas* (020-7939-9888; www.homesoverseas.co.uk) is a monthly worldwide magazine and Web site with property listings.

- The *Daily Telegraph* property section on Saturdays.
- The *Financial Times* on Saturdays.
- The *Sunday Times* property section.
- *World of Property* (01323-726-040; `www.outboundpublishing.com`) is a bi-monthly publication covering international locations; it features periodic sections on specific countries.

A growing number of English-language papers and news sheets are published and distributed in many of the countries I cover in this book. These publications target both the expat communities and property buyers in general. I list countries and cities where such publications are available in the corresponding country-specific chapter.

Working up your network

After you narrow down your search area, you can consider bypassing estate agents and try connecting directly with sellers. Sellers are almost certain to find the idea of selling direct to you appealing because doing so cuts out about 5 per cent of estate agent fees.

Start by seeing whether you can find a foreigner like yourself who wants to sell up. Don't panic: Just because someone is selling up doesn't mean that he or she has had a bad experience. In many cases, buyers are trading up after putting their toes in the water.

Start by asking your friends and acquaintances to see who has a property for sale. Even if you don't know anyone with a house in one of the countries you are interested in, by the time you do some preliminary research, you can uncover a veritable army of second-home owners in that country.

To widen your pool of contacts, draw on your skills as a networker. Everyone you find with a property abroad knows a couple of others, and they in turn know a couple more. Pulling on that thread soon leads to hundreds of people with whom you have some connection, however tenuous. Someone along the line probably knows someone else who is thinking of selling a home abroad.

Doing Hands-On Research: Rest, Recreation, and Reconnaissance

After you do all your background research, you're ready to see what the countries on your narrowed-down list are really like.

Unlike in Spain (and to a lesser extent Portugal) where property-inspection trips are high-pressure affairs and estate agents do not leave you alone until you sign on the dotted line, property inspection in the countries this book covers is usually a casual affair. Rarely will agents offer you any financial inducement, such as discount air travel or accommodation. Even where these are blandished, they are rarely worthwhile. The optimal approach is to make your own travel plans and fix appointments with estate agents and other contacts in the country beforehand. The Web sites I list later in this section can beat most other deals hands down in terms of cost and convenience.

When you make appointments with estate agents, make sure that you leave yourself plenty of time to wander around on your own. Agents want to keep you focused on their properties, but you want to get a broad appreciation of the whole property market in your chosen area.

Taking short breaks

The advent of low-cost airlines means that you can easily reach nearly all the countries in this book within a few hours from up to a dozen or so British airports. Improving hotel facilities throughout the region mean that for less than the cost of a modest weekend in a British holiday resort, you can get a four-day break in Prague, Sofia, and many of the other capital cities of Eastern Europe.

Check for bargain short breaks on Web sites such as Lastminute.com (`www.lastminute.com`), Travelocity.com (`www.travelocity.com`), and Expedia.com (`www.expedia.com`). Consider trying several new travel-focused search engines, including Kayak.com (`www.kayak.com`), Mobisso.com (`www.mobisso.com`), and Sidestep.com (`www.sidestep.com`).

Keep in mind that *when* you visit can be as important as *where* you visit. For example, the buzz of a seaside resort in the summer months may not be replicated in the winter and autumn. Not only are the tourists gone, but also many restaurants, cafés, and perhaps even the cinemas may have pulled the shutters down.

Tackling the tourist office

The people behind the counter usually speak English – an invaluable asset when you are seeking out useful information in a foreign land. Also, a tourist office is a reassuring indication that you may well have a holiday rental market for the property you plump for.

Following are a few subjects to probe those in the tourist office about to help you decide whether an area is worthy of your attention:

- **Accommodation:** Tourist offices normally maintain a database of local hotels, guesthouses, and private landlords willing to put you up. These recommendations are almost certainly cheaper than the places being plugged on the Internet or by travel agents.
- **Local attractions:** The more leaflets on display, the larger the office, and the more staff at work, the more certain you can be that the area is popular for visitors – a fact that you can't be quite so confident about just by reading a guidebook or searching the Internet. After you know just how popular an area is, you are more able to build a forecast of likely rental income.
- **Quality assessment:** Many tourist offices rate local properties using a star or other measurement system. Understanding how an area's tourist office assesses quality is the key to knowing how to pitch a rental for any property you may buy.
- **Transportation:** This is a topic that tourist office personnel are well geared up on. First, find out the routes, frequency, and rates of buses and trains. These answers give you a feel for how easily you can live in the area without a car – as well as how likely you are to attract potential business or holiday renters.

Driving the area

The optimal way to size up a region is to drive around it. Of course, driving in a new area is not always that easy, or for that matter safe for an unaccompanied foreigner. For example, in some countries the road signs are not only in a foreign language but also in a near-indecipherable alphabet such as the Cyrillic used in Bulgaria.

When you drive yourself, you can expand your search beyond the well-established developments. Get a good detailed map of the area you are interested in and systematically travel everywhere you find a cluster of buildings.

Contacting the locals

Start talking to local builders, lawyers, and surveyors and see whether they know of any properties about to come on the market. Take care not to be sucked into parting with any money until you have taken legal advice.

Going my way

I made one of my best property buys by just driving around a region I was interested in. All the agents in Bulgaria were steering me to buy in Bansko, a great ski resort that I cover in Chapter 12. But driving round the mountains, I found a small hamlet near Dobrinishte, 15 minutes from the ski gondola in Bansko, where property was less than half the price. Better still, in talking to the local mayor, I established that a chair lift linking the village to the main ski resort was planned in time for the next ski season.

None of the properties in the area was on any Web site or in the hands of any international estate agent. The locals had kept the town all to themselves – until I headed off the beaten track.

Be careful: Freelance *introducers* hang around estate agents' offices, banks, hotels, and bars in most of the countries I cover in this book. These individuals watch and listen to visitors, searching for foreign people who are obviously in the country on property-hunting visits. Introducers typically wait until an opportunity arises to introduce themselves – often as an obliging English speaker who just happens to know of a special bargain dream house that is not listed on the market at large. Of course, no one works for nothing. These people have arrangements with various estate agents who can load the deal to pay off the introducer's fees.

You do not need the services of an introducer. No vendor in his or her right mind is likely to surround the sale of a property in a veil of secrecy. By diligently ploughing round the estate agents yourself in your chosen area, you can do – for free – absolutely everything that introducers typically offer to do.

Narrowing Down Your Choices

After doing desk research and perhaps visiting one or two of the most promising countries on your radar screen, you may find your head swimming with a mass of decisions and choices. Don't worry – that's a good sign. It means that you are on the right track.

Your next task is to focus down to a handful of properties that are worthy of further investigation. Start by making the big decision first: Are you primarily out to make money, or are you hunting for something that you and your family will enjoy?

Then decide how much you are prepared to spend, taking account of extra costs that are certain to be involved, including brokers' fees, local property taxes, the costs of renovation, and so forth. Take time to consider what type of property and facilities (swimming pool, sea views, and so on) are essential to your needs. You may have to bounce back and forth between what is desirable in terms of a property and what is affordable.

Your decisions may even influence the country you end up choosing. For example €30,000 (£25,850) can buy you a pool, a view, and three bedrooms on the Black Sea coast, but you may need more than double that to get the same deal on the Dalmatian coast. And while you can also find this type of property on Poland's Baltic coast, you miss out on the long summer season and warm sea. Decisions, decisions!

This section gives you tools and tips for winnowing down to the best locations for you.

Refining your search

The 13 countries that this book covers spread across a land surface a dozen times greater than that of the entire UK. The region borders on five seas and is dissected by four time zones. If you already have a particular country or two in mind, so much the better. If not, by all means look at them all from the comfort of your armchair while reading this book and following the hundreds of Web sites I list.

But before you head out to the airport, you need to have a handful of specific destinations in mind.

- Your first decision is whether your main goal is to find a property as an investment or as somewhere for R&R (rest and recreation, or perhaps rest and retirement someday).
- The next factor to take into account is your appetite for risk. Whatever your intentions, buying a seaside apartment in Sebastopol, Ukraine, or anywhere in Northern Cyprus is a whole lot riskier than going for one in Malta, for example.

Figuring out your needs

Soon into your property search, you are likely to discover a wealth of attractive places to buy, but they all have something slightly different to recommend them. One may have a great garden and fantastic views but be located hours from a beach or airport. Another may need masses of work but have plenty of space for a bed-and-breakfast location so you can generate an income. You need to work out exactly what you really need – and are prepared to pay for.

The following questions can help you assess your basic personality and identify your most important needs in a new property. Take time and ask yourself – and your partner and family, if appropriate – the following questions. Consider writing down your answers to serve as a reminder and a tool for further planning:

- **Are you a town or country person?** No right answer here, but you need to know yourself before you splash out money for a sprawling farm or a hip urban loft.
- **Do you want to be inland, in the mountains, or on the coast?** Again, no right answer, but some nations in Eastern Europe are landlocked, have a limited coastal area, or lack significant residential development in mountainous regions.
- **Do you want to be isolated or have neighbours close at hand?** Keep in mind that being in the wilds with a partner may be fine, but consider what a property would be like if for some reason he or she wasn't there.
- **How important is outside space to you?** Urban dwellings have little outside space and what they do have, you probably have to share. By contrast, country properties may have too much space for you to maintain yourself.
- **How close do you want to be to shops, bars, and restaurants?** If you like to go out frequently, you probably want a property located in or near an active neighbourhood or town centre.
- **How important is public transport to living in a particular area?** If you plan to rely on public transport, find out your public transport options, including which are nearest, how much they cost, and how often they run.
- **How far away are leisure attractions?** While the distance to the beach or other sports facilities (golf, tennis, swimming, fitness centre, or riding) may seem like a minor issue for you, renters and visitors are likely to want to partake in these activities.
- **How good are the local health and social services?** Although healthcare is improving throughout the region, services still generally lag behind British standards. Try to locate English-speaking professionals.
- **What arts, cinema, and other entertainment are available in the area?** You may not need a property near museums and galleries, but a few intriguing entertainment options are usually necessary.
- **What are your potential neighbours like?** Do they have children and constant visitors? How much do you have to see them? Are they locals or foreigners? Does anyone speak English?

- **How far away is the nearest airport?** Also, find out whether budget airlines travel to the airport, region, or country.
- **Do properties in the area tend to sell quickly?** You may want to move up or out. Choosing an area with wide appeal and an active property market gives you options.

Deciding your budget

OK, so you are sold on a particular country in Eastern and Central Europe. But before you start to think seriously about looking at properties, you need to set your budget. You can waste an awful lot of time racing around a country looking at properties only to find that they cost more than you are prepared to commit. (Even searching on the Internet is frustrating when you haven't established a budget for yourself.)

Adding up how much you have

The average cost of a house in the UK is €257,000 (£180,000), and the average cost of a property in Eastern and Central Europe is €130,000 (£89,200). (You have to take averages with a pinch of salt, as by definition almost nothing is average. The great mass is above or below!) So if you intend to sell up and either downsize in the UK or abandon ship altogether and move abroad, in theory you need to have plenty of money to spare.

But if you do the sums carefully, you may not have quite as much as you would expect. The €127,000 (£87,100) you thought you may have as a result of selling in the UK so that you can buy abroad is more likely to be €99,990 (£68,500) when you take purchasing and moving costs into account (see Table 3-1).

Table 3-1 Calculating How Much Money You Really Have If You Sell Up and Move Abroad

Item	*Cost*	*Actual Cost*	*How Much You Have Left*
Sale price of UK home	€257,000	€257,000 - €7,710 (3%)	€249,290
Sale price of buying abroad for	€130,000	€130,000 + €14,300 (11%)	€104,990
Moving furniture	€5,000	€5,000	€99,990

So unless you are bringing other savings or reserves to the party – or you intend to take out a mortgage – going through the sums in a fashion similar to that shown in Table 3-1 is necessary to give you an idea of how the big numbers stack up. If you are seriously conservative with your money, then you can expect to earn interest on the €99,990 (£68,500) difference between selling in the UK and buying abroad, which amounts to around €3,000 (£2,050) a year. You will have to find an obliging friend or relative to live with, rent a house in your home country, or rent in your prospective country for the period in question, so you will also need to factor in that cost too.

Finding out how much you can borrow

If you intend to sell up in the UK and buy a similar property abroad, you probably don't need to borrow any money. However, if you have the income to support a loan, you can change the whole scenario.

Consider again the idea that you own an average €257,000 (£180,000) house in the UK. The UK has 11.5 million mortgages, totalling around £800 billion, which makes for an average mortgage of £69,560. That means that the average mortgagee has about £110,440 of equity available to borrow against.

Consider this situation another way: If you happen to be somewhere near the average figures, you can raise around 80 per cent of the amount of equity by remortgaging in the UK. That gives you €126,217 (£88,353) in funding from your British property, which is a very large slice of the €149,300 (£102,400) you need to buy an average Eastern or Central European house, pay all the legal expenses, and move your belongings.

In buying a property abroad, you acquire a new chunk of property equity against which you can borrow more. In theory, you can probably raise 70–80 per cent of the cost of your second property by way of a mortgage secured on that property. But before you get carried away and rush and buy a yacht, remember that any borrowing has to be serviced. That means that every month you get a bill from the mortgage company to pay for borrowing the money and to repay a slice of the borrowings. I look in detail at mortgage options in Chapter 18.

So if you feel you can afford – or can generate from your overseas and British properties – about £9,000 of extra income, then you should have little difficulty in raising all the money you need to keep your home in the UK and buy a house abroad. You also give yourself the flexibility to return to the UK at a later date by not getting out of the British property market.

In Chapter 18, I look in detail at the whole range of ways to fund your new property, including the risks and benefits of each option.

Setting your budget

Now for the $64,000 question: How much do you set aside for your purchase? The answer depends on your age, objectives, and appetite for risk. For example:

- If you and your partner are over 50, risk-averse, and plan to take up residence in the country you are buying into and live there for the rest of your life, then sell up in the UK, buy abroad for less, and bank the difference.
- If you and your partner are both under 50, want to keep your options open about returning to the UK, and don't want to take much of a risk, then downsize properties in the UK, buy an average house abroad, and take out just enough of a mortgage to fund the deal.
- If you are both under 50, want to keep open the option to return to the UK, and are happy to take a fair amount of risk, then keep your present house, rent it out, and buy a house abroad by taking out a sizeable mortgage.

Factoring in rental income

If you have properties in both the UK and abroad, you can rent out the location you're not living in, meet your mortgage costs, and perhaps even turn a small profit. (I look at the rental business in detail in Chapter 19.)

For example, if you have an average house in the UK worth £180,000 and an average mortgage of around £70,000, you want your rental income to exceed your costs:

Income	*Expense*	*Cost*
Rent £7,800	Mortgage on £70,000	£5,000
	Insurance	£500
	Agent's fees at 15%	£1,170
	Wear and tear, 10% of rent	£780
	Total expenses	£7,450

Given this scenario, your profit from renting is £7,800–£7,450, or £350. Okay, so you aren't going to get rich on the rent, but you do get to keep your British property and any capital appreciation.

However, adopting the strategy outlined in this section means that you must raise all the money you need from a source other than by selling up your

British home. That may mean less time on the beach and more in the bar – your bar, that is, pouring out the beers for paying punters.

After you decide on your strategy and set a budget, stick to it. However appealing a property is, you can't exceed your budget unless you can see a way to increase some other aspect of the equation, such as being able to rent out one of your properties for part of the year or earning additional money in some way (such as by taking a job or starting a business).

To renovate or not to renovate – that is the question

If you buy a property in need of renovation or extension to turn it into something that meets your needs, you need to be prepared for some significant additional costs.

Once upon a time, in the chaotic era before the European Union (EU) inspired a stronger legislative structure around property buying, almost every Eastern and Central European property came with a virtual guarantee of planning permission to extend, alter, or improve. Local mayors typically wanted development, and builders, lawyers, and surveyors all wanted work, so planning went through virtually on the nod. Today, however, you need to be very careful if you want to carry out major renovation work, as the rules have tightened up significantly throughout Europe.

Carrying out large-scale building work, even in your own country, is fraught with problems and dangers. Doing so with all the attendant problems of working in a foreign language, with an alien currency, and probably having to operate at a distance with only periodic site visits being possible, makes overseas remodelling work even more difficult. Add to the mix the people and organisations you have to deal with – an architect, a builder, perhaps a plumber and an electrician too. Plan to have your hands full for several months, dealing with the town hall, getting planning permission, and making sure that you can obtain the necessary building licences to cover the changes or designs you have in mind. Of course, there is always the option of hiring a project manager to supervise the renovation.

Aside from the strict legal aspects of planning and usage, renovation work may not be economically viable for several reasons. The most obvious, particularly in country areas, is the cost of providing usable water – and to a lesser extent power, sewage facilities, and telephone. Geographic reasons may render your plans unviable – the property may be too far from a good road, be on a steep slope, or have foundation issues.

Always keep in mind that one day you may want to sell your property, so it has to be both appealing and economically viable to someone else who may not be quite so enamoured with it as you are.

Building costs in all the countries this book covers are less than in the UK, with materials running up to two-thirds less and skilled local labour around one-third less. Plan to allow about €400–700 (£275–480) per square metre for renovation work, including planning permission. Councils may require up to 3 per cent of the value of the work in taxes, and architects' fees and planning and building permissions typically add about 14 per cent to costs.

Chapter 4

Weighing Up the Risks

In This Chapter

- Verifying property ownership
- Checking out value
- Reducing risks
- Taking out the cash

The Duke of Wellington called military intelligence 'the art of knowing what is on the other side of the hill'. The more you know, he reasoned, the more you can prepare for the ups and downs that come your way.

Like all property markets, Eastern and Central Europe offers an abundance of possible events that can cause problems. From dodgy new developments that block your view after you buy a property to doubtful ownership causing disputes as you try to buy, property-ownership trouble can quickly sour a seemingly sweet deal.

Before hassles come into play, you need to weigh up the prospects and risks for any country you are considering buying into. One of the biggest questions you must ask is whether you can make money, rather than lose money, on your purchase. Making money may not be your primary reason for buying this or that property in one country or another, but it is usually a qualifying condition. Few financially successful property buyers have anything else in mind.

Not all countries have property markets that are going to grow in value and deliver good rental income. In this chapter, I show you a simple technique that gives you a better than average chance of ensuring that your property purchase makes money.

Lots can get in the way of making a good return, so you need good advice. Your lawyer is perhaps the most important professional. Along the way, someone may tell you that you don't need your own lawyer or that a lawyer is a 'luxury' you must pay extra for. Don't listen. Work with a lawyer you trust throughout the purchase process.

Dealing with Ownership Issues

You need to be confident that your new dream home is actually yours and not the subject of a drawn-out legal dispute with a previous owner who claims to have been wronged by a previous regime. This section covers the potentially thorny issues associated with property titles and development plans.

Proving title

According to a prominent estate agent selling property in several Eastern and Central European countries, only one out of every three properties he sees is properly documented and ready for sale.

The best way, but not always an absolutely certain way, to find out who owns a property is by examining the *registered title deed* of the property as inscribed in the country's land or property registry. The title deed provides a description of the property, the details of the owner, and details of any mortgages or other charges against the property.

But two issues make proving title more difficult in Eastern and Central Europe than, say, in the UK:

- Some of the countries – Croatia and Cyprus for example – have experienced devastating civil wars. The victors in these conflicts widely regarded the land, homes, and other possessions of the 'losers' as part of the spoils of war. To secure lasting peace, property had to be restored to its rightful owners, and this has not always been successfully achieved.
- Many countries are grappling with the issue of restoring the concept of private ownership of land and property after decades of state ownership and the confiscation of estates. Many countries are struggling to re-create their land registries, a vital first step in proving title. After more than 40 years of neglect, this task is proving complex, expensive, and time-consuming. In Ukraine, for example, land is registered separately from buildings, essentially doubling the difficulty of the process.

The World Bank (`http://rru.worldbank.org`) has published a paper on registering property rights. The paper (available at `http://rru.worldbank.org/PapersLinks/Open.aspx?id=3598`) reviews countries' successes and failures as they update their land registries and procedures.

On average, the countries in this book take 180 days to accomplish the whole procedure of checking property title and registering a new owner. The fastest is 3 days and the slowest 956 days. (See Table 4-1 for country-specific time requirements.)

A number of countries speed up registration by offering a fast-track procedure. For example, by paying 25 per cent more in Lithuania, a buyer can cut down the process from 29 to 3 days.

In some countries (particularly Croatia and Slovenia), court backlogs can cause delays of more than a year in property registration. Often you can get a *provisional title on application*, a process favoured by many brokers. You can move forward on your purchase, you can even in some circumstances live in or rent out the property; but you don't know for certain that you own the property until you get the final title.

It is your lawyer's job to make sure that the title is correct and transferred to you on completion of the sale. Ask your lawyer for evidence of his or her professional liability insurance. In some countries, you may be offered insurance against a 'defective' title. Consider this option carefully and discuss it with your lawyer.

Table 4-1 Length of Time to Transfer Ownership Title

Country	*Average Number of Days*
Bulgaria	19
Croatia	956
Czech Republic	123
Estonia	65
Hungary	78
Latvia	54
Lithuania	3
Poland	197
Slovenia	391
Turkey	9
Ukraine	93
UK	21

*Source: World Bank, Doing Business (*www.doingbusiness.org*)*

Checking development plans

Several factors related to development plans can increase the risk in your investment by making the property harder to rent out and to sell when the time comes. You need to check out any proposed changes to roads, railways, airports, and so forth that could either enhance or detract from the attractiveness of the immediate locality.

Also, check that there are no plans to construct anything that may detract from either the value of the property or your pleasure in using it. Make sure that no buildings are scheduled to pop up directly in view and that no motorways are slated to weave past your door.

Checking development plans is easier said than done in many Eastern European countries. Ask your lawyer to investigate these matters by inspecting the town plan. You can also expect a house hunter to make these enquiries as part of his or her report. I cover using house hunters in Chapter 3.

Anticipating Insurance Risks

For a while – and perhaps permanently if you decide to keep your British property – you may need to insure in both the UK and abroad against the usual risks.

However, owning property in Eastern Europe offers a few new risks, such as having an unoccupied property for long periods or protecting yourself and your investment from earthquake damage (in Turkey, for example).

Insurance is a global business, and about 10 big pan-European insurance firms dominate the market. The insurers you are with now are very likely to have a branch or own a subsidiary company in the country you are considering.

Whatever insurer you select, you need to cover your risks with a business of substance. After all, the main purpose of insurance is to have someone to turn to when a disaster that would otherwise overwhelm you occurs. You don't want to find that the 10 per cent you saved on premiums by using a flimsy insurer results in your being landed with 100 per cent of the cost of rebuilding your house.

When searching for an insurer for your overseas property, use the same rules as you do in the UK. Check out any insurer by asking your professional contacts in both the UK and overseas. Bankers, accountants, and even estate agents can give you a steer here. You can also use the services of a specialist international property insurance broker such as Schofields Insurance (01204-365-080; `www.schofields.ltd.uk`) or Saga (0800-559-3230; `www.saga.co.uk`), which deals with a whole range of insurance matters for the over-50s living abroad.

The following are key considerations to make sure that you have adequate insurance:

- **Insuring belongings in transit.** Make sure that you cover your belongings on either your or your removal company's insurance policy for the period between leaving one house and arriving at the other.
- **Insuring property and belongings abroad.** In the short term the 'all risks' element of your British property insurance, if you have any, may cover your belongings. However, you need to insure your overseas property from the moment of ownership.
- **Discussing additional risks.** Advise your insurance company about any additional risks, such as a swimming pool or a stable full of horses, and whether the property will be unoccupied for long periods of time.
- **Covering property within a development.** If you are buying an apartment or a property in a complex, a central insurance policy may be in place and your contribution may be included in any service charge.
- **Renting out your overseas property short or long term.** If you are renting out, check with your insurance provider and mortgage company that they are happy. Both may require a higher payment to reflect the change of use.
- **Renting out your British home short or long term.** If you are renting out your British home, you need to check with your insurance provider and mortgage company that they are happy. Both may require a higher payment to reflect the change of use.

Assessing Potential for Capital Growth and Rental Yield

A lot of factors determine whether the property in a particular country or even an area within that country can help you achieve high growth in capital value and high rental yield. I look in detail at these factors in Chapter 2.

Table 4-2 lists the major factors to consider. Your next step is to run through the list for any country you are considering and see how it stacks up. Any country that rates more than about 60 should make you a reasonable return; above 80, and you are on to a winner.

Table 4-2 Assessing the Potential for Capital Growth and Rental Yield

Factor	*Score out of 10 for Country or Area A*	*Score out of 10 for Country or Area B*
Amount of inward investment (little = 0; lots = 10)		
Growth in the economy (much lower than old Europe = 0; much higher than old Europe = 10)		
Level of unemployment (high and staying high = 0; low and getting lower =10)		
Amount of tourism (not much and of poor quality = 0; lots of the infrastructure is improving = 10)		
Political stability (always changing government = 0; regular elections, but governments last their term = 10)		
Local mortgage market (none to speak of = 0; well developed, lots of providers, keen interest rates = 10		
Cost of living (about the same as old Europe = 0; a fraction of that in old Europe = 10)		
Property and income taxes (higher than UK = 0; much lower than UK = 10)		
Access to country (one airline and one airport = 0; several budget airlines and several airports = 10		
Lifestyle and amenities (still like the developing world =0; almost like home, good cinemas, theatre, restaurants, and healthcare = 10)		
Total out of 100:		

Of course, the factors that Table 4-2 lists are not necessarily *all* the factors that can apply. Some dormant factors may exist that have not yet appeared on the horizon. You need to build these factors into your thinking when assessing the potential for a particular country.

The following are a few additional factors to get your mind around:

- **Counting on cheap flights.** Yes, the arrival of budget airlines such as Ryanair and easyJet can make an area more popular, driving up property prices. easyJet makes no secret of the influence it expects to have and publishes property stories in its inflight magazine regularly. As a property investor, however, you must consider what can happen if the budget airlines pull the plug on your route or go bust. Budget airlines dump routes at will and alter timetables and flight frequencies all the time. Make sure that at least two airlines service your destination. While you may be happy to track there by bus, those looking for a holiday home to rent will almost certainly not.
- **Depopulating countries.** Housing markets are finely balanced by supply and demand. Too many buyers combined with too few properties, and prices rise. If properties suddenly flood a market, prices can stall or even fall. Usually developers building new properties keep a careful watch and try the keep the equation in balance. But what if tens of thousands, perhaps even millions, of a country's citizens head for the exit? Fanciful? It has happened several times in Eastern and Central Europe. Bulgaria's population shrank by 1 million over the period between 1991 and 2002, leaving more than 300,000 homes empty and for the most part unsold. Could it happen again? Perhaps. In February 2006, Russia's President Putin commissioned a study to explore ways to repatriate 'compatriots' who were left abroad in 1991. His goal is to stem the decline in the Russian population, which has shrunk by 6 million since 1992. If the incentives on offer to return to Russia pull back many of the 675,000 Russians in Latvia, the 330,000 in Estonia, the 278,000 in Lithuania, or the 8.2 million in Ukraine, the effect on local property prices may be significant.
- **Missing deadlines.** Some of the steam in the economies (and property markets) of the nations hoping to entering the European Union (EU) in the future lies in their progress towards EU-established goals. If a country fails to meet one or more of the criteria for membership as laid down in the Copenhagen Criteria (`www.europa.eu.int/comm/enlargement`), then property prices may tumble. The same may also happen if new EU members miss their target dates for adopting the euro. You can keep abreast of all issues relating to important matters in the EU on the EurActiv website (`www.euractiv.com`).
- **Artificially inflated property prices.** There is a tendency for prices to be exaggerated by over-expectations of EU membership and for them to tumble just after EU accession takes place as occurred in Hungary for example.

Making Money on Your Investment

The military saying 'You should never get into anything that you can't see your way out of' is also an excellent maxim for overseas property buyers. You must consider whether any property you are buying is as appealing to others as it is to you.

You also need to consider what may happen to the relationship between your currency (pounds) and the currency of the country you are buying property in. If a property transaction takes months or years to complete (as it can sometimes), your money is subject to all the vageries of the currency markets.

Finally, remember that you must pay some of any profit you make to those helping you buy and sell – and to the tax authorities.

Buying versus selling

The average ownership period of an overseas property, based admittedly on personal observation, is about nine years. My own average is half that. Maybe you'll own your property for a longer period, maybe shorter. But one day in the probably not too distant future, you will swap roles from buyer to seller. To maximise your potential to earn a profit on your investment, in any property purchase you need to consider the views of other potential buyers, or you may have difficulty selling and getting your money out.

Put yourself in the buyer's shoes. Consider how idiosyncratic your own needs are compared with the potential needs of others. While some features may give you great pleasure, the very same things may have limited appeal for others. For example, you may not mind that your property has no shower, only a bath. Or that your house is located miles from any neighbours and a few hours from an airport. Or, if you don't have school-age children, that the nearby schools are lacklustre. But most potential buyers do care about all these things – and more.

Dealing with capital gains

One of your goals in buying a property is to make a bit more money than you paid for it. Nothing wrong in that, and most people who buy and sell property overseas in the markets I examine in this book do quite well in this respect.

You have, however, to take into account a few factors before you can pocket your gain:

- **Selling expenses:** Although buying property can cost as little as 3 or 4 per cent of the purchase price, selling involves rather more costs. (See each country chapter for buying costs.) Estate agents take 4–5 per cent of the selling price, property taxes can eat up another couple of per cent, and legal fees may consume another 1 per cent or so. Total selling expenses can easily eat up 10 per cent of your selling price.
- **Paying for gains:** In many countries I cover in this book, local capital gains tax rates are either low (around 10 per cent) or non-existent if you own a property for three to five years. However, unless you are *domiciled* for tax purposes in the overseas country (see Chapter 17), you are still liable for capital gains tax in the UK at a rate of 25–40 per cent, depending on your tax code.
- **Currency costs:** Unless you plan to keep the proceeds of any sale in the country you buy in, you must transfer the funds back to the UK. If the exchange rate of the local currency has moved against sterling, you can potentially have costs for changing the currency *and* lose out on the exchange rate. (See the section 'Coping with fluctuating exchange rates' later in this chapter for more information.) In recent years, the pound has moved adversely by as much as 10 per cent against the euro, the principal currency used for property in the countries discussed in this book.

Handling rental risks

Around 450,000 Brits who own properties abroad hope to generate at least some rental income from their properties. Few are anywhere near as successful as they hope because a number of events often occur to eat up any profit:

- Optimism triumphs over realism when most people estimate how much money they can make. I look at how to prepare a realistic and prudent forecast for rental profit in Chapter 19.
- With a gross rental yield of 6–10 per cent (before expenses and taxes), you haven't exactly got a lot of margin for error. So if your rental income is to be converted back into pounds before you spend it, you need to build that cost into your equation. I look at exchange rate issues in the following section.

One way to minimise this risk is to hold rent money in the currency of the country where your property is and use it when you are in the country, or for repairs and refurbishments. In that way your rent's purchasing power is preserved.

Chapter 19 covers the ins and outs of renting out properties in the UK and overseas.

Avoiding e-mail-based scams

First-time landlords must be wary of a variety of rent-based scams that abound in today's burgeoning overseas property market.

For example, imagine the joy you'd experience as a potential overseas landlord if you received an e-mail asking to rent your property for six months at a better than average rate. To your further surprise and delight, the prospective renter sends a cheque, usually though not always using a foreign bank account, for more than double the agreed rent. Overpaying may put you on your guard, but what can possibly go wrong if you bank the money?

If this situation sounds too good to be true, that's because it is. Here's why: In the next phase of the scam, the prospective tenant sends you another e-mail a couple weeks later asking for the surplus funds to be transferred to their bank account. (The tenant typically offers some excuse about misunderstanding the original rental amount.) You check your bank statement and see that the funds have been credited to your account, so you oblige and send the balance back.

Unfortunately, at this point, you've been had. The funds in your bank are not *available funds*, to use the banking jargon. They are just a bookkeeping entry in the bank's records. International cheques – such as those issued on a bank overseas (even an international bank) – can involve a delay of up to eight weeks before the actual cash is transfer. This processing time gives the fraudster ample time to get your money into their hands.

The way to protect yourself from this scam is to ensure that you get confirmation from your bank that the cash has actually been transferred to your account before you send back any money to your prospective tenant.

Being wary of regulated rents

If you are buying an older property, be careful of *regulated rents*. Up to a fifth of all properties in the post-Communist countries of Central and Eastern Europe have rents regulated by the government rather than set by the landlord.

Regulated rents are set at around a fifth of the market rent. The purpose of this regulation is to keep accommodation affordable for all citizens in a country. Tenants in regulated properties often offer to be bought out by the landlord for sums equivalent to between three and four years of the full market rent. A case before the Strasbourg Court of Human Rights in 2005 ruled in favour of a Polish landlord who accused the government of violating her human rights by maintaining rent controls, stating that the government's action of regulating rents at the expense of property owners was illegal and against human rights. But landlords can't relax just yet, as an appeal is underway. Also the Court has power over non-EU members such as Turkey, Bulgaria, Romania, Ukraine, Croatia, which are all members of the Council of Europe.

Being on guard against guaranteed rents

Don't be fooled by *guaranteed rents*, in which a new development offers you a guarantee of receiving a set return (usually 7 or 8 per cent) over the course of your investment. Not only are these guarantees usually poor value, but also they provide no assurance that a good rental market for the property exists.

Nothing is for nothing. You can be sure that the rent, or at any rate a large proportion of it, is loaded back into the property's selling price.

Some developers are open about this type of price structuring and offer properties at two prices, one with a rental guarantee and a lower one without such a guarantee. A close examination of the figures usually shows that the developers are either taking no risk (as they add the full amount of the guaranteed rent back on to the property purchase price) or that they have added most of the cost back and are themselves at risk for only 1 or 2 per cent.

Coping with fluctuating exchange rates

Buying, selling, or renting out a property in Eastern and Central Europe means handling money in at least two currencies – pounds sterling and the currency of the country you are buying property in. You may even need to deal in euros, as many major transactions, including buying and selling property, are now conducted exclusively in that currency.

The amount you set aside in pounds can vary in its purchasing power in another currency by several percentage points and perhaps by as much as 10 per cent over an extended period. Any property purchase takes time and the longer it takes the longer you are exposed to currency market forces that can make your payments unpredictable.

The same potential for loss occurs when you sell a property or when you receive rent. Aside from the change in value of one currency against another, your bank or currency exchange service levies a transaction cost.

Changing money is a highly competitive business, and rates vary greatly. For a full discussion of your options – as well as advice on how to minimise negative exchange terms – see Chapter 18.

Limiting Your Risks

Everything in life is a risk, but it doesn't have to be a gamble: You can stack the deck in your favour. This section offers proactive advice for minimising many of the downsides related to property purchases.

Choosing a lawyer

You need a lawyer for various reasons. A lawyer helps ensure that you get good title to the property in question and assists you in making other important decisions, such as whether you should own the property yourself or share it with others. Your lawyer can also advise you on the perennial problem in Eastern European markets – being asked to under-declare the property price in order to minimise tax. (See 'Declaring the buying price' later in this chapter for more information on the pros and cons of undeclaring.)

All too often buyers of overseas properties are told (often by estate agents) that all their legal work can be done by a notary who happens to speaks perfect English. Buyers are often also told that using a lawyer only duplicates the work of a notary and doubles any fees. This advice is just plain wrong. Estimates indicate that more than three-quarters of foreign buyers don't take independent legal advice when they buy a property abroad. Often buyers rush out to find a lawyer only when they hit some snags *after* they have paid a deposit or, worse still, signed a contract. Don't be part of this statistic: Get professional legal assistance early on in your property-buying endeavour.

Differentiating between notaries and lawyers

Most of the countries in this book require the services of a notary at some point in a property purchasing deal. When this is the case, you absolutely must include a notary in the proceedings because under the country's laws only deeds of sale witnessed and authorised by a notary can be registered at the Land Registry. Without such registration no ownership transfer is complete.

You can find a local notary in the local telephone directory, or you can use one recommended by a friend or your estate agent.

Who you choose as a notary doesn't matter much for one simple reason: He or she isn't working for you. Unlike your own lawyer, who you expect to be looking after your interests, the notary is neutral. He or she carries out some checks on the property and makes sure that all the paperwork is in precisely the correct order for smooth processing by the land registry so that registration can take place. He or she also has a responsibility to make sure that the appropriate property transfer taxes are paid on time.

Knowing when you need a lawyer

The short answer here is always. You need a lawyer to look after *your* interests in the transaction, not just someone to see that what happens is of itself legal. That is the notary's function.

Essentially, your lawyer performs two vital functions.

- Your lawyer draws up the initial pre-sale contract and handles the payment of the customary 10 per cent deposit. Your lawyer is the only party to the sale likely to carry liability insurance that protects your deposit money in the event that things go wrong. (See the section 'Paying the deposit' later in this chapter.)
- Your lawyer ensures that you end up with a property that is legally yours, correctly described in terms of boundaries, access, and rights of way, and free of a mountain of debts.

Aside from knowing the law of the land in question, you need a lawyer who is competent and who speaks English. How do you find such a paragon? Start by trying to find someone you respect and trust who has used a lawyer in that country before. Not always an easy task, but if you stretch that definition a bit to someone you know who knows someone, you may have more success. (In Chapter 3, I cover building up your network of business contacts.)

If you have no luck after tapping into your network, try the following:

- **The Federation of Overseas Property Developers, Agents and Consultants** (`www.fopdac.com`) has a listing of lawyers in the UK with international property expertise.
- **The British Embassy in Kiev** (`www.fco.gov.uk`; in shortcut menu go to UK Embassies Overseas and select the country in which you are interested in buying a property) lists English-speaking lawyers.
- **The Martindale-Hubbell Lawyer Locator** (`http://lawyers.martindale.com/marhub`) and the **International Law Office** (`www.internationallawoffice.com/Directory`) also offer lists of English-speaking lawyers.

You can also find a handful of lawyers in the newspapers and magazines that I recommend for research purposes in Chapter 3.

Giving power of attorney

If you are not going to be in the county in which you are buying during all or even some of the purchase process – or you want to be sheltered from the mind-numbing bureaucratic process that so often prevails – consider giving your lawyer *power of attorney*. This document authorises an appointed person to act on your behalf in certain prescribed matters, as though he or she were you. In effect your appointee assumes the full responsibility for making your decisions and committing you irrevocably by signing documents on your behalf. Granting this power means signing a document in front of a notary, either in the country concerned or sometimes in the British Embassy of the country in question. Setting up power of attorney costs €10–25.

Even if you grant power of attorney, you can sign documents yourself. As well as being an experience in itself, you can have a last look around the property to make sure that everything you think is included in the sale is actually present and correct.

Declaring the buying price

In much of Eastern and Central Europe, a practice exists that involves paying some of the purchase price under the table. In effect, the vendor is asking to pay some of the purchase price in cash, undeclared to the authorities, and the balance in the normal visible manner. This strategy is attractive to both parties. Both you and the vendor lower your property tax bills to some extent, and the charges by professionals, which are based on the declared selling price, are lower too. So in theory, only the government, a lawyer or two, and the estate agent are the losers.

There are, however, a few snags with under-declaring the price, especially if the proportion of the total purchase price under-declared is large. For a start, the process is illegal in many countries and severe penalties are often imposed for under-declaring. The practice can also leave you with a larger capital gains tax bill when you sell up, unless you can persuade your buyer in turn to under-declare by the same proportion. You may also find it rather difficult with anti-money laundering regulations so prevalent to make a large sum of cash just disappear.

You are highly likely, especially in rural areas where you are buying a property that has been in the same hands for a long time, to be pressurised into agreeing to some level of under-declaring. The reason for this is simple. The vendor may have a large capital gains tax liability, which in effect is taking a big slice of the money they hope to get from the sale of the property concerned.

Overseas estate agents indicate that at present sellers are seeking somewhere between 20 and 50 per cent as the under-declared amount. Informally, this is considered acceptable, much as doing 75 miles per hour on the motorway is – though of course, strictly speaking, you are still breaking the law.

In this area, more than any other, you need to get sound legal advice and follow it.

Deciding who owns the property

You may be forgiven for thinking that the only way to own a property is for you to buy it. That's just too simple.

In general, you have five main types of ownership structure, each with a number of variations. Choosing the right structure for you requires professional advice from a lawyer or accountant conversant with British tax and inheritance law and the law in the country in which you are buying a property.

At stake is the potential to liberate thousands of pounds while you are alive and to save your dependants a small fortune in tax when you die. But to secure these savings, you may have to relinquish a degree of control over your property – not something many of us are too enthusiastic about.

If you are considering putting the property in your children's or partner's name, make sure that you give yourself a *life interest* in the property. A life interest protects your right to reside in the property for as long as you live, while saving your dependants a hefty inheritance tax bill when you die. Your lawyer can arrange this for you.

Paying the deposit

Early in the buying process, you are invited to demonstrate your commitment to buying by putting down some hard cash. Reservation deposits and any payments made to an agent, whether the agent is licensed or not, are not legally binding on the vendor.

There is no point in paying any reservation deposits to an agent. Only after a sales purchase contact has been agreed and signed by both parties and 10 per cent paid is the vendor legally bound to sell you the property. Reservation deposits for new developments should be made directly to the developer.

Make any and all payments via or under the supervision of an independent lawyer. Only in this way will your interests and your money always be protected. You can also be sure that the sales purchase contract is in your name and not in the name of the agency. This type of contract may be convenient for the agency because it allows them to control the sales process and speed things up, especially if you are out of the country, but you have no legal claim on the property. Try to ensure that any money you pay goes in an *escrow account* – that is, an account that keeps your money and the lawyer's general funds separate. Funds in an escrow account can be used only for the purpose of buying your property.

If you pay money to an agency and the deal falls through, the only way you may get your deposit back is to stick with that agent until he or she finds you another property you like and can afford.

Undertaking the survey

Property surveys in many of the countries in Eastern and Central Europe are neither usual nor a legal requirement. Unlike in England, where offers subject to survey are allowed, you are expected to get your ducks in a row *before* you shoot in Eastern Europe. The vendor expects you either to take the risk or to get the property surveyed before you put in an offer.

You may well find that the seller claims that a property has been surveyed – particularly when a developer is offering properties with mortgage finance included. This survey has probably been carried out by an estate agent and is confined to comparing the price of the property to similar ones nearby. (If you have done your research thoroughly, you already know better than anyone how much comparable properties cost. The lender, however, wants to ensure that the amount you are borrowing is less than the value of the property. Any mortgage that is offered to you is based largely on the results of this survey.) In practice, such a survey is almost valueless to you. While a mortgage valuation survey can highlight any glaring catastrophes waiting to happen, you have no comeback if you do have subsequent problems.

Going for the Full Monty

A useful and comprehensive survey gives you a full picture of the construction and condition of a property and is the most thorough and detailed report on the condition of a property that you can buy. You are likely to need this type of survey if the property is of unusual construction – dilapidated or extensively altered – or if you are planning a major conversion or renovation. (See the country-specific chapters on how to find a surveyor for your property.)

The surveyor checks for structural problems, including dampness, timber decay, roofs, roof spaces, walls, floors, woodworm, and gutters, and identifies all the significant structural defects and items of disrepair in a property. You should also ask your surveyor to check that the electricity and water supply are sufficient for your needs, including extra bathrooms, any swimming pool, and air-conditioning. (Some developments are set up so quickly and extensively that the water supply is insufficient for baths, so only showers can be used in the entire resort – a fact not given out in any property details.)

The surveyor's report, up to 30 pages long, includes a table of costs for major defects and problems. The report also suggests the order in which work should be carried out and an estimate of time and expense associated with each repair. With this information, you can know with a reasonable degree of certainty the cost required over and above the asking price to make the property habitable and secure. Armed with this information, you can go back to the negotiating table and hammer away at the vendor's aspirations.

Get the measurements right!

Nothing can reduce a property's value as much as getting the measurements wrong. In the UK, you buy properties by the number of rooms, usually counting just the bedrooms. Europeans use the number of square metres and price in relation to that figure. So you need to make sure that a property is as big as it is described.

Just because a property floor plan looks professional, don't believe that it is accurate or even correct. I once found that the plan of a ski apartment I was buying was for a different property in a different village. Sure, the apartment was by the same developer, but the actual layout and internal sizes were quite different. The result was that while the apartments were nominally the same size, the useful size in terms of living accommodation was 10 per cent adrift. The developed was asking me in effect to pay €5000 for space that didn't exist.

Another wheeze that some developers practice is to include the space occupied by the walls in the available floor space. Including the balconies and a share of any common parts into the square metreage of properties is pretty much standard practice.

To ensure that all measurements are correct, go round the property and measure it up yourself. You can buy an electronic tape measure for around £40 from hardware outlets and this can do all your measuring if you just point it at the walls. These handy devices can also convert the measurements into both area and volume (which is useful for working out how much a property costs to heat).

A valuation is not normally included as part of a surveyor's report, but you can request one to be included at a modest additional charge.

By seeking the opinion of a trained professional, you get peace of mind. If anything crops up later that the surveyor did not spot and draw to your attention, you can hit the surveyor with the bill for putting the defect right. That is why surveyors carry professional indemnity insurance.

If you are seriously interested in a property, you should be able to persuade a local builder to come round and give you a rough estimate of what he or she thinks repairs or conversion costs may be. The contractor may well do this in the hope of getting the job of carrying out any repairs and renovations, but if not, any fee for the estimate is likely to be very modest. The estimate, however rough, forms a vital part of your house-purchasing arithmetic.

Inspecting a property yourself

You can employ a surveyor to make sure that you are not buying an absolute lemon, but you can also do some of the spadework yourself by looking around the property with a critical eye. Aspects you can check yourself include:

- **Measurements.** Verify that the description of the property and the plan correspond to the property itself. Estate agents and vendors can be less than rigorous in terms of both measurements and descriptions, so you need to make sure that they are not short changing you.
- **Roofs, joists, and guttering.** Although hard to see from the ground, these areas can be the most expensive to remedy. Look out for missing or slipped tiles, damp patches on ceilings and walls, and timbers showing signs of rot. Check that gutters are in place and functioning.
- **Floors.** Unlike in the UK, you are unlikely to encounter any carpets in the property, so you can inspect both on and below the surface of the flooring. Where it is possible check the joists for rot, and make sure that there is some effective form of ventilation.
- **Windows and doors.** Check for obvious signs of rot. Do windows and doors open and close easily, and do the catches and locks work? Look for signs of condensation, which can mean poor ventilation, which in turn can lead to rot.
- **Electrics, gas, and plumbing.** Most holiday homes have a power rating of 3.3 kilowatts to keep costs down. This is not sufficient if you plan to live there full time, so you need to check the capacity of the power supply and ensure that you can increase it without undue cost. Check the wiring and fuse box, which will give you some idea of how old the wiring is. Make sure that sufficient plug points are present. Gas is almost certain to be bottled. Check that the tank is in a secure place and that a back-up valve is in place. Check out the water supply and establish whether it is reliable and whether you have a back-up water tank. Check drainage to see whether it is through a septic tank and, if so, what condition that is in.
- **Heating and air-conditioning.** How is the house heated in winter and kept cool in the summer? Wood stoves may be economical, but are you able to keep stocked up with wood? Also, this form of heating is impossible to have 'turned on' before you arrive. Keeping a house cool economically in the summer heat depends on the direction the main rooms are facing (towards the midday sun makes them harder to keep cool). Stone-flagged floors and shuttered windows can also help keep a place cool.
- **Access roads and paths.** How do you get to and from the property? Who owns the right of way, and who is responsible for its upkeep? A 500-metre drive may guarantee privacy and add a certain charm, but in the winter it may be impossible to use except with a four-wheel drive vehicle.

- **Common areas.** Are there any areas that you have to share with neighbours? In an apartment complex, this may include lifts, gardens, and swimming pools. In the countryside, it may be garden walls, fences, and paths. You need to find out when work was last carried out, what may need to be done soon, how much it may cost, and how costs are to be shared.
- **Swimming pool, outbuildings, and gardens.** These can be a bonus or a burden, depending on their condition. Remember that even when you are not there, gardens and pools need attention. If a pool is old or does not have adequate safety features to stop people, children in particular, from stumbling into it, you may have some big bills arriving soon. Outbuildings may look charming, but if they are in disrepair and dangerous, you can have a big unwanted bill on your hands just to stop the buildings falling down.
- **Disputes and defects.** You need to check that no disputes exist with neighbours over common ground, access, or services such as water, power, telephone, and drainage running across your or their property. Also check that all equipment that the vendors are leaving behind is in good working order, that outstanding defects have been made good, and that you have details of any guarantees and warranties.

Engaging a translator/interpreter

All the professionals you work with in the process of purchasing property have their own languages, supplemented liberally with the jargon of their trade. As if this isn't hard enough to handle, your communication is also (most likely) going to be conducted in a foreign language.

In vast swathes of rural Eastern and Central Europe, you are unlikely to find a notary or lawyer who speaks sufficient English to explain anything much of the buying process to you. Important matters, such as inheritance-related questions, almost certainly require advice that you can understand. The estate agent can help, if he or she speaks good English, but an agent is hardly a source of unbiased advice or legal expertise. Even in cases where the notary you are using speaks good English, he or she almost certainly knows little or nothing of the international dimensions of the transaction.

Even if you or your partner speak the language of your new country, you may not feel up to handling multiple, technical conversations. Insist on a translator being present as you sign documents so that you know exactly what you are getting into and are confident that you are not straying into a minefield.

Documents such as your surveyor's reports, contracts, building certificates, planning consents, and property registration documents all need translating. Your lawyer may be able and prepared to summarise the areas that he or she thinks are important in a letter or even have translated any areas of potential concern. But unless your lawyer or the person he or she relies on for translation is reasonably competent in the technical aspects of surveying or building work, much vital information can be lost.

Four organisations can provide you with someone to translate technical documents or provide a translator for crucial meetings:

- **Association of Translation Companies** (020-7930-2200; `www.atc.org.uk`), founded in 1976, vets members before admission and all are required to carry full professional indemnity insurance cover to safeguard the interests of the translation purchaser. Its Web site offers a members' directory as well as a quotation request form.
- **Association of International Conference Interpreters** (`www.aiic.net`) has 2685 interpreters on its books.
- **Institute of Linguists** (020-7940-3113; `www.iol.org.uk`) has 6600 members and runs a company, Language Services Ltd, with its own Web site: `www.languageservicesltd.com`.
- **Institute of Translation & Interpreting** (`www.iti.org.uk`) has a directory of members on its Web site who can provide translation and interpreter services.

Translating documents costs between €100 and €200 per 1000 words, depending on such factors as the complexity of the work and where the work has to be done. Fortunately, most translation work does not involve travel, so expect usually to be paying towards the lower end of these figures.

Part II

Examining the New Europeans

"The good news is we've just heard we've secured the property in Slovenia, so we can move there straightaway. The bad news is Gerald's spent the last two years learning <u>Slovakian</u> instead of Slovenian by mistake."

In this part . . .

In this part every aspect of the latest entrants to the European Union is examined, from the perspective of owning a home there. You will get a quick overview of the country, covering the whole lot from climate, cost of living, culture, and currency, through to budget airline access, property purchase procedures, taxes, and the prospects for the economy. Then comes a more detailed review of the handful of parts of the country that are believed to offer the best prospects for foreign buyers. These places will be those considered highly desirable to tourists, business people, and the more progressive elements of the local population. This 'desirability' factor will be what ensures you'll enjoy being there and if you want to let the property out or to sell it later, there will be a ready market. There is also an indicative price guide for properties in each area. But keep in mind this is a fast changing environment so use the country property websites and the other sources of property price statistics given, to keep current on the state of the market for both buying and renting.

Chapter 5

Czech Republic

In This Chapter

- Understanding the potential of the Czech Republic
- Discerning where you want to look
- Going through the purchase process
- Making the purchase work for you

Back in 1905 Václav Laurin and Václav Klement manufactured their first motorcar, the Voiturette, a stunner and the first of a steady stream of innovative vehicles to pour out of their factory. From 1950 to 1990 this tradition suffered something of a hiccup, and in the 1980s the Škoda became the subject of a series of jokes. For example: 'How do you double the value of a Škoda? Chuck a penny into it.' But now, with Volkswagen's help, the company is back on track producing world-class cars, making the Czech Republic the only country in new Europe to do so. In fact, only four carmakers in the world have been making cars uninterruptedly for more than 100 years, and Škoda is one of them.

The history of the Škoda motorcar is in many ways a metaphor for the Czech Republic as a whole – a sort of sleeping beauty awaking from a long slumber. Yes, the country has experienced problems along the way. The Czech Republic was part of Czechoslovakia from 1918 to January 1993, at which point it had a slightly acrimonious separation from Slovakia, also known as the Slovak Republic.

The Czech Republic is made up of the exotic-sounding former provinces of Bohemia, Moravia, and Czech Silesia, collectively known as the Czech Lands. The very names conjure up images of castles, mediaeval towns, and – rather more prosaically – very drinkable beers. Most of the world only knows Prague (certainly an exciting and fast-developing property market), but the nation has a lot more to offer than its capital. To rephrase the Škoda joke, 'How do you double the value of your property in Czech? Buy now and sit back for five years.'

Fast facts about the Czech Republic

Area: 78,864 square kilometres, slightly larger than Ireland and smaller than Austria.

Population: 10,241,000.

Location: Landlocked – the Czech Republic lies at the very heart of Europe. It has 1,881 kilometres of borders: 362 kilometres with Austria to the south, 215 kilometres with Slovakia to the southwest, 658 kilometres with Poland to the northwest, and 646 kilometres with Germany to the north and northeast.

Language: Czech belongs to the western group of Slavic languages and is related to a greater or lesser extent to Slovak, Polish, Ukrainian, Belarusian, Russian, Bulgarian, Macedonian, Slovene, Serbian, and Croatian. Worldwide just 10.5 million people speak Czech – and all but around 200,000 of them live in the Czech Republic.

History and geography require many Czechs to speak more than just their own language. Older citizens (60 years and up) speak German. Those between 30 and 70 can usually speak Russian, given that most studied it at school during the nation's Communist era. Students and young people speak English, or are eager to learn.

The quirky Web site Bohemica.com (`www.bohemica.com`) has a Czech dictionary online and a database of translators.

Currency: The official currency is the Czech crown (*korun* or *koruna*, abbreviated Kč, and with the international abbreviation of CZK). The crown is made up of 100 *haléř* (abbreviated hl). The currency is floating but tied loosely to the euro since the Czech Republic joined the EU. The euro is worth about 28 crowns, while £1 is worth 41 crowns.

Time zone: GMT +1.

European Union standing: The Czech Republic joined the EU as a full member in May 2004. The country is relatively prosperous and is harmonising its economy well with EU requirements. However, the nation is currently fighting for an extension of the phase-in period in which it can continue to apply a reduced value-added tax (VAT) rate to housing construction and heat supplies – factors that have an important bearing on the property market.

Emergency services: Emergency switchboard staff may not speak good English. If you need to call for assistance, do so through your local contacts or hotel receptionist. Alternatively, use the following emergency phone numbers:

Ambulance: 155

Directory enquiries: 1180

Emergency: 112

Emergency road service: 154 or 1240 on which English is spoken

Fire: 150

Police: 158

Visas: If you are a British citizen with a British passport, you don't need a visa to enter the Czech Republic as a tourist. If you are not a British citizen, contact your nearest Czech Embassy (020-7243-1115; `www.mzv.cz`) to see whether a visa is required. For identification purposes, all visitors are advised to carry a passport or photocopies of the data page of their passport at all times. EU and European Economic Area citizens staying in the Czech Republic for more than 30 days need to register with the Alien and Border Police. If you are staying in a hotel, ask the front desk staff to help arrange this registration for you.

EU citizens can contact the Foreign Police Department in Prague East (Pražská 18, 250 66 Zdiby; +420-974-820-950) or Foreign Police Department in Prague West (Zborovská 13, 150 00 Prague 5; +420-974-882-690). Citizens of other countries should contact the Foreign Police Department at Sdružení 1, Prague 4 (Pankrác 140 00; +420-974-820-925).

By air from the UK: The Czech Republic is well served by budget and other airlines with dozens of flights each day from various British airports. In addition, to the usual suspects, check out Czech Airlines (+420-239-007-007; `www.czechairlines.co.uk`). Prague is reasonably central and provides the best way to reach most places in the country. Ruzyně International Airport, located about 12 miles to the west of Prague, is serviced by a shuttle bus service between the city centre and city airport buses, which link up with the city's metro. A taxi to the airport costs around 120 Kč (£3).

By train from the UK: Travel from London to Prague by train involves going first by Eurostar to Brussels and then to either Cologne, Berlin, or Frankfurt. From these cities you can get a sleeper train to Prague. The Man in Seat Sixty-One (`www.seat61.com`) provides an overview of the possible routes. The whole journey takes between 20 and 24 hours. The simplest way to book is by phone using either Deutsche Bahn's UK office or European Rail.

Other routes from the UK: TravelCoach through pan-European Eurolines runs between London and Brno, Plzen, and Prague. The trip takes 20–27 hours.

Accommodation: Accommodation in the Czech Republic is plentiful and inexpensive, particularly outside Prague city centre and other key tourism areas. Hotels Czech (`www.hotelsczech.com`) specialises in hotels throughout the country, including the ski resorts. The hotels range from luxury to fairly basic with prices to match. Expect to pay €30–200 (£20–135) a night. Czech Travel Guide (`www.czech-travel-guide.com`) is a portal with links to a number of hotel and apartment Web sites with nightly rates starting from €16 (£11) per night per person. The Czech Expats Web site (`www.expats.cz`) has an accommodation portal where you can find apartments for long-term rental from €350 (£240) per month and hostel accommodation from €10 (£6) a night.

The Czech Republic is stable economically and politically and has been a full member of the European Union (EU) since 2004. However, it's not all a bed of roses. The nation still experiences a high degree of corruption and plenty of investors are looking to make a fast buck, especially in the *off-plan* section of the property market. I cover purchasing off-plan property in Chapter 18.

Getting to Know the Czech Republic

The Czech Republic is on a roll. It has everything going for it. The economy is growing fast, people have jobs, and wages are rising in line with increasing productivity. Companies, particularly American ones, are rushing to set up factories and operations in the country to take advantage of a skilled labour force. And the Czech Republic itself has much to offer, as the growing tourist population demonstrates.

Cultural considerations

Hundreds of flights come in each day – winter, spring, autumn, and summer – to the country's capital, Prague. The Czech Republic is that rare phenomenon – an all-year destination. What the country lacks in beaches (it is landlocked), it more than makes up for in historic attractions.

Old hands who 'discovered' Prague a decade or so ago often complain about not having the city to themselves any more. While Prague's bustling street life has proved a magnet to the 'booze-cruise' market, that audience has steered clear of the city's architectural treasures, including its magical blend of bridges, cathedrals, and church domes that straddle the Vltava river and nestle among seven hills.

While Prague undoubtedly dominates Czech culture, visitors can still explore virtually uncharted waters outside this exhilarating city. The country has an amazing number of cultural monuments. For a start, you can enjoy more 2,000 castles and chateaux, as well as numerous spa towns that have been frequented for medicinal purposes for more than five centuries. (Check out the later section 'Splashing in a spa' for more about the Czech spa experience.)

The Czech Tourism Web site (`www.czechtourism.com`) provides a valuable backdrop to everything cultural, incorporating information on the latest tourism initiatives, including eco-tourism.

Climate and weather

Though continental influences are evident, the climate of the Czech Republic is variable and does not conform readily to one particular category. Aside from areas of high ground, temperatures are relatively uniform across the country. The mean annual temperature at Cheb in the extreme west is 7°C and rises by only a couple degrees in Brno in southern Moravia. High temperatures can reach as high as 33°C in Prague during July, while in Cheb temperatures can get down to –17°C in February. Table 5-1 lists average temperatures for various Czech locations.

The growing season – when plants are actively growing – is about 200 days in the south but less than half that in the mountains. Annual rainfall varies from around 18 inches in central Bohemia to more than 60 inches on the Krkonoše mountains. Tables 5-2 and 5-3 show average rainfall and snowfall throughout the country.

Table 5-1 Average Daily Temperatures in the Czech Republic

Location	Jan–Mar	Apr–June	July–Sep	Oct–Dec
Prague	1°C	12°C	16°C	4°C
Ostrava	1°C	12°C	16°C	4°C
Liberec	0°C	11°C	15°C	3°C
Plzen Line	0°C	11°C	15°C	4°C
Karlov Vary	0°C	10°C	14°C	3°C

Table 5-2 Average Number of Rainy Days per Month in the Czech Republic

Location	Jan–Mar	Apr–June	July–Sep	Oct–Dec
Prague	9	9	8	9
Ostrava	7	10	10	8
Liberec	9	10	9	9
Plzen Line	11	12	11	9
Karlov Vary	8	10	8	7

Table 5-3 Average Number of Snowy Days per Month in the Czech Republic

Location	Jan–Mar	Apr–June	July–Sep	Oct–Dec
Prague	6	0	0	2
Ostrava	7	0	0	4
Liberec	8	0	0	3
Plzon Linc	8	1	0	4
Karlov Vary	7	1	0	3

English-language media

Finding an English newspaper outside the major cities is difficult. Where available, English papers typically arrive a day or two late and cost around 80 Kč ($2).

You can pick up local and some international news in English on the following Web sites, some of which also provide print versions:

- **Prague Daily** (www.praguedaily.com) is a World News (WN) network portal bringing together a range of information sources throughout the country. The real-estate section is worth a look.
- **Prague Monitor** (www.praguemonitor.com) is an online daily paper that carries small ads from expats for just about everything – rooms to let, cars for sale, second-hand furniture, language tutoring, and mortgage advice.
- **Prague Post** (www.praguepost.com) is a weekly print newspaper that also appears online. It has a useful section on properties for sale and rent, but it covers only Prague.
- **Prague Tribune** (www.prague-tribune.cz) provides a range of reports on new business tools and practices in human resources, marketing, finance, and technology and includes a small section on real estate. This is a subscription magazine published monthly in both Czech and English, but online it is free.
- **The Czech Business Weekly** (www.cbw.cz) has an in-depth property section with archived articles covering a wide range of real estate opportunities, including residential, retail, industrial, and distribution.

Radio Prague (www.radio.cz/english) broadcasts online in English with local and international news. Radio frequencies vary throughout the day, so check the listing available on the Web site's Frequency page.

You can also receive the BBC World Service locally on FM and short wave at various times of the day. Find details on frequencies on the BBC World Service Web site (www.bbc.co.uk/worldservice).

Tourism

Tourism is an important source of income for the Czech Republic. Yet in contrast to countries such as Malta, Croatia, and Cyprus, a broad industrial base also underpins the economy as a whole. Nevertheless, the Czech Republic is attracting more foreign tourists every year, reaching a record 6.4 million visitors in 2005.

Few foreign visitors stray far from Prague. Keep this fact in mind if you are hoping for significant rental income from your property. Some regions are working hard to attract more tourists; I discuss these areas in the section 'Choosing Where to Buy'. But other areas are still far too basic to appeal to affluent tourists.

The Czech Ministry for Regional Development is beginning to develop a major new tourist market by encouraging Czechs to holiday at home. Czechs spent a record 28 billion Kč ($6.72 billion) on overseas holidays in 2005, up 30 per cent from the preceding year.

To capture some of this revenue, Czech television advertising shows various spots in the republic with the message 'Come and spend time with people who really understand your needs.' The Czech government is proposing a change of legislation that encourages businesses to help fund employees' holidays within the Czech Republic and then write off the contribution in tax cuts. This plan may boost the home tourism market, but don't hold your breath. The Czech Republic has no coastline, and the lure of beaches and the sea is always strong.

Sports and leisure

Around Prague you find all the usual paraphernalia of urban leisure life – first-rate stage plays, opera performances, classical and jazz music, discos galore, art exhibitions, and poetry readings. You can see the latest films in English or their original language, with Czech subtitles, and a monthly film club shows Czech films subtitled in English.

The Prague Post (`www.praguepost.com`) offers up-to-date listings of entertainment events in English, in print and online.

The whole sports and fitness sector is enjoying better financial conditions thanks to a massive drop in (VAT) for services in fitness clubs, gyms, and saunas, from 19 per cent to 5 per cent as of 1 January 2006. Aerobics, bowling, dance, fighting sports, squash, tennis, swimming, table tennis, yoga, and golf are all on offer throughout Prague. Unfortunately, gym memberships are not a great bargain at around 45,000 Kč ($1,000) a year.

Czech is renowned for ice hockey, and its team is among the best in the world. The **Czech International Ice Hockey Camp** (`www.hockeycamp.cz`) is a unique facility located in the Bohemian town of Nymburk, 40 kilometres east of Prague. The programme aims to pass on hockey skills to children of all nationalities, and includes sessions taught in English.

Although landlocked, the Czech Republic has 50 sailing clubs.

For the UK property buyers, the country's ski and winter sports facilities can be very attractive:

- **Špindlerův Mlýn** in the Krkonoše ('giant') mountains in northeast Bohemia near the border with Poland is the largest and most visited ski resort in the country, with downhill and cross-country ski runs.
- **Boží Dar** and neighbouring resorts have a reputation as good family ski areas, offering more than 30 kilometres of cross-country trails through the snow-covered pine forests.

I cover property opportunities related to Czech ski resort areas in greater detail in the section 'Skiing areas'.

Talking Business

The Czech Republic is one of the most stable and prosperous of the post-Communist states of Eastern and Central Europe. The economy has been growing at 4–5 per cent. Though growth may slow slightly, the Czech National Bank (ČNB) expects gross domestic product (GDP) to grow by 3.3–4.5 per cent for the next few years.

Reasons for being so bullish on the economy rest on several factors:

- **Strong interest from the USA: The Czech Republic has proved an ideal base for American companies looking for access to European markets.** Some $10.9 billion (£6.3 billion) poured into the country between 1990 and 1998 alone. This influx of business continues to create demand for higher-quality rentals, apartments, and houses.
- **The EU effect:** The benefits of joining the EU are just beginning to take effect in the Czech Republic. The country has utilised only roughly 20 per cent of the 75 billion Kč allocated from EU funds. A spending spree in the not-so-distance future may fuel growth and spur the property market further.

Examining the cost of living

The cost of living across the Czech Republic is much lower than in the UK. For example, a 33-centilitre bottle of beer costs 20 Kč (50p), a three-course meal for two with wine 500 Kč (£12), and a city centre bus ticket 8 Kč (20p). Even an ticket to see a European football match rarely costs more than 400 Kč (£10).

Prague is very expensive compared with other cities in the Czech Republic, including Brno (the second largest city) and Ostrava.

The Czech Republic ranks 30th out of the 177 countries listed in the UN's Human Development Index (`http://hdr.undp.org/reports/global/2005`), so the country is not only inexpensive but also a good place to live.

Identifying areas of value

The Czech Republic still ranks among the best-value areas in Europe despite some hefty price hikes in recent years.

For example, a new residential development of 400 apartments in the docklands area of Holesovice, Prague 7 – an established residential area that is being extensively redeveloped with new up-market commercial offices and shops – is on offer with starting prices of €53,900 (£37,500). The area is close to the city centre and has good tram and metro links. (You need to add a zero to the end of those figures to buy a comparable property in, say, London's Docklands.)

Move 80 kilometres from Prague city centre and prices drop by a third; move to the countryside around Brno or further afield and prices are half those in Prague. Of course, locations away from the capital enjoy fewer facilities and transport options. But with prices for new-build properties starting at €23,000 (£15,700), good value can definitely be had.

Assessing potential rental yields

Foreign buyers tend to look for properties in the city centre (I discuss Prague in the section 'Choosing Where to Buy'). These areas have some of the most desirable city-centre properties, but prices are high and demand is great; think Mayfair or Kensington in London, rather than Streatham or Dagenham.

According to local estate agents, rental yields in the city centre are very low, often under 2 per cent. But, as indicated by these same agents, the market average gross rental income in Prague is around 7.7 per cent – and closer to 10 per cent in other regions of the country. This is because other major cities, the ski resorts, and other areas also attract an influx of tourists.

Aside from the incoming executive market, which is strong in Prague, a thriving local market is also clamouring for rented properties. Yields on these rentals can make sense if you buy a little away from prime areas but keep close to the tram or metro routes. Most locals have for years lived in cooperative housing introduced in 1959 by the state. These pre-fabricated high-rise buildings, known as *panelaky,* were quickly assembled and intended to last for generations. The buildings are ugly and dilapidated and have almost no soundproofing or thermal insulation. Now that the average monthly wage has grown almost 50 per cent since 1998, young professionals who can't yet buy but want to live in something better are actively seeking rentals. Their need is your opportunity.

Of course, don't overlook those the old *panelaky* buildings entirely – you can still make some money off them. Some investors are buying several top-floor apartments in these blocks, converting them into larger loft apartments, and then renting them out to locals who can't afford to refurbish themselves. Most investors concentrate on top-floor apartments as a way of minimising noise intrusion from neighbouring apartments. They only have to improve the insulation in the floors and one adjoining wall to eliminate sound problems.

Considering property appreciation

According to the Czech Statistical Office (`www.czso.cz/eng`), which has been monitoring property prices since 1995, prices have risen on average at around 12 per cent annually.

CSO calculations are based on the declared prices actually achieved rather than from brokers' selling prices, which should make the statistics more reliable. Unfortunately, some distortion results when the declared price is not the same as the price actually paid. The view of brokers in the market is that prices are slowing down and will stabilise below 5 per cent for the next few years. But even that is better than the 1–2 per cent forecast for the British property market.

Young Czechs, like young Bulgarians, Turks, and Croatians, are deserting the smaller villages and towns in search of better job opportunities in big towns and cities. The result is thousands of very cheap properties in theoretically undesirable places. If you are happy to live a long way from the luxuries of Prague, €8,000–20,000 (£5,400–13,650) can buy you a potentially desirable property. The cost of renovation is still low, with professional labour (bricklayers, plumbers, electricians) coming in at less than €2 (£1.37) per hour and general labour at half that.

Properties in small towns and rural locations have two other potential advantages in the coming years: First, with increases in property prices and the cost of living, affluent Czech retirees are beginning to look to buy property in villages in order to make their pensions go further. Second, who knows – the government's strategy of encouraging Czechs to take holidays at home may just work, adding impetus to the rural property market.

Choosing Where to Buy

Although quite a large country, the Czech Republic has no region more than a couple hours from its main international airport in Prague. So from a travel perspective, anything goes when seeking out a property that suits your purse and your purpose.

I divide the country's property markets options into three buying zones, starting with the safest, if most expensive, Prague, and then straying into more exotic if risky areas of Bohemia and Moravia, where skiing, spas, and mediaeval charms abound. Table 5-4 lists some example price ranges for various cities and regions in Czech.

Table 5-4 Indicative Purchase Prices and Monthly Rents for a Three-bedroom Property in the Czech Republic

Location	*Purchase Price*	*Weekly Rent (Low/ High Season)*
Prague	€250,000 (£170,000)	€300/600 (£205/410)
Ski areas	€120,000 (£82,000)	€200/400 (£135/270)
Spa and mediaeval towns	€150,000 (£102,500)	€250/450 (£170/307)

Prague

Known as 'the Golden City', Prague straddles the Vltava river with Prague Castle towering high above the city. Prague is rightly considered one of the most beautiful cities in the world, combining Bohemian, Gothic, Baroque, Cubist, and Art Nouveau influences into a visual feast. The city is listed by UNESCO as a World Heritage Site, which means that it is an area of outstanding beauty and worth preserving.

Prague is comprised of six towns: Staré Město (Old Town), Josefov (the preserved part of the former Jewish Town, today a part of the Old Town), Nové Město (New Town), Malá Strana (Lesser Town), Hradcany, and Vyšehrad, where Prague Castle is located.

Old Town Square, Tyn Church, the astrological clock tower, and the cobbled streets contrast with the opulence of Parizska Street's designer shops and fantastic bistros. In addition to its historic monuments, Prague has every benefit of a modern city – theatres, cinemas showing films in English, an international airport with dozens of daily connecting flights, and good metro and tram services.

The city enjoys an enduring tourist market as well as a steady stream of incoming foreign executives to underpin property prices.

After that build-up, you can be forgiven for thinking that property prices are through the roof! While prices are certainly higher than in some other capital cities in the region – Sofia, Bulgaria, for example – they are still very affordable by British standards. A new one-bedroom apartment in the west of the city commands prices upwards of €60,000 (£41,000), while a similar-sized one in Old Town Square costs €220,000 (£150,200). Head out of town a mile or two (but still on the tram and metro routes), and a small studio in a 12-year-old building costs €26,000 (£17,750) – you'd be lucky to find a property anywhere on the London transport system for seven times that amount.

Skiing areas

Skiing, snowboarding, cross-country skiing, telemark or 'free-heel' skiing, and – more recently – night skiing are all popular in the Czech Republic. The Czech Republic offers seven main ski areas, but none is a serious match for the French, Austrian, or Italian resorts yet.

At €80 (£55) for a seven-day ski pass, Czech skiing is still a relative bargain – although the large numbers of Austrian and German tourists are helping push up prices.

Czech ski areas to concentrate your property search on include:

- **Beskydy-Javorníky:** A number of cross-country routes and 12 kilometres of downhill slopes run from Pustevny. Bílá, which hosts the Czech and European downhill competitions, is also in this area.
- **Jeseníky:** The Malá Morávka ski region claims to have Czech's best snow conditions. Červenohorské sedlo and Ramzová are also popular with the locals.
- **Jizerské hory:** Centred around Liberec, these ski slopes – including Bedřichov, Tanvaldský Špičák, Severák, Desná, and Ještěd – are the nearest to Prague. Ještěd has a cable car service to its 1012-metre peak and offers paragliding in addition to skiing.
- **Krkonoše:** Pec pod Sněžkou, Špindlerův Mlýn, and Harrachov are the resorts here, and all are close together and lie about an hour north of Prague. Harrachov is one of few ski resorts where snowboarders can use all the ski runs. Cross-country skiing enthusiasts can find 110 kilometres of well-maintained tracks.

- **Krušné hory:** Boží Dar, one of the highest villages in Central Europe (1028 metres), has the Neklid ski slopes running below it and is close to another centre, Klínovec, which has extensive snow-making equipment.
- **Orlické hory:** Deštné and Říčky in the Eagle mountains have fairly limited skiing, but they have some good tobogganing, boarding, and night skiing plus links to long cross-country trails.
- **Šumava:** Železná Ruda is a national park with extreme skiing on moguls. Kramolin has a large winter sports centre.

Find out all you want to know about these ski areas – facilities, lift pass costs, travel direction, and more – on the Czech Holiday Information Web site (`www.holidayinfo.cz`).

The Czech ski areas are still not saturated with new developments, so you have to do much of the legwork yourself to find properties. New-build apartments near the slopes cost upwards of €35,000 (£23,900) for a one-bedroom property. Older family houses (*rodinnè domy*) in need of some restoration work in neighbouring villages sell for €25,000 (£17,000), but for that price you get two or three bedrooms and a bit of land.

The best of the rest

No location in the Czech Republic is all that far from Prague airport, so this hub is likely to be the prime route in and out of the country for tourists and business people alike. The airport's central location opens up a wealth of villages, towns, and rural areas in Moravia and Bohemia for possible property buying. Aside from the appalling remnants of Soviet-inspired architecture, you can find dozens of places brimming with rustic charm, along the lines of neighbouring Austria.

If your prime desire is to find somewhere interesting and affordable to buy – and you're willing to accept that rental income is limited – read on. Much of the tourist traffic outside Prague takes the form of locals with limited cash to spend or foreign day trippers spending time away from the capital or motoring in from nearby Austria and Germany. Bottom line: This is not the ideal market for holiday home letting.

Splashing in a spa

An hour or so's drive from Prague takes you to western Bohemia, close to the German border and at the heart of the Czech Republic's renowned spa area.

The seeming civilised appearance of these large spa hotels – majestic colonnades, tranquil surroundings, and the promise of health and recovery – conceals the ruthlessly competitive nature of the industry. Czech spa entrepreneurs have long battled for clients, introducing newer treatment methods and bolder claims for their effectiveness. Early clients included Tsar Peter the Great, King Edward VII, Goethe, Schiller, Chopin, Beethoven, and Wagner, as well as prominent aristocrats, industrialists, business people, and bankers.

Today, spa towns are enjoying something of a revival as new forms of relaxation and regeneration, beauty stays, and stress-reducing programmes are being introduced. You can also find a range of sports and fitness activities such as golf, cycling, hiking and walking, tennis, fitness centres, swimming pools, and other activities.

The three spa towns to concentrate your property search on include:

- **Karlovy Vary:** Situated on the western border of Bohemia in the Teplá River valley, 130 kilometres west of Prague, this is the biggest, best-known, and most visited spa in Bohemia and was founded before the 14th century by King Charles IV.
- **Františkovy Lázně:** Located in a forest, 5 kilometres from Cheb.
- **Mariánské Lázně:** Situated within the Slavkovský les national park.

In Karlovy Vary you can find a luxurious, newly converted two-bedroom apartment for around €90,000 (£61,400) and more modest properties (or those in need of renovation) for €20,000 (£13,500) or so. Prices for properties just a short distance from any of these spa towns are considerably lower.

Going mediaeval

Southern Bohemia lies along Czech's border with Germany and Austria. The area is awash with small mediaeval towns and cities, beautiful countryside, and impenetrable forests. The area has fortunately been protected from the worst ravages of industrialisation.

The following two towns are good choices to concentrate your property search on (if you drive around the area, only an hour or so from Prague, you can find many other similar towns):

- **České Budějovice,** built in a curve of the Vltava river, is the second best-preserved historical town in Bohemia after Prague and is designated a UNESCO World Monument. A fortified wall was erected around the city at the start of the 14th century and the town itself is built on a mediaeval grid plan. Popular features include a Dominican cloister, a Gothic cathedral, and more famously the Budvar Brewery, which claims to make the original Budweiser beer.
- **Český Krumlov,** a few miles from České Budějovice, has one of Europe's largest castles perched on a hilltop with centuries-old townhouses below. The town has become something of a magnet for artists and draws in a large number of day trippers from Prague.

Properties for sale in the centres of these mediaeval towns are rare and relatively expensive. A few miles out, however, a three-bedroom cottage in very good condition costs around €30,000 ($20,480).

At the other end of the spectrum, expect to pay €300,000 ($205,000) plus for properties described as 'chateaux' or 'manor houses'. These stunning old buildings on sizable acreages often need major restoration work. Also, always have the ownership of this type of property checked out carefully (see the following section 'Buying into the Czech Republic') because many such houses were confiscated from their owners during the Communist era. Although most of these 'restitution cases' as they are known have been settled amicably, there could still be the occasional problem property.

Buying into the Czech Republic

An EU citizen may only purchase property and land, but not agricultural or forest land, after acquiring a *residence permit*. This condition is a five-year exemption negotiated when the Czech Republic joined the EU in 2004 in an effort to ensure that only people who actually want to live or work in the Czech Republic can buy property. Some 'favoured nations', including Norway, Switzerland, Liechtenstein, and the United States, enjoy similar property buying rights as EU citizens. Everyone else must go through a slightly more complicated and costly route and buy through a limited company. I cover using a company later in this section, as this option may be desirable for EU citizens.

You can apply for a residence permit at the Foreign Police Department (see the sidebar 'Fast facts about the Czech Republic' for more information about visas), or through the Czech Embassy (`www.mzv.cz/wwwo/?zu=London`) in your home country.

Find a lawyer who has a good command of both Czech and English and who is independent of the estate agent or developer that you are dealing with. Ideally they should be based somewhere near where the property you are investigating is located. That will ensure that they are well versed in local matters such as prospective building activities that could interfere or even enhance the value of the property, such as new developments planned or roads to be built. You need to find the lawyer before you make an offer on a property so that they can be involved in every stage of the transaction. Look for lists of English-speaking lawyers on the Martindale-Hubbell Lawyer Locator (`http://lawyers.martindale.com/marhub`), the International Law Office (`www.internationallawoffice.com/Directory`), or Legal500.com (`www.icclaw.com`). You can also find lawyers on the Web site of the British Embassy in Prague (`www.britain.cz`).

The basic procedures in the property-purchasing process are:

1. **Research the market.**

   Chapter 3 explains how to find properties, but many estate agents in the Czech Republic have someone in their offices who speaks English.

   Some agents with an extensive range of properties both for sale and to let include the following:

   - **Prague Real Estate** (www.praguerealestate.cz) is an English site with prices in either euros or the local currency. It has an extensive range of properties for sale and to rent in all areas in the city, as well as a Vicinity section that covers surrounding towns. You can also find listings for auctions, land, whole apartment blocks, and foreclosures.
   - **Loyd Realty** (+420-353-222-227; www.loyd-realty.com) has an English-language Web site and sells properties in and around the spa town of Karlovy Vary. It has been in business since 1991, claims to have closed more than 1,000 successful real-estate transactions, and has opened offices in Prague and in Germany.
   - **Reality Skekrum** (+420-387-318-824; www.realityspektrum.cz) covers the mediaeval town areas around České Budějovice. The Web site is not in English, but it does offer photos and basic descriptions of all the properties.
   - **Bohemian Country Homes** (020-8123-8353; www.bohemiancountryhomes.com) has a Web site in English and a UK phone number. The agency covers the whole country with a map-based database of properties. It can also locate properties to your specification and arrange surveys.

   Always check that the estate agent you are dealing with is a member of a professional association such as the Federation of Overseas Property Developers, Agents and Consultants (www.fopdac.com), the National Association of Estate Agents, UK (www.naea.co.uk), or locally the Association of Real Estate Offices of the Czech Republic (www.arkcr.org).

   Founded in 1991, the Association of Real Estate Offices of the Czech Republic is the largest professional association in the country with more than 200 members. Its Web site contains a database of contacts and links organised by region and an interactive map for finding information about specific areas and cities.

   On Czech Web sites, look for the word *nabidka*, which means 'property on offer'.

2. **Find a property and carry out a thorough inspection.**

   Buyers do not generally carry out building surveys on new properties in the Czech Republic because these locations come with guarantees of quality.

Have any old building (or one that you want a mortgage on) surveyed. Your estate agent, lawyer, or mortgage provider can put you in touch with a local surveyor. Other options for locating a surveyor include the following:

- **Czech Association of Certified Property Appraisers** (+420 224-808-310; www.cscom.cz) offers a database of surveyors throughout the country. The association's Web site is in Czech, but if you click the words *Ceny pozemků* and then *Vstup do databáze cen pozemků*, you can utilise the site's database.
- **Royal Institute of Chartered Surveyors** (0870-333-1600; www.ricsfirms.com) has a searchable database, and its contact centre is open between 8:30am and 5:30pm GMT, Monday to Friday.
- **Czech Yellow Pages** (www.zlatestranky.cz) is available in English and lists surveyors, architects, and more or less every other service provider in the property field throughout the country. Start by following the Building thread.

Try to seek out a professional through the personal recommendation of someone whose judgement you respect. I cover this subject in Chapter 4.

3. **Negotiate and agree on the final price with the current owners.**

After viewing a property, you can negotiate directly with the owners or through the estate agent. Keep in mind that the total price you pay also includes the following:

- **Actual cost of buying:** This varies slightly but usually works out to between 3 and 4 per cent of the purchase price. Where VAT is due on new-build properties, buying costs can be significantly higher.
- **Real estate transfer tax:** This is 5 per cent (equivalent of UK stamp duty), which is paid by the seller, with the buyer as guarantor in the case of default. Hopefully you don't have to pick up this bill – it is your lawyer's responsibility to see that you don't.
- **Estate agency fees:** Around 4–5 per cent. Little competition exists at present, so expect to pay towards the higher end. Fees may be negotiable on larger purchases and when fees are quoted at or around 5 per cent may be negotiable. These are usually though not always paid by the seller. It is not unheard of to share the cost.
- **Fees related to a limited liability company:** Buying an off-the-shelf company costs around 60,000 Kč (£1,500), plus about 15,000 Kč (£375) in tax, accounting, and administration charges. See the sidebar 'Using a limited liability company' for more information on this process.
- **Value added tax:** Currently 5 per cent of the purchase price on new properties, and 19 per cent for new garages and parking spaces.
- **Notary fees:** 1 per cent of the purchase price, payable by the buyer.

- **Legal fees:** Around 2 per cent of the purchase price – €1,000–1,500 (\$680–1,025) on average.
- **Annual property tax:** 0.035 per cent of the purchase price (or €35 per €100,000 (\$24 per \$68,275).
- **Property management charges:** €300–700 (\$205–478) per year, due on new properties in most holiday complexes. Of course, this fee depends on the level of property management services you select.

4. **Draw up and sign the initial contract.**

   After you and the seller agree to a price, your lawyer draws up an *initial contract* that outlines the details and any conditions that must be met before the sale completes (for example, repairs).

   After you and seller sign the initial contract and you pay a deposit of 10 per cent, the sale is legally binding. You normally have up to three months for your lawyer to complete property checks and to apply for and receive your residence permit.

   Should you fail to go ahead with the purchase for any reason, other than that allowed by law, you forfeit your deposit.

   If you are not going to be in the Czech Republic when the contract has to be signed, you need to give your lawyer power of attorney, which I cover in Chapter 4.

5. **Carry out the last checks and sign the final contract.**

   After the initial contract, your lawyer carries out the necessary checks and searches and ensures that the vendor provides all the relevant title documents, permissions for use, and information on any mortgages and loans outstanding.

   Your lawyer must see your residence permit before the final deed of transfer of the property is signed.

Using a limited liability company

Technically, EU citizens can own property in their own name, following changes in Czech law in 2004. However, brokers are still recommending using a limited liability company, known in the Czech Republic as a *společnost s ručením omezením* or SRO, because a company offers considerable protection of personal assets, which can be at risk if you become inadvertently involved in a fraudulent transaction. Using a limited liability company also offers some possible taxation advantages on selling. It also has the advantage of getting around the need for a residency permit. Of course, seek out impartial legal advice in the Czech Republic if you intend to use a company and never just rely on a broker's recommendation.

Clear up property ownership questions early

Ben (not his real name) had put down his deposit on a bargain apartment in Prague and believed all was going well with his purchase until his lawyer rang him with some alarming news. The vendor didn't actually own the property he was selling – it belonged to his two daughters after a transfer the seller had made seven years earlier as a tax-planning strategy. Previously, the vendor had both his daughters sign agreements giving him the right to sell their property at a time of his choosing.

The notary, however, had ruled that this agreement was too old to be safely considered valid and that the daughters needed to sign a new letter of agreement. One daughter, still living with her father, readily signed again, but the other, now living in Canada with her husband, had second thoughts and refused to sign. Ben's deal was put in limbo – where it remains today, more than two years after the initial agreement.

Without timely legal advice Ben could have wasted a lot more time and money in trying to proceed with this purchase. Had he relied only on the broker he could in the worst case have ended up buying a property with a defective ownership title. Something he may not have discovered until he came to sell.

6. **Pay for your property.**

   After you receive you residence permit, you must pay the balance of the purchase price to the seller in Czech currency.

   To do this, you can either instruct your own bank or buy currency through a specialist company, which may offer more competitive rates (see Chapter 17 for more on moving money around). You can either have the purchased currency sent directly to your own bank account in the Czech Republic or you can use your lawyer's escrow account (this is a client account in which your funds are kept separate and cannot be accessed without your permission).

7. **Transfer utilities.**

   Registering for electricity, gas, water, telephone, and refuse collection is a time-consuming process in the Czech Republic, involving lots of paperwork. Sorting out the issues can take several days and in some cases weeks. Before moving in, try to deal with everything well in advance – or assume that for some days you will be in your new property without electricity and gas.

   Transferring utilities is definitely not something to tackle on your own, unless you are fluent in Czech. Get your estate agent to make all the necessary arrangements on your behalf. Agents typically expect to take on this responsibility.

Getting Settled in the Czech Republic

The Czech Republic is not too difficult to settle into. The internal transport systems are reliable, inexpensive, and interconnected. In fact, a single Web site lists timetables and routes for all buses, trains, and planes. Banking too is user-friendly, and English-speaking branches (in the cities at least) are easy to find.

This section covers the major topics you need to address when making yourself at home in your new Czech property.

Taxing matters

Czech taxation concerns related to property include:

- **Individual tax:** The Czech Republic has a progressive taxation system under which individuals are taxed at between 15 per cent on the first 109,200 Kč (just over £2,600) and 32 per cent on income above 331,200 Kč (£7,950).
- **Business tax:** Corporate tax is 24 per cent (down from 45 per cent a decade ago).
- **Capital gains tax:** This is not charged on the sale of a property that has been the owner's main residence for at least two years. If the property is not a main residence or is being sold less than two years from the date of purchase, tax is applied at the same rate as individual personal tax, up to a maximum of 32 per cent.
- **Value-added tax:** Charged at 19 per cent. The registration threshold is 1,000,000 Kč (£24,000).
- **Double taxation treaties:** Czech has a double-taxation treaty with the UK and with many other countries, which ensures that you don't end up paying tax twice on the same income or paying more tax than you should. (See Chapter 16, where I cover double taxation treaties.)
- **Death duties:** The rates of inheritance tax and gift tax range from 0.5 to 40 per cent. These depend on the relation between inheritor/donor and acquirer/heir/donee.
- **Local taxes:** Several administrative and local taxes, covering environmental fees for air and water pollution and waste deposit fees, are assessed. The sums are small, and the thing to keep in mind with all such local taxes is that the average annual wage is still less than £6,000 a year and such taxes are based on that amount.

To find out more about the tax regime in Czech, visit the Pricewaterhouse Coopers Web site (www.pwc.com/ua/eng/main/home/index.html). The Publications page provides a comprehensive and up-to-date guide to tax and much else besides. Or refer to the World Wide Tax Web site (www.worldwide-tax.com).

Opening a bank account

Opening a bank account in the Czech Republic is easier than doing so in the UK. All you need is a passport and some other form of identification, such as a driving licence. You also need to make a modest deposit of 200–2,000 Kč (£5–50), depending on the bank. You can find an application form in English on the eBanka Web site (www.ebanka.com), which gives you an idea of what information banks ask for.

Česká Spořitelna (www.csas.cz) has a special division designed exclusively for expats, offering everything from mortgages to Internet banking. You can find an excellent evaluation of Czech banks on the Czech Expats Web site (www.expats.cz/prague/article/money/bank-comparisons), which rates the ten largest local banks on friendliness, customer service, and charges. See also Chapter 17, where I cover offshore financing.

Staying healthy

The Czech Republic has a good Western-style medical service with some English-speaking doctors and dentists. However, staff members at the majority of Czech medical facilities do not speak English.

If you do not speak Czech and experience a sudden serious illness or emergency, call the central emergency services line on 112. Operators here speak English and, after establishing your problem, can contact appropriate emergency services on your behalf, staying with you to interpret when necessary.

You may find that doctors, dentists, hospitals, and even ambulances expect cash payment for services, so get receipts and seek reimbursement. The Centre for International Reimbursements (www.cmu.cz) has advice on what you can and can't expect of Czech health services, a full description of services, and a directory of hospitals. On the Prague TV Web site (prague.tv/prague/health), you can also find a list of doctors, dentists, and 24-hour pharmacies in Prague, most of whom speak at least some English.

Getting around the country

You have several options for conducting daily business and travelling within the Czech Republic. This section covers your major transportation options.

Car

Your UK driving licence is valid in the Czech Republic, but it must have a photo, otherwise an International Driving Permit is also required.

Vehicles in the Czech Republic drive on the right and observe the following speed limits: in built-up areas, 50 kilometres (31 miles) per hour; outside built-up areas, 90 kilometres (55 miles) per hour; on motorways, 130 kilometres (80 miles) per hour. Wearing seat belts is compulsory, and drinking and driving is absolutely prohibited.

Motorways run from Prague to Plzen, and from Podebrady to Bratislava (Slovak Republic) via Brno. You have to buy a vignette (season ticket) that costs approximately 800 Kč (£20) annually. A 10-day vignette is also available for approximately Kč100 Kč (£2.50).

The best roads in the Czech Republic generally meet European standards, but off the main roads surfaces are often uneven and potholed. Street signs and road markings are erratic and driving standards are poor. Overall the Czech Republic has one of the highest incidences of road fatalities in Europe. The road emergency service is available by calling 154.

Bus

Buses are a fast and comfortable way to get around the country. You can see the timetables for buses (as well as trains and planes) on `www.vlak-bus.cz` – the National Information System for Public Transport.

To actually book tickets, however, you must either to go the appropriate station or to a travel agent.

Taxi

Taxis are plentiful and usually cheap. The basic rate is about 25 Kč (£0.60) per kilometre (more at night).

However, many taxi drivers in Prague, and in other Czech cities, are dishonest and try to take advantage of foreigners. To avoid being overcharged, try when possible to book a radio-taxi from a reputable firm such as AAA, Profitaxi, City Taxi, or Radio Taxi, and always negotiate fares in advance.

If you have no choice but to use a taxi in the street, make sure that the vehicle is visibly marked with the company or commercial name of the taxi owner, together with the identification number. Keep a careful eye on the meter to make sure that it isn't set to 'fast forward'.

Train

The Czech rail network is very comprehensive, going to even the most remote locations. But despite the introduction of a new high-speed Pendolino train that has been tested at speeds of up to 237 kilometres per hour (147 miles per hour), most journeys are slow and involve going through Prague.

Czech Railways (`www.cd.cz`) publishes a national timetable and fare structure on its Web site. Fares are very inexpensive by British standards.

Plane

Czech Airlines (+420-239-007-007; `www.czechairlines.co.uk`) operates an extensive domestic service with regular domestic flights from Prague to Ostrava, Brno, and Karlovy Vary.

Other options

Prague has a comprehensive metro, bus, and tram service throughout the city and suburbs. Buses, trolleybuses, and trams also run in Brno, Ostrava, Plzen, and several other towns.

Chapter 6

Hungary

In This Chapter

- Understanding the potential in Hungary
- Discerning where you want to look
- Going through the purchase process
- Making the purchase work for you

Economically and politically, Hungary has been a full member of the European Union (EU) since 2004. The tourist market in the country is strong, and Hungary has received significant inward investment over the past decade – both important factors in driving an appealing property market. But the story here is not all a bed of roses: The nation still has a degree of corruption and you can find some people out to make a fast buck, especially selling *off-plan properties*. (I cover the pros and cons of off-plan property in Chapter 18.)

A substantial portion of the Hungarian property market is based in and around the capital, Budapest, which is hardly surprising as it has the country's only international airport and many of the nation's most alluring tourist attractions. However, after five or six years of strong price growth in the region, most brokers believe that the market is taking a breather.

Hungary's slightly slowed-down market means that now is a good time to hunt out *value* because you are under no pressure to buy. (That's not to say the brokers aren't going to try and create a little pressure of their own. But you can check up on the market yourself using the resources I describe in the later section 'Talking Business'.)

While you may be tempted to confine your property search to Budapest, Hungary has much more to offer, including an inland sea area that enjoys much warmer weather than the rest of the country. That area – not unlike a Mediterranean beach resort – is quite a surprise for a landlocked country. See the section 'Lake Balaton' later in this chapter for details.

Fast facts about Hungary

Area: Total: 93,030 square kilometres, about the same size as Portugal and a third larger than Ireland. Lake Balaton, the largest lake in Central Europe at 690 square kilometres, is located in the western portion of the country and is known as the 'Hungarian Sea'.

Population: 10,006,000, much the same as the Czech Republic.

Location: Landlocked and bordered by seven other nations, Hungary claims to be at the heart of Europe. (This assertion will certainly be more credible after Ukraine and Turkey join the EU.) Hungary has 2,171 kilometres of border: 366 kilometres with Austria to the northwest, 677 kilometres with Slovakia to the north, 103 kilometres with Ukraine to the east, 443 kilometres with Romania to the southeast, 151 kilometres with Serbia and Montenegro to the south, 329 kilometres with Croatia to the southwest, and 102 kilometres with Slovenia to the west.

Language: If you speak Finnish or even Turkish, you may recognise an odd word or two of Hungarian. The language, also known as Magyar, is part of the Finno-Ugric group of languages. Without getting too technical, this means that it is related to the Finnish language, among others. Additionally, many of Hungary's ancestors passed through Turkey, and Turks occupied Hungary for 150 years, which is why many Hungarian words sound similar to Turkish. Some 4 million people outside of the country, predominantly in Romania, Slovakia, Serbia and Montenegro, and Ukraine, speak Hungarian. It is even an official language in some provinces of Austria. An English–Hungarian dictionary is available at the Department of Distributed Systems Web site (`http://dict.sztaki.hu/english-hungarian`).

People throughout the region speak Russian widely as well, because many studied the language at school courtesy of their former Communist ruler. German is also reasonably common as the country was for centuries part of the Austro-Hungarian Empire. Students and young people speak English, and many others are eager to learn.

Currency: The official currency is the forint (abbreviated to Ft and with the international abbreviation of HUF). Originally the money was minted in Florence as golden coins, known as *fiorino d'oro*. A bout of hyperinflation in 1999 eliminated the *fillér*, of which there were 100 to the forint. At the time of writing, £1 is equivalent to 382 HUF, and €1 equals 2,632 HUF.

Time zone: GMT +1.

European Union standing: Hungary joined the EU as a full member in May 2004. The country is relatively prosperous but is struggling to harmonise its economy and public administration with EU requirements. By 2008, many predict that Hungary's public deficit will reach 10 per cent of gross domestic product (GDP), which is three times the acceptable level for the European Central Bank. The EU has agreed to let Hungary off the fines that should be imposed; however, as a consequence, Hungary will be among the last of the new EU countries to adopt the euro.

Emergency services: Staff at the main emergency number (112) usually speak English, but other switchboard personnel may not speak good English. Consider using your hotel operator for assistance. Important phone numbers include:

Ambulance: 104

Directory enquiries, in English: 191

Emergency (English usually spoken): 112

Fire: 105

Police: 107

Visas: EU citizens don't need a visa to stay in Hungary for up to 90 days during any six-month period, as long as they have valid passports. If you want to stay longer than 90 days, either apply through the Hungarian Embassy (`www.huemblon.org.uk`) for a *tartózkodási vízum* (long-term stay visa). If you are in Hungary and want to extend your stay, contact the Hungarian Immigration and Nationality Office (+36-463-9102; `www.bm-bah.hu`) at least two weeks before your 90 days are up. The Office of Immigration and Nationality of the Ministry of Interior is located at Harmat u. 131, 1102 Budapest. Non-EU citizens should contact their nearest Hungarian embassy or consulate to see what visa conditions apply.

By air from the UK: Budapest lies in the north-central part of Hungary and provides the best way to reach most other destinations. Ferihegy International Airport is 16 kilometres southeast of the capital. A minibus shuttle service between the airport and the capital costs around 2,300 HUF (£6). Taxis generally apply a transfer fare, which is a lump-sum fare of 5,000–8,000 HUF (£13–21) to take passengers from the airport to any Budapest destination. Public transport is the cheapest way to reach the city centre – rides take around 30 minutes and cost 150 HUF (£0.39).

Hungary is well served by budget and other airlines, with dozens of flights each day from various British airports. As well as the usuals, consider Malév (Hungarian Airlines (+36-1235-3888; `www.malev.hu`).

By rail from the UK: Travel by train means going first to Paris by Eurostar, and then overnight on the Orient Express (not the posh one – that's the Venice–Simplon Orient Express) to Vienna. From there, you have a three-hour journey on the Avala InterCity train to Budapest. The whole journey takes about 25 hours. The simplest way to book is by phone with either Deutsche Bahn's UK office or European Rail. The Man in Seat Sixty-One (`www.seat61.com`) provides an overview of the route.

By coach: The pan-European Eurolines runs between London and Budapest and to Györ, located halfway between Vienna and Budapest and Siófok, a tourist resort near Lake Balaton. The journey time is 27–30 hours.

Accommodation: Accommodation in Hungary is plentiful and inexpensive, particularly outside of Budapest city centre and other key tourist areas. In Budapest, you can find rooms for €100 (£69) per month and small apartments from around €250 (£170), but you have to look long and hard after reaching the country, using newspapers and Web sites that I list in the later section 'English-language media'.

Getting to Know Hungary

Hungary, perhaps even more so than the Czech Republic, is on a roll. The country has everything going for it: The economy is growing fast, people have jobs, and wages are rising (in line with increasing productivity, of course). Companies, in particular German-American ones, are rushing to set up factories and operations in the country and take advantage of its skilled labour force.

And Hungary itself has much to offer, as its growing tourist population demonstrates. Hungary is that rare phenomenon – an all-year destination. Hundreds of flights come in each day to the capital, Budapest.

B&B dreams

Originally from Halifax, Darren Kingsmith, a carpenter, and his partner Teresa, a bank manager, always dreamed of running a bed and breakfast abroad. For a long time they talked about moving to Spain, but they ended up missing the boat as prices rose too far to make economic sense. They then started to look further afield and eventually chose Hungary because of the country's fine reputation for horses. The Kingsmiths envisioned a house with a bit of land where Teresa, an avid horse lover, could run a riding stable.

The couple finally put their house in England on the market and took the plunge towards making their dream reality. Their house sold sooner than expected and within weeks they whittled dozens of Hungarian properties down to two viable options, both needing lots of work and located near Pécs in the warmer southern region of the country near the Croatian border.

The Kingsmiths had worked hard to renovate their home in the UK, so they had fairly realistic expectations for their Hungarian property. Still, settling into a new country and developing a new business have been challenging. Darren is adjusting to their new lifestyle gradually and has had to be patient while networking with new suppliers and understanding the ways in which official things are done in Hungary. For their bed-and-breakfast business, Teresa currently prepares meals and does the books. She has bought a horse and rides herself, but opening the stables is still a few years off. When asked if they have any regrets, Daren says simply, 'No, but it is not quite what we expected. We simply have to accept the long hours and different lifestyle.'

Cultural considerations

About the only activity that Hungary is short on when compared with its neighbours is some good down-hill skiing – a pity, because the country receives considerable snow in the winter. Aside from hitting the slopes, you can enjoy a wide range of activities, from opera to sports to some of the best wines in the world.

More than 3 million people a year visit Hungary, and nine out of ten stay within the city limits of Budapest. Part of the appeal lies in the fact that the capital is really three cities in one. In 1873, Buda and Óbuda on the east bank of the Danube river joined with Pest on the west bank, resulting in an amazing city with 237 monuments, 223 museums and galleries, 35 theatres, 90 cinemas, 2 opera houses, 12 concert halls, and an awful lot of great restaurants, shops, and places just to chill out.

Around Budapest, you find all the usual paraphernalia of urban leisure life – first-rate stage plays, opera performances, classical and jazz concerts, discos galore, art exhibitions, poetry readings, and live entertainment of every variety. Cinemas show the latest films in English, or whatever their original language, with Hungarian subtitles.

You can find listings of entertainment events in the English-language newspaper the *Budapest Sun* (`www.budapestsun.com`), which also has a comprehensive guide to the city's 28 cinemas and cinema complexes and information on metro and bus routes.

Budapest is just a fraction of what Hungary has to offer. There are many other great places, such as:

- Hortobágy and Kiskunság are vast national parks of exceptional natural beauty.
- The city of **Debrecen** is the country's second largest city and serves as a sporting venue and host to Hungary's premier jazz festival.
- Historic **Kecskemét** is famed for its Art Nouveau influences.
- **Lake Balaton** is Hungary's top summer retreat with 170 kilometres of shoreline and thermal lakes, including those at Hévíz, which are warm enough for a winter dip.
- Internationally renowned wine towns include **Eger,** the source of the popular *Bikavér* (Bull's Blood), and **Tokaj,** home of superlative dessert wines.

Climate and weather

Hungary has a continental climate, with cold, cloudy, humid winters and warm to hot summers. Temperature can get as high as 38°C in the summer, but average temperatures even in August rarely go much above 25°C. Winters can get as cold as –29°C. See Table 6-1 for more information about typical temperatures throughout the country.

Hungary experiences an average of six or seven days a month with some rain. Most regions get some snowfall between November and March, with Miskolc, near Ukraine, experiencing the heaviest falls. See Tables 6-2 and 6-3 for precipitation information.

Around Pécs, in the southern region of the country near the Croatian border, the climate is somewhat Mediterranean. Summers and autumns are slightly warmer than elsewhere in Hungary, and the region receives a day or so less average rain each month.

Table 6-1 Average Daily Temperatures in Hungary

Location	*Jan–Mar*	*Apr–June*	*July–Sep*	*Oct–Dec*
Budapest	2°C	16°C	19°C	4°C
Pécs	3°C	16°C	20°C	6°C
Györ	2°C	15°C	18°C	3°C
Miskolc	1°C	14°C	18°C	4°C
Szeged	2°C	16°C	19°C	5°C

Table 6-2 Average Number of Rainy Days per Month in Hungary

Location	*Jan–Mar*	*Apr–June*	*July–Sep*	*Oct–Dec*
Budapest	6	8	6	6
Pécs	4	7	5	4
Györ	7	7	7	7
Miskolc	5	8	7	6
Szeged	6	8	7	6

Table 6-3 Average Number of Snowy Days per Month in Hungary

Location	*Jan–Mar*	*Apr–June*	*July–Sep*	*Oct–Dec*
Budapest	3	0	0	2
Pécs	2	0	0	1
Györ	3	0	0	2
Miskolc	4	0	0	2
Szeged	3	0	0	2

English-language media

English newspapers are available primarily in Budapest. They arrive a day or two late and cost around 800 HUF ($2). English-language print media are difficult to find outside of the capital.

You can pick up all the local and some of the international news in English on the following Web sites, some of which also provide print versions:

- **Budapest Business Journal** (www.bbj.hu) is locally owned and claims to be a one-stop shop for business information about Hungary. The Web site has an archived database of articles dating back to 1994, with bags of information on property.
- **Budapest Sun** (www.budapestsun.com), partly owned by Associated Newspapers of Great Britain, offers a weekly subscription paper that is also available online for free. The *Budapest Sun* carries lots of classified ads with properties for sale and to rent, along with a useful guide to the facts about property in each district of Budapest and a section on apartments, hotels, and hostels.
- **Budapest Week** (www.budapestweek.com) is a general news online paper, with a small classified ads section.
- **Expat Loop** (www.xpatloop.com) is a Web site that keeps English-speaking foreigners informed of events and activities throughout Hungary.

The BBC World Service is available locally on FM and short wave at various times of the day. Find details on the BBC World Service Web site (www.bbc.co.uk/worldservice).

Tourism

Hungary was the world's fourth most popular tourist destination in 1990, with more than 20 million visitors annually, according to World Tourism Statistics. This ranking put Hungary just behind Italy and ahead of the UK and Austria. Unfortunately, for Hungary at any rate, these visitors were mostly from Eastern Europe, or day-trippers from neighbouring Ukraine and Croatia, who couldn't afford to go on holiday anywhere else and who consequently spent very little money in the country.

The past 15 years have seen a sea change in Hungary's fortunes. By capitalising on its great location close to wealthy neighbours and its fantastic history, the country has become a magnet for Western tourists curious to see how the other half lived for nearly 50 years behind the Iron Curtain. Hungary is still among the most important tourist destinations in the world, now receiving 13 million visitors annually. It ranks as the 15th largest tourist destination globally and the eighth in Europe, ahead of Greece, Portugal, and Switzerland.

Even more important than Hungary's sheer tourist numbers is the fact that its new visitors spend serious money and the country's facilities are rising to meet the higher expectations of affluent tourists. These tourists present a good opportunity for property buyers who want to enter the potentially lucrative holiday rental market.

The only fly in the ointment is that Hungary is basically still a one-horse town – or a one-trick pony, depending on your point of view. Budapest acts like a sponge for the nation, keeping most Western tourists within its boundaries. Some of these come with the promise of wild stag-night parties, but Hungary – and Budapest – has a lot more to offer than clubs promising 365 days of partying every year. The silent majority of tourists come to travel on the river, go shopping, and just soak up the rich cultural heritage.

Sports and leisure

Within Budapest, you can find more or less every leisure and athletic activity, from aerobics and fitness centres to paint balling and wine tours. The city offers squash clubs galore, half a dozen golf clubs (www.virtualhungary.com/lists/golfing.htm), 48 paragliding areas (www.kfki-isys.hu/pg/repter/enit.htm), and 140 tennis clubs.

Hungary features dozens of fishing opportunities (www.mohosz.hu/angol) in the two big rivers in the Carpathian basin, the Danube and the Tisza, along with hundreds of backwaters and three big lakes, Lake Balaton, Lake Velence, and Lake Tisza.

Hunting, riding, cycling, hang-gliding, hot-air ballooning, and hiking are all well served throughout Hungary. Down-hill skiing is the country's second most popular sport, but because Hungary's highest mountain is only 1,015 metres, most locals go abroad. Instead, content yourself with cross-country skiing on one of Hungary's 51 cross-country skiing tracks (www.sielok.hu/English).

The Hungarian Tourist Board (www.hungary.com) and Virtual Tourist Hungarian (www.virtualtourist.com/travel/Europe/Hungary/TravelGuide-Hungary.html) provide between them a comprehensive guide and tons of links to tourism and leisure facilities throughout every region and almost every town in the nation.

Talking Business

Of the 10 countries that joined the EU in May 2004, Hungary has proved to be the most economically dynamic, stable, and prosperous. Low operating costs, low business tax, a well-educated population, and a progressive government are the ingredients in this success. The economy has been growing at a rate of between 4 and 5 per cent, and though this rate may slow slightly in the coming years, the nation is on a long-term growth path.

In less than 16 years, the Hungarian government has managed to reduce inflation from 17 per cent in 1989 to 3 per cent in 2006, while increasing productivity by an average of 13 per cent every year. These economic indicators have, in turn, made Hungary the recipient of more than one-third of all foreign direct investment flowing into the region (including from the former Soviet Union).

All the major credit-rating agencies rank Hungary as *investment grade,* which means that international banks are happy to lend the nation money at the lowest possible interest rates. This status means that interest rates within Hungary are low and mortgage finance is plentiful and inexpensive. More than €24 billion (£16.5 billion) of foreign investment has been pumped into Hungary.

All these economic factors bode well for the property sector of the economy for three reasons:

- Hungarians are getting wealthier because the economy is export-led, with the nation selling manufactured products, machinery, equipment, food, and even electricity to other EU countries. Hungarians are beginning to enjoy their nation's prosperity and are forming a potential market of property renters and buyers.
- Strong business activity results in a high number of foreign executives visiting Hungary to help establish local enterprises. These executives need somewhere to stay – often of higher quality and recently built – for the few years that they are in Hungary.
- The city attracts many people to study – medicine is very popular, for example, as it can be taught in English as well as Hungarian. Lots of universities attract students from all over the country.

Examining the cost of living

The cost of living across Hungary is lower than in the UK. For example, a three-course meal with wine for two people in a mid-range restaurant in Budapest runs to an average of £21. A basket of food and household products costing £20 in the UK would cost around £17 in Budapest.

Budapest is very expensive compared with other cities in Hungary. On the same basis, if you live in Miskolc you need only earn £550, if you live in Pécs £1,000, or if you live in Szeged a mere £520.

Hungary ranks 35th out of the 177 countries listed in the United Nations' Human Development Index (`http://hdr.undp.org/reports/global/2005`), so the country is not only inexpensive but also a good place to live.

Identifying areas of value

Hungary still ranks among the best value in Europe for property, despite some hefty price hikes in recent years. Local brokers suggest that the best way to appreciate the value in the property market in Budapest is to look back to house prices in the UK ten years ago – then go back another five to ten years and you have the prices for the rest of Hungary. For example:

- A two-bedroom flat on the seventh floor in Budapest's third district sells for around £26,000. This district, the oldest in Budapest, is located in the northern part of the capital and is known as Budapest's Manhattan for a recent influx of young, dynamic businesses. (Chinese companies are planning a shopping centre here too.)
- A one-bedroom apartment in a new block in District XIII, which contains Budapest's largest shopping centre, Duna Plaza, sells for £56,000. Vodafone Hungary has its new headquarters in this district, and the apartment is located on the Danube river marina with a swimming pool and tennis court. (Think of this area as London's Chelsea Harbour, but with £500,000 still in your bank account!)
- A renovated two-bedroom flat with a new kitchen in the historic centre of Budapest, District V, sells for £130,000. This area is where much of Hungary's literary, artistic, and historic heritage has its roots. Apartment buildings here can get significant subsidies of up to 80 per cent of the costs paid to refurbish façades. The district is a cross between London's Kensington and Mayfair, with a couple of zeros lopped off the prices.
- A three-bedroom property on the edge of Lake Balaton, with a wine cellar and mooring for two boats, is on the market for €42,000. There is a small kitchen garden, and electricity, water, and sewage are already connected to the property. The house has been renovated but would need further improvements to make it an attractive rental possibility. Allow a further €10,000 for such work.

The city is divided into 23 districts marked by Roman numerals I to XXIII. The *Budapest Sun* Web site (`www.budapestsun.com/propguide.asp`) has a district-by-district guide to the city with both a historic perspective and some information on the current property market.

Assessing potential rental yields

According to the Budapest Property Finder (`www.filolog.com`), rental yields of 6–8 per cent are still possible in Budapest. For €100,000 (£68,800), you can still buy and furnish a one-bedroom apartment in District VI or VII, a studio apartment in a top location such as the northern end of District V, or a two-bedroom apartment in one of the up-and-coming outer areas such as Districts VIII, IX, and XIII. The site also contends that you can rent out these properties for €6,000 (£4,120) a year.

Of course, a lot depends on the actual location, appeal, and furnishing standard. Also, the preceding estimates may be seriously adrift if you have to carry out extensive refurbishment or wait several months to find a tenant. Unless you are going to let the property yourself, you must also budget for an agency fee of one month's rent plus 20 per cent VAT and management fees of up to 12 per cent plus 20 per cent VAT on the annual rental income.

Whatever way you choose to rent out your property, you need to apply for a tax ID through the National Tax Office, APEU (`www.apeh.hu`), and pay tax of 20 per cent on profits.

Factoring in the preceding costs means that you need to rent out a property for at least €8,000 (£5,500) a year or €670 (£460) a month, and an awful lot of property is already available on the market for less than that. Instead, you can work hard and find a property for less than €100,000 (£68,800), which is possible, or just accept that your yield is likely to be nearer to 4 or 5 per cent, rather than 8 per cent.

Away from Budapest, no one is venturing even tentative figures for rental yield. Bearing in mind that most tourists and business opportunities are in and around Budapest, budget for a figure between a half to two-thirds of the yield that you can obtain on property within the capital.

Considering property appreciation

According to almost all the brokers in the Hungarian property market, property appreciated an average of 63 per cent across the country between 1999 and 2003. Between 2003 and 2005, this rate steadied to a very respectable 15–20 per cent.

While these figures may be true anecdotally, in some instances the big picture is not quite so rosy. Unfortunately, many investors currently feel that the Hungarian property market is over-developed, with supply exceeding demand. This prognosis need not be doom and gloom for you. Now is still a great time to hunt out *value* as a property buyer. Don't let yourself be pressurised into buying by a broker. Time is on your side to find an appealing property at the lowest price possible. See the sidebar 'Time to hunt for value' for more information.

Time to hunt for value

GKI Economic Research Company (www.gki.hu), formerly the Hungarian Economic Research Institute, has conducted quarterly real-estate market surveys of Hungary since spring 2000 with the aim of finding out the plans, intentions, and perspectives of developers, brokers, and households in the real estate market. According to GKI, the market has declined since 2000 and only started growing again in March 2005. GKI's latest study, which is downloadable free of charge from its Web site, states that about a quarter of managers of real-estate firms report strong oversupply and 60 per cent some oversupply, while only 15 per cent feel that the market is balanced.

On a positive note, GKI's study shows that small is beautiful – with the strongest growth (more than 30 per cent a year) in new flats under 60 square metres in size. CKI believes that smaller units are an indication of where the market is heading.

The Hungarian market is still a big one, with around 30,000 new homes being built and bought each year and building permits running at 40,000 a year. Those figures offer an important clue: They suggest that supply and demand are going to be out of kilter for a while.

So now for the $64,000 question: What will happen to property prices in the future? The best estimate is that taking a five-year view, you may see appreciation in value of between a quarter and a third – respectable if not startling.

Of course, all these sums and estimates are based on figures for the property market as a whole. Chapter 3 provides you with information on researching the market and hunting out better than average value.

Choosing Where to Buy

Hungary, though quite a large country, has no region more than two or three hours from its main international airport, just outside Budapest. From a travel perspective, anything goes in terms of seeking out a property that suits your purse and your purpose.

I divide the country's property market options into two buying zones: Budapest, which is the safest (and usually most expensive) region; and then areas around Lake Balaton, which has the most developed tourist infrastructure after the capital. Table 6-4 lists some example prices and rents for these two regions.

If rental income and capital appreciation are not so important to you, the rest of Hungary is a rich opportunity for purchasing seriously low-cost property. The Virtual Tourist Web site (www.virtualtourist.com/travel/Europe/Hungary/TravelGuide-Hungary.html) has a comprehensive guide to every district, city, and town in the country. Browse through the listings, create a short list of possible candidates, and research a few in more detail. I cover research methods in Chapter 3.

Table 6-4 Indicative Purchase Prices and Monthly Rents for a Three-bedroom Property in Hungary

Location	*Purchase Price*	*Weekly Rent (Low/ High Season)*
Budapest	€150,000 (£103,000)	€300/600 (£206/412)
Lake Balaton	€70,000 (£48,000)	€150/400 (£103/275)

Budapest

Construction of the Chain Bridge (*Lánchíd*), the first bridge to connect Buda with Pest over the Danube, took seven years. When the bridge opened in 1849, it was considered one of the world's wonders, which is hardly surprising considering that the next bridge of any substance over the Danube was in Vienna. Since then, the united city of Budapest has flourished.

But crossing the Danube is not Budapest's only water attraction. Known as the 'City of Spas', the capital is richly endowed with natural thermal water springs, including its 16th-century Turkish baths. Budapest is also home to the best of the fine arts, including major international music festivals, theatre, art, opera, and musicals. Broadway and West End staples (such as *The Phantom of the Opera*, which runs year-round at the Madách Theatre) are popular attractions. The Merlin Theatre hosts mostly English-language productions, while the Buda Vigadó and Duna Palota Theatres host folk-music and dancing shows.

In short, Budapest is a capital city with everything you can reasonably require. It's easy to get to and easy to get around after you are there. Yes, property prices are high relative to the rest of the country, but the city still offers value, particularly when you compare it with other Eastern and Central Europe capitals.

If you are a capital-city person, which I am when buying property for purely investment purposes, then Budapest is the place to start your search. The Tourism Office of Budapest (`www.budapestinfo.hu/en`) provides a comprehensive picture of what the city has to offer its residents, be they you or the clients renting your property.

Lake Balaton

Lake Balaton, some 60 miles southwest of Budapest, is Hungary's number-one vacation resort and a major wine-producing region. Forty small cities and towns dot the lake, including the following:

- **Keszthely:** The largest town in the Balaton region, which lies west of the lake. Popular tourist attractions include the Baroque Festetich Castle, the Gothic style Parish Church, and the Balaton Museum.
- **Buzsák:** A small town famous for its folk art.
- **Várhegy:** A centuries-old Turkish hill fortress near Fonyód.
- **Balatonboglár:** A resort dating back to 1211, with the remains of Roman occupation and Iron Age earthworks.

The high tourist season runs from June until the end of August, when the average water temperature is 25°C, which makes for very enjoyable bathing and swimming. Fishing, sailing, and trekking around the wineries are other popular pastimes.

The region is serviced by a small international airport, with Ryanair flying the route three times a week.

Around the lake, you can find plenty of properties in good condition for sale for between €150,000 and €250,000 ($103,000–172,000), but these are typically grand palaces compared with what you can secure in Budapest for the same money. Three-bedroom weekend cottages sell for around €60,000 ($42,200). Parcels of land and ruins are available within a few kilometres of the lake for €10,000 ($6,900) or so. Land with electricity and water, but with doubtful planning consent, is on offer from upwards of €2,000 ($1,375) for a building plot. (The word 'doubtful' has a wide range of meanings. Rely on your lawyer to advise you whether a property you are considering is potentially valuable.)

Buying into Hungary

EU citizens living in Hungary can buy a residential property as their primary residence, provided that it does not include agricultural land, without any special permission. Currently, non-Hungarian EU citizens who want to buy more than one property must get permission from the local authorities. (At some point in the near future this restriction is supposed to be lifted, but no one knows when this will happen.)

Getting permission to purchase multiple properties can be time-consuming – sometimes taking up to 60 days – and applicants are never absolutely certain of having permission granted. You must first apply to the mayor of the local government (*Önkormányzat*), and then to the Administration Office (*Közigazgatási Hivatal*) of the county. After these bodies agree that the purchase 'does not interfere with any municipal or other public interests', they grant a permit. Your lawyer is responsible for carrying out this work, for which he or she charges a fee.

Find a lawyer who has a good command of both Hungarian and English and who is independent of the estate agent or developer with whom you are dealing. Ideally the lawyer should be based somewhere near the property you are investigating: This ensures that the lawyer is well versed in local matters such as prospective building activities that could interfere or even enhance the value of the property, for example new developments planned and roads to be built. You need to find the lawyer before you make an offer on a property so that they can be involved in every stage of the transaction. Look for lists of English-speaking lawyers on the Martindale-Hubbell Lawyer Locator (`http://lawyers.martindale.com/marhub`), the International Law Office (`www.internationallawoffice.com/Directory`), or Legal500.com (`www.icclaw.com`). You can also find lawyers on the Web site of the British Embassy in Budapest (`www.britishembassy.hu`).

Many buyers circumvent the need for permission by creating a Hungarian company as a vehicle to buy property. Your lawyer creates a company (which you own) and the company purchases and owns the property – and everyone is happy.

Creating a Hungarian company offers some tax advantages too:

- The purchase tax on the property is 2 per cent, rather than the 6 per cent that individuals pay.
- Income from rents is taxed at the business tax rate, which is lower than for individuals.
- You enjoy more favourable allowances for offsetting business expenses, such as being able to charge your trips out to Hungary against your income.
- When you sell up, capital gains tax for companies is lower than for individuals.

Unfortunately some, though not all, of the preceding tax advantages require you to become a tax resident in Hungary – a status that has pros and cons of its own. I cover the ins and outs of residency in Chapter 17.

To create a Hungarian company, all you need is your passport and a photocopy of a passport for anyone else who is to be a *director* of the company (your spouse, for example). You lawyer or broker can complete the whole process for you in a day, but keep in mind that the Court of Registry, where company details are recorded, is only open from 8.30 a.m. to 3 p.m. Monday to Thursday.

After you create your company, you must have its accounts audited and filed each year at a cost of around €350–400 (£240–275). You need an accountant to help with filing. Find an accountant through your lawyer or broker or by using the Hungarian Yellow Pages (`www.yellowpages.hu`).

The basic procedures for purchasing property in Hungary are:

1. **Research the market.**

   Chapter 3 explains how to find properties, but many Hungarian estate agents have someone in their offices who speaks English. You can also keep a lookout for signs with the word *Eladó* (for sale) on buildings as you travel around the country.

   Agents with an extensive range of properties both for sale and to let include the following:

   - **Budapest Property Finder** (`www.filolog.com`), run by Krisztina Palhegyi, is jam-packed with useful information on the property-buying process, prices, trends, potential rental yields, capital appreciation, and other helpful resources for settling into your new life in Hungary (including a database of international schools).
   - **Bridge Properties** (+36-1269-2845; `www.bridgeproperties.hu`) specialises in prime-location classical properties with good rental and capital appreciation potential in downtown Budapest. The site has useful information on the process and costs of setting up a company to buy property.
   - **Hungaromax** (`www.hungaromax.com`) is a real-estate portal with links to brokers who sell property around Lake Balaton and a few other places.
   - **Hungary Property** (01293-541-667; `www.hungaryproperty.net`), founded by property investor Martin Padfield, concentrates on selling off-plan properties. (See my thoughts on buying off-plan in Chapter 20.)
   - **Somogi Kuria** (`www.somogyi-kuria.info`) specialises in properties on the south side of Lake Balaton down to Pécs.

   Confirm that any estate agent you deal with is a member of a professional association such as the Federation of Overseas Property Developers, Agents and Consultants (`www.fopdac.com`) or the National Association of Estate Agents, UK (`www.naea.co.uk`). Locally, the Hungarian Real Estate Association, HREA (+36-1336-0072; `www.maisz.hu`), has a membership list, code of ethics, and approved fee structure, which the Web site details in English. Founded in 1991, the association has nearly 500 brokers throughout Hungary.

2. **Find a property and carry out a thorough inspection.**

   Generally in Hungary, buyers do not carry out building surveys on new developments, as these properties come with guarantees of quality.

Survey any old building or one that you want a mortgage on or that you have any concerns about.

Your estate agent, lawyer, or mortgage provider can put you in touch with a local surveyor. RICS Magyarország, the local Hungarian association (+36-1327-8446), formed in association with the UK's Royal Institute of Chartered Surveyors (RICS), can put you in contact with a surveyor. You can search the RICS online database (0870-333-1600; `www.rics.org`).

Alternatively, search the Hungarian Yellow Pages (`www.yellowpages.hu`), following the Building and Financial Service threads. You can find almost every type of service provider in the property field throughout the country. You can also find furniture suppliers, translators, tax consultants, and everything else under the sun. Of course, you are usually best off finding a professional through the personal recommendation of someone whose judgement you respect and who is impartial. I cover this subject in Chapter 4.

When you are doing your homework, find out whether the district council has grants for renovating facades, stairwells, roofs, and courtyards. Many of these are in dire condition. Some councils pay up to 50 per cent of the costs; the rest is gathered from the owners. However, in some of the poorer parts of town, this is simply not an option.

3. **Negotiate and agree on the final price with the current owners.**

   After viewing a property, you can negotiate directly with the owners or through the estate agent. Keep in mind that the total price you pay also includes the following:

   - **Cost of buying:** May vary slightly but usually works out to 3–4 per cent of the purchase price (selling costs 8–10 per cent). Where VAT is due on new-build properties, buying costs can be significantly higher.
   - **Purchase tax (equivalent of stamp duty):** If you are buying as an individual, the purchase tax is 2 per cent of the market value, up to HUF 4,000,000 (£11,000), and 6 per cent on any amount over that figure.

     Companies pay only 2 per cent purchase tax, whatever the value of the property. If your company's activities include building and selling properties, you may be exempt from paying any purchase tax up to a property costing no more than HUF 30,000,000 (£81,000).
   - **Annual property tax:** A maximum of HUF 942 per square metre per year – or around €350 (£240) for a typical three-bedroom property.
   - **Estate agency fees:** Usually 3–5 per cent. Typically the seller pays these fees, but if you employ a local broker to search out properties

for you, the buyer may be landed with a bill for 1–3 per cent of the purchase price for such a service.

- **Fees related to forming a company:** Around €800 ($550), including lawyer fees, notary fees, stamp duty, and bank charges.
- **Legal fees:** Between 1.25 and 1.5 per cent.
- **Notary fees:** Usually €20 ($13).
- **Property management charges:** €300–700 ($206–480) due on new properties in most holiday complexes and apartment blocks, depending on the services you select.
- **Value-added tax:** This is due on new-build properties, currently at the rate of 25 per cent but due to drop in 2006 or 2007 to 20 per cent. Be sure to check whether this tax is included in the selling price listed in the broker's details. Private individuals selling their own properties do not have to charge VAT.

Some developers are introducing annual charges for the right to use the land on which a property stands. The idea appears to have been hijacked from the UK's ground rent, charged by the owner of a freehold to leaseholders. If you come across this charge, walk away from the deal. You can find plenty of other developers who are less rapacious.

4. **Draw up and sign the initial contract.**

   After you and the seller agree to the price, your lawyer draws up an the initial sale and purchase contract, or *Adásvételi Szerzödés*, which outlines the details and any conditions that must be met before the sale completes (for example, repairs).

   After you and the seller sign the initial contract and you pay a deposit of 10 per cent, the sale is legally binding. You normally have up to three months for your lawyer to complete the property checks with Land Registry Office (*Területi Földhivatal*). If you fail to go ahead with the purchase for any reason other than that allowed by law, you forfeit your deposit. If you are not going to be in Hungary when this contract has to be signed, you need to give your lawyer Power of Attorney, which I cover in Chapter 4.

5. **Carry out the last checks and sign the final contract.**

   After the initial contract, your lawyer carries out the necessary checks/searches and ensures that the vendor provides all the relevant title documents, permissions for use, and information on any mortgages and loans outstanding.

Your lawyer needs to see your permission from the local authorities or company registration documents before you sign the final deed of transfer of the property.

6. **Pay for your property.**

   You need to pay for your property in Hungarian currency. To do this you can either instruct you own bank or buy currency through a specialist company, which may offer more competitive rates (see Chapter 17). You can send your purchased currency directly to your own bank account in Hungary or you can use your lawyer's escrow account. (*An escrow account* is a client account in which your funds are kept separate and cannot be accessed without your permission.)

7. **Transfer utilities.**

   Registering for electricity, gas, water, telephone, and refuse collection are time-consuming processes involving lots of paperwork. The process can last several days and in some cases weeks. Before moving in, deal with everything well in advance, or take into account that for some days you will be in your new home without electricity and gas.

Register the change of ownership in the land register, and then you receive a printout identifying you as the new owner. You won't be able to transfer the utilities if you don't have this printout. Unless you are fluent in Hungarian, transferring utilities is definitely not something to tackle on your own. Your broker can, if asked, arrange for all utility meters to be read and recorded and then transferred to your name. Most brokers expect to do this as part of their general service, but you may still need to ask them to do so.

Getting Settled in Hungary

Hungary is not too difficult to settle into. The internal transport systems are reliable, inexpensive, and nicely interconnected. A single Web site (`www.bkv.hu`) lists information and timetables for all buses, trains, and planes in Hungary. Banking too is user-friendly, and finding a branch with English-speaking staff in the cities at least is not difficult. Health care is adequate by Eastern European standards, but you need to hunt out English-speaking medics.

In the following sections, I cover all the little details you need to attend to make your new residence in Hungary feel like home.

Taxing matters

Hungarian taxes related to property include the following:

- **Individual tax:** Hungary has a progressive taxation system under which individuals are taxed at between 18 per cent on the first HUF 1,500,000 (£3,920) and 38 per cent for income above that figure.
- **Business tax:** The tax rate for companies is 16 per cent, payable in advance throughout the tax year. For a new company, the advance tax is calculated from the profit forecast made by the director(s). If the profit forecast is in excess of HUF 3,000,000 (£7,840), advanced payments are made monthly; otherwise payments are made quarterly. You must pay any difference between the tax forecast and the tax due by 20 December each year.
- **Capital gains tax:** A company pays a tax rate of 16 per cent when selling a property, compared with 20 per cent when a private individual sells a property.
- **Death duties:** The rates of inheritance tax and gift tax range from 2.5 to 21 per cent, depending on the relation between inheritor/donor and acquirer/heir/donee.
- **Double taxation treaties:** Hungary has a double taxation treaty with the United Kingdom and many other countries, which ensures that you don't pay tax twice on the same income or pay more tax than you should. (I cover double taxation treaties in Chapter 17.)
- **Local taxes:** Several administrative and local taxes cover other matters, such as environmental fees for air and water pollution and waste deposit fees. These sums are small. The factor to keep in mind with all such local taxes is that the average annual wage in Hungary is HUF 156,375 a month (less than £500). Such taxes are based on this wage.
- **Tax on rental income:** Companies pay tax at a rate of 16 per cent on profit – that is, rent minus expenses including a depreciation expense allowance of 2–5 per cent annually. Individuals pay tax at 20 per cent on the full rental income and can only deduct a depreciation expense after owning the property for six years.
- **Value-added tax:** VAT is charged at 20 per cent, and the registration threshold is HUF 1,000,000 (£2,610).

To find out more about the tax regime in Hungary, visit the Pricewaterhouse Coopers Web site (`www.pwc.com/ua/eng/main/home/index.html` and follow the Publications link. You can find a comprehensive and up to-date guide to tax and much else besides. Or refer to the World Wide Tax Web site (`www.worldwide-tax.com`).

Opening a bank account

Opening a bank account in Hungary is easier than in the UK.

- **To open a forint-based bank account** (*forint számla*) – which pays no interest on any money deposited – all you need is a passport. You need to deposit at most €300 (£206), and frequently nothing at all to open the account. If you want a credit card, the bank asks you to lodge a sum equal to what you may spend.
- **To open a hard currency account** (*deviza számla*) in euros or sterling – which *does* pay interest – you need a passport and some other form of identification. You need to deposit at least €300 (£206).

Banks to consider include OPT (`www.otpbank.hu`), the largest Hungarian bank with 441 branches; Általános Értékforgalmi Bank Rt (`www.gbt.hu`), known in English as the General Banking and Trust Co., Ltd; the German-owned Magyar Külkereskedelmi Bank Rt (`www.mkb.hu`); and the US-owned CitiBank Rt (`www.citibank.hu`). All have English Web sites that explain their full range of services and costs. Additionally, check out Chapter 18, where I cover the whole subject of financing offshore.

Staying healthy

Medical treatment available in Hungary is adequate but in no way comparable to services in the UK. Life expectancy is about 10 years less that in the UK – among the lowest in the region. Hungarian doctors are well-trained, but emergency services are barely adequate and a language barrier can exist. Health services are currently stretched because all Hungarians are entitled to full health care. Private facilities, except for foreigners, are virtually unheard of.

The Hungarian Ministry of Health advises foreign residents to take out private medical insurance. I cover private medical insurance in greater detail in Chapter 20.

EU nationals resident in Hungary are eligible to receive free medical treatment from government-funded hospitals and clinics. You may find that doctors, dentists, hospitals, and even ambulances expect cash payment for their services, so be sure to get receipts. The US embassy in Budapest (`www.budapest.usembassy.gov`) offers information on health-care services.

If you do not speak Hungarian and experience sudden illness or serious injury, call the emergency services on the central number, 112. Operators on this line speak English and, after establishing your problem, can contact appropriate emergency services on your behalf, staying in contact with you to interpret where necessary.

Getting around the country

Hungary is a large country, and you have a variety of options to get from town to town – or to explore several of the larger cities. This section covers your travel options within Hungary.

Hungary does not have a scheduled internal air service. Instead, plan to travel by bus or car between major cities.

Bus

Buses are usually a fast and comfortable way to get around the country. Volanbusz (`www.volanbusz.hu`) operates buses within Hungary and to international destinations. It operates 500 coaches and travels to 170 cities and towns throughout Hungary daily. Its English-language Web site offers timetables, information, fares, and online booking services.

Car

Your British driving licence is valid, but it must have a photo, otherwise an you also need a International Driving Permit. Vehicles in Hungary drive on the right. Speed limits are 50 kilometres (31 miles) per hour in built-up areas, 110 kilometres (67 miles) per hour outside built-up areas, and 130 kilometres (80 miles) per hour on motorways. Wearing seatbelts is compulsory and drinking before driving is absolutely prohibited.

Seven of the country's eight motorways run from Budapest. You have to buy a *vignette* (season ticket), which costs HUF 1,900 (£5) for a weekly pass or HUF 3,200 (£8) for a monthly pass. The Hungarian Autoclub (*Sarga Angyal*) runs the motorways; its phone number is 188.

Hungarian motorways and major urban roads are generally good. In the countryside, the roads are often narrow, poorly maintained, and heavily used by agricultural machinery, animals, and pedestrians. Take care driving in Hungary, and expect to be stopped frequently by police checking documents whilst hunting for illegal aliens.

Taxi

Taxis are plentiful and usually cheap throughout Hungary. However, many Hungarian taxi drivers, particularly in Budapest, are dishonest and try to take advantage of foreigners. To avoid them overcharging you, try when possible to book a radio-taxi from a reputable firm, such as City Taxi or Fotaxi, and negotiate the fare in advance. If you have no choice but to use a taxi in the street, make sure that it is visibly marked with a company or commercial name and has an identification number. Keep a careful eye on the meter to make sure that it isn't set to 'fast forward'.

Taxi fares are set to rise in 2007 to HUF 240 (£0.63) per kilometre, with a pickup charge of HUF 300 (£0.78) and an additional tariff of HUF 300 for telephone orders.

Info taxi (`www.infotaxi.org`) is an online resource for information on reputable taxi companies. The site offers contact information for services in most major Hungarian cities.

Train

The Hungarian rail network is very comprehensive, going to even the most remote locations, but most journeys are slow and involve going through Budapest. Hungarian Railways (`www.elvira.hu`) publishes a national timetable and fare structure on its Web site. You can check out international travel on this Web site too, including journeys to London, but you can't get price information or book such journeys online.

Train fares are very inexpensive by British standards, with journeys typically costing less than £12 to cross the entire country.

Metro and tram

Buses, trolleybuses, and trams run in Budapest and several other major cities and towns. Budapest's system is the most comprehensive, with a wide range of options connecting the city's districts and suburbs. The BKV Web site (`www.bkv.hu`) – look carefully in the bottom centre of the home page for an English-language link – has details, timetables, and fares for all Budapest's transport systems – buses, trams, metro lines, boats, and even its funicular railway.

Chapter 7

Poland

In This Chapter

- Understanding the potential in Poland
- Discerning where you want to look
- Going through the purchase process
- Making your purchase work for you

Life in Poland continues to improve. The country's economy is growing at a rapid pace, unemployment is falling, and budget airlines are opening up new routes on a regular basis. All this and more make Poland an attractive market if you want to invest in overseas property.

Despite large areas that still suffer the blight of Soviet-era building blocks, many cities have been painstakingly restored to their pre-war glory – and in some cases even better. In terms of housing stock, the biggest pressure for new housing in Krakow and Warsaw is from the university students who come from the surrounding regions and that has been going on for years now.

Some issues regarding Polish property, like any investment, may certainly make you wary, but by and large many of the risks have been mitigated since the country's full admission to the European Union (EU) in 2005. Galloping inflation, a total collapse of the currency, and failure to address still-worrying environmental issues now seem more remote scenarios than they were just a few years back.

As I outline in this chapter, if you study the market carefully and take a few basic precautions, buying a property in Poland can be both fun and profitable.

Fast facts about Poland

Area: 312,685 square kilometres, roughly the size of Italy and about a third bigger than the UK.

Population: 38.64 million.

Location: Central Europe, east of Germany and bordering Belarus, the Czech Republic, Germany, Lithuania, Russia, Slovakia, and Ukraine. Poland also enjoys a 430-kilometre stretch of Baltic coastline.

Language: Polish. Most Poles on the street do not speak English. However, Poland has one of the youngest populations in Europe, with more than a third of its inhabitants under 25 years of age. English is a very popular language in schools, so many young educated Poles and some businesspeople speak some English. In addition to Polish, older people are more likely to speak German and Russian, the languages of their closest physical and historical neighbours.

Currency: The zloty, which translates literally as 'golden', abbreviated to Zl, is divided into 100 groszy, abbreviated to gr. In 2005, £1 was equivalent to 5.89 Zl. Beginning in 2008, the country hopes to move over to the euro. The new zloty, dating from 1995 after a period of hyperinflation, is abbreviated as PLN. Generally, international financial activity is designated in PLN, while local transactions are in zloty.

Time zone: GMT +1.

EU standing: Poland joined the EU on 1 May 2004.

Emergency services: Emergency switchboard staff rarely speak good English. If you need assistance, get help through your local contacts or your hotel receptionist, or call the Tourist Police, who speak English and are dedicated to the issues associated with tourists, including theft and accidents. Emergency phone numbers:

Ambulance: 999

Directory assistance: 913

Fire: 998

Police: 997

Tourist police: 0800-200-300

Visas: EU citizens do not need visas to visit Poland and can stay indefinitely. You can find visa regulations for individuals outside the EU on the Polish Embassy Web site (`www.poland.embassyhomepage.com`).

By air from the UK: In addition to the usual airlines, try Poland's national carrier Lot (0845-601-09-49; `www.lot.com`).

By train from the UK: You can get from London to Warsaw by train with just one change at Brussels. The journey takes 20 hours and costs about £300.

Other routes from the UK: The pan-European Eurolines bus network is playing the no-frills airlines at their own game with a concept termed *ultra low-cost* European travel. Bus travel time from London to Warsaw is around 27 hours and costs around £66.

Something you'd better know: Apartments for rent in Poland are often poky and spartan. The plumbing and heating systems may be very old, so make sure that everything is in working order before moving in. Advertised by the square metre, apartments are designated one room, one-and-a-half rooms, two rooms, and so on. A one-room apartment is comparable to a studio. 'One-and-a-half rooms' typically indicates an additional small room or area between the sleeping quarters and kitchen area.

Many landlords who rent to foreigners operate 'informally', which means that they don't declare their rental incomes to the tax authorities and avoid paperwork if at all possible. It is prudent to get some sort of written receipt from your landlord just in case there are any problems.

Accommodation: Hotels in Poland are plentiful, cheap, and varied. A good-quality three-star hotel in Warsaw or Krakow costs around £60 a night for two, but you can search out adequate hotels for half that figure. Orbis (www.orbis.pl) is the largest hotel chain in Poland, with 60 hotels and 12,000 rooms. Local tourist offices can make bookings for you, or you can book some rooms online at Staypoland.com (www.staypoland.com). Ask your estate agent for his or her recommendations, checking first that he or she has actually stayed at that hotel.

If you're staying for a week or longer, negotiate a good discount in a hotel. Alternatively, look out for rooms (*pokoje*) or lodgings (*noclegi*) that are advertised at the entrances to houses; these can cost as little as £5 a night or £200–300 a month – many with a breakfast of sorts thrown in.

Getting to Know Poland

Poland has a lot to offer tourists and residents alike:

- Cultural giants from composer Frédéric Chopin to author Joseph Conrad have called Poland home, and the country's world-class film industry has operated for more than 60 years.
- Poland has hundreds of castles, as befits a country that has been in the wars for centuries.
- While the climate is not exactly Mediterranean, much of Poland's climate is continental, which usually means that cold winter weather is balanced by some good warm spells.
- Geographically, the country has a bit of everything to offer – from ski slopes in the Carpathian Mountains in the south to long golden sandy beaches along the Baltic Sea.
- Transportation is good and getting better. Low-cost airlines from the UK and Ireland and new Eastern European budget carriers run regular flights to eight Polish cities. Fast trains and a host of bus services make getting around Poland easy and inexpensive.
- Tourism and investment from overseas are accelerating fast, spurred on by Poland's entry to the EU in May 2004. Fortunately, the cost of living in Poland (see Table 7-4) is still relatively low by UK standards.

Polish culture

Located at the very centre of Europe, Poland has been coveted and conquered by neighbouring countries on more than a few occasions over the centuries. These various visitations have added to an already diverse wealth of attractions. Poland has culturally and historically always lain somewhere between Western and Eastern Europe.

Poland has the usual run of museums and galleries, but what it boasts in spades is castles. There are 406 castles, 1,966 palaces, and 2,749 historical manor houses in Poland. It is possible to spend the night and eat superb old Polish cuisine in many. Over 250 of these are listed on the Wikipedia free encyclopaedia Web site (`en.wikipedia.org/wiki/List_of_castles_of_Poland#B`).

In the 13th century, Europe was faced with the threat of Mongol invasion. The Mongols' spread westwards from their barren homeland between China and Russia was a terrifying experience for those unlucky enough to get in their way. The Teutonic Knights, founded by German pilgrims and crusaders around 1120 and who played a major role in defending the Christendom of northeastern Europe, had several fortified castles in Poland. The brick castle of Malbork, former seat of the Grand Master of the Teutonic Order, was the biggest structure of its type in mediaeval Europe and is now on the UNESCO World Heritage List. The castle at Bylow built between 1395 and 1407 is now a museum and puts on knights' tournaments, largely as a tourist attraction. Nidzica, another Teutonic castle, is now a hotel.

If you fancy the idea of buying your own castle, you can find dozens for sale from £50,000 upwards all over Poland on the International Castles for Sale Web site (`www.castles.glo-con.com`) and on the Polish Estates Gateway (`www.polish-estates-gateway.co.uk`). If the castle you are buying is registered as a national heritage, you may get financial help from the local authority and be able to recover VAT paid out on renovation materials. But before you get too carried away, think of the running costs. One 'satisfied' customer who had bought a castle complained of his £8,000-a-year heating bill!

Climate and weather

Poland's climate has features of the maritime mild climate of Western Europe (mild summers and winters, lot of rain, clouds) combined with the more severe continental climate of Eastern Europe (warm dry summers and cold winters).

Overall the coldest area is the northeastern *Suwalki* region and the warmest is the southwest. Throughout the year, the warmest temperatures reach the upper end of 30° C, but the lowest can drop to –40°C. In January, average temperatures range from about 1°C in the western, more maritime zone to about –5°C in the southern mountains. In summer, average temperatures decrease as you head in a northwesterly direction, from about 20°C in the southeast to about 17°C near the Baltic. Warsaw's July temperatures average 2–25°C; winters are cold, with average January temperatures ranging from –5 to –1°C. Table 7-1 lists average temperatures for various locations in Poland.

Rainfall in Poland averages about 610 mm (24 inches), ranging from about 1,200–1,500 mm (47–59 inches) in the mountains to 450–600 mm (18–24 inches) in the lowlands. Snow can lie on the ground for up to three months, but occasionally a winter has almost no snow at all. You can be absolutely certain of snow in the southern mountains during the winter. Tables 7-2 and 7-3 show average rainfall and snowfall throughout the country.

Table 7-1 Average Daily Temperatures in Poland

Location	*Jan–Mar*	*Apr–June*	*July–Sep*	*Oct–Dec*
Warsaw	0°C	12°C	17°C	3°C
Krakow	1°C	12°C	16°C	4°C
Gdansk (Baltic Coast)	–1°C	10°C	15°C	3°C
Bialystok (Mazurian Lakes)	–1°C	12°C	16 °C	2°C

Table 7-2 Average Number of Rainy Days per Month in Poland

Location	*Jan–Mar*	*Apr–June*	*July–Sep*	*Oct–Dec*
Warswa	8	10	9	9
Krakow	7	7	7	10
Gdansk	9	10	9	9
Bialystok (Mazurian Lakes)	7	8	8	8

Table 7-3 Average Number of Snowy Days per Month in Poland

Location	*Jan–Mar*	*Apr–June*	*July–Sep*	*Oct–Dec*
Warsaw	8	0	0	4
Krakow	8	0	0	4
Gdansk	7	1	0	4
Bialystok (Mazurian Lakes)	9	1	0	4

English-language media

Finding an English newspaper in most Polish cities is fairly easy. Papers arrive a day late and cost around 15 Zl ($2).

Read up on local and some international news in English on the Warsaw Voice Web site (www.warsawvoice.pl) or its English-language print version, which is published weekly. This indispensable guide for foreigners in Poland offers cinema listings, property small ads, a restaurant guide, and information on life in various foreign communities in Poland. The paper claims a readership of 45,000 and has been in circulation since 1988. A year's subscription to *Warsaw Voice* – the most cost-effective way to buy it – runs 260 Zl (£46), but one copy on the street costs 10 ZL (£1.79).

Additionally, the *Warsaw Business Journal* (www.wbj.pl) is designed as a one-stop shop for business information about Poland, such as banking, finance, industry news and legal issues. Printed editions in English can be found at newsstands, priced 10 ZL (£1.79), and are often provided free by airlines and in hotels and cafes.

The BBC World Service can be received locally on FM and short wave at various times of the day. Find details of frequencies on the BBC World Service Web site (www.bbc.co.uk/worldservice).

Tourism

Tourism in Poland is surprisingly strong. In fact, Poland ranks eighth in Europe as a tourist destination (based on the number of arrivals it accepts annually). Additionally:

- Poland has outpaced more traditional tourist destinations such as Greece and Switzerland.
- Top tourist nationalities are German (25 million), Czech (8.8 million), Ukrainian (4.8 million), Belarus (3.8 million), and Slovakian (2.9 million). Brits, Americans, and French account for barely a million visitors.
- The average stay is less than five nights, with average spending around £20 per day.

Although tourism and the hotel infrastructure are still underdeveloped, the situation looks set to change rapidly as around 40 per cent of all foreign private investment in Polish is in tourism. This in turn should mean plenty of holiday rental opportunities for property owners.

Sports and leisure

While Poland has a bit of everything – seaside, beaches, lakes, mountains, forests, lakes, protected park areas, cultural sites, and historic sites – 75 per cent of all visitors stay in cities. Having said that, a number of new leisure-oriented locations are growing fast, which should provide holiday rental opportunities for property owners:

- Zakopane in the Tatra mountains, considered to be Poland's winter skiing capital, has a series of outstanding trails, jumps, and lifts. Skiing competitions are regularly held here, and the town has several hotels, lodges, and chalets catering to the needs of skiers.
- The Sudeten mountain region in south Poland has enjoyed recent good snow conditions, transforming the area into a popular skiing destination.
- In the north, around the Mazurian Lakes (near Goldap) and Kaszuby (near Wiezyca), cross-country skiing has taken off.
- Other popular winter sports centres include Wisla, Szczyrk, and Ustron in Beskid Slaski and Szklarska Poreba.

Talking Business

This section covers several important economic and business factors that, from a property-owning perspective, are important considerations.

Examining the cost of living

While in Poland you can enjoy a standard of living comparable to that of many more-developed EU economies – and it doesn't cost you nearly as much. Wages in Poland have been increasing very slowly due to high unemployment, which has kept the lid on costs. (Average monthly wages in the private sector are around £490.) Table 7-4 outlines the cost of living in Poland.

Although not quite the bargains they once were, household goods, food, clothing, transport, eating out, and other leisure activities cost about 40 per cent less than in the UK. How long Poland can remain relatively cheap is hotly debated. The most recent Worldwide Cost of Living survey by the Economist Intelligence Unit raised Warsaw's ranking from 92nd to 55th, overtaking a number of US cities, including Miami, Boston, Seattle, and Atlanta. Fortunately, much of the rest of Poland has a long way to go before it becomes as expensive as Warsaw.

Estimating potential yield

Rental yields in the more developed city areas in Poland have seen a decline during the past five years according to Ober Haus (`www.ober-haus.lt`), one of the region's largest estate agencies operating more than 30 offices across the Baltic and Central European region, including Poland, Estonia, Latvia, and Lithuania. Ober Haus research shows that rental yields have declined in benchmark areas such as Warsaw, from a high of 12.5 per cent five years ago to around 11 per cent today. This figure is an average; better yields can still be had. One developer, for example, is offering at the time of writing apartments for sale in Warsaw city centre for £43,000, which they guarantee to rent on your behalf for £5,375 per annum, a yield of 12.5 per cent, for at least ten years.

Polish property prices grew rapidly in the run-up to the country's entry to the EU, and supply got a bit ahead of demand. With nearly 17,000 new apartments built each year in Warsaw alone, compounded with a dip in the world economy, property price rises have slowed down in recent years. However, developers appear to have over-compensated for the slow-down and cut back on new building to such an extent that a shortage of supply seems to be taking effect. According to the Ober Haus review, market prices are now moving ahead at 10 per cent per annum.

No residential property market in old Europe offers yields anywhere near 10 or 11 per cent, so although the Polish market has slowed a bit, it still appears to have a head of steam.

Choosing Where to Buy

With the Polish property market still in its infancy from the perspective of non-Polish overseas buyers, prudence suggests confining your search to areas served by airports and those with strong leisure and business appeal. While limiting yourself in this way may rule out some great bargains, you can be more certain of getting a good rental yield (if that's what you want) and finding an interesting and enjoyable destination. Also, you're more likely to get a decent return on your investment when you choose to sell up.

In this section, I divide Poland into chunks that make good sense based on transportation, leisure, and business interests. For the purposes of researching properties in an easy, organised manner, I anchor the best places to look for property in Poland around the major cities. If you're clutching a travel guide, you may not recognise my divisions as being the classic way to split the country.

Table 7-4 offers some typical prices and rental yields for newly built apartments and older apartments in and around several major cities. While the actual figures you encounter when you do your own research will undoubtedly vary from the costs in the table, the relative pricing between various areas probably will be similar.

Table 7-4 Indicative Purchase Prices and Monthly Rents for a Three-bedroom Property in Poland

Location	*Purchase Price*	*Weekly Rent (Low/ High Season)*
Warsaw	€320,000 (£220,000)	€350/800 (£240/550)
Krakow	€260,000 (£175,000)	€280/600 (£190/410)
Baltic Coast	€74,000 (£50,000)	€200/400 (£136/270)
Masurian Lakes	€70,000 (£48,000)	€200/400 (£136/270)
Zakopane	€70,000 (£48,000)	€150/350 (£102/238)

The major cities

Poland's cities also have the lion's share of cultural and leisure resources in the country, making them appealing if you want to own property and spend time there too. Aided by good airports, tourism in many Polish cities is also growing apace, which makes the following locations attractive investment opportunities.

Warsaw

As Poland's largest city, Warsaw is the nation's economic, cultural, and political hub. Situated in the Mazowieckie province in east-central Poland, the city span's the Vistula river. It is easily one of Europe's most underrated cities with an impressive cultural scene and an ever more lively nightlife.

Warsaw is easy to get to (a critical factor in choosing a property location):

- **Frederic Chopin airport** has almost 190 regular daily connections with a few dozen cities on four continents, as well as a fast-growing number of low-cost airline connections to major UK cities. The airport carries twice as many passengers as all the country's other airports combined.
- **Daily trains** operating out of the conveniently located central railway station connect Warsaw via a rapid and regular service to European capitals such as Berlin (6 hours away), Vienna (8 hours), Prague (9 hours), Moscow (21 hours), and Kiev (15 hours). More information on trains is available at `www.pkp.pl`.

'New' Old Town

After the Second World War, more than four-fifths of Warsaw lay in ruins, and most of the population had been killed or deported. To the surprise of people at home and abroad, much of Warsaw's historic centre was meticulously re-created in the years after the war by the Communist authorities. Critics have unkindly dismissed the 'new' Old Town as being an unconvincing fake, despite the fact that many of today's Old Town buildings are closer to the original architecture than they were before destruction. The rebuilding of the Old Town was rewarded in 1980, when it was added to the UNESCO World Heritage list. The Old Town is dominated by the Royal Castle, and the area is awash with museums, palaces, and churches, as well as restaurants and hotels. The area is more of a tourist attraction than an area with great property bargains, but it adds appeal to the city and the country as a whole.

Not only is the city easy to get to and bustling with things to do, but also the new property market is booming. More than 16,000 new apartments are built each year, both to accommodate incoming business executives and diplomats and to replace the poorly built blocks thrown up during the Soviet era. The city also has a thriving market in older properties, though these are less likely to appeal to foreign long-term residents such as diplomats and business people.

Krakow

Krakow, Poland's fourth largest city, is a major tourist destination, housing almost a quarter of the country's museums and a cultural scene that surpasses that of Warsaw and the other cities.

Situated in the southeast of the country on the banks of the Vistula river, between the Jura uplands and the Tatra mountains, Krakow has one of the best-preserved mediaeval city centres in Europe. Left intact since the Tartar raids of the 13th century, the city has dozens of churches, monasteries, and abbeys spanning every architectural period. Laid out in 1257, the *Rynek Glowny* (main market square), dominated by the 16th-century *Sukiennice* (cloth hall), is one of the largest mediaeval market squares in Europe. It is still a bustling trade area, with myriad market stalls and street cafés.

The city's Jagiellonian University, the oldest in Poland, is just one of a number of colleges that bring almost 100,000 students to the city. The large student population stimulates the area's lively nightlife and creates a strong property rental market.

Although Krakow is delightful, the surrounding countryside is less so. Auschwitz is not far away, and coal-mining and other industries have devastated the area, now called the 'Black Triangle', between Poland, Germany, and

Bohemia. The concentration of heavy industry has imposed high costs on human health in the heavily populated areas of Upper Silesia around Krakow and Katowice. Nevertheless, there is a huge salt mine just outside of Krakow – Wielicka – which gets about a million tourists a year, and there is a great national park, so it's not all bad.

Krakow has cold, snowy winters, which are in part compensated for by long and balmy summer nights.

Communications and transportation are good, with Krakow's John Paul II airport – the country's second largest international airport – only 18 kilometres (20 minutes) west of the city centre.

Other cities

Poland's other major cities with good air links to the UK include the following:

- **Poznan,** which began life as a small settlement clustered around a wooden castle on the island in the 9th century. In the 15th and 16th centuries, the city became one of the most important commercial centres in Europe and for a while was effectively the country's capital. Today, it is a busy and prospering city renowned for its international trade fairs. There is a thriving tourist market as well as a healthy influx of business travellers. There are museums, an attractively restored old town, and sufficient cultural activities to sustain interest. Flights from the city's Lawica airport connect regularly to Copenhagen, Dusseldorf, Hanover, Nuremberg, Stansted, Vienna, and Warsaw. Trains link to Berlin and Warsaw in about three hours.
- **Lodz,** Poland's second largest urban centre, is 130 kilometres southwest of Warsaw. In the 19th century, the city enjoyed an economic boom as one of Europe's major textile producers, on a par with Manchester. It is certainly not on the tourist trail, but it has an attractive city centre. The city is home to Poland's biggest film studios and Europe's most famous film schools. Ryanair has a daily flight from the UK to Lodz.
- **Bydgoszcz,** in north-central Poland on the Brda river, is one of Poland's major inland ports. Chartered in 1346, the city developed in the 15th and 16th centuries to become an important commercial centre. Strong on beer production, the city is trying hard, with some modest success, to become a tourist attraction. If you are up for buy-to lets in Manchester or Leeds, then Bydgoszcz may appeal to you. Tourists and property hunters alike may find the city better to use as a jumping-off point for Toruń, some 50 kilometres away. Toruń is one of the most beautiful cities in Poland, built on both banks of the Vistula river. Gothic buildings in Toruń's Old Town won the designation of World Heritage Site from UNESCO in 1997. Ryanair flies to Bydgoszcz from Stansted.

- **Wroclaw,** the capital of Lower Silesia, is built on 12 islands on the Orda river at the foot of the Sudeten mountains. Numerous tributaries of the Odra and canals cut through the town, which includes 112 bridges. Wroclaw is one of the oldest and most beautiful cities in Poland and enjoys a lively cultural, social, and business life. The city is also home to 13 academic schools, including Wroclaw University and technical university. Ryanair flies from Stansted to Wroclaw.

The Baltic coast

If you are in the market for a coastal cottage at about a fifth of the price you pay in Cornwall, then Poland's Baltic coast may be the place to look.

Stretching for more than 500 kilometres with broad expanses of beautiful amber sand, this coast has the potential to be the envy of many other countries, including those on the Mediterranean. Unfortunately, the region has two major drawbacks: The weather here is more changeable than in southern Europe, and both air and sea temperatures are lower (water temperatures hover around 20°C in July and August). Nevertheless, long warm summers are not uncommon, and overall the climate – though nothing like sizzling Spain or Portugal – is broadly comparable to that of Cornwall and Devon.

Another thing to be mindful of is pollution in the Baltic, particularly in the Bay of Gdansk. (Poland's central coastline is far cleaner.) Of course, pollution is not a problem unique to Poland, and new environmental projects sponsored by the EU are already under way to improve the situation.

The Baltic coastal region is rich in attractions – from picturesque fishing villages such as Tolkmicko and Puck to the 150-year-old Elblag canal and Malbork, site of the Gothic fortified castle of the Grand Master of the Teutonic Order. The town of Sopot features a fine beach, a promenade pier to rival Brighton's, a casino, and an open-air opera house, which is also home to annual song festivals. The Slowinski National Park, a waterfowl sanctuary, is a distinctive natural attraction, with wandering dunes and a desert-like landscape.

Gdansk, Sopot, and Gdynia, commonly called the Tri-City, are next to each other on the Baltic coast and serve as the main way into the region. Situated at the mouth of the Wisla river, Gdansk grew to be one of the biggest and richest of the Hanseatic League ports in the 14th and 15th centuries. It is now a key commercial city, developing fast thanks to large-scale inward investment.

Gdansk Lech Walesa airport, the third largest airport in Poland, has regular flights to the UK. The Prussian city of Szczecin, at the German end of the Polish Baltic coast, also has flights to the UK.

The Lake District, Mazurian style

If you're prepared to take a bigger gamble, spend some time exploring Poland's version of a combination of the Lake District and the Norfolk Broads. Mazuria, also known as Mazury, is a great district to visit for fishing and cycling through remote villages and dense forests. Around 20 per cent of Mazuria is lake, including the two largest in Poland – Sniardwy (113.8 square kilometres) and Mamry (104.4 square kilometres). Forest covers another 30 per cent. The main lakes were joined together by canals in the 19th century, and many others are joined by rivers, which forms one great waterway system that can be explored by canoe, dinghy, yacht, or local pleasure steamer.

Start your local research in Mikolajki, situated on Lake Sniardwy. The town is a veritable tourist trap and in the summer months becomes very crowded. The Olsztynski Klub Golfowy (golf club) has a course a little shorter than serious players may be used to but is testimony to the approaching westernisation of the leisure market.

The quickest way to get to the lakes is from Gdansk, some 60 kilometres away, which has good direct air connections from the UK.

Winter wonderland

If you fancy a ski chalet with year-round appeal – and a much smaller price than those in Switzerland or France – look no further than Zakopane. Originally a 17th-century forestry settlement, this rambling town, 100 kilometres south of Krakow on the edge of the Tatra mountains national park, is a popular centre for Polish intellectuals.

Although billed as Poland's premier mountain resort, Zakopane is not the skiers' paradise that the locals would have you believe. It does have some decent pistes to keep most people happy for a few days, but the skiing is fragmented and the lift infrastructure antiquated (although reportedly undergoing some modernisation). The nearest ski slopes are 3 kilometres (2 miles) away at Kasprowy Wierch and in Gubalowka and Nosal. Poles and other visitors from Eastern Europe make up most of the skiing population.

What makes the area appealing from a property investor's point of view is that Zakopane is a year-round resort. Each year more than 2 million people hike, camp, climb, paraglide, raft, and otherwise enjoy its splendid natural scenery. Additionally, the area is home to *goralska muzyka* (highland music) and the distinctive Zakopane mountain architectural style, pioneered by Stanislaw Witkiewicz. These houses, built loosely along the lines of a classic Swiss chalet, protect the locals from storms, gales, and the cold and are beautiful in a fundamentally Polish way.

The real estate register

In Poland, concern still exists that a displaced Jewish family or their relations may turn up one day to reclaim property you have bought if the property was built before 1939. Until a definitive national property register has been compiled with comprehensive information concerning land, buildings, and reported property prices, these nagging doubts linger. Your lawyer's task is to steer you away from such problems. Your lawyer's professional indemnity insurance is intended to recompense you should he or she make any mistakes in the property-buying process.

Unfortunately, after this register is complete, brace yourself for some hefty changes in local property taxes. Under the current Polish system, property tax rates are related to land area and usable space, regardless of whether a property is a brand-new city-centre apartment or a derelict house in the middle of a field. That means the tax burden is identical or similar for most properties of equal size. The new system will incorporate an element to cover the amenities in an area. For example cities with good urban transport, museums, theatres, and so forth will be taxed at a higher rate than is applied to rural properties without such 'luxuries'.

Like all mountain areas, Zakopane is not easy to get to. The nearest international airport is in Krakow. The train route from the city is tortuous and takes four hours. Buses are quicker, taking two hours out of peak hours and costing 8–10Zl ($1.42–1.77). However, the ride along twisting roads is not comfortable, and in heavy traffic (almost every Friday and Sunday) the trip can take three to five hours.

Buying into Poland

Despite the country's membership of the EU, buying a property in Poland still carries a few restrictions. Unless you happen to have Polish nationality, if you are buying a holiday or investment property (rather than planning to live there permanently) you have to apply for permission from the Polish Home Office, which you must obtain before you complete your purchase. You can find information on how to do this (in English and Polish) at `www.mswia.gov.pl`.

If you are buying property as a foreigner and plan to move permanently to Poland, you first have to apply for permanent residency. Information on how to apply is available on `www.mswia.gov.pl`.

The basic procedure for purchasing property in Poland is as follows:

1. **Research the market.**

   Chapter 3 explains how to find properties, but you can find a number of English-speaking estate agents who specialise in Polish properties and who have offices in Poland, including the following:

   - **Leach Property Consultants** (+ 48-692-183-369; `www.leachpropertyconsultants.com`), headed by Tom Leach, an Oxford graduate who has been working in the Polish property market since 2003.
   - **Letterstone** (020-7384-7488; `www.letterstone.com`), a British firm specialising in Eastern European buy-to-let property developments in several up-and-coming areas of Poland.
   - **Property-Krakow** (`www.property-krakow.com`), established in 2003 by Robert Watkins, focuses exclusively on Krakow properties.

2. **Find a property and carry out a thorough inspection.**

   Generally in Poland, buyers do not have building surveys carried out. You can see from property details when a house was built and examine what state it is in at present. If a property requires a lot of renovation work, ask a building company to inspect and quote for any repairs and renovations before you make an offer. The company may charge you a modest fee – perhaps £50 or so for a two-page report on a small property. They may even carry out the work free of charge in the hope of you appointing them to carry out the renovation work. It is more likely that the builders will speculate on getting the renovation work for themselves.

3. **Negotiate and agree on the final price with the current owners.**

   After viewing a property, you can negotiate directly with the owners (unless the agent requires you to sign a contract prohibiting this) or through the estate agent, which may be more convenient if any language difficulties exist. Keep in mind that the total price you pay also includes:

   - **Actual cost of buying:** May vary slightly but usually works out to 7–9 per cent of the purchase price.
   - **Property tax:** 2 per cent of the purchase price (equivalent of UK stamp duty).
   - **Estate agency fees:** Usually around 3 per cent, though some newer agencies that deal directly with developers aim for a slightly higher figure. With larger purchases and where fees are quoted above 3 per cent, these may be negotiable.
   - **Notary fee:** Approximately 1.5 per cent.

- **Court fees to register your property:** 1.5 per cent (a ceiling on court fees of 20,000 PLN (£3,579) is in effect).
- **Property management charges:** Due on new properties in most holiday complexes, these charges are 40–80 PLN (£7.16–14.32) per square metre.

4. **Draw up and sign the initial contract.**

   After you agree to a price, you have to see a notary (*notarusz*) and draw up an *initial contract*, which outlines the details and any conditions that must be met before the sale completes (for example, repairs). After you and the seller sign the initial contract and you put down a 10 per cent deposit, the sale is legally binding.

   Both buyer and seller typically use the same notary, and generally meetings are held with all parties present, which makes sorting out any queries and problems much easier, faster, and cheaper than in the British conveyancing system. But using the same notary means you do not receive independent legal advice. If you feel that you need legal advice, appoint your own lawyer.

   Find a lawyer who has a good command of both Polish and English and who is independent of the estate agent or developer that you are dealing with. Ideally the lawyer should be based somewhere near the property you are investigating. That ensures that the lawyer is well versed in local matters such as prospective building activities that could interfere or even enhance the value of the property, for example new developments planned and roads to be built. You need to find a lawyer before you make an offer on a property so that he or she can be involved in every stage of the transaction. Look for lists of English-speaking lawyers on the Martindale-Hubbell Lawyer Locator (`http://lawyers.martindale.com/marhub`), the International Law Office (`www.internationallawoffice.com/Directory`), or Legal500.com (`www.icclaw.com`). You can also find lawyers on the Web site of the British Embassy in Warsaw (`www.britishembassy.pl`).

   If a buyer pulls out of a purchase, they will lose their deposit. If the vendor pulls out of the sale, it is usual to stipulate that the vendor pays double the deposit by way of a penalty. A date by which the *final contract* (completion) must take place is also stated in the initial contract.

   Unless you are fluent in Polish, you need to have an official translator present. A translator ensures that you understand the documents and everything that goes on in the discussions. They do not offer legal advice or help you make decisions – they just transmit the words. The translator's signature also appears on the signed documents to show that everything was properly explained. Translators charge around £30 an hour. You can easily locate one through a local telephone book or your notary or estate agent.

You can make a start by trying to recognise a few key words with the help of an online translator, such as that available at www.poltran.com.

5. **Carry out the last checks and sign the final contract.**

   After the initial contract, the notary carries out the necessary checks/searches and ensures that the vendor provides all the relevant title documents, permissions for use, and information on any mortgages and loans outstanding. This usually takes 3–6 weeks.

   When the final contract is signed by both parties, you must pay the remaining 90 per cent of the money due. In Poland, loans secured on a property remain attached to the property and not the owner, and so it is vital to ensure that the vendor provides a document from the council offices on that day confirming that there are no loans secured on the house.

6. **Pay for your property.**

   You must pay for your property in Polish currency. To do this, you can either instruct your own bank or buy currency through a specialist company, which may offer more competitive rates. You can have the purchased currency either sent directly to your own bank account in Poland (see the section 'Opening a bank account' later in this chapter). You can also use the notary's *escrow account*, which is a client account where your funds are kept separate and cannot be accessed without your permission. This latter payment method is better when you are giving your lawyer power of attorney to act on your behalf (see Chapter 4). Once the money changes hands and the contract is signed, the property is yours.

7. **Transfer utilities.**

   After you become the owner of your Polish property, expect to spend a day with the old owner trailing round the electricity, telephone, and water provider offices to put all the utilities in your name. Unfortunately, you can rarely conduct a transfer by telephone or letter; nor are bank standing orders to pay for them totally reliable. Ideally, you need someone in the country to help with these matters. If you are letting the property after sale, then you can expect the local letting agent you engage to handle all these matters within the fee. Otherwise speak to your estate agent, notary, or – better still – neighbours and come to some equitable arrangement.

Since EU accession, the variety and availability of Polish mortgage products (*hipoteczne*) available to foreign investors have widened from basic home loans, buy-to-let mortgages, and commercial loans. You can, relatively easily, get up to 80 per cent of the purchase price advanced over 30 years. Specialist companies such as Poland Mortgage Direct (www.poland-mortgage-direct.com) and Fiscus Mortgages (www.fiscusmortgages.co.uk/mortgages-abroad/Poland) can help here.

You would be wise to shop around: The up-front fees can be huge and the degree to which the mortgage company wants to get in on the purchase varies enormously. Some companies insist on you having their survey and insuring the place and the loan with their own products.

If you are not a Polish national, you can only take out a loan in Poland if you have a card of habitual or temporary residence in Poland. See the Web site of the Polish Home Office (www.mswia.gov.pl) for further details.

Getting Settled in Poland

Buying a property is in many respects the easy part of getting into Polish life. Plenty of people, such as estate agents and lawyers, have something to gain by smoothing your path to purchase, so that is what they do. After that, you are to some extent on your own. This section covers things that you need to address after your purchase is complete.

Although some matters – for example capital gains tax, which I discuss in the following section 'Taxing matters' – may seem a distant concern, the actions you take early on can mitigate pain later on.

Taxing matters

Polish tax matters concerning property that you should consider are as follows:

- **Business tax:** Business taxes are a flat 19 per cent. You should file an estimated return for business taxes to the tax authorities by 31 March.
- **Capital gains tax:** Tax on property gain, after deducting the costs for renovation and the like, is 10 per cent. After owning a property for five years, you have no capital gains liability. Capital gains from the sale of investments other than property are charged at 19 per cent.
- **Double taxation treaties:** Poland has a double taxation treaty with the UK and with many other countries, which ensures that you don't end up paying tax twice on the same income or paying more tax than you should. (I cover double taxation treaties in Chapter 17.)
- **Individual tax:** If you earn money in Poland – either from employed or self-employed activities, or from renting out property – you are liable to pay tax in Poland.

  If you are resident in Poland for tax purposes, you must also pay Polish taxes on your worldwide income. (In Chapter 17, I explain the rules on residency.)

Non-residents are liable to pay tax on earned income at rates that vary from 19 per cent on the first 37,000 PLN, up to 40 per cent on income above 74,000 PLN.

- **Value-added tax:** This is currently 22 per cent, but it is under review and may be reduced to 18 per cent.

To find out more about the tax regime in Poland, visit the Polish Information and Foreign Investment Web site (`www.paiz.gov.pl/index`), which provides a comprehensive up-to-date guide to tax and much more.

Opening a bank account

Opening a personal bank account in Poland is essential for all property-related activities. You can open accounts in both Polish currency and a foreign currency, such as euros or sterling. Most likely, you need a Polish currency account for regular local transactions and one in sterling for transferring larger sums for buying property. Some banks require a minimum amount to be deposited, usually around £70.

Bank accounts are normally opened in person in Poland, and you have to present a valid passport; some banks also require an additional document with a photo, such as a driving licence. Take an interpreter or someone else who can help you to communicate with the bank staff, who are unlikely to be English speakers. The National Bank of Poland (`www.nbp.pl`) has a full list of local and international banks that operate in Poland, with links to their Web sites.

Banks in larger cities are usually open from 9am to 4pm on weekdays and until 1pm on Saturdays. Banks in smaller towns and villages have more limited business hours, usually from 9am to 1pm. *Kantors* (private currency exchange offices), which often offer the best exchange rates, are usually open from 9am to 7pm weekdays and until 2pm on Saturdays. 24-hour services are usually available in major tourist areas such as train stations, border crossings, and airports.

You can use credit cards in Polish hotels, tourist offices, expensive restaurants, and some bigger shops. However, credit cards are not as popular as in Western Europe, and people generally pay with, and ask for, cash, either local currency or euros. Polish shoppers often put down small cash deposits on more expensive purchases and return later with the balance after visiting their bank.

Staying healthy

In many respects, health care in Poland falls well below the standards to which Westerners are accustomed. Plan to fly home if serious illness strikes, or call your health insurance company. (In Chapter 20, I cover major health-care choices in Eastern Europe.)

The Polish health-care system suffers from a shortage of resources and a lack of service improvements, which results in high levels of public dissatisfaction and medical personnel strikes. You must have a European Health Insurance Card (EHIC) to access health care in Poland. Polish health care is provided by units that have contracts with the National Health Fund, or *Narodowego Funduszu Zdrowia* (NFZ).

If you are ill, go to the nearest basic health-care general practitioner (GP). Make sure the GP is contracted with the NFZ. If the GP is not contracted with the NFZ, you are charged as a private patient and cannot receive a refund. In an emergency, go directly to a state hospital, where you can receive treatment and medicines free of charge.

On the whole, pharmacies and drugstores are well stocked with Polish and imported medicines and health products. However, you should bring an adequate supply of any prescription drugs that you may be taking. Medicines (and cosmetics) are *lekarstwa* or *leki* in Polish, while a pharmacy is *apteka*. Pharmacies usually feature a large green cross above their entrances.

If you need dental treatment, be sure that the dentist is contracted to the NFZ, otherwise you will be charged privately. Only basic emergency dental care is provided free of charge.

Getting around the country

Poland offers a variety of transportation methods to travel around the country after you arrive. This section details your major transportation options.

You can find out more about travelling around Poland on the official tourism Web site (`www.poland.dial.pipex.com`).

Train

With more than 24,000 kilometres of track, the Polish state railway PKT is one of the largest in Europe. The service, in a bid to streamline, has split up into a number of operating companies, and unfortunately tickets on one service are rarely usable on another.

Trains range from slow local trains (*Pociag osobowy*) that stop at every station to European intercity trains (*Pociag IC/EC*) that zoom between major cities both inside and outside the country. The costs and service levels vary greatly, ranging from moderately uncomfortable, refreshment-free local trains to air-conditioned, near-luxury cars with full restaurants aboard.

Tickets are modestly priced by UK standards. You can buy tickets on some but not all trains. The safest approach is to get a ticket from a branch of the Orbis Polish Travel Bureau (www.orbistravel.com).

You can find comprehensive chatty information on Polish Train Page (www.polrail.com), a privately maintained Web site run by Jeffrey Dobek, or by visiting the PKT Web site (www.pkp.pl), which has an English-language section and an online timetable and booking service.

Plane

LOT Polish Airlines (0845-601-09-49; www.lot.com) operates internal flights between a dozen Polish cities. You can take daily flights from Warsaw to all the regional cities, but flights between other cities usually connect through Warsaw and can be less than convenient. One-way flights between cities cost around 140–285 Zl (£24.80–50). You can purchase tickets on the LOT Web site or at Orbis Travel Bureau (www.orbistravel.com).

Car

Traffic drives on the right in Poland. The number of cars on the road has increased substantially in recent years. Fuel costs are about 20 per cent lower than in the UK. Roads are generally narrow, badly lit, and frequently under repair (especially in the summer months). Pedestrians and animals make heavy use of Polish roads as well. All these factors make driving, especially after dark, a hazardous affair. All in all, Poland is not a place for faint-hearted drivers.

Alcohol consumption while driving is effectively prohibited, as Polish law restricts blood alcohol levels to below 0.05. Penalties for drunk driving include a fine and probation or imprisonment for up to two years. In fact, drivers involved in any accidents can expect severe penalties – and in an accident causing injury or death, the penalty can be imprisonment from six months to eight years.

Speed limits in Poland are 60 kilometres (40 miles) per hour in built-up areas, 90 kilometres (57 miles) per hour on major roads, and 110 kilometres (69 miles) per hour on motorways. Wearing a seat belt and carrying a warning triangle are compulsory. Trams have right of way. Always have your driving licence, insurance documents, and passport with you when driving.

The Polish Automobile and Motorway Federation (*Polski Zwiazek Motorowy Auto-Tour*) has multilingual operators and provides assistance countrywide. You can reach the Federation by calling 981 or 9637 or visiting its Web site (www.pzm.pl).

Buses and trams

Most public transport operates from 5.30am to 11pm, with generally good and reliable bus services between and within all towns, though the state of cleanliness is variable. In larger urban areas, trams and trolleybuses are available as well. All buses charge a flat fare, and you can pre-purchase tickets and passes. Drivers do sell tickets, but you pay a higher price (2.50 Zl; £0.44) rather than the 2 Zl (£0.35) charged at street kiosks.

After you board a bus or tram, punch your ticket in one of the special machines located on posts throughout the bus. Polish trams and buses do not have conductors, but inspectors check tickets periodically. The fine for not having a ticket is 70 Zl (£12.39).

You have to buy a city bus ticket for each piece of luggage you are carrying. You plus backpack equals two passengers! And yes, they will fine you if you do not!

Taxi

Taxis are available in all major towns. You can usually find them at ranks or you can order one by phone. The current rate is around 3 Zl (£0.53) per kilometre, though a surcharge is in effect from 11pm to 5pm, on weekends, and for out-of-town journeys. Taxi drivers prefer payment in hard currency and expect tips.

Chapter 8

Slovenia

In This Chapter

- Understanding the potential in Slovenia
- Discerning where you want to look
- Going through the purchase process
- Making the purchase work for you

The good news about Slovenia is plentiful. It is stable economically and politically and became a full member of the European Union (EU) in 2004. Corruption is relatively low, and fast, inexpensive travel to and around the country abounds. The tourist market is strong, and Slovenia has been the recipient of much inward investment – two factors that help create an appealing property market.

Slovenia's complex policies and procedures once deterred foreign buyers from purchasing property. After joining the EU, most of the confusion was swept aside. I cover the few remaining obstacles later in this chapter.

One important factor that differentiates Slovenia from every other country in the region is the low cost associated with buying property. Only 2 per cent covers all buying costs, though you may feel a little nervous allowing the estate agent to do your survey. To protect yourself, always check the land registry (*Zemljiška Knjiga*) and appoint a lawyer on your behalf. (Unfortunately, Slovenia's low property transaction costs may be short-lived. A new real-estate tax may be introduced in the next two years.)

To begin discovering whether Slovenia is right for you, read on.

Fast facts about Slovenia

Area: 20,246 square kilometres – almost exactly the same size as Wales and Israel, and a little larger than Kuwait.

Population: 2,011,000 – a third less than Wales.

Location: Slovenia is bounded to the north by Austria, to the northeast by Hungary, to the southeast by Croatia, and to the west by Italy. It has a small strip of sea coast (46.6 kilometres) on the Adriatic.

Language: The official language for most of the country is Slovenian, spoken by more than 90 per cent of the population, with Serbo-Croatian spoken by 5 per cent. In a recent survey, 6 per cent of the Slovenian population claim to be fluent in English, 18 per cent claim to be fairly fluent in English, and 33 per cent consider their English to be non-existent. Small Italian ethnic communities appear throughout the western territory of Slovene Istria, close to the Italian and Croatian borders, while a Hungarian community resides in the area of the Slovenian-Hungarian border. In these regions, the minority languages are preserved as semi-official. Italian and German are also widely understood.

Slovenian is reputed to be very difficult for foreigners to learn, with dozens of dialects, many of which are not mutually understandable. Despite the language's difficulty, courses organised by the Ljubljana Faculty of Arts have grown from serving 200 people a year in 1990 to more than 3,000 a year in 2005. You can find a Slovenian–English (*Anglické*) online dictionary at `www.otpalca.sk`.

Currency: The official currency in Slovenia is the tolar, abbreviated to SIT. The tolar is made up of 100 stotins. £1 is equivalent to 350 SIT, and €1 is equivalent to 239 SIT. The Bank of Slovenia intends to adopt the euro in 2007.

Time zone: GMT +1.

EU standing: Slovenia joined the EU as a full member in May 2004. The country is one of the most prosperous of those that joined the EU at that time, with an average wealth of three-quarters that of the original EU members.

Emergency services: Emergency switchboard staff may not speak good English, so you may need help from others. Emergency phone numbers include:

Ambulance: 112

Fire service: 112

Police: 113

Rescue services: 112

Slovenian Auto Association (AMZS): 1987.

Visas: Citizens of EU member states do not need a visa to enter Slovenia. If you intend to stay longer than three months, apply for a residence permit with the Administrative Unit (`www.mnz.gov.si`). If you are not a citizen of a EU country, check your visa obligations through the consular section of the Slovenian Embassy (0207-222-5400; `www.slovenia.embassyhomepage.com`), which offers downloadable visa application forms.

By air from the UK: Ljubljana, the capital, is reasonably central and provides the best way to reach most places in the country. Brnik, Slovenia's only international airport, is 23 kilometres from Ljubljana and 7 kilometres from Kranj. Frequent buses connect the airport and Ljubljana city (45 minutes) and Kranj (15 minutes), with fares at around 1,000 SIT (£3). A taxi fare from the airport to Ljubljana costs approximately 7,000 SIT (£20). In addition to the more usual airlines, try Slovenia's national carrier Adria Airways (+385-1369-1304; `www.adria-airways.com`). Ryanair has regular flights to Trieste, Italy, a few miles from the frontier and just an hour or so's drive from Ljubljana. You can also fly into Zagreb, the capital of neighbouring Croatia (see Chapter 13), and connect by train or bus to Ljubljana.

By rail from the UK: The train route from London to Ljubljana involves changing at Paris and either Munich or Venice. The journey takes the best part of two days. Book tickets in the UK through European Rail or Deutsche Bahn's British office. The Man in Seat Sixty One (www.seat61.com) provides an overview of the route.

Other routes from the UK: The pan-European Eurolines runs between London and Maribor, and to Ljubljana in the summer. Journey time is between 32 and 38 hours.

Accomodation: Lodging in Slovenia is plentiful, but it is often fairly basic and yet not particularly inexpensive. Standards are fast improving, particularly outside of the centre of Ljubljana and other key tourism areas. In Ljubljana, you can find rooms for €150 (£102) per month and small apartments from around €400 (£272), but you have to look long and hard after you're in the country, relying on newspapers and Web sites I list in the section 'English-language media' later in the chapter.

The Slovenian Tourist Board (www.slovenia-tourism.si) has details and Web links to numerous new and renovated hotels, boarding houses, private rooms, apartments, and farm accommodation throughout the country. The Ljubljana Tourist Office (www.ljubljana.si) has details of hundreds of hotels, guesthouses, bungalows, studio apartments, and privately owned rooms in the city and surrounding areas. Ljubljana-hotels (www.ljubljana-hotels.1bigeurope.com) specialises in hotels throughout the country, covering most towns and cities. The hotels range from fairly basic to luxury, with prices to match. Expect to pay between €30 and €200 (£20–136) a night. Ask for special offers if you stay four nights or more. Hostel World (www.hostelworld.com/countries/sloveniahostels.html) has details on hostels in 18 towns and cities throughout Slovenia, from £10 a night.

Apartmaji Sobe (+386-1434-2660; www.apartmaji.si) is a small agency providing apartments to let long term. Sublet.com (www.sublet.com) connects owners and tenants worldwide with apartments and rooms for long-term rental and features a selection of Slovenian properties. Stoja Real Estate Agency (www.rent-a-realestate.com) lists more than 150 houses and apartments to rent, starting from €350 (£238) a month.

Getting to Know Slovenia

Slovenia packs an awful lot into a tiny space. A small patch of country enjoys a Mediterranean climate, while a large area can easily pass for the best bits of the Austrian or Swiss Alps.

Slovenian culture

Slovenia, though only half its size, has much in common with Switzerland: One minute you are jostling with rivers and mountains, the next rolling over vine-encrusted hills. Slovenia is the third most forested country in Europe, after Finland and Sweden, with the remains of primaeval forests still in evidence in the Kočevje area, along with occasional bears, wolves, and lynxes.

A family-friendly enterprise

Ian Samuels (35), a former electrician, his wife Louise (32), and their two children, Dylan (4) and Lennon (20 months), have set up a home and business in Prekmurje, a region of rolling hills and vineyards in northeast Slovenia, where the country borders Austria, Hungary, and Croatia. The geography itself tells you something of why the Samuels found Slovenia so compelling. Though you can reach Prekmurje by flying to Ljubljana, travel is far quicker and cheaper to fly to Graz, in neighbouring Austria just 75 kilometres away.

After the deaths of two close family members, Ian felt that life was too short to spend it in Staines. He and his family picked Slovenia for no better reason than Louise's father had visited and was impressed by the way it had recovered from the war and become a highly civilised country. Ian and Louise hit on Prekmurje specifically after scouring the area around the region's largest town, Murska Sobota. Eventually they found Vaneča, a traditional alpine-style three-floor Slovenian summer home with modern facilities, capable of sleeping up to six adults, plus space for two cots.

Their business vision was to create a family holiday environment. With young children of their own, Ian and Louise know at first hand the limited attraction that beautiful countryside can have for young ones. To this end, they have equipped their property with a bouncy castle, slide, game tables, a container full of play equipment, and a mass of DVDs – mostly bought on eBay to keep within a tight budget. The Samuels plan eventually to expand their venture when the time is right. For example, they are looking to set up a café in one derelict building and convert other buildings into holiday cottages.

Other enterprising Brits are starting businesses nearby. One outfit takes small groups underground cycling, with lamps on their heads, through hundreds of miles of disused mine shafts, while another offers one of Slovenia's popular activities, white-water rafting.

The country is brimming with traditional culture – and not just in the capital, Ljubljana, which is home to an annual festival and dozens of museums and art galleries. Almost every municipality has a museum or gallery, and major towns have theatre houses. For example, Ptuj, the country's oldest town, is a centre of Roman heritage, while smaller towns such as Kamnik, Kranj, Radovljica, and Škofja Loka have a rich mediaeval cultural heritage.

The nation even has an indigenous brand of pop music, with rock bands such as Zaklonišče Prepeva from Nova Gorica and local pop singers such as Robert Pešut (alias Magnifico). Music – with a heavy dose of irony – plays an important role in the country's ongoing recovery from years of what many consider to be a civil war. For example, the 'Slobo Songs' – music that samples parts speeches of former Serbian president Slobodan Milošević – are regularly performed in alternative clubs.

As part of the effort of Slovenians to distance themselves from other ex-Yugoslav nationalities (Serbs, Croats, Bosnians, Montenegrins, and

Macedonians), locals use a special proper noun to identify foreigners: *Neslovenci*, or non-Slovenes.

Slovenia has a rich and well-kept wine tradition. Much of Slovenia's best wine comes from the area between Trieste and the upper Soča Valley. Here you find that much of Italy's best culinary traditions spill over the border, blending cured hams with traditional local dishes such as Raznici, grilled pork tenderloin, and Cevapcici, or spicy meatballs. Paired with Slovenian wine, these Italian-influenced dishes make for some very enjoyable afternoons, even if you have a restoration project on your hands.

Climate and weather

Slovenia is a small country with some very different climates:

- The region around Maribor has an Alpine climate, much like its Austrian neighbour. In the late autumn and winter the region receives plenty of snow and for the rest of the year a fair bit of rain.
- The central area around the capital has a temperate sub-Alpine climate with hot, wet summers, averaging 18–20°C.
- The eastern part around Novo Mesto has a moderate continental climate, with summer temperatures a degree or two lower than in the capital and some snow in the winter.
- The coastal part of Slovenia, south of Nova Gorica, has a Mediterranean climate with warm to hot and dry summers, mild winters, lots of sunshine, and no snow. One disagreeable feature of winter weather here is a cold gusty wind, the bora, bringing cold air from Central and Eastern Europe down the coast for a few days at a time.

Table 8-1 covers average temperatures throughout the region, while Tables 8-2 and 8-3 detail precipitation averages.

Table 8-1 Average Daily Temperatures in Slovenia

Location	*Jan–Mar*	*Apr–June*	*July–Sep*	*Oct–Dec*
Ljubljana	1°C	13°C	17°C	4°C
Maribor	3°C	14°C	19°C	5°C
Nova Gorica	5°C	16°C	20°C	8°C
Novo Mesto	3°C	14C	18°C	5°C

Table 8-2 Average Number of Rainy Days per Month in Slovenia

Location	Jan–Mar	Apr–June	July–Sep	Oct–Dec
Ljubljana	5	10	9	7
Maribor	7	13	11	9
Nova Gorica	4	4	3	5
Novo Mesto	4	7	5	5

Table 8-3 Average Number of Snowy Days per Month in Slovenia

Location	Jan–Mar	Apr–June	July–Sep	Oct–Dec
Ljubljana	4	0	0	2
Maribor	4	0	0	4
Nova Gorica	0	0	0	0
Novo Mesto	2	0	0	2

English-language media

Finding an English newspaper outside Ljubljana is difficult. Available papers arrive a day or two late and cost around 350 SIT (£2). The country is currently not well served with English news media. In this respect, Slovenia is well behind almost every other country I cover in this book. Perhaps a business opportunity exists here? Slovenia is practically the only former Yugoslav republic that has made a virtue of keeping out of the news. Being neither a NATO member nor the next-door neighbour of a former Soviet republic or Balkans hotspot has assured it that few foreigners will be certain of such rudimentary facts as where it is.

You can just about keep up with current events, but news, information, and even classified ads related to the property market are almost non-existent. You can pick up local and some international news in English on the following Web sites, some of which also provide print versions:

- **Finance** (`www.finance-on.net`) carries an English summary of business and general news in Slovenia intended mainly for foreign readers.
- **Ljubljana Life** (`www.geocities.com/ljubljanalife`) is a free city guide and entertainment magazine published four times per year and

distributed on a complimentary basis at Ljubljana airport. Look for its regular section on ex-pat meetings.

- **Slovenia Business Weekly** (`www.gzs.si/eng`), an electronic weekly from the Chamber of Commerce and Industry of Slovenia, offers current news, including Slovenian economy and business. The site also has a Business Opportunities Exchange System with a database of people seeking to offer or purchase goods, equipment, capacities, services, technology, and more.
- **Slovenia News** (`www.uvi.si/eng/slovenia/publications/slovenia-news`) is a weekly e-newsletter covering politics, environment, culture, business, science, and sports. It's a polished, government-inspired product with comprehensive links to masses of information on the country.
- **Slovenia Times** (`www.sloveniatimes.com`) is published every two weeks on Thursdays and is available free of charge as a welcome for foreign visitors. The publication features a good entertainment listing and a virtually empty classified ads section.

The BBC World Service is available throughout Slovenia. Find details on the BBC Web site (`www.bbc.co.uk/worldservice`).

Tourism

Slovenia's tourist industry was the first to bounce back after the collapse of Communism and the subsequent civil war. In fact, it is the only former Yugoslavian country to actually have more overseas visitors now than it had during its pre-war peak. In 2005, more than 2.5 million holidaymakers came and used up 8.5 million bed nights between them. The largest number of tourists came from (in ranking order) Italy, Germany, Austria, the UK, Croatia, Hungary, and the Russian Federation.

The resiliency and popularity of Slovenia as a tourist destination are easy to understand when you consider that the country always offers something enjoyable to do or see year round – an important factor for potential property buyers to keep in mind.

Tourists spread themselves around the country fairly evenly. While many arrive in the capital, they don't all stay there. From the ski resorts in the east to the Mediterranean coast in the west, tourists fan out throughout the year to explore Slovenia's rich ancient, mediaeval, and baroque heritage, as well as its mixture of Mediterranean and Central European (Austro-Hungarian) influences. All in all, this trend makes for a healthy property market. Evidence suggests that many tourist attractions that are currently upgrading their facilities are doing better than those that do not.

Although tourism is important, less than 7 per cent of Slovenian workers are employed in the industry, and tourism accounts for just 3.5 per cent of the country's income. These figures mean that Slovenia can afford to take a relaxed and balanced approach to tourism, which allows the country to maintain its rural and near-idyllic feel. This attitude contrasts sharply with some countries in the region where tourism has come to dominate the economic landscape and, in the process, begun a process of possible self-destruction.

Sport and leisure

Slovenia is an exceptional place for sport and recreation. The Slovenian Tourist Board (`www.slovenia-tourism.si`) has an excellent Web site with information on every activity, as well as links and other contact details to venues and activity providers.

Slovenia has dozens of excellent ski resorts. The nation's top mountains include Triglav, the highest mountain in Slovenia at 2,864 metres in the Julian Alps, Grintovec at 2,558 metres in the Kamniske-Savinjske Alps, and Stol at 2,236 metres in the Karavanke mountains. Krvavec, not far from Ljubljana, is one of the most accessible and popular sites. Though a little overcrowded at weekends, Krvavec has trails for snowboarding, sledding, and cross-country skiing.

The mountains also provide opportunities for mountain biking, climbing, hiking, and hot-air ballooning (Slovenia hosted the 9th European Hot-Air Balloon Championships at Murska Sobota and Ptuj). The Soča and other clear, fast Alpine rivers give kayakers, canoeists, and rafters a run for their money. Nearby lakes provide an opportunity to fish in the wild, something of a rarity these days. You also can hunt brown bear (usually only with a camera), roe and red deer, wild boar, chamois, fallow deer, and small game such as hare, pheasant, and duck.

Away from the mountains, eight golf courses are spread around the country. Working across to the coast, you can find a lot more to do than just lie on a beach, though of course you can do that. The Bay of Piran, close to Croatia, pulls in pleasure sailors, while marinas in Portorož, Koper, Izola, as well as dozens more around the Italian and Croatian coast, attract all sorts of boating. You can also visit the Škocjan Caves, which are on UNESCO's list of natural and cultural world heritage sites. The 1,400-metre cave is cut through by a 150-metre-deep underground rift of the Reka river.

Talking Business

Slovenia has proved to be an economically dynamic, stable, and prosperous EU member. Low operating costs, low business taxes, a well-educated population, and a progressive government are the ingredients that have led to this success. The economy has been growing at between 4 and 5 per cent per annum and, although it may slow slightly, is on a long-term growth path. Unemployment at 10.7 per cent is not too far from the EU average, and Slovenia ranks 14 out of the 25 EU member states for innovativeness, making it the second-best performer (after Estonia) among the ten new member states, according to the European Innovation Scoreboard (EIS).

The factors driving the economy are resilient and bode well for the property sector. First, Slovenians are getting wealthier because their economy is export-led. Slovenia sells textiles, manufacturing, timber products, and agricultural products throughout the EU. Second, overseas executives continue coming to the country to help set up enterprises locally; these people need somewhere to stay for the few years that they are in Slovenia.

Examining the cost of living

The cost of living throughout Slovenia is lower than in the UK. Average monthly pay in Slovenia in 2005 was 3,199,200 SIT (£9,300), which drops to 2,029,600 SIT (£5,900) after tax and social security. Food and non-alcoholic beverages are the greatest expense, taking around 20 per cent of income, followed by transport costs at around 14 per cent, which includes expenditure on buying and maintaining a car and paying for bus and train tickets. Housing costs (rent, maintenance, electricity, water, gas, and municipal utility and other services) take up around 11 per cent. So that means that the average Slovenian manages to survive in terms of staying fed, housed, heated, and transported for 913,200 SIT (£2,655) a year. All these facts and figures mean that the average British pensioner can live fairly comfortably in Slovenia.

Slovenia ranks 26 out of the 177 countries listed in the United Nations' Human Development Index (`http://hdr.undp.org/reports/global/2005/`), so the country is not only inexpensive but also a good place to live.

Identifying areas of value

Slovenia does not rank as the best value in Eastern Europe if you simply look at property prices on a size-for-your-buck basis. For example:

- Small, three-year-old, one-bedroom apartments situated in a scenic area in the centre of the Triglav National Park on the road leading from Bovec to the Vrsic Pass and featuring some good skiing sell for €85,000 (£57,800). This is about twice the price of a comparable property in Bulgaria.

- A four-bedroom villa on the coast sells from €250,000 (£170,000), a good 20 per cent more than similar houses in Turkey – and there you have a longer summer and milder autumn.
- In Ljubljana, the new Rozna Dolina apartments, situated close to the park, the American embassy, and only a five-minute walk from the city centre, are for sale at €350,000 (£238,000) for a two-bedroom property with parking. You can certainly find cheaper comparable properties in Ukraine, Poland, and Hungary.

But value is more than just price. Slovenia is a lot closer to the UK than Bulgaria and Ukraine, and it is already a paid-up member of the EU, which is likely to guarantee stability and future prosperity. Three diverse countries – Austria, Hungary, and Croatia – are literally on your doorstep, which means that Mediterranean beaches, Alpine ski resorts, and Italian cooking are only an hour or two away.

Plus, you can still find good-value properties (often in need of a bit of tender loving care) away from the main tourist areas. For example, an old ski house near Cernko, built circa 1984 with three bedrooms, is on the market at the time of writing for €28,000 (£19,000). The house is one of a number in the Idrija region, a wealthy area during the time of the Hapsburgs, when mercury mining was a prosperous industry. While you can't ski from the door (it's a half-hour drive), properties in this area are typically three times the size and half the price of new apartments next to a ski lift.

Assessing potential rental yields

Slovenia does not have reliable, centrally collected information on rental yields. However, by using data from a couple of sources, you can make some educated guesses:

- Europa Gateway to the European Union (`www.europa.eu.int`) lists, among other useful information on living and working throughout the EU, the rent for houses in Ljubljana. Average rents are around €1,400 (£960) in the city and €1,000 (£686) in the surrounding area. One-room flats start at around €360 (£247).
- Find a Property (`www.findaproperty.com`) lists 70 properties for sale around Slovenia and shows the average price for a two-bedroom house as €53,000 (£36,400) and a three-bedroom house as €91,000 (£61,400).

Slovenia has a lot less property available compared with many other countries I look at in this book. Also, the Slovenian market is less well developed. Both of these factors can push up rental yields.

Choosing Where to Buy

According to data provided by Slovenia's Tax Administration, DURS (`www.sigov.si/durs`), more than 500 foreigners have purchased real estate since Slovenia joined the EU. The favourite areas for foreigners are the coastal municipality of Koper and Murska Sobota in the northeast, followed by Kranj and Nova Gorica in the west. In the region of Gorenjska, foreign buyers (mainly from Britain and Ireland) purchased 70 per cent of all properties in Kranjska Gora, Bohinj, and Bled. In terms of nationality, about 29 per cent of all properties were purchased by Brits, while Italians, Austrians, and Germans also had significant representation.

In 2006, according to the DURS report (`www.uvi.si/eng/slovenia/publications/slovenia-news/2394/2398/`), the minimum price of new property in Slovenia is €100,000 (£68,000).

Statistics and the views of brokers on the ground point to three smart places to buy property:

- **Ljubljana and its surrounding area** continues to attract incoming executives, eager to set up businesses in the country. Also, the Slovenian populace continues a general move towards the capital from the countryside in search of better-paying employment.
- **Maribor,** to the north, offers great skiing in the Julian Alps around Lake Bled to the northwest.
- **The coastal region** between Koper and Piran and inland to Kras (if you don't mind a drive to the beach) is a popular area. Neighbouring Italy and Germany offer interesting side trips and international air travel options through nearby Trieste.

I cover these three areas in the following section, plus a few other intriguing possibilities. Table 8-4 offers some indicative prices throughout the country.

Table 8-4 Indicative Purchase Prices and Monthly Rents for a Three-bedroom Property in Slovenia

Location	*Purchase Price*	*Weekly Rent (Low/High Season)*
Ljubljana	€350,000 (£238,000)	€1,000/2,000 (£680/1,360)
Maribor	€150,000 (£102,000)	€400/600 (£272/408)
The coast	€150,000 (£102,000)	€500/700 (£340/475)
Lake Bled area	€150,000 (£102,000)	€400/600 (£272/408)

Ljubljana

Ljubljana, Slovenia's capital, has had a chequered history. Formerly a Roman province, Emona, the city passed to the Hapsburgs and became the main city in the Austrian province of Carniola. It was devastated by an earthquake in 1511, rebuilt in the Renaissance style, occupied by Napoleon, severely damaged by another earthquake in 1895, and rebuilt again in Art Nouveau and Baroque styles. In 1919 following the First World War it passed to Yugoslavia and became the capital of Slovenia. During the Second World War, the Italians put 32 kilometres of barbed wire around the city and turned it into the largest prisoner-of-war camp in Europe. Finally in 1991, it became the capital of the newly independent republic of Slovenia. Throughout much of this time, Ljubljana Castle (*Ljubljanski grad*), formerly a Roman stronghold and mediaeval fort, has towered over the city from its hill-top position.

More than half of the money spent by tourists in Slovenia stays in the capital, which supports a population of 330,000. More than €5 billion (£3.4 billion) has been invested in the country since 1997, with companies such as Bayer, Renault, Bosch, Siemens, Henkel, Simobil-Mobilkom, Goodyear, Microsoft, Oracle, and Bank Austria setting up operations in and around Ljubljana. Austrian companies account for more than 30 per cent of all inward investment and the British companies just 2 per cent. These two factors alone are sufficient to put a strong upward pressure on the housing market, creating opportunities for both long- and short-term rental as well as good prospects for capital growth.

The city has a wide range of old and new properties, and developers are already making serious inroads into the limited land bank. You can't find much property for sale for under €200,000 (£136,000), and new three-bedroom apartments with good letting potential start from €300,000 (£204,000).

The Tourism Office of Ljubljana (`www.ljubljana-tourism.si`) provides a comprehensive picture of what the city has to offer residents – be they you or the clients renting your property. Invest in Slovenia (`www.investslovenia.org`) has up-to-date information on business and inward investment.

Maribor

Maribor, close to the Austrian and Hungarian borders, is Slovenia's second city, with a population of 103,000. The city lies on the Drava river and is a centre for some fairly unattractive heavy industries, in the chemical, engineering, and electrical fields. These industries, however, employ lots of people who need places to live.

Before the First World War the city was populated by roughly equal numbers of Germans and Slovenians. By the 1930s, the German population had dropped to a quarter, though the city and region still boast a sizeable, if much smaller, German presence.

The city has a 12th-century Gothic cathedral, a 15th-century castle, a fine Renaissance town hall, a large university, and the country's second airport, with flights by Slovenian Spirit (`www.slovenianspirit.com`) to Paris and some Austrian cities. While nothing is currently in the works, a budget airline may be interested in including this airport in the future, an important factor in driving up property prices.

The region's main tourist attraction is skiing – and for that matter, anything to do with mountains. Snow guns and careful grooming virtually guarantee 100 days of skiing each year, and the area has the longest (5 kilometres) illuminated night ski run in Europe.

You can find more leisurely pursuits during warmer weather by following one of the region's many wine trails. Maribor claims to be home to the oldest vine tree in the world, the more than 400-year-old *Stara trta*.

You can find plenty of old ski lodges, small hotels, and increasingly an expensive selection of new ski apartments close to the ski lifts. Newer properties can be relatively expensive, with small apartments near a ski lift selling from €80,000 (£54,400) and renovation projects from €25,000 (£17,000).

The coast

The Italians and Croatians have rather ungenerously left Slovenia with a mere 30 kilometres of shoreline and with beaches that are more rock than sand. Grandiosely called the Slovenian Riviera, the area is more a token coast than anything else.

However, you can find some very attractive old towns:

- **Koper** is a jewel of Mediterranean urban planning, with its Prešeren and Carpaccio squares, renovated Praetorian Palace, and Gothic cathedral.
- **Piran,** once ruled by Venice, is reputed to be one of the best-preserved towns anywhere on the Adriatic. With its narrow mediaeval streets flanked by boutiques, craft shops, and good seafood restaurants, this old port has charms aplenty.

Inland a mile or two, you find a rolling limestone plateau scattered with farming villages, woodland, and large green meadows. Astounding geological sights, including the world famous Škocjan Caves, attract tourists throughout the year.

In the region's many excellent restaurants, you can enjoy cooking that blends Slovenian and Italian flavours to mutual advantage. Seek out the distinctive Teran dark ruby-red wine (traditionally, it should be 'black as rabbit's blood') and *prsut*, an air-dried ham similar to prosciutto.

Needless to say, as Trieste and Venice are nearly within sight, Italians and Germans are buying property in this region. You can still find older properties in need of some work, but for the most part, new developments and buildings already refurbished by local entrepreneurs dominate the market. Property prices on the coast range from €90,000 (£61,200) for a fairly pokey studio to €375,000 (£255,000) for three bedrooms and a sea view. Inland properties cost about a quarter less.

You can still find near-wrecks in need of complete rebuilding from €20,000 (£13,600). However, for investors, such low prices may be a false economy, as renting to tourists seems sketchy. But if you just love the place and want the property largely for yourself, go for a bargain.

Other possibilities: Lake Bled and the Julian Alps

Bled, which celebrated its thousandth anniversary in 2005, has been a health resort since the Middle Ages. It captures the essence of the region set against the backcloth of the serrated summits of the Julian Alps. You can quickly understand why it calls itself 'the healthiest spot in Europe'. The whole area is set in Triglav National Park and offers some pleasant mountain walks to old villages. If you arrived blindfold, you would swear you were in Switzerland, Austria, or northern Italy.

Lake Bled itself is only about three miles in circumference, with a foot and bicycle path circling the lake that you can cover in about an hour. The island in the centre, by the way, is the only island in Slovenia. The late President Tito kept a summer residence here, which is now a four-star hotel.

When you're not swimming, rowing, sailing, windsurfing, or enjoying the heated thermal waters that most hotels seem to have, you can go walking, climbing, fishing, kayaking, canoeing, or rafting on Alpine rivers. In the winter, skiing is available on Mount Kanin and Kranjska Gora.

Ski properties in the region start from €80,000 (£54,400) for a studio, going up to around €350,000 (£238,000) for a new chalet-style building. You can still find older properties in need of renovation and located a few miles away from €25,000 (£17,000). Around the lakes, newer properties are available, starting at around €200,000 (£136,000).

Buying into Slovenia

Before Slovenia joined the EU on 1 May 2004, foreigners were allowed to buy property only after going through a lengthy process, often taking up to nine months and requiring personal permission from the Ministry of Justice. In practice, few foreigners succeeded in jumping through the hoops, and prosperous locals bought many of the holiday homes in the mountains and on the coast. (Germans, Italians, and Austrians were the most successful foreign buyers during this time.) Since Slovenia joined the EU, buying property has become a relatively straightforward and uncomplicated activity for all member country nationals, rarely taking more than a few weeks from beginning to end.

To purchase property, you must get an EMŠO (Identity) number and a tax number, as do all Slovenians. These items cost about €15 (£10) each and take no more than a couple of days to organise. You can expect your broker to get these on your behalf within his or her fee. Find out more about tax numbers on the Slovenian government Web site (`www.gov.si/durs/index.php?lg=en`). Find out about applying for a residence permit with the Administrative Unit (`www.mnz.gov.si`) by following the link to the Internal Affairs Inspectorate and then selecting 'Useful Information'.

Slovenia is keeping its options open and can, should it wish, make use of a general safeguard clause provided for in Article 37 of the European Union Accession Treaty allowing the country to reapply restrictions on property and land purchases by non-nationals until 2011.

Find a lawyer who has a good command of both Slovenian and English and who is independent of the estate agent or developer that you are dealing with. Ideally the lawyer should be based somewhere near the property you are investigating. This ensures that the lawyer is well versed in local matters such as prospective building activities that could interfere or even enhance the value of the property, for example new developments planned and roads to be built. You need to find the lawyer before you make an offer on a property so that they can be involved in every stage of the transaction. Look for lists of English-speaking lawyers on the Martindale-Hubbell Lawyer Locator (`http://lawyers.martindale.com/marhub`), the International Law Office (`www.internationallawoffice.com/Directory`), or Legal500.com (`www.icclaw.com`). You can also find lawyers on the Web site of the British Embassy in Ljubljana (`www.british-embassy.si`).

The basic procedures for purchasing property in Slovenia are as follows:

1. **Research the market.**

   Chapter 3 explains how to find properties, but you can find many Slovenian estate agents with someone in their offices who speaks

English. Agents with an extensive range of properties both for sale and to let include the following:

- **Agency Barbara** (+386-1434-4325; www.agencijabarbara.com) is run by a Slovenian-Canadian who has returned to Slovenia and offers a selection of properties from around the country.
- **Imobilai** (+386-1241-7020; www.imobilia.si) sells and rents houses and apartments throughout the country.
- **Property Real Estate** (+386-1434-9000; www.property.si) sells and rents houses and apartments around the country, with about 300 properties on its Web site.
- **Property Slovenia** (+386-2585-1344; www.propertyslovenia.si) concentrates on selling houses in the region around Maribor.
- **Slovenian Properties** (www.slovenianproperties.com) offers no phone number but has a user-friendly Web site with properties around the country. It also provides some useful information on the buying process in Slovenia.
- **Stoja Real Estate** (+386-1439-8170; www.rent-a-realestate.com) specialises mostly in rental properties in and around Ljubljana, but it also has a small selection of apartments and houses for sale.
- **Think Slovenia** (020-845-9439; www.thinkslovenia.com), with offices in London and Ljubljana, has a very comprehensive Web site that you search by price or area.

For a Web site listing almost every estate agent in Slovenia, visit www.matkurja.com/en/directory/business_and_economy/real_estate/real_estate_agencies.

Unlike other estate agent links in this section, many of the sites may well not be in English. Someone in most of the offices should be able to speak English well enough to help you.

Always check that the estate agent you are dealing with is a member of a professional association such as the Federation of Overseas Property Developers, Agents and Consultants (www.fopdac.com) or the National Association of Estate Agents in the UK (www.naea.co.uk).

2. **Find a property and carry out a thorough inspection.**

   Estate agents in Slovenia do their own basic valuation surveys. However, generally in Slovenia buyers do not carry out building surveys on new developments, as these come with guarantees of quality. Have a survey conducted on old buildings, buildings that you want a mortgage on, and any structure you have any concerns about. Your estate agent, lawyer, or mortgage provider can put you in touch with a local surveyor. Structural surveys cost between €150 and €300 (£102–204).

Alternatively you can search the Royal Institute of Chartered Surveyors' online database (`www.rics.org`) or call the contact centre at 0870-333-1600 between 8.30am and 5.30pm (GMT), Monday to Friday.

You're usually best off trying to find a professional through the personal recommendation of someone whose judgement you respect and who is impartial. I cover this subject in Chapter 4.

3. **Negotiate and agree on the final price with the current owners.**

   After viewing a property, you can negotiate directly with the owners or through the estate agent. Keep in mind that the total price you pay also includes the following:

   - **Cost of buying:** This may vary slightly, but it usually works out to 2–3 per cent of the purchase price. (Selling costs are typically 4–6 per cent.) Slovenia is one of the least costly places in which to buy property anywhere in the world.
   - **Purchase tax (equivalent of stamp duty):** 2 per cent, paid by the seller.
   - **Estate agency fee:** Usually around 4 per cent, plus 20 per cent VAT. Paid half by the seller and half by the buyer. In theory, you get a lot for your money – this price usually includes the cost of drawing up the contract and *Zemljiška Knjiga* (Land Registry) searches.
   - **Notary fee:** Included in the estate agent's fees.
   - **Legal fees:** €500 (£340) if you use a lawyer of your own. Estate agency fees typically include basic lawyer services related to closing the deal. (See also Chapter 4.)
   - **Annual property tax:** Around €50 (£34) per year for a three-bedroom house.
   - **Property-management charges:** €250–600 (£170–408) on new properties in most holiday complexes and apartment blocks, depending on the services you select.

4. **Draw up and sign the initial contract.**

   After you and the seller agree to a price, your lawyer draws up the *initial sale and purchase contract*, which outlines the details and any conditions that must be met before the sale completes (for example repairs). After you and the seller sign the initial contract and you put down a 10 per cent deposit, the sale is legally binding.

   You normally have two months for your lawyer to complete the property checks with the Land Registry Office (*Zemljiška Knjiga*), but in Slovenia the estate agent usually does this basic work before putting the property on the market. If you fail to go ahead with the purchase for any reason other than that allowed by law, you forfeit your deposit.

If you are not going to be in Slovenia when the initial contract has to be signed, give your lawyer *power of attorney*, a topic I cover in Chapter 4.

5. **Carry out the last checks and sign the final contract.**

   After the initial contract, your lawyer carries out the necessary checks/searches and ensures that the vendor provides all the relevant title documents, permissions for use, and information on any mortgages and loans outstanding.

   Your lawyer must see your EMŠO (Identity) number and tax number before you and the seller sign the final deed of transfer of the property and you pay the seller the balance of the purchase price.

6. **Pay for your property.**

   You must pay for your property in Slovenian currency. To do this, you can either instruct your own bank or buy currency through a specialist company, which may offer more competitive rates. (See Chapter 18 for more information.)

   You can send your purchased currency directly to your own bank account in Slovenia or you can use your lawyer's *escrow account*. This is a client account in which your funds are kept separate and cannot be accessed without your permission.

7. **Transfer utilities.**

   Registering for electricity, gas, water, telephone, and refuse collection in Slovenia is a time-consuming process, involving lots of paperwork. Sorting out the issues can take several days and, in some cases, weeks.

   Before moving in, deal with everything well in advance, or you may be in your new home for some days without electricity and gas.

   Utility transfer is definitely not something to tackle on your own, unless you are fluent in the Slovenian language. Your broker will, if you ask, arrange for all utility meters to be read and recorded and transferred to your name. Brokers expect to do this as part of their general service, but clients still normally have to ask.

Getting Settled in Slovenia

Slovenia is not too difficult to settle into. The internal transport systems are reliable, inexpensive, and reasonably joined up. Health care is more than adequate by Eastern European standards, but you still need to hunt out English-speaking medics. Banking, too, is user-friendly, and finding English-speaking bank staff is easy, in the cities at least.

This section covers the major topics that you need to address when making yourself at home in Slovenia.

Taxing matters

Unfortunately, personal taxes in Slovenia are high, with a top rate of 50 per cent, so you may well decide against moving your permanent financial base there. I cover the ins and outs of choosing where to base your tax affairs in Chapter 17.

Slovenian tax matters concerning property that you need to consider include the following:

- **Business tax:** The tax rate for companies is 25 per cent.
- **Capital gains tax:** In Slovenia, capital gains are added to income for tax purposes.
- **Death duties:** The rates of inheritance tax and gift tax range from 2.5 to 21 per cent and depend on the relationship between inheritor/donor and acquirer/heir/donee.
- **Double taxation treaties:** Slovenia has double taxation treaties with the UK and many other countries, which ensures that you don't end up paying tax twice on the same income or paying more tax than necessary. (See Chapter 17 for more on double taxation treaties.)
- **Individual tax:** Slovenia has a progressive taxation system under which individuals are taxed between 16 and 50 per cent.
- **Local taxes:** Around €50 (£34) per year for a three-bedroom house.
- **Tax on rental income:** Taxed as individual income.
- **Value-added tax:** Charged at 20 per cent.

To find out more about the tax regime in Slovenia, visit the PricewaterhouseCoopers Web site (`www.pwc.com/ua/eng/main/home/index.html`) and follow the Publications thread. The site provides a comprehensive and up-to-date guide to tax and more. Or refer to the World Wide Tax Web site (`www.worldwide-tax.com`).

Opening a bank account

In Slovenia, individuals who have been granted a residence permit can apply for all banking services available to residents of Slovenia. Find out about applying for a residence permit with the Administrative Unit (`www.mnz.gov.si`); look for the Residence Permit – Application of Aliens form.

Non-residents can open a *multi-currency account* (for Slovenian tolars and foreign currencies) by applying in person with an original photographic identification document, such as a passport, national identity card, or driving licence. This account limits transactions to depositing and withdrawing money. You can see full details of the distinction between these accounts on the SKB Banka Web site (`www.skb.si/eng`).

The Bank of Slovenia (`www.bsi.si`) has a full list of all banks operating in Slovenia. Bank Austria (+386-1587-6600; `www.ba-ca.si`) is a member of the HVB Group, the largest banking network in Central and Eastern Europe. SKB Banka (+386-471-5100 `www.skb.si/eng`) is owned by the French bank Société Générale SA and has a good banking network and Web site with information in English. See also Chapter 18 for information on offshore financing.

Staying healthy

Slovenia is the only Central or Eastern European country that did not completely neglect its health care during the financial turmoil that followed the change from Communist to free-market economic systems in the early 1990s. While the standard of health care is relatively good, it is overstretched. According to a report on the Slovenian Government Press and Media Web site, the Health Minister Andrej Brucan is considering hiring foreign medical staff, especially doctors, to work in under-staffed Slovenian hospitals.

If you do not speak Slovenian and experience a sudden serious illness, call for emergency services on the central number 112. Operators on this line speak English and after establishing your problem can contact the appropriate emergency services on your behalf, staying in contact with you to interpret where necessary.

EU nationals who are resident in Slovenia are eligible to receive free medical treatment from government-funded hospitals and clinics. However, you may still find that doctors, dentists, hospitals, and even ambulances expect cash payment for their services, so obtain receipts.

The Web site of the British embassy in Ljubljana (`www.british-embassy.si`) has a list of English-speaking doctors in Ljubljana. The Web site of the US embassy (`www.ljubljana.usembassy.gov`) has a list of doctors and dentists throughout the country who speak English.

Getting around the country

You have several options for conducting daily business and travelling within Slovenia. This section covers your major transportation choices.

Slovenia does not have a scheduled internal air service.

Car

Your UK driving licence is valid, but it must have a photo – otherwise you also need to carry an International Driving Permit. Vehicles in Slovenia drive on the right and observe the following speed limits: 50 kilometres (31 miles) per hour in built-up areas, 90 kilometres (55 miles) per hour outside built-up areas, and 130 kilometres (80 miles) per hour on motorways. You must wear a seat belt. Police can collect all traffic fines on the spot.

The road system in Slovenia is comprehensive and of a reasonable quality. Stretches of the main Ljubljana–Koper, Ljubljana–Maribor, and Ljubljana–Jesenice routes are motorways (*avtoceste*); tolls are levied on these routes.

The Slovene Automobile Club (`www.amzs.si`) operates a 24-hour emergency service (call 987). Most major towns have technical centres.

Bus

Buses are usually a faster and more comfortable way to get around the country than driving. Avtobusna Postaja Ljubljana (+385-9093-4230; `www.ap-ljubljana.si/eng`), the national carrier, runs a comprehensive service throughout the country. You can check out timetables online, but you have to make bookings by telephone. You need to pick up and pay for the reserved ticket two hours before departure for local journeys and six hours before departure for international destinations.

Fares are inexpensive, and the service is frequent between major towns and cities. For example, six buses a day each way travel the 140-kilometre trek between Ljubljana and Maribor.

Ljubljana is a small, pedestrian-friendly city. It has an inexpensive and efficient bus service that covers most destinations in the city and beyond. The service runs from 5am to 10.30pm, with some central lines running later. Tickets for a single journey cost SIT 300 (a little less than £1). You can also buy tokens from the bus station, post offices, and other shops around the city. You must have the exact fare. Most bus drivers don't speak English, so you need to know where you are going.

Taxi

Taxis are plentiful and usually cheap. Info taxi (`www.infotaxi.org`) is an online resource on reputable taxi companies and taxi phone numbers worldwide. HIT Taxi (+386-1-430-3000) and Gea Taxi (+386-1-433-3444) are two reliable local firms.

Train

Slovenian Railways, Slovenske železnice (+385-1291-3332; www.slo-zeleznice.si/en) runs a extensive rail service throughout the country. The Web site features a comprehensive timetable. A ski train to Bohinjska Bistrica runs from Ljubljana every day during the skiing season.

Fares are very inexpensive by British standards, with journeys typically costing less than £12 to cross the entire country. You can check out national and international travel on the Web site.

Chapter 9

Cyprus

In This Chapter

- Understanding the potential in Cyprus
- Figuring out where you want to look
- Going through the purchase process
- Making your purchase work for you

Cyprus is the third largest island in the Mediterranean after Sicily and Sardinia. The climate is near perfect, with a claimed 300-plus days of sunshine each year and a sea temperature that rarely drops below 16°C. Beautiful scenery, tranquil waters, rocky coves, sandy beaches, and historic monuments fill the nation with natural and manmade wonders. Much property on the island is still a bargain, despite several boom years.

All these factors ensure the island's reputation as a playground if you're seeking a combination of relaxation, water sports, and exploration. They also make Cyprus an appealing location for purchasing property for your own pleasure and possibly to turn a profit.

So what is the problem with Cyprus? Well, the island has been divided since 1974, when Turkey invaded after a short-lived Greek Cypriot coup. The northern (Turkish) and southern sides of the island have glowered across an artificial border since then, arguing bitterly over properties they were forced out of. (1974 is a date you hear frequently when you start looking for property in Cyprus, as ownership of land and older properties after that date can be a problem.)

Additionally, moving between Northern and Southern Cyprus has been problematic – and even now the only way into Northern Cyprus by air is via Turkey, with charter flights required to touch down in Turkey before continuing to the island. (Airlines are not allowed to fly directly to Northern Cyprus because it is not officially recognised by any country other than Turkey.)

Fast facts about Cyprus

Area: 9,250 square kilometres, of which 3,355 square kilometres are in Turkish-controlled Northern Cyprus. In total, the island is slightly larger than Jamaica and about two-thirds the size of Northern Ireland.

Population: 780,200, of which around one-fifth live in Northern Cyprus. This is about 100,000 less than the population of Birmingham.

Location: Cyprus has 650 kilometres of coastline. The island is 60 kilometres from Turkey, 264 kilometres from Damascus (Syria), 350 kilometres from Egypt, and 800 kilometres from Athens. Mount Olympus, at 1,951 metres, is the highest point on the island.

Language: Greek is the official language in the south, and Turkish is used in Northern Cyprus. English is widely used and understood in official and commercial circles throughout the island.

Currency: In Southern Cyprus (also known as the Republic of Cyprus), the currency is the Cypriot pound (CYP), which is sub-divided into 100 cents. At the time of writing £1 is equivalent to 0.84 CYP. In Northern Cyprus, the new Turkish lira (YTL) is used as the local currency, currently converting at a rate of about 2.58 YTL to £1. Inflation is still a problem in Turkey, so you need to check the exchange rate regularly.

Time zone: GMT +2.

EU standing: Southern Cyprus joined the EU in 2004, leaving a large question mark over the inclusion of Northern Cyprus in the EU. Technically, Northern Cyprus is a country that no country other than Turkey recognises. The EU set some hurdles for Turkish Cyprus to jump before it could have direct access to the benefits of membership, including trade and investment. But on 8 December 2005, the European Commission withdrew these preconditions. Also in 2005, the EU agreed to start membership talks with Turkey. Although these talks are expected to last more than 10 years, relations between Turkish Cyprus and the rest of the island have begun to thaw.

Emergency services: Emergency switchboard personnel may speak adequate English. However, if you need assistance, you may be best calling through your local contacts or hotel receptionist. Emergency phone numbers are as follows:

In Southern Cyprus:

- Fire 112
- First aid: 112
- Forest fire: 1407
- Phone directory: 192
- Police: 112

In Northern Cyprus:

- Fire: 119
- First aid: 112
- Forest fire: 177
- Phone directory: 192
- Police: 155

Visas: Citizens of the EU, the European Economic Area (EEA), Australia, Canada, Japan, and the USA do not require a visa to enter either part of Cyprus. If you enter the island through Northern Cyprus and have a Northern Cyprus stamp in your passport, you may have difficulty getting into Southern Cyprus. You can get around this inconvenience by requesting to have a stamped *visa form* that is loosely inserted into your passport and can be removed on departure by the customs officials. Tourists can stay for three months, but if you want to stay longer you must apply for a residency permit. You can obtain information on applying for a permit from the FAQ sections of the Web sites of the Republic of Cyprus (`www.cyprus.gov.cy`) or the Turkish Republic of Northern Cyprus (TRNC) (`www.trncgov.com`).

By air from the UK: Southern Cyprus has a comprehensive air service, including two international airports. Cyprus Airways (8000-0808 Cyprus toll free, +357-22-365-700; www.cyprusairways.com) runs daily flights between Cyprus and the UK. Other airlines to consider include British Airways, GB Airways (01923-664-000; www.gbairways.com), Libra Holidays (0871-226-0446; www.libraholidays.co.uk), and Helios Airways (0870-750-2750; www.flyhelios.com).

Northern Cyprus has no direct flights other than from Turkey. These go through Ercan International Airport (tel: +90-392-231-4806) near Nicosia.

Other routes from the UK: No direct sea routes exist between the UK and Cyprus. Scheduled ferryboats travel from Girne (Kyrenia) and Gazi Magusa (Famagusta) to Turkey's south-coast ports of Mersin, Alanya, and Tasucu. Fast boats take around two hours and slow about five hours. Contact Fergün Shipping (+90-392-815-1770; www.fergun.net) for fares and timetables.

Accommodation: In Cyprus you can find lodging to suit all pockets, from hostels at £5 a day through to quality short- and long-term accommodation ranging from £10 to £200 per day or £110 to £3,500 per month. One- to five-bedroom apartments, houses, and villas are available, many luxuriously furnished with both air conditioning and winter heating. The Web sites of the Cyprus Tourist Board – Southern (www.visitcyprus.org.cy) and Northern (www.tourism.trnc.net) – are good starting points. Other Web sites with a good range of accommodation include www.cyprusonline.com and www.a1tourism.com/Cyprus.

Cyprus Apartments (+357-25-320-905; www.cyprus-apartments.net) has accommodation online throughout the island from CYP19 (£23) per apartment per night and hotels from CYP20 (£24) per person per night, as does Accommodation Cyprus (0800-783-6852; www.accommodationcyprus.com). Ask your estate agent for recommendations, checking first that he or she has actually stayed there.

Since 2003, the situation has steadily improved, spurred by Southern Cyprus's membership of the European Union (EU) and Turkey's desire to join. Various parts of the Northern–Southern Cyprus border have opened. In November 2005, bulldozers began dismantling an important symbol of a divided Cyprus when the Turkish Cypriot authorities started removing their roadblock on Ledra Street, the famous shopping area in Nicosia that was split for four decades.

Buying property in either part of Cyprus does have its risks, but these are diminishing faster than property prices have risen. Bottom line: Bargains can still be had in Cyprus for the well informed.

Getting to Know Cyprus

Cyprus has a lot to offer tourists and residents alike. The climate is great, and communications are good to excellent between the UK and Southern Cyprus. (Relations are also improving between the UK and Northern Cyprus.) Low-cost air travel is not quite available yet, but several airline options are getting closer to offering a service to Southern Cyprus.

Unfortunately, not all of Cyprus, north or south, is equally appealing to everyone. The following sections sort through the pros and cons of various aspects of life in Cyprus.

Cypriot culture

Cyprus stands at the crossroads of three continents – Europe, Asia, and Africa – and has one of the region's most exotic histories. Geographically and culturally, the country is a rich mixture of cuisine, castles, and coastline.

Since the Mycenaean Greeks settled in Cyprus more than 3,000 years ago and established a Greek civilisation on the island, the Phoenicians, Romans, European Crusaders, Franks, Venetians, Ottomans, and other conquerors (including the recent and most controversial Turkish invasion) have all left their mark and helped to shape the island's character.

The most obvious influences today are from the British colonial era, from the 19th century to 1960. Cars drive on the left, three-pin electric plugs are the norm, English is widely spoken, and the legal system is modelled in part on English law.

Small as the island may be, Cyprus is rich in cultural attractions. The countryside is dotted with glorious castles, such as those at Buffavento, St Hilarion, and Kantara. A spectacular Greco-Roman theatre is built into the bluffs overlooking the Mediterranean Sea. The city of Kourion features an early Christian basilica, an ancient forum, public baths, and a house of gladiators.

Climate and weather

December and January are the only months when rain is likely in Cyprus – and even then, four or five rainy days each month are typical (compared with the UK's 14 per month). Snow is virtually unheard of anywhere on the island, except in the Troodos mountains, where you can ski for about eight weeks in the winter.

In February, the island's 1,950 flowering species spring into life. Orchids, almond trees, pink cyclamen, and red anemones lead to a refreshingly different atmosphere from that resulting from the cold wind, rain, and snow that hit much of the UK about this time of year. After February the weather continues to get pleasantly warmer, with summer extending from mid-May to mid-October. Tables 9-1 and 9-2 list typical temperatures and precipitation levels throughout the year.

Table 9-1 Average Daily Temperatures in Cyprus

Location	*Jan–Mar*	*Apr–June*	*July–Sep*	*Oct–Dec*
Akrotira	13°C	21°C	26°C	17°C
Larnaca	12°C	21°C	26°C	17°C
Nicosia	13°C	25°C	31°C	18°C
Paphos	12°C	20°C	25°C	17°C

Table 9-2 Average Number of Rainy/Snowy Days per Month in Cyprus

Location	*Jan–Mar*	*Apr–June*	*July–Sep*	*Oct–Dec*
Akrotira	7	2	0	5
Larnaca	7	2	0	5
Nicosia	4	1	0	2
Paphos	8	3	0	5

English-language media

You can easily find an English newspaper anywhere on the island, but they may arrive a day or two late and cost around CYP1.90 ($2).

You can keep abreast of local and international news in English online. The following Web sites carry classified ads sections, which list apartments to rent, translation services, and tourist guides:

- **Cyprus Mail** (www.cyprus-mail.com)
- **Cyprus News Agency** (www.cna.org.cy)
- **Cyprus Today** (www.cyprustoday.net)
- **Cyprus Weekly** (www.cyprusweekly.com.cy)
- **Financial Mirror** (www.financialmirror.com)

You can receive the BBC World Service locally on FM and short wave at various times of the day. You can find details on frequencies on the BBC World Service Web site (www.bbc.co.uk/worldservice).

Tourism

For the Crusaders, Cyprus was a place to relax before or after making the dangerous trip to the Holy Land. Ever since then, tourism has been the mainstay of the island's economic life. Each year tourists spend more than £650 million in Cyprus, and tourism accounts for as much as 10 per cent of the nation's gross domestic product (GDP).

However, these substantial figures mask something of a crisis in the tourism industry. The glory years for tourism were from 1998 to 2001, when tourism income went up by 51 per cent. Since then tourism has declined by more than 10 per cent. Reasons cited for the decline include the war in Iraq, terrorism, and escalating food and accommodation prices. Other serious problems, in the eyes of tourists at any rate, include the fact that Cyprus is still divided (causing confusion and uncertainty) and a distinct lull during the winter months when the island offers few unique reasons to visit. Also, Cyprus has failed to make much of an impact on the all-important American tourist market.

But Cyprus is fighting back. The island has a strategic plan for tourism development 2003–2010, which includes as a principal goal making Cyprus a year-round tourist destination. The strategy seems to be making some impact – total visitor numbers are up 2 per cent in the last year to 2.34 million. While rates for tourists from the UK and Ireland are still down slightly, rates for visitors from Germany, Greece, Austria, Italy, and Spain are up.

For prospective property owners, these statistics are still something of a mixed blessing. Specifically, you may not be able to base your rental income on having tourists in your property for much more than six months of the year. On the other hand, you can enjoy the island pretty much to yourself from November to April as these are still the slow months.

Sports and leisure

The most prevalent leisure activities on Cyprus are loafing around the beaches and sailing. However, you can enjoy a wealth of more active endeavours, though often on a smaller scale than in other Mediterranean resort areas.

- Cyprus has its share of popular mass leisure and sporting activities, with water parks, jet skiing, bungee jumping, hang gliding, go-carting, and nearly every other form of adventure activity.
- The island's single ski resort includes a modest six runs.

- In Northern Cyprus you can shoot partridge, wood pigeon, and hare – with a government-issued licence, of course. You can also fish for carp, roach, bass, silver bream, catfish, zander, and trout.
- If the tourist board has its way, Cyprus may end up having the highest density of golf courses in the world: 11 golf courses are proposed over the next few years, adding to the island's current three.

The government is also hard at work, thinking up new things to do. A 2005–2007 plan for sports tourism includes plans to create facilities for canoeing in the Yermasoyia dam, water skiing in the Polemidhia dam, rowing in the Kourris dam, and sailing in Larnaca.

Talking Business

Since 2004 (when Cyprus entered the EU) and November 2005 (when Turkey, the dominant influence on life in the north of the island, was accepted as a candidate for EU membership), business life in Cyprus has improved dramatically.

- Annual GDP is growing faster in the north (8 per cent) and the south (3 per cent) of the island than in the UK (2 per cent).
- Foreign direct investment (FDI) – money invested by companies setting up operations in Southern Cyprus (including investments from the EU) – is around £1 billion a year. This figure has shown little growth in the past few years, in part due to concerns about the country's loss of offshore tax status on entering the EU. (Being 'offshore' provides businesses and individuals with opportunities for tax minimisation).
- More than £2 billion of foreign investment has poured into Northern Cyprus in the past two years, up significantly on anything seen previously. Around 9,000 individual overseas buyers have bought properties there.

In the past, Northern Cyprus acted as a brake on Southern Cyprus achieving its full potential. This dynamic seems to be changing now, with both parts of the island attracting large sums of inward investment, which is being used to make the infrastructure better for tourists and businesses. And as a consequence, the conditions for owning property are improving as well.

In the following sections, I discuss important factors to consider before purchasing property in Cyprus.

Examining the cost of living

Prudential's International Costa Living research study calculates the cost of a weekly basket of ten weekly shopping items in ten of the most popular countries for British retirees. The study ranks Cyprus as the most costly at £20.06.

Cyprus municipality taxes have risen from £80 to £100 annually, but these figures are nothing compared with the £1,200 that is typical for Council Tax in the UK. Cyprus income tax is also cheaper if you elect for local tax domicile.

However, public transport is limited, so a car is essential. Free health care is only on offer to people on very low incomes and government employees.

Assessing value

In the south of the island, good-value property is becoming increasingly hard to find. That is not to say you can't get good value in Cyprus, but you have to hunt rather harder than you did a few years back.

Today, run-down properties in Cyprus, located in not particularly attractive areas and requiring £50,000–60,000 of repairs, are on the market at asking prices of £60,000 or more. These same houses five or so years ago would probably have gone for £8,000–10,000 or even less.

Locals trot out a much-vaunted statistic that for the £250,000 price of a two-bedroom apartment in Cannes or St Tropez, you can get a four-bedroom house with a pool in Paphos. True, to an extent. But in an area of France with living conditions comparable to those in Paphos, £250,000 still buys a very substantial house, with probably 10 or more rooms, land, and outbuildings. A liveable village house in such an area of France mostly costs no more than £40,000 and takes half the time – and a fifth of the airfare – to get to, compared with Cyprus, which all in all may be more convenient if you are just looking for a holiday home to visit several times a year.

Renting out a property in Cyprus

If you're thinking of purchasing property with a view to renting it out, rental returns in Cyprus are about 5 per cent annually for long-term (6 months and over) rentals and upwards of 8 per cent annually for short-term (holiday) rentals. For the UK these figures are 3 and 5 per cent, respectively. Put another way, you can reasonably expect to rent a property you bought for CYP120,000 (£145,000) for about CYP500 (£602) a month for an annual renewable term and for CYP800–1,000 (£964–1,205) or even more for shorter periods.

Remember that local estate agents also charge you a fee equivalent to the first month's rental to help find a tenant. Additionally, if you want the property managed, expect to pay a management fee of 20–25 per cent for short-term rentals and 9–10 per cent for long-term rentals.

Anticipating appreciation

Prices in Southern Cyprus for both property and land are about 40 per cent higher than in Northern Cyprus. According to 2005 research by S. Platis Economic Research (`www.splatisecon.com`) and sponsored by the Peace Research Institute of Oslo (PRIO), the gap between north and south is closing fast. Property prices in Southern Cyprus have been growing at around 18 per cent since 2002. Land prices in Northern Cyprus have rocketed by 172 per cent in two years, and prices of housing units have leapt 36 per cent.

Only 15 per cent of properties in Cyprus are holiday homes, with around 60 per cent of those in foreign ownership, so the overall market is not unduly weighted towards investors. Even so, local opinion is that property price rises will slow down because Cypriots have greater difficulty financing properties at current prices and demand for second-hand properties (often priced about 30 per cent lower than new properties) will increase.

Choosing Where to Buy

Cyprus is not large, and most parts of Southern Cyprus are within reasonable travelling time of the two main international airports. The north part of the island is still much less accessible, with no direct flights from Europe. However, the north represents excellent value in terms of property buying and cost of living, albeit with a greater degree of risk.

Fortunately, the barriers between north and south appear to be coming down, as the influence of the EU's largesse spreads throughout the island. The following sections explore location options over the island.

Southern Cyprus

Southern Cyprus, now fully integrated into the EU, is home to the coastal resorts where most foreigners have chosen to set up home and where most tourist activities take place. The area has a heavy infusion of Brits, most of whom have concentrated their property purchases within an hour or so of the two international airports, Paphos and Larnaca, at either end of the coast.

This part of the coast stretching from the northern part of the island round the west coast and on to the well established southern beach resorts around Lemessos is well served by Paphos international airport.

Table 9-3 gives prices for a typical three-bedroom property in various towns throughout Southern Cyprus. Actual prices may vary quite a bit. For example, homes on a beach front or golf course or with a bit of land can cost up to double the prices listed in the table. By contrast, inland properties in some less accessible villages may be a third less. Less costly properties are still available as well. For example, older apartment blocks in Lemmasos still offer small two-bedroom apartments for around CYP60,000 ($72,300).

Table 9-3 Average Purchase Prices and Monthly Rents for a Three-bedroom Property in Southern Cyprus (Prices in CYP)

Location	*Purchase Price*	*Monthly Rent*
Ayia Napa	175,000	800–1,100
Larnaca	135,000	900–1,500
Lemassos	60,000	800–1,100
Paphos	200,000	900–1,500
Pirgos	120,000	750–1,000
Polis	130,000	750–1,000

Polis

Polis, which was an important town for merchants in ancient times, is the least developed area along the coast, with a beach area that runs up against the Northern Cypriot (Turkish) border. Polis itself is a little inland, but nearby Latchi is a delightful old fishing harbour with adjoining long sandy beaches. The area has a number of fish tavernas on the beach, as well as cafés and restaurants in the town.

This oasis of calm is ideal if you want to keep well away from nightclubs, theme parks, and rowdy revellers. The Akamas peninsula attracts hikers, bird watchers, and picnickers. The Baths of Aphrodite, where mythology claims the goddess bathed in a grotto pool in the shade of a fig tree, is a major tourist draw.

Polis has some attractive older houses, but these are rarely for sale. When considering new-build apartments, bungalows, and villas, keep the following factors in mind:

- The potential exists for some radical uplift in property prices after the new motorway to Paphos international airport opens.
- Improving relations with neighbouring Northern Cyprus should have a positive knock-on effect for the whole area.
- One potential downside: This area is likely to be very quiet out of season. While that may be fine for you, property in Polis may not produce high rental yields.

Paphos

Soaring cliffs, translucent blue water, amazing caves, coastal views, and beautiful beaches make Paphos a popular but expensive area. The town itself is home to an international airport and a population of 50,000, of which an estimated 7,000 are British.

The town has an abundance of swanky five-star hotels hogging the beach front and several 18-hole golf courses nearby. Properties around the golf courses are prestigious, with village-style houses and apartments dominating. Golf-course properties cost upwards of CYP500,000 (£602,500), which is fine if you love golf but makes little sense from a rental-yield perspective – Spain is the leading market for golfing holidays and Bulgaria is the leading up-and-coming location.

Small villages such as Emba and Pegia may be attractive for some buyers, but realise that these areas have been totally overrun by foreign buyers, more than 90 per cent of whom appear to be Brits.

Lemassos (Limassol)

Lemassos (Limassol) is an area dominated by the British sovereign base at Akrotiri, which is still an important staging post for military forces, gaining new significance due to its proximity to Iraq.

The city also has a well-established tourist industry, fuelled recently by an influx of Russian businesspeople. With a population of around 150,000 and an active port, the city is home to a range of year-round business activities.

Lemassos is not a beautiful city, but you can find some attractive beaches and small villages, such as Dhora and Mousere, in the foothills of the Trudos mountains. While the old stone houses in these areas usually need serious renovation, you can often find good property deals.

Pirgos, Larnaca, and the surrounding area

Pirgos, in the middle of the southern coast, is equally accessible from Paphos and Larnaca international airports. However, the real property and tourism action takes place further along the coast between Larnaca and Protaras.

In 1974 when the Turkish-Greek battle over Cyprus hotted up, the population of Larnaca grew rapidly, with Greek nationals pouring in from the war frontier a few miles to the north. The town now has a population of about 75,000 and a leisurely pace.

Other attractive towns in the area include the following:

- **Lefkara,** an important lace-making town, lies a dozen miles inland and is an attractive option if you don't mind a trek to the beach. Old stone houses in this area still occasionally come on to the market at prices reflecting their scarcity and desirability.
- **Maroni, Kalavassos, and Tokhni** are all places where foreigners have bought into newer, though still attractive, developments.
- **Pervolia, Kiti, and Tersafanu** have pockets of development, and the smarter locals are building here.
- **Zygi,** a village west of the airport, offers a healthy choice of fish tavernas. It is perhaps the least developed coastline in the southern part of the island.

Ayia Napa

Ayia Napa, at the far eastern end of the island, is full of strip bars, hotels of the less than luxurious variety, and many unimaginative restaurants. Still, the area has somehow become a magnet for younger foreigners, many of whom have bought properties here.

The area enjoys a strong holiday let market, and rental yields and capital values appear sound, particularly in places such as Protaras and Paralimni, which are quieter and more refined. These two areas have the added bonus of being near Famagusta, an important city in the Turkish-occupied zone. As north–south tensions continue to reduce, property prices here should see a fillip.

Northern Cyprus

Northern Cyprus is every bit as beautiful as the rest of the island, but even its most ardent supporters agree that the region is in something of a time warp.

For example, despite the introduction of the metric system of weights and measures, the old Ottoman system is still much in use. Land in Northern Cyprus is still measured in dönüms. (1 dönüm = 4 evleks, 1 evlek = 3600 square feet. 1 dönüm = 1,388 square metres or 14,400 square feet. 3 dönüms = 1 acre.)

Jenny and Bob Nicholls have had a two-week timeshare in the Canary Islands for the past ten years. They have used it every year and enjoyed their stay on the island immensely. The tennis court and swimming pool are a particularly attractive feature for their ten-year-old daughter. They had no expectation of being able to sell their timeshare on for a profit, despite the sales brochure claiming that timeshares were an investment as well as a holiday. They have treated their timeshare as a pre-paid holiday. The £2,000 capital cost for a 30-year timeshare and annual maintenance charges of £350 has effectively given them a two-week holiday for around £400 a year.

On a recent holiday in Northern Cyprus, the Nicholls found a two-bedroom apartment in a five-year old development in Kyrenia for sale for £32,000. There is a communal swimming pool and the beach is within walking distance. The Nicholls decided to buy the property after only a cursory examination of the property and the surrounding area. They are aware that Northern Cyprus is a more risky proposition than Southern Cyprus, but as the sum involved is relatively small they are happy to take that risk. They are not looking for capital appreciation, and even if the property is difficult to sell on or is actually worth less than they paid for when they come to sell, they still consider it will prove no more costly than their timeshare.

Their reasoning is that borrowing the whole sum at 6 per cent will cost less than £2,000 a year. If they can rent it out to friends and family for just six weeks a year at £300 a week, a discount on the prices generally available, they will recover most of their costs and have a holiday home available to them for the rest of the year for less than the cost of their two-week timeshare. Cyprus is also only about 4 hours flying time from the UK, an additional attraction.

Northern Cyprus is only for brave property investors right now. While it offers many unquestionably attractive properties, and several recent political omens are encouraging, the risk of losing your investment is still a serious threat. See the sidebar 'Slow growth in Northern Cyprus' for more details. Without an iron-clad guarantee to the title, you face the possibility of losing your property to a former owner. See the following section 'Buying into Cyprus' for more information on protecting your investment.

Table 9-4 lists some prices and rental rates for areas in Northern Cyprus.

Table 9-4 Average Purchase Prices and Monthly Rents for a Three-bedroom Property in Northern Cyprus (Prices in £)

Location	Purchase Price	Monthly Rent
Girne (Kyrenia)	70,000	630–840
Nicosia (Lefkosa)	120,000	280–420

Nicosia (Lefkosa)

This divided city is home to about 200,000 people in the 'Greek' side and 50,000 in the Turkish-controlled area. The nearest airports are Larnaca in the south and Ercan International, with its currently restricted range of flights only to mainland Turkey.

The main reason to consider property in Nicosia is the potential for the city to become the heart of the whole country, if and when the island becomes united. At present, the division gives a feel reminiscent of the Berlin Wall, with streets cut in two and windows looking out over a virtual no-man's land. Still, some beautiful stone houses have the potential to be transformed into great homes or rentals for international business people when 'normal service' is resumed.

Slow growth in Northern Cyprus

Northern Cyprus's slow development is the result of being divided politically since the Turks invaded the region in 1974. Although encouraging steps towards a political settlement are happening – people and goods can now move fairly freely between north and south – no one knows for sure when the island will become fully integrated.

The effect of this division and the forced exodus of various ethnic groups across the north–south demarcation line have left a cloud of uncertainty over property titles throughout the border regions, particularly in the less prosperous Turkish enclave. The Cyprus government puts the number of Greek Cypriots affected by the exodus at more than 200,000 individuals and estimates that between them they hold valid titles to approximately 82 per cent of the privately owned land in the occupied areas.

The Cyprus government has issued periodic warnings to foreign nationals that they face possible 'grave legal and financial consequences' if they buy property in the Turkish-controlled part of the island. Legal cases to resolve title disputes are dragging their way through the European Court of Human Rights, with apparent victories being awarded to both Greek and Turkish property owners.

It is particularly important that you use a lawyer from the outset of any property transaction and make sure that they carry professional liability insurance (see chapter 4).

Girne (Kyrenia)

Most new property development in the north has been in and around Girne, which enjoys views of the eastern Mediterranean's crystal waters. The sea around Girne offers some of the finest and safest bathing in the Mediterranean. The area's long diving season benefits from several exciting reef formations and exotic marine life, including the loggerhead, listed as an endangered species, and green turtles.

Girne itself lies under the walls of a mediaeval castle, along a coastline backed by the spectacular Beşparmak mountains. The town has an attractive harbour surrounded by old stone houses, fish restaurants, and a modest clutch of mercifully small hotels. The area is a welcome relief from the tourist towers that clutter some parts of the southern coast.

Buying into Cyprus

Buying property in Cyprus is not a complicated process, but ensuring legal title to property can be a hazardous occupation. Under no circumstances buy a property in either the north or south without engaging a lawyer who carries sufficient professional indemnity cover to make good any loss you incur if things go wrong.

Find a lawyer who has a good command of both the local language and English and who is independent of the estate agent or developer that you are dealing with. Ideally the lawyer should be based somewhere near the property you are investigating. This ensures that the lawyer is well versed in local matters such as prospective building activities that could interfere or even enhance the value of the property, for example new developments planned or roads to be built. You need to find the lawyer before you make an offer on a property so that they can be involved in every stage of the transaction. Look for lists of English-speaking lawyers on the Martindale-Hubbell Lawyer Locator (`lawyers.martindale.com/marhub`), the International Law Office (`www.internationallawoffice.com/Directory`), or Legal500.com (`www.icclaw.com`).

The basic procedure for purchasing property in Cyprus is as follows:

1. **Research the market.**

   Chapter 3 explains how to find properties. A number of English-speaking estate agents, some with offices in the UK, specialise in property in Cyprus. The following agents mostly cover proprieties in the north:

   - **Boray Estate Agency** (+90-392-822-2919; `www.borayestates.com`) is a Cypriot-owned company, initially set up in Nicosia (Lefkosa) in 1995. In 2000, as foreign buyers were becoming increasingly interested in properties within the Kyrenia (Girne) area, the agency opened offices there. Its English-language Web site lists more than 200 properties, from £20,000 to £385,000.

- **Northern Cyprus Homes** (01933-626-876; www.northern-cyprus-homes.co.uk) operates from permanent premises in Stanwick, Northants, with business partners near Kyrenia. The agency is fully conversant with building, purchase, and legal procedures and can also introduce you to professionals in the fields of finance and insurance.
- **Unwin Estates** (+90-392-822-3508; www.unwinestates.com) is a British-owned and managed agency with an eight-person team operating out of Girne.

The following agents mostly cover proprieties in the south:

- **Cyprus Estates** (www.cyprusestates.com) is an Internet portal with links and information on most major estate agents in Cyprus.
- **Cyprus Yellow Pages** (www.cyprus-yellowpages.com) carries an exhaustive directory of estate agents on the island.
- **Lloyd Bruce** (+357-25-396-633; 01268-726-919; www.lloydbruce.co.uk) is a family-run business with an extensive range of new development properties throughout the island.

Estate agents are usually though not always licensed by the Cyprus Real Estate Agents Association (CREAA) (+357-25-367-467; e-mail: solo@cytanet.com.cy). CREAA requires licensed estate agents to provide insurance of £50,000 per contract, and some agents of their own accord carry insurance of £100,000. Check that the agent – and indeed any professional you end up dealing with – carries such professional indemnity insurance, which safeguards you if something goes wrong with your purchase.

2. **Find a property and carry out a thorough inspection.**

   Generally in Cyprus, buyers do not get a building survey carried out, but this is largely because most purchases are of new properties. If you are buying an older property or just want peace of mind, you can easily and inexpensively (£150–400) obtain a survey.

   The Cyprus Civil Engineers and Architects Association (www.cceaa.org.cy) and the Association of Valuers and Surveyors (+357-22-751-221) can put you in contact with a surveyor.

   If you want to be confident of finding someone who speaks and writes in English, search the Web site of Cyprus Anglo Info (+357-25-812-476l http://cyprus.angloinfo.com) to find a Royal Institute of Chartered Surveyor (RICS)-qualified surveyor.

3. **Negotiate and agree on the final price with the current owners.**

   After viewing a property, you can negotiate directly with the owners or through the estate agent, which may be more convenient if any language difficulties exist. Keep in mind that the total price you pay also includes the following:

- **Actual cost of buying:** This may vary slightly but is usually 9–15 per cent of the purchase price.
- **Land registration transfer fees:** 3–8 per cent (equivalent of UK stamp duty).
- **Estate agency fees:** Usually around 3–5 per cent. Little competition exists at present, so expect to pay towards the higher end. Fees may be negotiable for larger purchases and when initially quoted fees are above 3 per cent.
- **Legal fees:** 1–2 per cent, depending on the complexity of the transaction. Older properties tend to cost more.
- **Value-added tax:** Due on new properties with building permits issued after 1 May 2004. Currently 15 per cent, but usually paid by the developer.
- **Survey and valuation fee:** 0.5–0.75 per cent.
- **Property management charges:** Due on new properties in most holiday complexes. These fees run between CYP300 ($361) and CYP750 ($903) annually, depending on the level of service you want.
- **Annual property tax:** Typically 0.2 per cent, but ranges between zero and 0.35 per cent, depending on the property value.

4. **Draw up and sign the initial contract.**

   After you and the seller agree to a price, you have to see a lawyer (see Chapter 4) and draw up an initial contract that outlines the details and any conditions that must be met before the sale completes (for example, any repairs). After you and the seller sign the initial contract and you put down a deposit (usually 10 per cent of the total sale), the sale is legally binding.

   The initial contract also includes a date by which the final contract, or completion, must take place. When you sign the final contract, you must pay the remaining 90 per cent of the money due.

5. **Carry out the last checks and sign the final contract.**

   After the initial contract, your lawyer carries out the necessary checks and searches and ensures that the seller provides all the relevant title documents, permissions for use, and information on any mortgages and loans outstanding.

   The crucial element to check in Cyprus, particularly in Northern Cyprus, is the title to the property. Estate agents may be reluctant to tell you much about title until you are well into the purchase process. You can do some preliminary research into the *tapu* (title) deeds yourself. The Land Office in Nicosia has a record of all deeds in the north, and the District Land Office in each major town in the south holds the deeds for its area. See the sidebar 'Title deeds in Cyprus' for more information.

Title deeds in Cyprus

Because of the partition of Cyprus in 1974, you need to pay attention to certain important factors when researching title deeds:

- Early on, check the number of the title deed in the lower right-hand corner of the deed. If it has TRNC (Turkish Republic of Northern Cyprus) in front of the number, proceed with care.
- Freehold title deeds issued before 1974 to any foreign owner are unlikely to be challenged and can be considered reasonably safe – subject, of course, to usual legal inspections.
- Freehold title deeds issued before 1974 to Turkish or Greek Cypriots are also usually safe. However, the TRNC places some restrictions on subsequent foreign ownership of such properties. In any event, the amount of land that can be transferred with such properties is restricted to one dönüm (1,330 square metres), and government permission is needed for such purchases, taking up to six months to obtain.
- TRNC title deeds are those issued for properties that usually belonged to Greek Cypriots before 1974 and were exchanged for land in the south after the invasion. This practice of exchange took place in the south too, though to a lesser extent. Various legal cases on such disputed title deeds are rumbling through the courts. Cyprus's EU accession, which allows court judgements in one member state to be carried out in another, has added a new danger to the purchase process because UK citizens can theoretically place their UK assets at risk in a dispute over title in Cyprus. For a comprehensive explanation as to how land exchange between north and south was handled and why it can still be a problem, visit the Shelter Offshore Web site (`www.shelteroffshore.com`) and type 'Title deeds in North Cyprus' in the search box.

6. **Pay for your property.**

   You need to pay for your property in Cypriot pounds (CYP) in the south and Turkish lira (YTL) in the north. To do this, you can either instruct your own bank or buy currency through a specialist company, which may offer more competitive rates (see Chapter 18). Purchased currency can be sent directly to your own bank account in Cyprus, or you can use your lawyer's escrow account, which is a client account where your funds are kept separate and cannot be accessed without your permission.

7. **Transfer utilities.**

   Getting utilities connected or transferred into your name is a simple process that your lawyer or estate agent can advise you on. The cost of transfer is modest; even arranging for a new supply of electricity and water is unlikely to cost more than £200–600, depending on size and location of property and whether you have a pool or garden irrigation system.

Getting Settled in Cyprus

While you're purchasing property, plenty of people – such as estate agents and lawyers – have something to gain by smoothing your path before you hand over your cash. After that, you are, to some extent, on your own. Although some matters, for example capital gains tax, may seem a distant concern, the actions you take early on can mitigate the pain later. This section covers day-to-day material for establishing yourself comfortably in Cyprus.

Taxing matters

Since Cyprus joined the EU, the whole tax and VAT system is in the process of being harmonised. Changes are afoot in the north too, as Northern Cyprus edges closer to being integrated with the EU.

The northern part of the island follows the Turkish tax code (see Chapter 15), except where indicated in this section. Tax matters for property bought in the south of the island are as follows:

- **Business tax:** Currently 10 per cent of profits.
- **Capital gains tax:** On the sale of properties, the first CYP50,000 (£59,565) is exempt from tax if you have owned the property for more than five years. Otherwise, the tax rate is 20 per cent.
- **Double taxation treaties:** Cyprus has a double taxation treaty with the UK and many other countries, which ensures that you don't end up paying tax twice on the same income, or paying more tax than you should. (I cover double taxation treaties in Chapter 17.)
- **Individual tax:** Cypriot residents (see Chapter 17 on rules of residency) pay a progressive income tax, running from 0 per cent on incomes up to CYP10,000 to 30 per cent on incomes of CYP20,001 and over. Residents are subject to tax on investment income – including rentals, dividends, and so forth at rates between 3 and 15 per cent.
- **Value-added tax:** In the north, VAT rates vary between 0, 3, 9, 13, and 20 per cent. In the south a flat rate of 15 per cent applies.

To find out more about the tax regime in Cyprus, visit the Worldwide Tax Web site (`www.worldwide-tax.com/cyprus/cyprus_tax.asp`), which provides a comprehensive and up-to-date guide to tax.

Opening a bank account

Opening a personal bank account in Cyprus is essential for all property-related activities. You can open accounts in both the local and a foreign currency such as euros or sterling. You probably need a local currency account for regular local transactions and a sterling account for transferring larger sums for buying property. You can use credit cards with reasonable ease throughout Cyprus.

The procedure for opening a bank account is simple and requires only a passport or a local ID card. The following banks operate a range of accounts, including a *sight account,* roughly equivalent to a current account, which provides you with a chequebook to make payments and withdraw money, access to automated teller machines (ATMs), direct banking, Internet banking, and payment of standing orders.

In the south, try the following:

- **Bank of Cyprus** (+357-22-848-000; `www.bankofcyprus.com`) operates more than 280 banking outlets, 172 of which are in Cyprus, 96 in Greece, 6 in the UK, 8 in Australia, and 1 in the Channel Islands.
- **Universal Bank** (+357-22-883-333; `www.usb.com.cy`) has a smaller network of banks, confined to Cyprus.

In the north, try Limasol Bank (+392-22-803-333; `www.limasolbank.com`). See also Chapter 15 for information on Turkish banks.

Staying healthy

Cypriots tend to complain about their health service, but services compare well with those in the UK. In fact, the Cyprus government is looking into ways to exploit opportunities for medical tourism. In addition to hospital beds being five times cheaper in Cyprus than in the UK, Cyprus offers somewhere warm and sunny to recuperate.

You need a European Health Insurance Card (EHIC) for subsidised emergency treatment at government hospitals now that Cyprus is a member of the EU. Unless you are on a very low income or are a pensioned citizen of an EU country and have transferred your residence to Cyprus, all medical treatment is charged for. See the sidebar 'What your EHIC entitles you to in Cyprus' for more information on EHIC benefits.

Major hospitals on the island include Nicosia General Hospital (+30-22-801-400), Paphos General Hospital (+30-26-940-111), Limassol General hospital (+30-25-330-333), and Larnaca General Hospital 'Archbishop Makarios III', (+30-04-630-300).

Your EHIC is not valid in Northern Cyprus, so you must take out medical insurance. In fact, most foreign residents in Cyprus take out medical insurance. See Chapter 20 for more information.

You can find good pharmacists, doctors, dentists, and hospitals throughout the country, though the standard is undoubtedly higher in the south.

Getting around the country

Cyprus does not have an internal rail or air network, so travelling around the country is all done by road. Today, good roads exist or are being built to connect Nicosia, Larnaca , Limassol, and Paphos. The roads in the south are in better shape than those in the north, but that situation is set to change as EU money starts to flow in.

Car

Driving is on the left and the road signs are mostly in English. The maximum speed on motorways is 100 kilometres per hour. The roads are much emptier than in the UK, but that doesn't seem to help the patience of the local drivers, who make a habit of driving too close for comfort and leaning heavily on the horn.

Unless you plan to live on the island, you may find it cost effective to hire a car. You can get a small four-seat car with air-conditioning, an essential feature for much of the year, for around £200 a month.

Getting back and forth across the border between Northern and Southern Cyprus is less of a hazard than it used to be, but you still need car documents. Also, customs regulations limit what you can take either way across the border. For example, unlike throughout the EU, between Northern and Southern Cyprus you cannot take any quantity of tobacco, alcohol, or perfume back and forth. However as the North becomes more integrated into the EU, such restrictions should decline.

Public bus

Cyprus offers a comprehensive and efficient public bus service. Unfortunately, the services generally stop before the sun goes down (around 6pm), and they don't run on Sundays.

Intercity bus services connect major towns. Urban buses run within most larger towns and tourist centres. Rural buses connect smaller villages to neighbouring towns. Bus timetables and schedules are available from tourist offices or directly from the bus companies.

Two bus companies with a good coverage of routes and timetables in English are Intercity Buses (www.intercitybuses.com) and Nicosia Buses (www.nicosiabuses.com.cy). The Cyprus Anglo Info Web site (cyprus.angloinfo.com) has a comprehensive list of bus companies throughout the island.

Taxi

Various taxi services are available, ranging from conventional personal service to shared inter-urban services that offer more comfortable surroundings than the public buses. The Cyprus Anglo Info Web site (cyprus.angloinfo.com) has details on these services.

Chapter 10

Malta and Gozo

In This Chapter

- Understanding the potential in Malta and Gozo
- Figuring out where you want to look
- Going through the purchase process
- Making your purchase work for you

'Property' is the second most popular term typed into the Web site Search Malta (`www.searchmalta.com`), the country's most used search engine – and 'Real estate' comes seventh. Therein lies the secret that underpins the value of investing in the Maltese property market: The locals are still the dominant force in the market. Unlike Spain, for example, where the predominant buyers are Brits and Germans and when they stop buying the market takes a dive, the property market in Malta just seems to keep on rising.

You quickly encounter a few additional revelations when you begin investigating the Maltese property market, including:

- Malta is not one island but two – or even three, if you include Comino, a small but inhabited island between the larger islands of Malta and Gozo.
- Malta is extremely Brit-friendly. Everyone speaks English, the post boxes are reassuringly red, and cars drive on the left. The legal process for buying property is conducted in English. Even the title deeds are published in English, and so you do not need to hire translators during the purchasing process.
- Malta offers some amazing tax concessions. Foreigners – both visitors and those domiciled in Malta – pay tax at a miserly 15 per cent. The country does not have local or council taxes. And Malta places no restrictions on how much time you must spend in the country each year to take advantage of tax policies, as is the case with some other nations. (I cover tax domicile and related topics in Chapter 17.)
- Malta is stable economically and politically. Also, the nation became a full member of the European Union (EU) in 2004.

Fast facts about Malta and Gozo

Area: 316 square kilometres, slightly larger than the Maldives and smaller than Grenada. Two of the three islands, Malta (246 square kilometres) and Gozo (67 square kilometres), make up 99 per cent of the land mass.

Population: 396,000.

Location: The Maltese Islands, as they are sometimes referred to, lie 85 kilometres south of the Italian island of Sicily and 300 kilometres to the northeast of Tunisia in the Mediterranean Sea. The archipelago includes three inhabited islands (Malta, Gozo, Comino) and four uninhabited smaller islands.

Language: Malta has both Maltese and English as official languages. Italian is widely spoken as well due to close historical and geographical ties (Italian media have also recently penetrated the country). Many islanders have good knowledge of French and German. A basic English–Maltese dictionary is available online at the About Malta Web site (`www.aboutmalta.com/language/engmal.htm`).

Currency: Maltese lira (LM), known locally as the Maltese pound. Divided into 100 cents; each cent is further divided into 10 mils. Expect to convert to the euro by 2010. The lira is worth €0.43 or £1.6.

Time zone: GMT +1.

European Union standing: After some heated internal debate, Malta joined the EU as a full member in May 2004. In negotiations with the EU, Malta obtained a number of concessions, one of which is a permanent right to restrict EU citizens to buy only a single property in Malta. Currently, EU citizens can purchase a *second* property in Malta (outside specially designated areas) only after residing in Malta for a continuous period of at least five years.

Emergency services: Emergency switchboard staff speak good English, so you can easily get help. Important emergency phone numbers include:

Ambulance: 196

Fire: 199

Phone directory: 118 2

Police: 191

Visas: Citizens of EU countries and a large number of other countries do not require a visa to enter and stay in Malta for up to 90 days. See Malta's Ministry of Foreign Affairs Web site (`www.mfa.gov.mt`) for details and visa application forms. If you want to stay longer than 90 days, you need to apply for a residency permit. Two types of permit exist: *temporary permits*, which have to be renewed every year, and *permanent permits*, which never require renewal. You must fulfil certain income conditions of at least LM10,000 (£16,000) a year and have a character reference from someone of standing such as a lawyer, banker, doctor, or accountant. The fee for residency permits is modest, at about LM50 (£80). The process takes up to three months to complete. You can see the regulations in full and download an application form on the Maltese Ministry of Justice and Home Affairs Web site (`www.mjha.gov.mt`).

By air from the UK: Air Malta (020-8788-5164; `www.airmalta.com`) flies between the archipelago's only international airport in Gudja (6 kilometres from the capital Valletta) and the UK. Try also British Airways and Alitalia (0870-544-8259; `www.alitalia.co.uk`).

Direct flights to Gozo do not exist, but Helicopteros del Sureste S.A. (+356-2156-1301; `www.helisureste.com`) operates a helicopter shuttle service for Air Malta, running every 15 minutes or so throughout the day between 5.45am and 1.45am to Xewkija Heliport in Gozo. Check out the full schedule of direct and indirect flights to and from Malta on the Malta Airport Web site (www.maltairport.com).

Other routes from the UK: No direct sea route exists from the UK to Malta, but after you get to Sicily you can take a ferry to Valletta. The Cemar Agency Network in Genoa (+39-010-573-1750; www.cemar.it/dest/ferries_malta.htm) has details of ferry routes to and from Malta. Fares to Sicily are around £60 return. The journey takes at least 90 minutes on a fast boat. There are no services in November and December.

Accommodation: Hotel accommodation runs the gamut – from budget hotels at around €17 (£11) a night up to the Xara Palace, a Relais and Chateau five-star luxury experience, starting at €212 (£145) a night. The Choose Malta Web site (www.choosemalta.com) lists all the island's hotels by location and category.

For longer-term accommodation, you can find apartments or villas to rent for from €400 (£275) a month for a two-bedroom fairly basic property up to €2,000 (£1,370) or more a month for a villa with views and a swimming pool. Dhalia (www.dhalia.com), a well-established Maltese company, has details on more than 3,800 properties to rent short and long term throughout the two main islands. Malta Budget (www.maltabudget.com) runs a service putting visitors into host family homes, with long-term rates for a couple starting at around €250 (£170) per month. Ask your estate agent for recommendations, checking first that he or she has actually stayed at any recommended location.

All these factors, when combined with a warm climate, rich culture, low crime rate, and reasonably short travel time from the UK, make Malta an uncommonly attractive country for anyone looking for somewhere to settle, retire to, or just spend a few weeks a year relaxing and enjoying a reliable return from their property.

Getting to Know Malta and Gozo

Malta has much of the feel of the UK, particularly the Scilly Isles, 30 years ago – only Malta is consistently about 10°Celsius warmer.

Although the islands are small, you can find plenty to see and do. After you start exploring, you're sure to feel like you're abroad, despite the many familiar elements and the fact that almost everyone speaks English.

Cultural considerations

Malta has culturally and historically always lain somewhere between Africa and Europe. The Maltese language draws heavily on Arabic, urban Tunisian, and other north African dialects. Add to this the fact that Italian was the official language until 1936, including during a period of British control, and you can begin to appreciate the country's unique flavour – reassuringly Western European, with strong African and Arabic undercurrents, as well as remnants left behind by Phoenicians, Romans, Normans, and Ottomans, among the many who have landed at this strategic sea-route crossroads.

Malta is an archaeology lover's paradise, with many sites and structures dating back to 1,000 years before the Egyptian pyramids:

- The two main islands feature seven megalithic temples, considered by many to be the oldest free-standing constructions in the world. The Ggantija complex on Gozo is a relic from the Bronze Age and the temples at Ta'Hagrat, Skorba Hagar Qim, Mnajdra, and Tarxien are just some of the examples of the temple tradition in Malta.
- The Hal Saflieni Hypogeum on Malta is an enormous subterranean structure dated at around 2,500 BC. This labyrinth of underground chambers was used as a burial site, temple, and shelter.
- Mysterious 'cart tracks' attributed to prehistoric humans mingle with the remains of Roman villas, Punic tombs, and towers such as the structure that the knights of St John built at Xlendi Bay on Gozo in 1650.

Additionally, Malta is also renowned for its *festi,* or village festivals, held throughout the summer when the 64 towns on Malta and the 14 on Gozo celebrate their patron saints. All *festi* are three-day affairs, starting on Friday when the saint's effigy is displayed in the church. On the Saturday local bands turn out, fireworks are let off, and feasting lasts well into the night. Sunday brings more fireworks (the Maltese don't need much encouragement to let off fireworks), followed by a High Mass, a procession, and more food and drink.

You can get a full timetable for the year's *festi* at the Malta Culture Web site (`www.maltaculture.com`) by typing 'feast' into the search box on the home page.

Speaking of food and drink, the popular local dish is *pastizzi,* a small boat-shaped delicacy of ricotta cheese and egg wrapped with thin crisp pastry that is sold on street corners and in village bars everywhere. *Ravjul* (ravioli) is the local pasta – and a reminder that Malta's nearest neighbour is the Italian island of Sicily. Maltese wines wash down just about any meal.

Climate and weather

Malta's climate is Mediterranean throughout and similar to the weather in neighbouring southern Italy – but with the benefit of cooling sea breezes to relieve daytime temperatures at the height of summer. Two seasons dominate:

- **Summers** are warm (usually around 30°C), dry (three-quarters of the island's entire rainfall of 22 inches falls between October and March), and very sunny (more than 10 hours of sunshine a day). The weather starts hotting up in April. By July and August, Malta's hottest months, daytime temperatures are often above 35°C.
- **Winters** are mild, with daytime temperatures rarely falling below 10°C and the sun shining for an average of 6–7 hours a day. The occasional blast of north and northeast wind from Central Europe brings night-time temperatures close to (but not below) zero. Unlike in Cyprus, a near neighbour, snow never falls in Malta. Even in November, sea temperatures are above 19°C, great for diving at the end of the tourist season when the waters are less crowded.

Another dominant feature of the Maltese climate is the winds, which are strong and regular. The three prevailing winds are the cool northwesterly (*majjistral*), the dry northeasterly (*grigal* or *gregale*), and the hot, humid southeasterly (*xlokk* or *sirocco*).

English-language media

British newspapers are difficult to find outside the major cities, and even then they arrive a day or two late and cost around £2.

You can pick up all the local and some international news in English on the following Web sites:

- **Business Today** is published by the *Business Times* (www.businesstimes.com) weekly on Wednesdays. Its Web site is updated weekly on Thursdays. The site carries all the island's commercial news, as well as the Malta Stock Exchange (MSE) trading statistics.
- **Malta Business Weekly** (www.maltabusinessweekly.com.mt/) gives another slant on business life on the islands. It is published by the Standard Group, which also produces the *Malta Independent.*
- **Malta Independent** (www.independent.com.mt/) has an online version with an extensive classified section incorporating details of properties to rent and buy, with topics including home improvements, furniture, craftspeople, and the like.
- **Malta Today** (www.maltatoday.com) is a sister publication to *Business Today* concentrating on more general local news.
- **Times of Malta** (www.timesofmalta.com), published by Allied Newspapers, carries extensive local and world news. Its archive search engine is probably its most useful feature, enabling you to check up on almost any topic related to property.

Bay Radio (89.7FM), owned by the Eden Leisure Group, went on air in 1991 and now broadcasts 24 hours a day in English and Maltese. Radio Malta (93.7 FM) and Campus Radio (103.7 FM) carry large quantities of the BBC's World Service.

You can receive the BBC World Service itself locally on FM and short wave at various times of the day. Find details of frequencies on the BBC World Service Web site (`www.bbc.co.uk/worldservice`).

Tourism

An estimated 25 per cent of Malta's wealth depends on tourism. The number of tourists coming to the islands peaked at about 1.25 million in 2000. Despite a recent slight increase in the number of tourists visiting, the amount of money tourists are spending has dipped by around 4 per cent. The good news for holiday property owners is that tourists appear to be spending fewer nights in hotels and more nights in apartments and villas.

Malta's primary tourist market is the UK, which accounts for 40.5 per cent of total tourists, growing at about 3 per cent a year. Germany, Scandinavia, the USA, Austria, and France are other growing markets. The numbers of tourists from Italy, Belgium, the Netherlands, Switzerland, Russia, and Libya are declining.

A point to keep in mind when doing your research is that despite being a little more difficult to get to than the island of Malta, 25,000 tourists opt to stay in Gozo – a number that has increased by more than 21 per cent in recent years.

Sports and leisure

Malta's climate is ideal for almost every type of sporting and leisure activity. Top of the list has to be anything to do with the sea:

- **Beaches:** You can find beaches for everyone and every occasion. Many beaches are easy to reach via public transport, but some are harder to get to – you then have the added bonus of privacy once there. The most popular beaches are Mellieha, Ghajn Tuffieha, Golden Bay, Paradise Bay, and Armier or Ramla l-Hamra on Gozo.
- **Boating:** You can rent or charter a luxury sailing boat, a small dinghy, or anything in between.
- **Diving:** Malta's safe tide-less sea is above 20°C for much of the year. Dozens of caves, wrecks, caverns, and swim-throughs make the region an excellent place for scuba diving. Snorkelling is also popular.

You must have a local diving permit, referred to as the C-card, to dive in Malta. The permit is issued by the Department of Health and costs LM1 (£1.60). To obtain the permit, you need to present a medical certificate, two passport photographs, and your dive logbook.

- **Other activities:** Windsurfing is a major sport in Malta, attracting international contestants for competitions such as the Sicily–Malta Race. Parakiting is offered at most beaches, as are paragliding and fishing trips.

Away from the coast, you can enjoy hiking, jogging, riding, cycling, and more than 1,200 established rock-climbing routes. All the usual suspects such as squash, tennis, bowls, swimming pools, and fitness centres are on offer, and the island has a professional 18-hole golf course.

The Visit Malta Web site (`www.visitmalta.com/en/what_to_do/rech_sportfac.html`) includes a searchable database of all the island's sports and recreational facilities by activity, location, and provider.

Talking Business

With economic growth at more than 4.5 per cent annually and unemployment at 4 per cent, Malta is one of the most successful, albeit small, countries in the EU. In particular, heavy investment in infrastructure since 1987, in part inspired and financed by EU membership, has stimulated Malta's economy.

With few indigenous raw materials, Malta produces only about 20 per cent of its food needs, has limited freshwater supplies, and has no domestic energy sources. The economy is dependent on foreign trade, manufacturing, and tourism. While Malta has based its economic development on the promotion of tourism since the mid-1980s, labour-intensive exports are also key to its economy: The country has attracted more than 200 foreign-owned manufacturing companies in the past two decades.

In this section, I cover important business and economic factors to bear in mind when searching for and purchasing property in Malta.

Examining the cost of living

Compared with the UK, the cost of living in Malta is a quarter to a third lower. Food is inexpensive, taxes are low, and local property taxes do not exist. The benign climate also means that staying warm in the winter costs a fraction of that in the UK.

High rating on the human development index

The United Nation's human development index (HDI; http://hdr.undp.org/reports/global/2005) is a composite index that measures countries on three basic dimensions: A long and healthy life; knowledge, as measured by the adult literacy rate and enrolment ratios for schools; and a decent standard of living. Malta ranks 31st out of the 177 countries listed in the HDI, and so the country is not only inexpensive but also a good place to live.

Since Malta joined the EU, prices have started to rise and the country is not quite the inexpensive paradise it once was. According to a survey reported in *Malta Business and Financial Times* (www.businesstimes.com.mt/2005/03/09/focus.html), inflation rose for 14 months in a row, and utilities and fuel were up by 18 per cent (though food costs were down by 1 per cent). The survey also noted that 64 per cent of Maltese were dissatisfied with recent increases in the cost of living.

Identifying areas of value

With some new kids on the block such as Bulgaria, Turkey, and Slovenia offering two- and three-bedroom apartments for sale for €80,000 (£55,000), some of Malta's estate agents are anxious about a possible drop in the number of international property buyers. But according to Frank Salt, who established Malta's biggest estate agency 26 years ago, only about 1,000 foreigners a year buy a property as a holiday or retirement home in Malta, and around 70 per cent of these investors come from the UK.

Don't expect Maltese property prices to compete with budget destinations. The appeal of owning property on Malta lies elsewhere. Specifically, properties on the island are quite individual – even quirky. Even many of the new developments retain this charming architectural tradition.

Although not as cheap as in other countries, property prices in Malta are still about half the entry price for comparable property in the UK. Expect to find property on the islands beginning at around €75,000 (£51,000) for small apartments and €130,000 (£89,000) or so for villas.

Assessing potential rental yields

Although Maltese estate agents claim to have a ready supply of long-term tenants who they can sign up to rent your property within a week, substantiating rental yields is difficult because no consolidated figures are available in Malta.

Determining how much money you stand to make from renting out your Maltese property requires consideration of several factors:

- Maltese properties are typically achieving yields of 5–6 per cent gross – that is, before agent's fees of around 15 per cent of rent and maintenance expenses, which eat up another 15 per cent. Taking those two factors into account, you lose close to a third of your yield, making returns before tax between 3.5 and 4 per cent.
- While the rents associated with short-term holiday lets are much higher, the letting season is not 52 weeks but 20–25 weeks long.

A trawl of Web sites offering Maltese properties both for sale and rent suggests that real yields may be as little as 2 per cent. For example, an estate agent offers a three-bedroom and two-bathroom property with great views in Qui Si Sana Beach in the heart of Sliema for £355,000 or for long-term rent at £473 per month. Assuming 100 per cent occupancy, this rent shows a return of just 1.6 per cent.

Considering property appreciation

The Maltese housing marketing has to some extent followed the British model. In 1948, just 23 per cent of the population owned their homes; by 2001, this had risen to 70 per cent. Substantial local demand makes for a healthy market. Because Malta is a small set of islands with limited land, property prices almost always rise.

Property prices have been rising at between 10 and 15 per cent a year in recent years, fuelled by a number of factors, including the local population's desire to replenish dilapidated housing stock, continued growth in tourism, new growth from multinational businesses such as Vodafone and Microsoft establishing operations in Malta, and the Maltese government's efforts to encourage citizens to repatriate money by investing in local property.

Local estate agents suggest that property price rises will slow down to around 8 per cent a year. Malta's National Statistics Office (`www.nso.gov.mt`) shows the House Price Index growing at a more modest 4.6 per cent a year.

Dealing with corruption

According to the EU's 2003 monitoring report, Malta has made few developments in fighting corruption. The nation does not have an official body to combat corruption. As recently as 2002, a former chief justice and another judge had cases instituted against them over allegations of bribery.

Transparency International (TI), a global organisation that monitors corruption, has found that out of 159 countries surveyed, two-thirds scored less than five out of a top score of 10 (lower scores indicate less corruption). Malta ranked 25th, scoring 6.6, which is higher than any of the other nine new entrants to the EU. Still, Malta's rating was 0.2 lower than its score the previous year.

From a property perspective, corruption revolves around securing planning permissions that could detrimentally affect another property, for example interrupting a view or increasing road usage. Using a local lawyer with an inside track on what can and cannot be done in the planning field will go some way to limiting the potential damage. But in the words of Bob Dylan, 'Money doesn't talk: it screams.'

Choosing Where to Buy

From a travel perspective, almost anything goes when seeking out property in Malta that suits your purse and your purpose. The country is small, and no location is all that far from the nation's only international airport.

In order for local buyers to be able to compete with international investors, the Maltese government has established a law restricting foreign buyers to purchasing just one property outside certain zones. International buyers can purchase additional property if they become residents or live on the islands for at least five years.

I divide the islands' options into three buying zones: Malta, Gozo, and what I call the 'Investors' Zone'. This zone includes areas in which foreigners are allowed to buy more than one property. Table 10-1 lists indicative prices and rents for these various areas.

Table 10-1 Indicative Purchase Prices and Monthly Rents for Three-bedroom Property in Malta

Location	*Purchase Price*	*Weekly Rent (Low/High Season)*
Malta	£150,000	£280/520
Gozo	£120,000	£230/440
Investors' Zone	£350,000	£500/1,750

Malta

Working up the large island from south to north, areas worth investigating on Malta include St George's Bay and the fishing ports of Marsaxlokk and Birzebbugia, known for its sandy beach. Other well-liked zones include Zejtun, which is built on top of a hill and overlooks the harbour of Marsaxlokk, and the bays of St Thomas and Marsascala. Around here, the cheapest apartments start at ₤78,000 for a two-bedroom shell (a newish structure in need of bathroom, kitchen, and other fittings). Prices are more typically between ₤180,000 and ₤400,000.

Further inland, you find less pricey properties in areas that are popular with locals from Valletta looking for weekends away from the city. Mqabba is the home of the island's only natural resource, globigerina limestone. Most Maltese houses include this material in their construction. Neighbouring villages include Qrendi, Zurrieq, Siggiewi, Kirkop, Safi, and Luqa. In this area, small finished apartments start at ₤72,000, with prices more typically between ₤90,000 and ₤120,000.

Properties around the capital, Valletta, and neighbouring St Julien's and Sliema – all at least with the potential for sea views – are among the most expensive on the islands. Portomaso, a waterfront development comprising luxury apartments, yacht marina, and Hilton Hotel leisure facilities, is a typical example of the newer developments on the islands. Portomaso is a prestigious development, with prices to reflect its desirability, ranging from a small one-bedroom apartment without a sea view at ₤150,000 up to large three-bedroom apartments at around ₤450,000.

Cottonera, another new development, is built on the historical waterfront at Vittoriosa, formerly home to the British navy's Mediterranean fleet, with Fort St Angelo beyond. Apartments here are smaller but not all that much cheaper than Portomaso when you consider what you get for your money. Despite views over the Grand Harbour to Valletta, Vittoriosa has no beaches. The nearest beach is in Rinella Kalkara.

In the centre of the island, towns worthy of attention include Mosta on the main route from Valletta to Cirkewwa, a heavily developed and prosperous town. Mosta offers plenty of business premises for sale, with small shops selling for between ₤30,000 and ₤50,000 and apartments starting at ₤50,000 and ranging through to around ₤70,000 for a three-bedroom property with balconies. Surrounding villages and towns worth exploring include Lija, Burmarrad, Rabat, and Naxxar.

The northern part of the island contains a mixture of inexpensive inland properties in towns such Mellieha and Bugibba, where building plots start at

£25,000 and two-bedroom apartments go for £50,000–65,000. More expensive and exotic properties are available in St Paul's Bay and Mellieha Bay.

Gozo

Gozo is barely half an hour by ferry or 20 minutes by helicopter from Malta. Most of the island's villages are high up and feature good sea views. This small island (14 kilometres long and 7 kilometres wide) was once shunned by all but the Maltese. But now it is fast becoming developed – some say over-developed. Prices are still a little lower than on the main island, but they are catching up fast.

The principal town, Victoria, with a population of around 27,000, is close to the centre of the island. Other villages and towns to explore for property include the following:

- **Sannat,** known as Ta'Cenc, is famous for its spectacular cliffs and crags, as well as being the natural home of many wildlife species.
- **Xaghra,** to the northeast of Victoria and encircled by the beautiful bays of Ramla, Ghajn Barrani, and Marsalforn, is rich in history. Its beach with distinctive honey-red sand is perhaps the most popular on the island.
- **Nadur,** with its spectacular baroque church and green valleys, is close to the bays of San Blas, Dahlet Qorrot, and Ramla, the largest sandy beach on the island.

Property in Ghajnsielem, a town that offers properties on par with many of the areas on the island, starts at around £55,000 for a two-bedroom flat overlooking a large communal pool and within walking distance to Mgarr harbour. But don't expect every property to be this cheap. A converted three-bedroom house with many of its original features and swimming pool and deck area located on the outskirts of Gharb, another area on Gozo with highly desirable property, sells for around £300,000.

The Investors' Zone

The government has designated certain areas of Malta as zones in which overseas buyers may purchase an unlimited number of properties, without going through the complexity of forming a holding company or having to wait until they have lived on the island for at least five years. Investors' Zone areas include the following:

- **Manoel Island and Tigne,** which many consider two of Malta's most ambitious development projects. By 2012, these once-derelict areas will have been transformed into two of the most prestigious residential and retail areas in Malta, according to the project's developers.

- **Portomaso and Cottonera waterfront projects in Malta and the Fort Chambray project in Gozo:** Prices here start at ₤130,000 for a modest studio and rise to more than ₤400,000 for three bedrooms and a sea view.

Areas designated for multiple purchase tend to be new and fairly soulless. If you think of London's Docklands circa 1990, you can imagine something of the flavour. But look what happened there: Fortunes were made by those with the foresight to get in early.

Buying into Malta and Gozo

The process for buying, selling, and renting property in Malta is generally well-ordered, secure, and safe. You may encounter more problems with titles than in the UK, but Malta has far fewer title-related issues than Cyprus and Hungary. Unlike in Turkey, where the military has to vet every property transaction, Malta's regulations follow a pattern that is reasonably familiar to British buyers.

You still need to take legal advice and heed all the usual precautions as you do for any transaction involving a large sum of money.

Find a lawyer who has a good command of English – not too difficult in Malta, as almost everyone speaks English. Your lawyer should be independent of the estate agent or developer that you are dealing with. You can find lists of English-speaking lawyers on the Web sites for the Martindale-Hubbell Lawyer Locator (`lawyers.martindale.com/marhub`), the International Law Office (`www.internationallawoffice.com/Directory`), and Legal500.com (`www.icclaw.com`).

The basic procedures in the property-purchasing process in Malta are as follows:

1. **Research the market.**

   Chapter 3 explains how to find properties, but you can also find estate agents who specialise in Maltese property. English-speaking agents with an extensive range of properties both for sale and to let include the following:

   - **Dhalia** (+356-2149-0681; `www.dhalia.com`) claims to be the Maltese Islands' largest estate agency and property consultancy organisation, operating from 14 offices spread throughout Malta and Gozo.

- **Frank Salt Real Estate** (+356-2135-3696; `www.franksalt.com.mt`) is an agency established in 1969 and now run by Salt's two sons and a number of Maltese directors.
- **Property Line Malta** (+356-2138-3970; `www.propertylinemalta.com`) was incorporated in 1986 by three brothers: Clarence Busuttil and Graham Busuttil (both doctors in law) and Trafford Busuttil (managing director).

Verify that any estate agent you deal with is a member of a professional association such as the Federation of Overseas Property Developers, Agents and Consultants (+08703-501-223; `www.fopdac.com`), the National Association of Estate Agents, UK (01926-496-800; `www.naea.co.uk`), the Malta Chamber of Commerce (+356-2123-3873; `www.chamber.org.mt`), or the Association of Estate Agents, Malta (+356-343-730).

2. **Find a property and carry out a thorough inspection.**

   Generally in Malta, buyers do not carry out building surveys on new developments, as these come with quality guarantees. You should have old buildings, locations that you want a mortgage on, and locations that you have any concerns about professionally surveyed. Your estate agent, lawyer, or mortgage provider can put you in touch with a Maltese surveyor.

   In Malta, the nearest thing to a professional association for surveyors is the Kamra tal-Periti, formerly the Chamber of Architects and Civil Engineers (+356-2131-4265; `www.ktpmalta.com`). Alternatively you can search the Royal Institute of Chartered Surveyors' (RICS) online database or call its contact centre (08703-331-600; `www.rics.org`).

   Malta Yellow Pages (`www.yellow.com.mt`) lists eight pages of architects and civil engineers, but you're usually better off trying to find a professional through recommendations from someone whose judgement you respect and who is impartial. I cover the topic of locating surveyors in Chapter 4.

3. **Negotiate and agree on the final price with the current owners.**

   After viewing a property, you can negotiate directly with the owners or through the estate agent. Keep in mind that the total price you pay includes the following:

   - **Acquisition of Immovable Property (AIP) permit fee:** LM100 (£160). See the sidebar 'AIP permits' for more information.
   - **Actual cost of buying:** May vary slightly, but usually between 10 and 12 per cent of the purchase price.
   - **Estate agency fees:** Usually 3–5 per cent. As there is little competition at present, expect to pay towards the higher end. With larger

purchases and where fees are quoted above 3 per cent, you may be able to negotiate.

- **Legal and notary fees:** 1 per cent of the purchase price, payable in two stages: 33 per cent with the signing of the preliminary agreement and 67 per cent with publication of the final deed.
- **Property management charges:** €200–700 (£135–475) per year due on new properties in most holiday complexes. These fees vary depending on the level of services you select.
- **Research into title, liabilities, and so on:** LM250 (£400), which is included in the legal fees if you use a lawyer.
- **Stamp duty (equivalent of UK stamp duty):** 5 per cent, which the notary is responsible for paying on your behalf to the tax authorities. This is payable in two stages: 1 per cent with the signing of the preliminary agreement (which must then be registered with the Inland Revenue to have validity) and 4 per cent with publication of the final deed.

4. **Draw up and sign the initial contract.**

   After you and the seller agree to a price, your lawyer draws up an *initial contract* that outlines the details and any conditions that must be met before the sale completes (for example, repairs). After both you and the seller sign the initial contract and you put down a 10 per cent deposit, the sale is legally binding.

   You normally have up to three months for your lawyer to complete property checks and to apply for an AIP permit, if required. See the sidebar 'AIP permits' for more information.

   If you fail to go ahead with the purchase for any reason other than those allowed by law, you forfeit your deposit. If the vendor defaults, they are liable to pay double your deposit.

   If you are not going to be in Malta when the contract has to be signed, you need to give your lawyer power of attorney, which I cover in detail in Chapter 4.

5. **Carry out the last checks and sign the final contract.**

   After you sign the initial contract, your lawyer carries out the necessary checks/searches and ensures that the vendor provides all the relevant title documents, permissions for use, and information on any mortgages and loans outstanding.

   If an AIP permit is required, your lawyer must see this document before you sign the final deed of transfer of the property.

AIP permits

As a foreign buyer, you usually need to acquire an Acquisition of Immovable Property (AIP) permit in order to purchase property in Malta. The application process usually takes about three months.

A few restrictions apply:

- The value of the property must exceed LM50,000 (£80,000), or LM30,000 (£48,000) for an apartment.
- The property can only be used as a residence, though you may accommodate guests.
- If you are bringing funds to Malta from abroad, you must do this through a bank.

Following Malta's accession to the EU in May 2004, the rules have been modified concerning AIP permits relating to citizens of EU countries. EU citizens can buy *one* property without needing a permit, provided that the property is intended to be a primary and principal residence, regardless of whether you actually choose to live in Malta. Non-EU citizens must still always apply for an AIP permit.

Review the regulations concerning AIPs and download an application form at the Maltese government's AIP Web site (`www.aip.gov.mt`).

You pay the seller the balance of the purchase price, together with the 10 per cent of the price you deposited on signing the initial contract.

6. **Pay for your property.**

   You need to pay for your property in Maltese currency. To do this, you can either instruct you own bank or buy currency through a specialist company, which may offer more competitive rates. See Chapter 18 for more information.

   You can have the purchased currency sent directly to your own bank account in Malta or to your lawyer's escrow account, which is a client account in which your funds are kept separate and cannot be accessed without your permission.

7. **Transfer utilities.**

   You can handle almost every aspect of transferring and paying for all utilities online. Malta's principal utility providers include Enemalta Corporation (`www.enemalta.com.mt`), which supplies electricity and bottled gas, and the Water Services Corporation (`www.wsc.com.mt`), which supplies water and disposes of waste water. Malta has no natural gas network. Domestic water and electricity use are metered, and bills are sent out every two months, based on twice-yearly meter readings with estimated readings in between.

You can transfer utilities easily, but you must pay a deposit of LM100 ($160) if you don't have a local Maltese ID card or aren't a citizen of an EU country.

Malta.com (`www.malta.com`) provides telephone and Internet services, usually within 20 days of application and at an initial cost of LM23.6 ($38) and a monthly line rental charge of LM2.57 ($4); call charges are on top of that. For new telephone contracts, a deposit of LM500 ($800) is required; the deposit is refundable when you close the contract. Having local ID or proof of citizenship of a EU country frees you from having to pay this deposit.

The Government of Malta Information and Services Online Web site (`www.gov.mt`) provides information on services and charges for all utilities as well as application forms, a fault-reporting service, the ability to check bills online, and – for Bank of Valletta and HSBC account holders – online payment options. The site also includes links to services offered by Malta Post, the Department of Customs, the Gozo Channel, and Air Malta, as well as information on bus, taxi, and minibus services.

Getting Settled in Malta and Gozo

Malta is one of the easiest Eastern European countries for Brits to settle into. The rules, language, and to some extent the culture are both familiar and benign. Britain influenced the course of affairs in Malta for more than 160 years, so the similarities aren't surprising.

This section covers a variety of topics that you need to address to get comfortable and situated in your new life in Malta.

Taxing matters

Maltese tax concerns related to property include the following:

- **Business tax:** Corporate tax is 35 per cent. There is no withholding tax on interest and royalties paid to foreign residents.
- **Capital gains tax:** This is not charged on the sale of a property that has been the owner's main residence for at least three years. If a house is not a main residence or is being sold less than three years from the date of purchase, tax is applied at the same rate as individual personal tax, up to a maximum of 35 per cent.
- **Death duties:** The Death and Donation Duty Act was repealed with effect from 22 November 1992, so as long as the property has not been in your ownership in any way from before that date, you are not liable for death

duties. However, if you inherit a property, you must pay a 5 per cent property transfer tax when moving the deeds into your name.

- **Double taxation treaties:** Malta has a double taxation treaty with the UK and many other countries, which ensures that you don't end up paying tax twice on the same income or paying more tax than you should. See Chapter 17 for more information on double taxation treaties.
- **Individual tax:** Malta has a progressive taxation system under which individuals are taxed between 0 per cent on the first LM3,100 (£4,960) through to 35 per cent of their income above LM6,751 (£10,800). Permanent residents are charged a reduced rate of 15 per cent on any income remitted into the country, subject to a minimum tax of LM1,000 (£1,600) per year.
- **Local taxes:** Malta does not have any local property taxes.
- **Value-added tax:** Charged at 18 per cent. The registration threshold is a low €10,000 (£6,800). As a comparison, the UK threshold is €86,000 (£58,700). The Maltese government VAT Web site (`www.vat.gov.mt`) has all the relevant information.

To find out more about the tax regime in Malta, visit the Maltese Inland Revenue Web site (`www.ird.gov.mt`).

Opening a bank account

Opening a bank account in Malta is a simple and speedy process. Take along an original copy of a banker's reference provided by your UK bank, a copy of your passport, and a utility bill proving your address.

All the usual types of bank account, including foreign-currency and Internet accounts, are available in Malta. Banks are usually open between 8.30am and 12:30pm Mondays to Fridays and until 11:30am on Saturdays. You can find plenty of automated teller machines (ATMs). Credit cards are widely accepted.

Find a full directory of all Malta's banks on the Malta Banks and Financial Institutions Web site (`malta.co.uk/malta/bank1.htm`). If you want to pay your utility bills online, plan to bank with HSBC (`www.hsbcmalta.com`) or Bank of Valletta (`www.bov.com`).

Staying healthy

Malta has a comprehensive and well-regarded health service that is funded from taxation and is free to patients. EU nationals resident in Malta are eligible to receive free medical treatment from government-funded hospitals and clinics.

The islands have six public hospitals, one of which is on Gozo, as well as three private hospitals, nine health centres, 214 pharmacies, 1,000 doctors, and 1,400 nurses and midwives. The main general hospital is St Luke's in Guardamangia (`www.slh.gov.mt`), where all major operations are performed. The St James private hospital (`www.stjameshospital.com`) is a state-of-the-art medical centre covering most treatments you would expect in the UK, including an extensive range of cosmetic surgery.

There are charges for prescription medicines, but people on low incomes and people with specified chronic diseases are exempt from payment. All drugs used in inpatient treatment and for the first three days after discharge are free of charge for the patient.

In the main, people pay for dental care in private dental clinics (licensed by the Public Health Authorities) much as they do in the UK. Only acute emergency dental care is offered free of charge in hospital outpatient and health centres.

The Ministry of Health Elderly and Community Care Web site (`www.sahha.gov.mt`) gives details on all hospitals, health centres, and dentists, as well as information on medical entitlement and links to reassuringly familiar services such as 'meals on wheels'.

Getting around the country

Although Malta is a small country, you have a variety of options to get around Malta and Gozo and to travel between the nation's seven islands.

Bus

The only public transport option is bus. Malta's railway system had a short life: Its single line from Valletta to Mtarfa opened in 1883 and closed in 1931.

Malta is divided into three bus zones spreading out from Valletta in Malta or from Victoria in Gozo. The further you go, the more you pay. You can see the routes, fares, and timetables on the Malta Transport Web site (`www.maltatransport.com`).

Car

Anyone over 18 holding a valid EU driving licence can drive in Malta. Driving is on the left-hand side of the road. A seat belt must be worn at all times. Malta and Gozo do not have highways or motorways. The upper speed limit in built-up areas is 40 kilometres (24 miles) per hour and outside built-up areas 64 kilometres (40 miles) per hour.

Malta is reputed to have the cheapest car-hire rates in Europe, with prices starting at LM5.50 ($8.80) per day, including mileage and insurance, for hire periods of more than 14 days in winter.

Taxi

The 250 Maltese government-licensed white taxis can pick up from anywhere on Malta and Gozo. Fares are fixed for the airport route and for several other destinations. Otherwise, always ask for an estimate before you get in.

Ferry

The Gozo Channel Company (www.gozochannel.com) operates three modern passenger and car ferries out of Cirkewwa and Mgarr. The shortest travel time to Gozo is 20 minutes, from Cirkewwa, Malta's most northern point. Sa Maison, near Valletta, to Gozo is a 75-minute journey.

In summer, a passenger-only service is available on Hovermarines (fast ferries) from Sa Maison in Malta to Mgarr in Gozo.

Helicopter

Helicopteros del Sureste SA (+356-2156-1301; www.helisureste.com) operates a helicopter shuttle service for Air Malta, running every 15 minutes or so throughout the day between 5.45am to 1.45am between Xewkija Heliport, Gozo, and Malta International Airport in Luqa.

Check out the full schedule of direct and indirect flights to and from Malta on the Malta Airport Web site (www.maltairport.com).

Chapter 11

The Baltic States

In This Chapter

- Understanding the potential in the Baltic States
- Discerning where you want to look
- Going through the purchase process
- Making the purchase work for you

The Baltic States – Estonia, Latvia, and Lithuania (before the Second World War, some people considered Finland to be a fourth) – are different countries despite often being seen as very similar. Their languages belong to two distinct language families, and the countries belong to different Christian camps. However, they have shared a common history ever since the Crusaders invaded in the 13th century up to 1918, when they became sovereign nations. Freed from Soviet influence in 1991, the three countries formed the Baltic Council, and in 1995 they created the Baltic Peacekeeping Battalion (*Baltbat*) to strengthen security in the region. However, they still remain three independent countries with their own governments.

From a property-owning perspective, the three countries also have much in common. They are geographically close, with all three located within an hour or so's drive from each other. They have similar-sized coastlines on the Baltic Sea and near-identical climates. They also all joined the European Union (EU) on the same date.

Perhaps most importantly from a property-purchasing perspective, the Baltic States' unspoilt sparsely populated land, attractive mediaeval cities, dynamic economies, and leisure amenities are all proving a magnet to tourists, business people, and people interested in relocating.

Fast facts about the Baltic States

Area: The Baltic States occupy 174,500 square kilometres in total. Latvia and Lithuania are much the same size, at roughly 65,000 square kilometres, and Estonia is about a third smaller, at about 43,000 square kilometres. The total area of the three nations is a little over the size of England, Wales, and Northern Ireland combined.

Population: 7,219,000 total. Estonia, 1,333,000; Latvia, 2,290,000; Lithuania, 3,596,00.

Location: Edging on to the Baltic Sea with a combined coastline of 4,330 kilometres, most of which (3,700 kilometres) belongs to Estonia, which also has more than 1,500 islands in the Baltic and Lake Peipus (*Peipsi-Järv*). Poland lies to the southwest, Belarus to the east, and Russia to the northeast.

Languages: Despite the three nations' similarities in culture and history, their languages belong to two distinct language families, and each of the countries has its own language. Lithuanian and Latvian share common roots, though speakers do not necessarily understand each other with ease. Estonians and Latvians use German widely as a second tongue, and many Lithuanians speak at least some Polish. The Estonian language has nothing in common with Lithuanian and Latvian but shares linguistic roots with Finnish.

Soviet influence throughout the 20th century left around a quarter to a third of the Baltic States' population speaking Russian. Most people only speak the language of their respective country, but fortunately many speak English.

Online language resources include:

- English–Estonian dictionary: `www.ibs.ee/dict`
- Latvian–English dictionary: `www.letonika.lv/DictForm.aspx`
- Lithuanian–English dictionary: `www.dictionaries.vnvsoft.com/en/index.html`

Currency: Estonia uses the Estonian kroon (EEK); €1 is equivalent to 15.72EEK and £1 is equivalent to 22.794EEK. Latvia uses Latvian lats (LVL); €1 is equivalent to 0.70LVL and £1 equivalent to 1.01LVL. Lithuania uses the litas (LTL); €1 is equivalent to 3.47LTL and £1 is equivalent to 5.03LTL.

The euro is widely used for all major transactions, and property-related transactions are priced in euros. The euro is likely to be adopted throughout the three counties by 2010, but each country is debating what to call the new currency. Latvia's government, for example, has voted to call the single European currency the 'eiro'.

Time zone: GMT +2.

EU standing: All three countries joined the EU as full members in May 2004.

Emergency services: Emergency switchboard operators may not speak good English, so you may need help from others to request these services. Alternatively, in all three Baltic States, call the International Emergency Number, 112, which usually has operators who speak English.

Estonian emergency phone numbers:

Ambulance: 112

Fire: 112

Police: 110

Latvian emergency phone numbers:

Ambulance: 03

Fire: 01

Police: 02

Lithuanian emergency phone numbers:

Ambulance: 112

Fire: 112

Police: 112

Visas: EU citizens do not need a visa to enter any of the Baltic States. If you intend to stay longer than three months, apply for a residence permit. After three years, you can then apply for permanent residence. For details of how to apply for these permits – or for a visa if you are not a EU citizen – contact the relevant country embassy (Estonia: 020-7589-3428; www.estonia.gov.uk; Latvia: 020-7312-0040; www.latvia.embassyhomepage.com; Lithuania: 020-7486-6401; www.lithuania.embassyhomepage.com).

By air from the UK: A number of airlines fly direct to the Baltic States. In addition to the usual suspects, try Air Baltic (+370-5235-6000; www.airbaltic.com), SAS, Scandinavian Airlines (020-8990-7159; www.scandinavian.net), and Estonian Air (020-7333-0196; www.estonian-air.ee).

By rail from the UK: You can travel from the UK by train to all three Baltic capital cities, changing in Brussels, Berlin, and Warsaw. Book tickets in the UK through European Rail or Deutsche Bahn's British office. You can also travel by rail and sea, crossing from Newcastle via Gothenburg and Stockholm to Tallinn and then on to Riga using DFD Seaways (0870-252-0524; www.dfds.co.uk). The Man in Seat Sixty One (www.seat61.com) provides an overview of these routes.

By coach from the UK: The pan-European Eurolines runs between London and Tallinn, Parnu, and Valmiera in Estonia; Riga in Latvia; and Vilnius, Kaunus, Marijampole, and Panevezys in Lithuania. The journey takes 50–60 hours.

Accommodation: Hotel accommodation is plentiful throughout the region and ranges from dirt cheap to very expensive. Tourist-class hotels are readily available from €30 (£21) a night for a double room. Baltic Hotels (+372-6266-233; www.baltichotels.com) covers all three countries. Hostel World (www.hostelworld.com) has details of hostels in 14 towns and cities throughout the Baltic States, costing from £10 a night.

Apartments for long-term rent throughout the region start from €40 (£28) for a night and €300 (£208) for a month. The *Baltic Times* (www.baltictimes.com) carries small ads for apartments in all three countries. Relocation Apartments (020-8944-1444; www.relocationapartments.com) carries a range of apartments and corporate housing for short and long stays in the major Baltic cities, as does Sublet City (www.sublet.com), which provides a global marketplace where tenants and landlords can match their housing needs.

For a selection of apartments in Estonia, contact ITES Apartments (+372-6310-637; www.ites.ee). For Latvia, contact Riga Apartments (+614-1914-9051; www.riga.lt), which runs out of an information portal in Ekaterinburg, Russia. For Lithuania, contact Nuomos Biuras (+370-5233-5577; www.nuomosbiuras.lt).

Getting to Know the Baltic States

The Baltic States have an awful lot of space and very few people. The region's history is rich and varied, which is proving a strong pull for tourists, but the recent resurgence in business activity is really fuelling the current property-buying frenzy.

Unemployment in many areas is down to 5 per cent (just more than half the EU average), the economies are growing at near to four times the rate for larger EU countries such as France, Germany, and the UK, and money is pouring into new investments and new businesses.

Price rises for new-build properties have been in double-figure percentages for several years, and buying off-plan is very popular. Developers don't seem to be able to keep up with a near-insatiable demand for property, and the off-plan system is a way to keep buyers in a queue while relieving them of their money. (I cover the pros and cons of buying off-plan in Chapter 18.)

The reason for the current buying bonanza lies partly in the shortage of quality hotel rooms in the region and partly in the urgent need to update dilapidated areas where the build quality was low. But a further big part of the boom is the availability of cheap mortgage finance, spurred on by wages that are growing at nearly 15 per cent.

All these factors mean that tourists, businesses, country nationals, and speculative investors are creating upward pressure on land and property prices. A few signs indicate that supply and demand are balancing out. So when a buyers' market returns, prices should stabilise and you may be able to find some bargains in the mix.

Cultural considerations

The Baltic States have always been attractive to international travellers, but the region's rich history and low prices – not to mention sheer curiosity about what the Russians have left behind at the end of the Communist era – have led to significant growth in this interest.

The Baltic countries seem a million miles from the packaged tourism markets of southern Europe and are refreshingly genuine. In short, the area has loads to offer visitors. Dramatic cliffs and jagged inlets line the thousands of kilometres of Baltic Sea coastline that joins the countries together. Large islands dot Estonia's coast, including Saaremaa and Hiiumaa and hundreds of smaller isles, such as Muhu, Kihnu, and Ruhnu, with windmills, thatched cottages, and tranquil fishing villages. Inland, you can enjoy vast forests and national parks such as those at Aukštaitija, Žemaitija, and Dzūkija in Lithuania and dozens of others in all three countries. Monasteries and churches (900 in Lithuania alone) mingle with Baroque palaces, ancient manor houses, and castles.

Truth be told, the Baltic beaches are not world-class and the skiing is limited. But in every other respect, the region has plenty to keep visitors occupied and eager to return. Proximity to much wealthier countries (Sweden, Finland, and Denmark) ensures a burgeoning tourist market, which in part explains the strong interest from overseas buyers in the property market here.

The Web site of Baltic Travel (020-7078-4122; `www.baltictravel.net`) provides details and links to most cultural, travel, and tourism activities in all three countries, as well as information on nearby Russia, Sweden, and Norway. The country-specific tourism Web sites are:

- **Visit Estonia** (`www.visitestonia.com`)
- **Latvia Tourism** (`www.latviatourism.lv`)
- **Lithuanian Travel Guide** (`www.travel.lt`)

Climate and weather

Winters in the Baltic are long, cold, and often dark. December can see daylight disappear by 4 pm and not reappear until 9 am the next day. Although not anywhere near as cold as parts of neighbouring Russia, midwinter mean temperatures are around –10°C and rise to only 17°C in southern parts of the region in midsummer. Like the British Isles, the Baltic States hardly have a typical summer or winter – summer days with temperatures reaching 30°C do occur, as do periods of continuous rain and, in the winter and autumn, snow. Tables 11-1 to 11-3 cover average temperatures and precipitation throughout the region.

The sea temperature in the Gulf of Finland is an average of just 1°C in May but rises to 16°C or higher approaching St Petersburg in August. Despite the region's thousands of kilometres of coast, innumerable islands, and lakes, Baltic waters are no substitute for the Mediterranean. Divers should definitely take a drysuit.

Table 11-1 Average Daily Temperatures in the Baltic States

Location	*Jan–Mar*	*Apr–June*	*July–Sep*	*Oct–Dec*
Tallinn (Estonia)	–2°C	9°C	14°C	1°C
Riga (Latvia)	–1°C	11°C	16°C	2°C
Vilnius (Lithuania)	–2°C	11°C	16°C	1°C

Table 11-2 Average Number of Rainy Days per Month in the Baltic States

Location	*Jan–Mar*	*Apr–June*	*July–Sep*	*Oct–Dec*
Tallinn (Estonia)	6	9	8	10
Riga (Latvia)	5	8	8	8
Vilnius (Lithuania)	9	9	9	9

Table 11-3 Average Number of Snowy Days per Month in the Baltic States

Location	*Jan–Mar*	*Apr–June*	*July–Sep*	*Oct–Dec*
Tallinn (Estonia)	11	1	0	6
Riga (Latvia)	8	1	0	4
Vilnius (Lithuania)	12	1	0	6

English-language media

English newspapers are available primarily in the capital cities, arrive a day or two late, and cost around £2.

The Baltic States are currently not well served with English-language news media. You can just about keep up with events through local media and online sources, but information about the property market – news, information, and even classified ads – is almost nonexistent. The Baltic States are well behind almost every other country in this book in terms of published real-estate information. Perhaps a business opportunity exists?

You can pick up all the local and some of the international news in English on the following Web sites:

- **Baltic Times** (`www.baltictimes.com`) is an independent weekly newspaper that covers the latest political, economic, business, and cultural events in Estonia, Latvia, and Lithuania, with offices in each capital. It has a classified advertisements section covering the property market. A subscription print version is available for around €110 (£76) a year, which includes access to more online resources.

- **City Paper** (www.balticsww.com) has an extensive range of news and information aimed at the expat community across the three countries, including property to rent and buy, information on the property market, buying procedures, banking, and the mortgage market. You can also find information on cinemas, restaurants, and online dictionaries for the three languages. The site also offers telephone directories in English for real-estate companies, property rental, and service providers in all three countries. A subscription print version is available for around €95 (£66) a year, which includes access to more online resources.
- **Expats Network International** (www.expatsnet.net) offers a range of discussion groups and Web links for the international community in the Baltics, covering immigration, employment, real estate, health care, travel, and business prospects.

The BBC World Service is available locally at various times of the day. Find details on the BBC World Service Web site (www.bbc.co.uk/worldservice).

Tourism

The growth in tourism for the Baltic States in recent years has been little short of stupendous. Across the three countries, the number of tourists coming in is growing by 20 per cent a year; for Estonia, the number of foreign visitors has grown by more than 30 per cent. Riga Airport reports that passenger numbers have almost doubled, while AirBaltic has posted a rise in profits of more than 80 per cent. The recent influx of budget airlines to all three capitals confirms that tourism is on a roll here.

Of the 10 million or so visitors to the region each year, by far the greatest number come from neighbouring Finland and Sweden on shopping expeditions. Estonia's elimination of restrictions on the quantity of alcohol and tobacco that you can take out of the country has helped here. Rural tourism has also enjoyed a recent boom, with the region's parks, ecotourism sites, spas, and historic monuments drawing in the crowds.

Many tour operators believe that the Baltic countries are set to provide a new, different, and relatively affordable destination for international travellers. Thirsty for unique locales, more than 150,000 North Americans and a similar number of Brits and Irish head to one of the three countries each year. You can now find Greek, Indian, Thai, French, Georgian, Italian, and English restaurants in major cities. (And so far, the strip-bars and gambling prevalent in other booming tourist destinations have been kept within bounds throughout the three countries.)

Sports and leisure

The Baltic States have a little of nearly everything – and an awful lot of some other sports and leisure activities. The region has only a handful of golf courses (Estonia has only one 18-hole golf course, located at Niitvälja, 33 kilometres southwest of Tallinn).

The region's downhill skiing is fun rather than world-class, but the locals have made their mark in cross-country skiing, winning numerous Winter Olympic medals. The first snow arrives in November, but the real skiing season begins around Christmas time and lasts until the end of March or early April. The heaviest snowfalls are in southern Estonia, around the hills in Otepää and Võrumaa, and in northeastern Latvia.

The long Baltic coastline has fantastic beaches and coves and is a great base for sailors, both day-trippers and bolder adventurers. You can charter a sailing boat and set sail for the spectacular islands of Estonia's west coast or go for a longer voyage to Helsinki, the Åland Islands, Stockholm, or further still.

The region really comes into its own as a place for walkers, climbers, bird watchers, horse riders, and bicyclers who want to explore areas of outstanding beauty that are seriously uncrowded. Even at the peak of the tourist season, visitors combined with the locals number less than the population inside the UK's M25 ring, but spread out in a region the size of England, Wales, and Northern Ireland combined. Space is something that the Balts do well. They also do rivers and lakes well – canoeing, kayaking, rafting, and fishing (with a permit, of course) are popular activities in the region's thousands of lakes and rivers.

Spas centred around sources of underground mineral waters containing compounds of bromine and sulphur and medicinal mud are starting to pull in tourists in search of a cosmetic uplift, a quick detoxification treatment, or just relaxation.

The country-specific tourism Web sites provide links to all these leisure activities and more. See the section 'Cultural considerations' earlier in this chapter for details.

Talking Business

Barely a year after joining the EU, Eurostat, the EU's central statistical body, stated that the Baltic States had recorded the fastest economic growth across the EU and that it expects the trend to continue. Although Latvia, the poorest country in the EU, has consistently outperformed its neighbours with current gross domestic product (GDP) topping 10 per cent, Estonia achieved 9.3 per cent, and Lithuania a very creditable 6.7 per cent. These growth rates are between three and five times the average for the EU as a whole.

The key drivers of this phenomenal growth include retail trade, manufacturing, and residential construction (up a staggering 71 per cent). The region saw inward investment of more than €40 billion (£28 billion) between 1995 and 2005, more than double the investment made into Russia over the same period. Companies setting up in the region come from neighbours such as Sweden and Finland as well as from the UK, France, Germany, the USA, and Hong Kong.

Even more importantly, the factors fuelling this growth are resilient, which bodes well for the property sector of the economy. In particular:

- The countries' populations are getting wealthier, with wages rising by 10 per cent a year. This is happening because their economies are export-led and sales to other EU countries are growing at more than 20 per cent a year.
- Lots of executives are coming in from big overseas companies to help set up enterprises locally. These individuals need somewhere to stay for the few years that they are in the region.
- The number of overnight stays in Baltic accommodation is growing by more than 30 per cent annually, and the pressure is strong to create more accommodation.

You can keep track of economic and business trends in the region by reading the *Baltic Rim Economies Bimonthly Review*, published by Finland's Turku School of Economics and Business Administration (`www.tukkk.fi/pei/bre`). This free review is published on the last week day in every even-numbered month and is available online.

Examining the cost of living

The cost of living across the region is lower than in the UK, with average monthly pay around €500 (£347). For example, a five-hour first-class rail journey costs around €15 (£10), and reasonable restaurant meals cost €3–5 (£2–3.5). The average British pensioner can live fairly comfortably here.

Estonia (38th), Lithuania (39th), and Latvia (48th) also rank high out of the 177 countries listed in the United Nations' Human Development Index (`http://hdr.undp.org/reports/global/2005`), so the countries are not only inexpensive but also reasonably good places to live.

Identifying areas of value

The Baltic States rank as having reasonably valued property when compared with the other Eastern Europe countries that are now in the EU. However, this situation is rapidly changing: A boom in prices in the city centres and the more popular tourist resorts is altering the value equation rapidly. For example:

- A new two-bedroom house in Jogevamaaand, Estonia, close to some reasonable skiing, sells for €30,000 (£20,800). This is about two-thirds the price of comparable property in, say, Bulgaria, which is not yet in the EU (though admittedly, the downhill skiing in Bulgaria is almost certainly better).
- New apartments in the Luther quarter of central Tallinn ranging in size from 27 to 170 square metres are on offer for prices between €53,000 (£36,760) and €255,000 (£177,000), which is about what you would expect to pay in Prague. Not great value when you consider that Prague gets 6.9 million foreign tourists a year, of whom 500,000 are British, compared with Tallinn's 38,903 British tourists and 1 million visitors.

Assessing potential rental yields

The latest (and perhaps last) real-estate market report prepared jointly by Latvia, Lithuania, and Estonia (`www.kada.lt/ntr/stat/review2004`) includes reports from various brokers in the three countries. Each indicates gross pre-tax rental yields of around 8–10 per cent, which reduce to 6–8 per cent after expenses such as depreciation and brokers' fees. The bodies responsible in each country for gathering real estate data include the Estonian Land Board (`www.maaamet.ee`), the State Land Service of the Republic of Latvia (`www.vzd.gov.lv`), and the State Enterprise Centre of Registers (`www.kada.lt`). Individually, these organisations don't offer any conclusive information on yields, other than to suggest that they are rising.

The growth in tourism has resulted in a shortage of hotel accommodation during the peak summer periods, which provides an opportunity for property investors to offer holiday apartments and fill the gap. Also, the growth in inward investment, bringing in ever more executives either for months or years at a time, adds to the demand for quality properties.

Considering property appreciation

Property prices have increased by 10–40 per cent a year for the past five years, albeit from a low base. Developers built 1,800 new apartments in

Tallinn alone in 2003, selling 1,650 in the same period. The following year, another 3,000 units were built and sold, and now the rate of sales is exceeding the rate at which new properties can be built.

The view in the market is that properties in the city centres of all three countries will continue to appreciate at around 8–9 per cent a year for the foreseeable future. The experts are so confident for a variety of reasons:

- Demand is outstripping supply. Investors are buying properties off-plan (see Chapter 18, where I examine this opportunity) that are not scheduled to be completed for up to two years ahead.
- Mortgage finance (at rates starting as low as 2.75 per cent for up to 90 per cent of a property's value for periods up to 30 years) is underpinning growth. In Estonia, for example, an area with some of the lowest mortgage rates, this type of borrowing accounts for only 17 per cent of annual GDP, compared with an EU average of 48 per cent of GDP.
- Salaries are rising fast, at about 7–10 per cent annually. Most locals live in substandard and very small apartments (the typical living area of 24 square metres is half the EU average). Increasingly well-off Balts are renting and purchasing new properties.
- Increased interest from outside property investors is making for a volatile market. Even Hong Kong property developers are entering the market.

The Estonian Land Board (`www.maaamet.ee`), the State Land Service of the Republic of Latvia (`www.vzd.gov.lv`), and the State Enterprise Centre of Registers (`www.kada.lt`) produce useful information on the state of the property market in their respective countries. Ober-Haus (`www.ober-haus.ee`), the largest real-estate agency operating across Estonia, Latvia, and Lithuania, produces a report each year giving a residential property update for each country, available free on its Web site.

Choosing Where to Buy

All three Baltic State capitals have aspirations to become the premier Baltic city, the place where foreign investors just have to be. So far, Tallinn (Estonia) and Riga (Latvia) probably have the most credible claims to being important business and financial cities. In this section, I focus on property opportunities in each of the capitals.

Tallinn's claim is supported by an impressive array of facts. The EU plans to invest €5.1 billion (£3.5 billion) in Estonia's infrastructure between now and 2011. The investment will go into roads, airports, hospitals, education, and

Estonian businesses generally, which will in turn lead to more jobs, expanding businesses, higher consumer spending, and more investment in property. The Global Growth Competitive Index (`www.weforum.org`) ranks Estonia 20th out of 117 countries in the world, higher than any other Eastern European country. Additionally, Estonia plans to cover the entire country with wireless Internet broadband and so become the first country in the world to be totally wi-fi.

But Latvia and its capital Riga are hardly slouches in terms of progress. The country is placed 44th in the Global Growth Competitive Index, ahead of such luminaries as China, India, and neighbouring Poland. The airport is buzzing, and trade with Sweden, Denmark, and Germany, all within 200 miles by sea and 30 minutes by air, is helping to fuel growth.

As a result of its less favourable position, Lithuania's capital, Vilnius is a longer shot in the battle to be the Baltic capital of choice. Still, the Lithuanian economy is growing faster than that of the other two states, and the increasing importance of Poland in European economics and politics certainly bodes well for Vilnius. As Lithuania is already placed 42nd in the world competitiveness stakes, you can't eliminate Lithuania from the race to be the region's top dog.

However exciting an opportunity they may appear – and the buzz is significant – Estonia, Latvia, and Lithuania are still very much niche property markets. For the time being, concentrate on looking for good-value properties in the three capitals, which attract up to 80 per cent of the tourist market, receive most of the inward investment, and are home to the most affluent nationals. Table 11-4 highlights comparative rents and purchase prices throughout the Baltic States.

Table 11-4 Indicative Purchase Prices and Monthly Rents for a Three-bedroom Property in the Baltic States

Location	*Purchase Price*	*Weekly Rent (Low/ High Season)*
Tallin (Estonia)	€150,000 (£104,000)	€800/1,200 (£555/830)
Riga (Latvia)	€140,000 (£97,000)	€600/1,000 (£415/693)
Vilnius (Lithuania)	€120,000 (£83,100)	€500/900 (£347/624)

Tallinn

Tallinn (population 400,000) is an undoubted treasure.

The historic town centre with a mediaeval cathedral on a hill above the picturesque walled lower town is now a UNESCO World Cultural Heritage site. Despite being assailed, sacked, flattened, and plundered over the centuries – the last time by the Soviet air force in the Second World War – much of the mediaeval old town has kept its charm. And the tourists who flood in throughout the year certainly share this view. You can get a full picture of what the city has to offer on the Tallinn Tourist Board Web site (`www.tourism.tallinn.ee`).

Talinn is compact, with the port and heliport a few minutes walk from the old town in Narva, the main commercial and diplomatic district of the city. Helsinki is only 1 hour 45 minutes by fast catamaran across the Baltic. Tallinn international airport can be reached by car in less then 15 minutes.

Property prices have been rising at more than 10 per cent a year, mostly in new developments, with two-bedroom apartments selling for from €56,000 (£38,800) in areas such as Viimsi, one of the wealthiest suburbs of Tallinn, 10 minutes from the city centre and a short walk from the beach. Closer to the city centre in areas such as the Pro Kapital Business Centre, which houses several embassies, two-bedroom apartments sell for from €81,000 (£56,000). A two-bedroom apartment in a renovated property in a 17th-century building located on the site of the Väike-Rannavarava (Portgate) bastion, which was destroyed after the Crimean War, is available for €120,000 (£83,100), a fairly typical price.

Though very attractive, most of the properties discussed above are small and rare. You also need to budget an additional €13,000 (£9,000) if you want a parking space, which is an essential for long-term tenants and makes future resale easier.

Riga

Riga is a vibrant, grand, and imposing city, characteristics that earned it the title of 'Paris of the North' from its pre-war visitors. It is the biggest (population 902,000) and most cosmopolitan Baltic capital, with reputedly the best night life and certainly the worst traffic. Cobblestone streets, with teahouses full of cakes, tortes, and the famous Latvian breads and pastries, are hallmarks of the city, as are its parks, beaches, spas, palaces, and fantastic opera house.

You can get a full picture of what the city has to offer in Riga This Week (www.rigathisweek.lv), a rather more focused guide to the city than you find on the main Latvian Tourist Board Web site (www.latviatourism.lv).

Riga has experienced strong and sustained growth in property prices in recent years, with new apartments realising a 20 per cent gain in the first half of 2005 alone, according to local brokers. The most popular suburbs, judging by the amount of property on offer, include Imanta, Purvciems, Plavnieki, Ziepniekklans, and districts such as Zolitude, just 10 minutes from the city centre. In these areas, a two-bedroom apartment sells for around €52,000 ($36,000), while close to the centre a new apartment costs €75,000 ($52,000). A tiny one-bedroom apartment in an older attractive building in the city centre sells for upwards of €80,000 ($55,500). These prices include parking spaces, at least with the newer properties.

Vilnius

For hundreds of years, the good citizens of Vilnius built their houses where they felt like, without any layout or order. In 1536, the duke ordered the houses to be built in rows following a plan. This worked well for a while, until a series of fires caused whole streets to change direction or disappear completely. Today the main tourist route starts at the Cathedral Square and goes to the Dawn Gate and through Pilies Street. This area, together with Didžioji Street, is packed with luxury shops, cafés, embassies, night clubs, and all the razzmatazz of city life. Squares, hills, courtyards, parks, and the only known monument to American composer, guitarist, and singer Frank Zappa are among the reasons to visit Vilnius.

The KGB Museum represents the city's recent past, with guides taking you on a tour through the same cells in which they were imprisoned. The future is best seen from the top of the Television Tower, where you can try a 280-metre bungee jump, or enjoy lunch at Paukščiùtakas, a restaurant 165 metres above the city. The Vilnius City Tourist Board (www.turizmas.vilnius.lt) can fill you in on all the details of what the city has to offer.

New three-bedroom apartments in the city centre with parking sell for between €90,000 ($62,300) and €150,000 ($104,000) and beyond in Užupis District, which is popular with artists as well as many wealthy citizens.

According to Lithuanian broker reports, the market for both old and new apartments is strong and has been growing at up to 20 per cent a year. However, the latest report states that the rental market is stagnant, which is an indication that property prices may be slowing down as supply meets demand.

Buying into the Baltic States

Estonia, Latvia, and Lithuania take a relaxed view to foreigners owning property, whether EU nationals or not. Purchasing in forest, agricultural, and some coastal areas is often more difficult, and the difficulties vary in each country. In Estonia, for example, foreigners can buy more or less any land they want as long as it is no more than 10 hectares. In Lithuania and Latvia, foreigners must live in the country for at least three years and have been involved in agriculture before.

Outside of agricultural and coastal land, the only constraint for foreigner buyers is how long you can stay in the country. If you intend to stay longer than three months, apply for a residence permit. After three years, you can then apply for permanent residence. For details of how to apply for these permits, or for a visa if you are not a citizen of the EU, contact the relevant country embassy (Estonia: 020-7589-3428; www.estonia.gov.uk; Latvia: 020-7312-0040; www.latvia.embassyhomepage.com; Lithuania: 020-7486-6401; www.lithuania.embassyhomepage.com).

Find a lawyer who has a good command of both the local language and English and who is independent of the estate agent or developer that you are dealing with. Ideally the lawyer should be based somewhere near the property you are investigating. This ensures the lawyer is well versed in local matters such as prospective building activities that could interfere with or even enhance the value of the property, for example new developments planned or roads to be built. You need to find the lawyer before you make an offer on a property so that they can be involved in every stage of the transaction. Look for lists of English-speaking lawyers on the Martindale-Hubbell Lawyer Locator (http://lawyers.martindale.com/marhub), the International Law Office (www.internationallawoffice.com/Directory), or Legal500.com (www.icclaw.com).

The basic procedures for purchasing property in the Baltic States are:

1. **Research the market.**

   Chapter 3 explains how to find properties, but many estate agents have someone in their offices who speaks English. Agents with an extensive range of properties both for sale and to let include the following:

   - **Arc Property** (020-7371-7633; www.arc-property.co.uk), based in London, offers properties in Estonia, Latvia, and Slovakia. It provides a number of property market intelligence reports and a useful buyer's guide.
   - **Estonia Properties** (www.estproperties.com) has an extensive range of properties in Tallinn only.

- **Invalda Real Estate** (+370-5273-0000; www.inreal.lt) operates out of Vilnius and has very comprehensive reports on property prices, trends, and rental yields on its Web site.
- **Ober-Haus** (+372-665-9700; www.ober-haus.lt) is one of the very few companies offering an extensive range of properties in all three countries. It also covers Poland. The site offers comprehensive data on all the relevant property markets, showing price movements and rental information.
- **Property in Estonia** (www.property-in-estonia.co.uk), run out of Cambridge by David Laity, offers property in Tallinn and also has a buyer's guide on its Web site.

Check that any estate agent you are dealing with is a member of a professional association such as the Federation of Overseas Property Developers, Agents and Consultants (www.fopdac.com) or the National Association of Estate Agents, UK (www.naea.co.uk) or is a member of its country's professional association:

- **Association of Real Estate Companies of Estonia** (+372-641-1516; www.ekfl.ee) has a directory of its 50 members on its Web site, as well as its members' code of practice.
- **Latvian Real Estate Association** (+371-733-2034; www.lanida.lv) has a directory of its 40 members, as well as information on property market trends.
- **Lithuanian Real Estate and Investment Management Association – LITIVA** (+370-5238-4420; www.litiva.lt) offers a directory of its membership.

2. **Find a property and carry out a thorough inspection.**

   Generally in these three countries, buyers do not carry out building surveys on new developments because these properties come with guarantees of quality. Survey any old buildings, buildings that you want a mortgage on, and building that you have any concerns about.

   Your estate agent, lawyer, or mortgage provider can put you in touch with a local surveyor. Estate agents tend to do their own basic valuation survey. Additional structural surveys cost €150–300 (£104–208).

   Alternatively, you can search the Royal Institute of Chartered Surveyors' (RICS) online database (0870-333-1600; www.rics.org).

   You are usually best finding a professional through the personal recommendation of someone whose judgement you respect and who is impartial. I cover finding professional assistance in Chapter 4.

3. **Negotiate and agree on the final price with the current owners.**

SOUTHAMPTON SIKH SEVA

Established in December 2014, we are a charitable organisation consisting of a small group of volunteers from the local Sikh Community. This is an ongoing project to help the homeless and disadvantaged people by providing food aid in this challenging financial climate. Our aim is to tackle the continuing problem of wide spread hunger and foster unity between communities.

Our voluntary service is delivered through the concept of Langar, free vegetarian food for everyone regardless of faith, gender age or status. We run the provisions for Langar purely on donations, with volunteers who prepare, cook, serve and clean as part of their Seva (selfless service).

Our team, along with the support from volunteers, go out every week to the streets of Southampton with freshly prepared vegetarian food and drink.

Throughout 2015 we have participated in a number of events in recognition of our Sikh beliefs and promoting Langar. These include Vaisakhi, Chabeel and National Langar week.

Fighting Hunger

Sikhs believe that no one should be hungry and langar is integral to the Sikh faith and lifestyle. It provides a daily lifeline for many people around the world, regardless if you are Sikh or not.

Equality

Langar was created by the founder of the Sikh faith, Guru Nanak Dev Ji over 500 years ago. It was designed to break down barriers and teach equality amongst all. This is why everyone regardless of religion, caste, colour, age, gender or social status eat together at the same level.

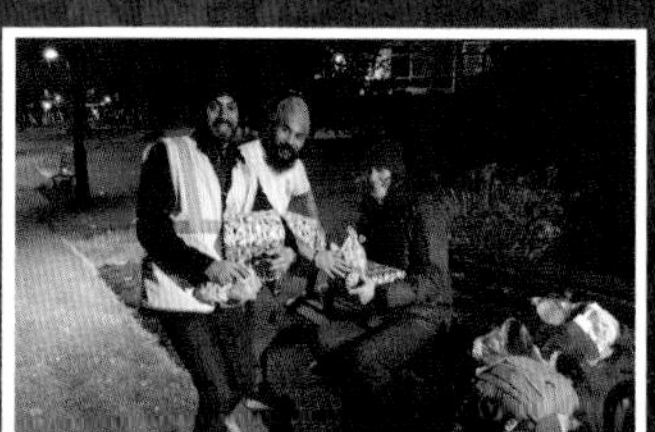

Teaching Compassion

Langar's are all run on donations of food, money and time. Anyone can volunteer to cook, clean or distribute Langar. This is seva (selfless service) and it teaches us the joy of sharing with others and have empathy with those less fortunate.

We rely purely on chairtable donations. Please donate now or get in touch

To donate:

Southampton Sikh Seva
Account No: 41476158
Sort Code: 56-00-68

 **07765166815 / 07748811912**

 **@s.s.s_khalsa_kitchen**

 **khalsa-kitchen@outlook.com**

 **Southampton Sikh Seva**

After viewing a property, you can negotiate directly with the owners or through the estate agent. Keep in mind that the total price you pay also includes the following:

- **Actual cost of buying:** This varies slightly between countries and according to your negotiating skills, but it usually works out to 3–6 per cent of the purchase price. Selling costs are 5–8 per cent.
- **Purchase tax (equivalent of stamp duty):** Paid by the buyer at 0.075 per cent in Estonia, 2 per cent in Latvia, and 1 per cent in Lithuania. These taxes are all currently under review.
- **Estate agency fees:** Usually 3–8 per cent, plus 18 per cent VAT. These are included in the selling price and deducted from the sum given to the seller.
- **Notary fee:** €20 (£14) in Estonia and Latvia, and around 1 per cent of the purchase price in Lithuania.
- **Value-added tax:** 18 per cent in all Baltic States and should always be included in the selling price.
- **Legal fees:** Around €500 (£347), unless you plan to depend entirely on the notary and the estate agent, which may be unwise. (See also Chapter 4.)
- **Annual property tax:** Property tax in Estonia is set by the local government; for Tallinn, this ranges from 0.2 to 0.7 per cent. In Latvia, property taxes are 1.5 per cent of the value assigned by the state to your property, which is usually lower than market value. Lithuania has no property tax on apartments or houses yet, but such a tax is on the way. Lithuanian land tax is 1.5 per cent of the property's value.
- **Property management charges:** €450–800 (£312–485) due on new properties in most holiday complexes and apartment blocks, depending on the services you select.

4. **Draw up and sign the initial contract.**

   After you and the seller agree to a price, your lawyer draws up an *initial sale and purchase contract*, which outlines the details and any conditions that must be met before the sale completes (for example, repairs).

   After you and seller sign the initial contract and you pay a deposit of 10 per cent, the sale is legally binding. Your lawyer normally has a month or two to complete property checks with the Land Registry Office. In Estonia, the land registration process can take up to four months to complete; in Latvia and Lithuania, it takes only 10–30 days.

If you fail to go ahead with the purchase for any reason other than that allowed by law, you forfeit your deposit. If you are not going to be in the county when this contract has to be signed, you need to give your lawyer power of attorney, which I cover in Chapter 4.

5. **Carry out the last checks and sign the final contract.**

   After the initial contract, your lawyer carries out the necessary checks/searches and ensures that the vendor provides all the relevant title documents, permissions for use, and information on any mortgages and loans outstanding. You and the seller then sign the final deed of transfer of the property, and you pay the balance of the purchase price to the seller, together with the 10 per cent of the price that you deposited on signing the initial contract.

6. **Pay for your property.**

   You must register the property in your name and pay for it in local currency. To do this, you can either instruct you own bank or buy currency through a specialist company, which may offer more competitive rates (see Chapter 18). You can either send the purchased currency directly to your own bank account in the Baltic States, or you can use your lawyer's *escrow account*, a client account in which your funds are kept separate and cannot be accessed without your permission.

7. **Transfer utilities.**

   Registering for electricity, gas, water, telephone, and refuse collection is a time-consuming process involving lots of paperwork. Sorting out issues can last several days or, in some cases, weeks. Deal with everything well in advance, or take into account that for some days you may be in your new property without electricity and gas.

   Transferring utilities is definitely not something to tackle on your own unless you are fluent in the language. Your broker can, if asked, arrange for all utility meters to be read, recorded, and transferred to your name. Brokers expect to do this as part of their general service, but you often need to remind them.

Getting Settled in the Baltic States

The Baltic States are not too difficult to settle into. The internal transport systems are reliable and inexpensive, though internal air travel other than between the three capitals is virtually non-existent.

Personal taxes are low, with a top rate of 25 per cent (which is set to get lower), so you may well decide to move your permanent financial base to the country you choose to buy in. I cover the ins and outs of deciding where to base your tax affairs in Chapter 17. Banking is user-friendly, and finding an English-speaking branch – in the cities at least – is not difficult.

Health care is adequate by Eastern European standards but is below what you expect in the UK. You need to hunt out English-speaking medics.

In the following sections, I cover all the little details you need to attend to in order to make your property in the Baltic States feel like home.

Taxing matters

Taxes related to property in the Baltic States include the following:

- **Business tax:** Estonia: 24 per cent. Latvia: 15 per cent. Lithuania: 15 per cent.
- **Capital gains tax:** Estonia: same as for individual income tax. Latvia: exempt from tax if you own the property for at least one year, otherwise taxed at same rate as for income. Lithuania: exempt from tax, provided that within any one year you sell only one asset.
- **Double taxation treaties:** All three countries have double taxation treaties with the UK and many other countries, which should ensure that you don't end up paying tax twice on the same income or paying more tax than you should. (See Chapter 17 in which I cover double taxation treaties.)
- **Death duties:** None of the three countries charges wealth taxes or inheritance taxes.
- **Individual tax:** Estonia: 24 per cent. Latvia: 25 per cent. Lithuania: varies by type of income, but usually around 15 per cent.
- **Local taxes:** Varies, but for a three-bedroom house this tax usually amounts to €50–100 (£35–70) annually.
- **Tax on rental income:** Same as for individual income tax in all three countries.
- **Value-added tax:** Charged at 18 per cent on all purchases.

To find out more about the tax regimes in these countries, visit the PricewaterhouseCoopers Web site (`www.pwc.com/ua/eng/main/home/index.html`) and follow the Publications link to find a comprehensive and up-to-date guide to tax and much else besides. Or refer to the World Wide Tax Web site (`www.worldwide-tax.com`).

Retiring and renting

Teacher Ian Jones and his wife Helen, age 56 and 50 respectively, bought an eight-bedroom property a few miles from the centre of Riga two years ago. While Ian was in the army, the couple moved around a lot, and one place they loved was Norway. Property in Norway was out of their league, but in Latvia their savings more than covered the €18,000 (£12,500) house they bought. Since buying their property, they have spent two long summer holidays in the country. Helen gives English lessons, and they have let out their finished bedrooms to tourists while working at renovating the rest of the property.

Their aim is to be able to live comfortably on a £20,000 annual income (£14,000 pension plus £6,000 they hope to make in Latvia) after they retire in a few years. While they are not confident that they can generate that much income from holiday lets in Latvia alone, the couple intend to keep their British property and let it out when they permanently move to Riga.

Living costs are rising much more slowly than they expected, so they are looking forward to a comfortable retirement rather than the frugal one they may have endured in the UK . (See Chapter 19 where I cover renting out properties.)

Opening a bank account

To open an account, you need identification, such as a passport, and a residence permit, if you have one.

The Baltic International Bank (`www.bib.lv/en`) is one bank that covers the region. Bennet, Bernstein & Partners Ltd (`www.bbp-net.com/en/cat/70`) has a directory of all the banks in the Baltic States.

Staying healthy

Health care is improving across the three countries, but emergency and medical services tend to fall below Western standards. There are emerging pockets of good care, and some Western-trained doctors have opened up practices in the capital cities, following the influx of wealthy business people and tourists. The British embassies in each country have lists of doctors and other English-speaking practitioners.

If you do not speak the local language, in the case of sudden serious illness call emergency services on the central number line (112). Operators on this line speak English and, after establishing your problem, they contact appropriate emergency services on your behalf, staying in touch with you to interpret where necessary.

EU nationals residing in the Baltic States are eligible to receive free medical treatment from government-funded hospitals and clinics. You may find that doctors, dentists, hospitals, and even ambulances expect cash payment for their services, so always get receipts.

Getting around the region

Estonia, Latvia, and Lithuania aren't large countries, and you have a variety of options to get from town to town – or country to country. This section covers your travel options within the Baltic States.

Bus

Buses are usually a faster and more comfortable way to get around the Baltic States. Tourism Web sites have links to all bus services around and between the countries: Visit Estonia (www.visitestonia.com), Latvia Tourism (www.latviatourism.lv), and Lithuanian Travel Guide (www.travel.lt).

Car

Your British driving licence is valid, but it must include a photo, otherwise you also require an International Driving Permit.

The road system throughout the Baltic States is, to say the least, patchy. The occasional motorway-quality highway, often requiring a toll, is a rarity compared with the miles and miles of potholed roads. Vehicles drive on the right and observe the following speed limits: 50 kilometres (31 miles) per hour in built-up areas, 90 kilometres (55 miles) per hour outside built-up areas, and 130 kilometres (80 miles) per hour on motorways. Wearing seat belts is compulsory, there is zero tolerance of alcohol before driving, and police are empowered to collect all traffic fines on the spot. Most people drive with dipped headlights on at all times.

Taxi

Taxis are plentiful and usually cheap and reliable throughout the three countries.

Info taxi (www.infotaxi.org) has information on reputable taxi companies and taxi phone numbers worldwide and covers some cities in the Baltic States.

Train

In Estonia, trains are operated by Edelaraudtee AS (www.edel.ee) and Elektriraudtee (www.elektriraudtee.ee), but the latter does not yet have an English-language Web site.

Latvian Railways (www.ldz.lv/en) and Lithuanian Railways (www.litrail.lt) both have English-language Web sites with timetables and fares. You can check out international travel on these Web sites too. Train fares are very inexpensive by British standards, with journeys typically costing less than £12 to cross an entire country.

Plane

Air Baltic (+370-5235-6000; www.airbaltic.com) flies a regular service between the three capital cities, as does Estonian Air (020-7333-0196; www.estonian-air.ee). Air Lithuania (+370-7007-0777; www.airlithuania.lt) runs a service between Vilnius and Palanga on the Lithuanian Baltic coast.

Within the three capital cities

You can get around most of the three capital cities on foot without much trouble. Trolley buses, trams, and minibuses run from before 6 am until after midnight. The following city tourism Web sites list links to all transport services: www.rigathisweek.lv, www.tourism.tallinn.ee, and www.turizmas.vilnius.lt.

Part III

Reviewing the Hopefuls

"Chernobyl? Never affected us here."

In this part . . .

In this part I talk about countries in the region that are not currently members of the European Union, from the perspective of owning a property there. Some of these countries are on track for membership in the near future, a couple are slated to join a little later but for two, Turkey and Ukraine, the prospects are more distant. Yet each country has a rich seam of property opportunities and if your attitude to risk is heading towards the adventurous then any of these could be for you.

In this part you will get a quick overview of the country, covering climate, cost of living, culture, and currency, through to budget airline access, property purchase procedures, taxes, and the prospects for the economy. Then comes a more detailed review of the handful of parts of the country that are believed to offer the best prospects for foreigners to buy in. These places will be those considered highly desirable to tourists, business people and the more progressive elements of the local population. This 'desirability' factor will be what ensures you will enjoy being there and if you want to let the property out or to sell it later, there will be a ready market. There is also an indicative price guide, for properties in each area. But keep in mind this is a fast changing environment so use the country property websites and the other sources of property price statistics given to keep current on the state of the market for both buying and renting.

Chapter 12

Bulgaria

In This Chapter

- Understanding the potential in Bulgaria
- Discerning where you want to look
- Going through the purchase process
- Making your purchase work for you

Bulgaria is emerging as a paradoxical investment location. While the country's population has dropped by a million in the past dozen years as people left to seek better lives elsewhere (leaving a glut of houses on the market), life in Bulgaria continues to improve. The country's economy, one of the most prosperous in the former Soviet bloc, has improved substantially in the past few years: The country enjoys political stability, and Bulgaria is on track to be admitted to the European Union (EU) in 2007.

Bulgaria certainly has some issues to be wary of, as with any investment. But by and large, if you study the market carefully and take a few basic precautions, buying a property in Bulgaria can be both fun and profitable.

Bulgarians nod their heads from side to side for 'yes' and up and down for 'no'. They sometimes swap this convention around when they're talking to foreigners.

Fast facts about Bulgaria

Area: 110,912 square kilometres, roughly the size of England.

Population: 7.97 million.

Location: Southeastern part of the Balkans peninsula, bordering Greece and Turkey to the south and the Republic of Macedonia and the former Yugoslavia to the west. The River Danube separates Bulgaria from Romania to the north; the country's natural eastern border is the Black Sea.

Language: Bulgarian (English spoken commonly).

Currency: The lev, which is divided into 100 stotinki. In 2004, around 2.8 leva (the plural of lev) was worth £1 and 2 leva equated to €1. All property transactions are done in euros.

Time zone: GMT+2.

EU standing: Bulgaria is actively seeking to join the EU and is on track to join in 2007.

Emergency services: Emergency switchboard staff rarely speak good English. If you need to call for assistance, do so through your local contacts or hotel receptionist. Emergency phone numbers include:

Fire: 160

Medical aid: 150

Police: 166

Roadside assistance: 146

Telephone information: 144

Visas: Until Bulgaria becomes a full member of the EU, UK citizens don't need a visa for one visit of up to 30 days in each six-month period. If you expect to stay in Bulgaria for more than 60 days a year, you need to apply for a visa. The Web site of the Bulgarian embassy (`www.bulgarianembassy.org.uk/visa`) has full details. After Bulgaria joins the EU, citizens of EU countries will not require a visa to visit or stay in the country.

By air from the UK: Try British Airways, Bulgaria Air (`www.air.bg/en`), Air France (www.airfarnce.co.uk), Lufthansa (`www.lufthansa.com`), Austrian Airlines (`www.aua.com`), and Alitalia (`www.alitalia.co.uk`).

By train from the UK: You can get to Bulgaria by train, but at best travel takes more than 40 hours. Contact European Rail or Deutsche Bahn's UK office for more information.

Other routes from the UK: No direct bus service is offered, although a weekly Eurolines coach (`www.eurolines.co.uk`) leaves the Gallieni international bus station in Paris at 8 am every Monday. The single fare is around £100, but travelling to Paris and spending a night there makes this an expensive and tiring option. The only direct sea route from the UK to Bulgaria is a container link to Varna.

Something you'd better know: Take great care when changing money in Bulgaria. Banks require passports and are slow, so you may be tempted to use one of the thousands of change shops. Make sure that you read the declared exchange rate and the commission on the notice outside before you hand over your money. Some change shops offer conversion rates that leave you with a third less than current national exchange rate, which is legal if that is the rate posted.

Accommodation: Hotels in Bulgaria are plentiful, cheap, and varied. A good-quality three- or four-star hotel in Sofia costs around £50 a night for two, but you can search out adequate hotels for half that figure. Staying for a week or longer – subject of course to having the appropriate visa – is unlikely to cost much. Private rooms cost as little as £3 a night or £200–300 a month, with a breakfast of sorts thrown. Local tourist offices can make bookings for you, or you can book some lodgings online at BG Globe.com (`www.bgglobe.net`). Ask your estate agent for recommendations.

Getting to Know Bulgaria

A large number of available properties is not the only reason to consider Bulgaria. With EU membership looming and the nation's Soviet bloc history a distant memory, the country's appealing cultural and business opportunities are becoming more apparent – and worth weighing up carefully if you're looking to buy property in Eastern Europe.

Bulgarian culture

Bulgaria's location as a geographic and historic crossroads, combined with a variety of ethnic influences and some stunning natural scenery, make for a rich cultural tapestry.

Bulgaria has more than 30,000 historical monuments from different epochs, and 330 museums and galleries form an impressive base for the development of cultural tourism. Over the centuries, the country has produced a steady stream of Thracian treasures and burial tombs, magnificent frescoes, and many examples of ancient applied arts. Rugs, carpets, painted ceramics, finely ornamented fretwork, and superbly fashioned jewellery make for a lively craft scene.

Bulgaria claims, with some justification, to be the country where wine was invented around 3,000 years ago, and some recent vintages are superb. Fortunately, only the mediocre escape the country, leaving the best for the locals – which can include you if you buy property here.

Climate and weather

Bulgaria has a generally moderate climatic zone, with two significant subzones, to the north and south of the *Stara Planina* ('Old Mountains') range. Winters are colder in northern Bulgaria and much milder in the southern part of the country. Winter temperatures vary between 0 and –7°C, with occasional plunges to –20 °C. The spring is continental and varied, with enough rain to ensure a good supply of cheap vegetables and fruit, for which Bulgaria has been renowned in Europe for centuries. Summer is hot and sweltering in northern Bulgaria, especially along the River Danube. Temperatures range between about 28 and 30°C, sometimes going above 35°C, with 40°C not unheard of on the Black Sea coast. Autumns are usually mild and pleasant, with a local version of an Indian summer ('Romany summer') occurring fairly regularly. In the south and at altitude in the mountains, the temperature is about 5°C cooler, though Plovdiv and Sofia can be warmer. Tables 12-1 to 12-3 list typical temperatures and precipitation levels throughout the year in Bulgaria.

Table 12-1 Average Daily Temperatures in Bulgaria

Place	Jan–Mar	Apr–June	July–Sep	Oct–Dec
Burgas	4°C	16°C	22°C	7°C
Rousse	3°C	18°C	24°C	6°C
Sofia	2°C	14°C	19°C	4°C
Vidin	3°C	17°C	21°C	3°C

Table 12-2 Average Number of Rainy Days per Month in Bulgaria

Place	Jan–Mar	Apr–June	July–Sep	Oct–Dec
Burgas	6	6	4	6
Rousse	3	5	4	4
Sofia	5	10	6	5
Vidin	2	3	3	4

Table 12-3 Average Number of Snowy Days per Month in Bulgaria

Place	Jan–Mar	Apr–June	July–Sep	Oct–Dec
Burgas	2	0	0	1
Rousse	2	0	0	2
Sofia	6	0	0	2
Vidin	1	0	0	1

English-language media

You can easily find English newspapers in most Bulgarian cities, but they arrive a day late and cost around 5 leva ($2). You can pick up all the local and some of the international news in English on the Sofia News Agency Web site (`www.novinite.com`), updated every five minutes, or on Bulgaria Online (`www.online.bg`).

The *Sofia Echo* (`www.sofiaecho.com`) comes out on the street on Thursdays and is the indispensable guide for all foreigners in Sofia. The publication offers cinema listings, news, and a restaurant guide. It is available free in most major hotels and costs $2 in bookstalls. It has a modest coverage of other major cities. The online edition has a good database of restaurant reviews covering Sofia and other cities.

You can listen to the BBC World Service locally on 91.0 FM.

Although plays and other live performances are performed in Bulgarian and are extremely hard to follow if you do not understand the language (even when you know the plot), the cinemas in Bulgaria hold a pleasant surprise. Because the Bulgarian market is too small for dubbing to be economical, cinemas show films in the language they were shot in with Bulgarian subtitles. This means that you can see any number of English-language films at Bulgarian cinemas on the cheap – a pound or two at most. Films come out in Bulgaria at much the same time as in other major cities around the world. For example, one Harry Potter film premiered in Sofia on the same day as it did in London.

Tourism

Tourism is one of the Bulgarian government's 'priority branches' – the other two are agriculture and the food industry, including wine. The number of foreign tourists visiting Bulgaria is growing rapidly. In 2004–2005 more than 3.5 million tourists arrived, up by 40 per cent in just two years.

Sports and leisure

The Black Sea coast has nearly 300 days of sunshine each year, making the area a natural for yachting, surfing, water-skiing, diving, underwater fishing, and other aquatic sports. Away from the coast there are plenty of opportunities for hiking, cycling, riding, photo tourism, and eco-tourism, with three national and nine nature parks and a number of reserves containing exceptionally beautiful features. Rila, Pirin, the Rodopes, Vitosha, and the Balkan mountains are all great places for skiing, trekking, and mountain climbing. Bulgaria also has more than 600 hot, warm, and cold mineral springs with curative properties and hotels with state-of-the-art equipment and skilled staff nearby.

Like to hunt? Bulgaria may be a country you should target. While hunting is being frowned on in the UK, in Bulgaria you can hunt deer, wild goat, bear, boar, grouse, hare, partridge, pheasant, and other game. In fact, Bulgaria ranks second in the world in terms of the quality of shot trophies.

Talking Business

While the Bulgarian economy was one of the most prosperous in the Soviet bloc, Bulgaria hasn't always been synonymous with prosperity in the post-Soviet years. Runaway inflation peaked at nearly 600 per cent in 1997, and unemployment reached as high as 38 per cent in 1999.

But since 1999, the laggard of the East European transition countries has experienced a prolonged period of economic and political stability. Unemployment has dropped by two-thirds in the past five years to 10 per cent, and inflation was just 4 per cent in 2005, which compares reasonably well with other countries in the region. Interest rates have eased rapidly, and economic growth is around double that of old Europe. In July 2003, the International Monetary Fund (IMF) called Bulgaria's economic performance 'excellent'.

This section considers the business implications of owning property in Bulgaria.

Examining the cost of living

The average monthly salary in Bulgaria is around £150–200, a lot less than your likely last pay cheque. Fortunately, nearly everything in Bulgaria costs a fraction of UK prices and at least 40 per cent less than in Spain, Italy, or Portugal.

Supper in an ordinary restaurant costs about 15 leva (£4.50), while the price of a 0.5-litre bottle of Rakiya, the local brandy, costs 3–15 leva (£1–4.50), depending on the quality of the product, the manufacturing technology, and the region of origin. A loaf of bread costs 40 stotinki (14p) and half a litre of milk about the same. A week's groceries for two runs to about 100 leva (£35), even if you have to throw in a Coca-Cola and a few Mars bars. The trams and trolleys that run through the capital Sofia and some other major cities are very inexpensive: A ride from one end of Sofia to the other costs a standard 0.5 leva (18p).

The cost of living in Sofia is higher than in the major cities by about 10 per cent. In the country away from major towns, the cost of living is lower. Utility bills, however, are both uniform and rising rapidly due to the increasing cost of energy throughout the world and the need to modernise water and drainage supply.

If the Bulgarian economy continues to grow at its present rate of 5 per cent and the EU countries keep growing at around 2 per cent, average Bulgarian wages will catch up with the UK in 64 years. So the bargain prices will be around for a while yet.

Estimating value and potential yield

Not surprisingly, given the cost of living difference, properties are cheaper in Bulgaria than in the UK and elsewhere. Consider Sofia, the capital. A three-bedroom, 166-square-metre apartment in Sofia's Lozenetz district (roughly equivalent to London's Kensington) runs to around £150,000. A similar property in Kensington would cost around £600,000 and in Prague £200,000–300,000.

And that's in Bulgaria's largest city. Most smaller cities and remote areas are even less expensive.

Savvy shoppers have the potential of getting a greater return on their investment in Bulgaria than in other countries. Take the preceding Sofia apartment example. That apartment can command a rental of £1,300 per month, or £15,600 per year. Given the purchase price of £100,000, that's an annual yield of almost 16 per cent. By comparison, a £200,000–300,000 Prague apartment probably yields around 10 per cent, while a £600,000 Kensington apartment yields about 3 per cent.

Real estate indices in Bulgaria are still in their infancy, but recent indications are promising:

- The Bulgarian Real Estate Market Index, or REMI, was established in September 2002 by the National Real Property Association of Bulgaria (+359-2988-6890; e-mail: nrpa@mb.bia-bg.com). In November 2004, the index stood at 162, up considerably from its base of 100 two years earlier.
- *The Economist* Intelligence Unit, in a 2004 review of world property markets, said of Bulgaria that the prospects were good and that prices should continue to rise, albeit at a slower rate that in the previous two years.

Weighing pros and cons

Bulgaria does have some challenges that you may not know about. Products that depend on imported raw materials or technology are not such a bargain. And the country has, not surprisingly, some infrastructure challenges. For example, the only heating that is cheap is the town heating system, provided from a super-heating station supplying whole neighbourhoods and available in larger cities. Several large stations pump hot water right to your door for washing and heating. The only snag is that the city council decides when conditions are cold enough to turn on the heat – and occasionally the hot water dries up.

Value near Veliko

Mary, 27, a former council worker from Harrogate, and Tony, 29, a civil servant originally from Scotland, went to Bulgaria on a touring holiday in 2003. The beauty and remoteness of the country captivated them. They stayed in Veliko Târnovo, Bulgaria's capital in mediaeval times before the Turks overran the country.

When Mary was made redundant, her payout and Tony's savings were sufficient to buy a two-bedroom house in a village 20 kilometres from Veliko. They paid £5,000 for the house and a small amount of land and spent a further £1,500 plus a lot of hard work to make the house habitable.

Bulgaria has a predominantly cash economy. Payment by cheque or credit card is not common, even in restaurants, hotels, and shopping. For day-to-day needs have some cash, but don't carry around too much. Shops are accustomed to buyers putting down a small deposit and returning later to conclude the purchase.

Choosing Where to Buy

Bulgaria has four key property categories – the major cities, the Black Sea area, the ski resort area, and everywhere else. Each offers different opportunities and different risks. The following sections examine each area in detail.

The major cities

Sofia, Plovdiv, Varna, and Bourgas all have droves of new apartments being built to accommodate incoming business executives and diplomats, as well as to replace the poorly built blocks thrown up during the Soviet era.

For more information on major towns and places of historical interest in Bulgaria, visit `http://get.info.bg` and click the Visit link.

Sofia

In addition to being the capital, Sofia is the country's financial centre, is home to 16 universities, and has dozens of excellent restaurants and a vibrant night life.

Sofia was a settlement for Thracians, Romans, Bulgarians, Byzantines, and Ottomans. Historic treasures include the Church of St Nedelya, the 13th-century Chapel of St Petka Paraskeva, the Banya Bashi Mosque near Sofia's mineral baths, the 14th-century sunken Church of St Petka Samardzhiiska, and the 4th-century Rotonda of St George (Sofia's oldest church).

While the capital has the most expensive property in the country, it is still a relative bargain compared with other large cities in Europe. For example, a new apartment in Lozenets, one of the smartest areas in Sofia, costs a third of what a similar property in Prague or Budapest goes for – and less than a tenth the price of one in London or Paris.

Sofia's appeal to property buyers is the large number of business people, diplomats, and, more recently, American service families who have been relocated from Germany, who are looking for new apartments and houses, a commodity still in scarce supply. Also, the capital draws in a substantial influx of tourists throughout the year and is the gateway into the country for many tourists heading to other parts of the country.

Plovdiv

Plovdiv is the second-largest city in Bulgaria, enjoying a prime location in the centre of the country and in the midst of a large agricultural region. The city hosted three different specialised exhibitions of the World's Fair from 1981 to 1991 and is the home today of many international exibitions and fairs, including Vinaria, the wine fair for central and southeastern European producers and traders. These fairs pull in business people throughout the year and have stimulated the local property market by creating increased employment and wealth.

Plovdiv is steeped in history with the ruins of a Roman stadium and forum, Turkish Baths, and the Dzhumaya dzhamiya (Friday mosque), with its impressive diamond-patterned minaret and lead-sheathed domes. Old Plovdiv, most of which is designated as an architectural-historical reserve, is a cobbled hilly village within the city boundary. Most of the new development building is away from the old area, but it is possible to find small houses and apartments there. Property prices in the old part of town are about a fifth higher than elsewhere in the city.

Varna, Bourgas, and other cities

Bulgaria features several other cities worth considering:

- **Bourgas** (also spelled Burgas) is a port city on the Black Sea coast (technically the largest port in the country). It boasts two universities.
- **Rousse** on the bank of the Danube is joined by the Bridge of Friendship with the Romanian town of Gyurgevo.
- **Sexaginta Prista** ('Port of the 60 Ships') was originally a Roman town and an important Ottoman harbour and fortress.
- **Smolian**, bordering Greece, has some of the best traditional-style houses in Bulgaria, but many of the newer houses being built mirror those found in the new town centre, completed in 1983. The area is famous for its seven lakes, the 'emerald eyes of the Rhodopes'.
- **Stara Zagora,** situated in southern Bulgaria, was founded on the former Roman settlement of Beroe. At the foot of Sredna Gora mountain, the city has leafy boulevards, lively open-air cafés, opera, theatre, and natural thermal hot springs.
- **Varna** is a port city on the Black Sea coast with coastal resorts nearby. In 2004 *FDI Magazine* proclaimed Varna 'South-eastern Europe City of the Future', citing its strategic location, fast-growing economy, rich cultural heritage, and high-quality education.

- **Veliko Turnovo,** the former mediaeval capital of Bulgaria, is famous for its archaeological and architectural heritage.
- **Vidin,** the oldest city on the Bulgarian side of the Danube, is linked with Kalafat Romania by a ferry. Formerly the Roman fortress of Bononia, the town was the capital of the Vidin Kingdom in 1371 under Tsar Ivan Sratsimir before being occupied by the Turks.

You can see many of these historic Bulgarian cities and towns by taking a cruise down the River Danube. The Danube connects nine countries from the Black Forest to the Black Sea; it is Europe's second-longest and perhaps most historic river. The Bulgarian Tourist Board Web site (`www.bulgariatravel.org`) provides all the information on the cities from Vidin in the west to Veche on the Black Sea coast, but it has no information on the Danube itself. For that, you have to rely on the Romanian Tourist Board (`www.romaniatourism.com/danube.html`), where you also find links to the major companies that run boat tours down the river.

The Black Sea coast

Once the playground for the entire Eastern bloc, this coastline has 380 kilometres of marvellous sandy beaches stretching the whole length of the country's eastern border, with Romania to the north and Turkey to the south.

This region is the most developed area for holiday property, with more than 30 resorts. Some of those resorts, such as Sunny Beach, Albena, and Golden Sands, are new and match the giant Spanish resorts of a decade or so ago in terms of quality, though that position is changing fast as high-quality apartment blocks mushroom. The area is approaching overdevelopment, so consider looking at some of the older fishing villages south of Varna and towards Turkey. In particular, Nessebar, situated on a rocky peninsula on the Black Sea, has notable charms. The 3,000-year-old town was originally a Thracian settlement (Mesembria) and became a Greek colony at the beginning of the 6th century BC. The town's fortress dates from the Middle Ages, when Nessebar was one of the region's most important Byzantine towns.

Sozopol, originally called Apolonia, was founded by the Greeks in 610 BC. Sozopol, 31 kilometres south of Bourgas, has a population of about 7,000, a little smaller than St Ives in Cornwall and of a similar tourist appeal. A 100-metre-long strip of land connects the cobbled old town to the mainland, which has expanded to create a much larger new town. Sozopol fills up with international tourists in the summer and with Bulgarians, Turks, and other Eastern Europeans out of season. The town is rarely empty. Apartment developments are springing up fast. A new two-bedroom flat with sea views, air-conditioning, and parking costs about €100,000.

The ski resort area

Bulgaria's ski resort area is in the southwestern part of the country, with Greece just to the south and Macedonia to the west. Aside from a four-month skiing season, these resorts are slowly building up an all-season appeal. Walking, hiking, fishing, and more extreme sports, such as rafting, mountain biking, and 4x4 off-road trail driving, are making an appearance. This in turn is extending the opportunities for holiday rental income.

Skiing is becoming a major tourism force in Bulgaria, with the annual number of Britons expected at Bulgarian ski resorts now estimated at 50,000 and rising. The Bulgarian government, seeking to build on the region's growing popularity, is investing more than £50 million in ski infrastructure, particularly at Bansko, which was a major contender for the 2012 Winter Olympics.

Property prices in the ski resort areas (other than Vitosha, which is more expensive due to its proximity to Sofia) range from £40,000 to £120,000 for new apartments near the gondola stations. Many of the new apartment complexes have private swimming pools, gyms, saunas, and restaurants. Properties in neighbouring villages can be had for as little as £10,000.

Bansko

Bansko is Bulgaria's newest ski resort, with a new gondola chair lift and 14 kilometres of ski runs, including slalom and giant slalom runs, a 5-kilometre cross-country track, and a Rollbahn track. This year-round resort also offers excellent walking, hiking, mountain biking, and other tourist attractions, such as the renowned Rila monastery and a narrow-gauge railway running through the spa resort of Velingrad to Septemvri.

The city, once an important way-station on trade routes linking the Aegean port of Kavalla with the Balkan hinterland, is now connected to Sofia via a new fast highway. Travel time from Sofia's airport is now only 90 minutes. With an additional hour of travel, you can reach the Greek border, and in one more you can be swimming in the Aegean Sea – and still easily be back in Bansko for supper.

Borovets

Borovets is the oldest and largest mountain resort in Bulgaria, situated 1,350 metres above sea level on the northern slopes of the Rila mountains. Located only 70 kilometres from Sofia and 126 kilometres from Plovdiv, the resort has twice hosted World Cup competitions in Alpine skiing; its biathlon track is one of the best in Europe. The resort features 18 ski runs, covering 40 kilometres on three separate but close areas.

Major developments appear to be under way in and around Borovets with huge investments flowing into neighbouring villages. The plan is to create a larger, interlinked skiing area, a sort of a mini-version of France's Trois Vallées. The best way to find out about these developments is to hire a car and stay in the region for three or four days driving around the villages.

Pamporovo

Pamporovo, the most southerly skiing resort in Europe, is situated in the heart of the Rhodope mountains, some 250 kilometres from Sofia and about 85 kilometres from Plovdiv airport. At an altitude of 1,650 metres, the resort's seven ski runs cover 25 kilometres of hills at varying levels of difficulty. Three nearby cross-country runs total more than 40 kilometres of trails. Plans exist for new ski runs to tie in local villages to the larger resort.

High-ups in the old Soviet regime greatly favoured Pamporovo, as some of the architecture suggests. Foreign investment is coming in fast, and French ski operators have been sniffing around looking for pastures new, so this is very much a resort on the up.

Vitosha

Vitosha, at 1,800 metres above sea level, is only 10 kilometres from Sofia and is the highest ski resort in Bulgaria. Unfortunately, the weather is variable and though the ski area is reasonably large and receives plenty of snow, the facilities lag behind the other areas and you have to trek back to Sofia for any après-ski life.

The resort does enjoy good transport links with Sofia, and a taxi ride out costs not much more than a couple of pints of beer in a London pub. Of course, this proximity to Sofia means that the slopes are very crowded during weekends and holidays.

Other Bulgarian opportunities

You can find the highest-risk and lowest-cost properties in Bulgaria away from the cities, the Black Sea area, and the ski resorts. The good news: Any property off the beaten track is extremely cheap. In fact, you can still find bargain prices of £1,000 or less. Be forewarned, though, that in many places the access roads are poor, provision of utilities limited or non-existent, and the chances of resale remote. Some vilages such as Granitovo (see the sidebar 'Granitovo on the go') are charming, but the towns are often dreary with overtones of post-Soviet architecture.

Granitovo on the go

Granitovo, a small town (population 2,000) in beautiful countryside between two small mountains and several lakes, lies just 120 kilometres from the Black Sea and Bourgas International Airport. According to an article in the *Trud Daily* (`www.trud.bg`), 53 British families have moved into houses in the area. The attraction is the low prices – properties can be had for £4,000 – as well as the town.

But the good news about Granitovo doesn't end there. Located just 25 kilometres from the border with Turkey, the town is set to receive major government investments in infrastructure and modernisation, including a first-class road to Istanbul and the Turkish sea coast. The neighbouring villages of Melnitsa, Maluk Manastir, and Lesovo, as well as the town of Elhovo, have also sold houses to British buyers.

There are a number of property developments, such as Vitosha Park, 6 kilometres from Sofia International Airport. Vitosha Park is a luxurious, modern gated residential complex of 330 apartments situated in Sofia's Simeonovo district at the foot of the Vitosha Mountain. Developments here are clustered around the cable car lift, with panoramic views of the city of Sofia and the mountain. Prices start at €75,000 for a one-bedroom apartment and go up to around €125,000 for a two-bedroom, two-bathroom property. This area is of great appeal only to the leisure and holiday market. For a wider all-year rental appeal, it is probably best to stick to central Sofia, where property prices are similar.

Chepelare

Chepelare, 10 kilometres south of Pamporova, is the smallest of the ski resorts and is 1,100 metres above sea level. It boasts the longest ski run in Bulgaria, at 30 kilometres. The skiing infrastructure is fairly basic, with only two runs: Chala (3,150 metres) and Turisticheska (5,250 metres).

Chepelare has the cheapest skiing in Bulgaria. A six-day adult lift pass is 45 levs (£22), with children going at half price.

Buying into Bulgaria

At the time of writing, foreigners cannot directly acquire ownership rights on land in Bulgaria, but don't think that your Bulgarian dream ends there. This rule is set to change in 2006 in preparation for EU membership, and even the existing restriction on foreign ownership of land is largely illusory.

One way to skate around the foreign ownership restriction is fairly inexpensive and takes only about four weeks. Bulgarian companies with foreign participation, irrespective of the percentage of foreign participation in the company, can acquire full land ownership rights, including ownership rights on agricultural land. In other words, all you have to do is have your legal team set up a company in Bulgaria that you own, much like a limited company in the UK, and you can buy land in Bulgaria through the company.

Fortunately, the process of buying property in Bulgaria is becoming more efficient. In October 2003, for example, a central national property register was established to replace localised registries. This central register is expected to speed up the buying and selling process and make transactions more transparent.

The basic procedures for purchasing property in Bulgaria are as follows:

1. **Research the market.**

   Chapter 3 explains how to find properties, but a number of English estate agents specialise in Bulgarian property and operate offices in Bulgaria, including the following:

   - **Balkan Ski Chalets** (+359-889-633-086; www.balkanskichalet.com)
   - **Stara Planina Properties** (+359-88-720-3364; www.stara-planina.com)

   The British Bulgarian Chamber of Commerce (www.bbcc.bg) lists a dozen or so estate agencies and property developers among its members, while the Bulgarian Embassy Web site (www.bulgarianembassy.org.uk) has links to more than 80 estate agents, half of whom are based in the UK.

2. **Find a property and check to see whether it is being sold with land.**

   If a property is being sold with land, you may need to set up a company in Bulgaria, as I describe at the beginning of this section. If not, as is usually the case with apartments, then setting up a company may not be necessary.

   Check that the space you are paying for is what you expect. You may think that buying property by the square metre is straightforward enough, but pay attention to the vanishing space. A 100-square-metre apartment in a new block might include 15 square metres of common parts (stairs, corridor, and so on), 8 square metres of space occupied by walls, and 10 square metres of balconies. If so, you have only 67 square metres of real living space – in which case, a quoted price of €1,000 per square metres for a nominally 100-square-metre property translates into a true cost of €1,492 per square metre for usable space.

Generally in Bulgaria, building surveys are not carried out on new developments as these come with guarantees as to quality. Old buildings, buildings that you want a mortgage on, and buildings that you have any concerns regarding should be surveyed. Your estate agent, lawyer or mortgage provider will be able to put you in touch with a local surveyor. If you require a structural survey, this will cost between €100 and €300.

Alternatively, you can search the Royal Institute of Chartered Surveyors (RICS) online database (`www.ricsfirms.com/vw/search/location.aspx`), call their contact centre (0870-333-1600 between 8.30 am and 5.30 pm, Monday to Friday), or email contactrics@rics.org.

Try to find a professional through personal recommendation of someone whose judgement you respect and who is impartial. I cover this subject in Chapter 4.

3. **Negotiate and agree on the final price with the broker or current owners.**

Most agents have a minimum charge of around £2,000, and some impose a reservation charge of £500–1,000 on hotter, newer properties, which is refundable when you complete the sale.

Keep in mind that the total price to you also includes the following:

- **Estate agent costs:** Both buyers and sellers pay commission to estate agents in Bulgaria, with charges ranging from 3 to 10 per cent.
- **Local taxes:** 0.15 per cent of the purchase price (which is unbelievably low in comparison with the UK). You must pay these taxes annually as soon as you own a property. So for a property costing £40,000, local taxes are £60 per annum.
- **Management charges and maintenance fees:** £8–15 per square metre due on new properties in developments and in some of the newer apartment blocks in the cities.
- **Miscellaneous costs:** For example, survey charges.
- **Municipal tax:** Known locally as 'country tax', this is about 2 per cent of the price (equivalent to UK stamp duty).
- **Refuse tax:** varies in the region of £15–30, depending on the location and size of the house.

Total charges, including agency fees, legal and translation costs, stamp duty, and survey costs, should be around 12 per cent of the purchase price for properties without land and 14 per cent for properties with land.

4. **After the verbal agreement, draw up the initial contract and get the property removed from the market (similar to 'sold subject to contract' in the UK).**

   At this stage, 10 per cent of the purchase price is due. If you don't complete the sale, you lose your deposit. If the vendors withdraw, they pay you double that sum. You should get a lawyer involved from the outset, and certainly before you make an offer to buy any property or put down a retaining deposit.

   Since 2004, you can raise mortgage finance through banks in Bulgaria. The interest rates are high (10 per cent) and the maximum loan is 70 per cent of the purchase price. You must set up a company locally to handle the process.

   Find a lawyer who has a good command of English and who is independent of the estate agent or developer that you are dealing with. Ideally, the lawyer should have offices near to where you are buying the property, as then he or she will have a good insight into local issues, such as new developments, road works, and any other factors that might detract from the value of your property. You can find lists of English-speaking lawyers on the Web sites of the Bulgarian Embassy in London (`www.bulgarianembassy.org.uk`), the British Embassy in Bulgaria (`www.british-embassy.bg`), the Martindale-Hubbell Lawyer Locator (`http://lawyers.martindale.com/marhub`), the International Law Office (`www.internationallawoffice.com/Directory`), and Legal500.com (`www.icclaw.com`).

5. **Using a lawyer, do the standard checks on legal documents pertaining to the property.**

   Items to check include:

   - Title documents.
   - Licences and permissions.
   - Debts on title.
   - Terms of contract.

6. **Sign the notary act (contract to purchase) in front of a Bulgarian notary public, along with the final legal contract, and pay for the property.**

   Your lawyer should insist that you have a copy of the contract translated into English and read out to you in their presence.

   At this point, the remaining 90 per cent of the purchase price is due. Transfer the sum in euros via your solicitor. (I cover transferring funds in Chapter 18.)

Although illegal, you are likely to be asked to declare a lower price than the one declared in the deed, so the vendor can reduce the tax on their gain. (I cover this common practice in these regions in Chapter 4.)

You are now the owner of a Bulgarian property. The title deeds for your property and the extract from the Land Registry arrive two or three weeks after the final completion date. These documents are in Bulgarian, so you need to have them translated. (I cover translations and using translators in Chapter 4.)

7. **Transfer the utilities.**

   Registering for electricity, gas, water, telephone, and refuse collection is a time-consuming process involving lots of paperwork. Sorting out the issues can last several days or in some cases weeks. It is advisable to deal with everything well in advance, or you have to take into account that for some days you will be in the property without electricity and gas. This is definitely not something to tackle on your own without being fluent in the language. Your broker will, if asked, arrange for all utility meters to be read and recorded and transferred to your name as part of their general service.

After you sign the notary act, you are responsible for insuring the property. Property insurance is relatively expensive and can include coverage for earthquakes, which are a risk in parts of Bulgaria. Expect to pay £200 a year for a property costing £30,000. The Bulgarian Internet Business Catalogue (`www.need.bg/en`) lists local insurance companies and brokers.

Getting Settled in Bulgaria

Buying a property is in many respects the easy part of getting into life in Bulgaria. After you purchase your property, you are to some extent on your own. This section covers things you need to address after your purchase is complete.

Taxing matters

Bulgarian taxes to consider include the following:

- If you rent out your Bulgarian property, you are liable for income tax. The issue as to exactly where the income has been earned is complex. If you employ a British sales agent who sells to British clients who pay in the UK, you may be able to argue that this is a taxable event in the UK. I cover tax matters in Chapter 17 and renting out your property in Chapter 19.

- **Business tax:** Under the Corporate Income Tax Act (CITA), all businesses are liable to corporate income tax. The corporate income tax rate is 15 per cent. Annual profits must be declared no later than 31 March of the year following the taxable year. If you use a company to buy your property, then any profit from rent will be liable to this tax.
- **Capital gains tax:** Bulgarian capital gains tax is currently 19.5 per cent of the profit on a sale, after deducting costs for renovation and the like. Your principal property is exempt from this tax after you own it for five years.
- **Double taxation treaties:** Bulgaria has a double taxation treaty with the UK and many other countries, which should ensure that you don't end up paying tax twice on the same income – or paying more tax than you should. (I cover double taxation treaties in Chapter 17.)
- **Individual tax:** Under the Personal Income Tax Act (PITA), tax-liable people are *individuals* – residents, non-residents, and sole-trader businesses. Residents are liable for their worldwide income. Non-residents (in Chapter 17, I explain the rules of residency) are liable only for their income derived from Bulgarian sources. Tax scales run from 18 to 29 per cent, depending on the level of income.
- **Value-added tax:** Any person or business, resident or non-resident, who has a sales turnover of more than BGN 50,000 (£17,500) during the preceding 12 months is obliged to register for VAT purposes by filing a standard registration form within 14 days after the end of the calendar month in which the threshold is reached. VAT is charged at 20 per cent, with a zero rate for exports and special preferential rates for some imports.

To find out more about the tax regime in Bulgaria, visit the Invest In Bulgaria Web site (`www.investbg.government.bg`), which provides a comprehensive and up-to-date guide to tax and much else besides.

Opening bank accounts

Opening bank accounts in Bulgaria is refreshingly simple. Take along your passport and you can be up and running in a day or two.

You need two or perhaps three accounts. Open separate accounts for euros and sterling, as well as levs, which you need to pay utility bills and other local expenses. The sterling and euro accounts are for transferring funds from and to the UK and elsewhere in Europe. Bank charges are around £1 a month.

The following Web sites have downloadable application forms for opening bank accounts:

- **ING** (www.ing.bg) is a Dutch global financial institution with significant presence in Bulgaria.
- **Bullbank** (www.bulbank.bg), originally state-owned, is now a private Bulgarian bank.

See also Chapter 19, where I cover international banking, mortgages, and other money matters.

Staying healthy

EU nationals resident in Bulgaria are eligible to receive free medical treatment from government-funded hospitals and clinics, but you need a European Health Insurance Card (EHIC). You may find that doctors, dentists, hospitals, and even ambulances often expect cash payment for their services, so you will need to get receipts.

The Web site of the US Embassy in Sofia (http://sofia.usembassy.gov/hospitals4.html) has a list of hospitals, doctors, and dentists throughout the country who speak English. If you have an urgent medical or dental problem, you can find a list of doctors, dentists, and clinics at www.need.bg/en or www.search.bg, which both have English sites.

The Bulgarian Ministry of Health (www.mh.government.bg) describes the services you can expect after you are resident if you decide to pay contributions to the local national health system.

Health care in Bulgaria falls well below the standards to which Westerners are accustomed, so either head for the airport and fly home if a serious illness strikes or call your health insurance company. (In Chapter 20, I cover health-care choices.)

On the whole, pharmacies and drugstores are well stocked with Bulgarian and imported medicines and health products. However, bring an adequate supply of any prescription drugs that you need.

In urban areas, keep out of the way of packs of stray dogs that roam the streets. A bite requires an unpleasant course of treatment against rabies.

Getting around the country

After you reach Bulgaria, you have a variety of transportation options to explore the region and to conduct daily business. This section covers your major transportation options.

You can find out more about travelling around Bulgaria on the official tourism Web site (www.bulgariatravel.org).

Plane

Bulgaria Air (+359-2-865-9517; www.air.bg) operates domestic services connecting Sofia with the coast and main cities. Trips from Sofia to Bourgas and Varna on the Black Sea take about an hour. Air travel is only slightly more expensive than rail travel.

River

Regular boat and hydrofoil services along the Bulgarian bank of the Danube link many centres, including Vidin, Lom, Kozloduj, Orjahovo, Nikopol, Svishtov, Tutrakan, and Silistra.

Train

Bulgarian State Railways connects Sofia with the country's main towns. A sleeper service runs from Sofia to the Black Sea coast and daily trains operate to Thessalonica, Istanbul, Kiev, Moscow, Bucharest, and nearly everywhere else in the old Soviet bloc. Travel across almost the entire country from Sofia to Varna costs between £12 and £30.

Reservations are essential, and first-class travel is advised. For details, contact the State Railway Office (www.bdz.bg). The Web site is in English but does not include booking services. To book, you either need to go in person to the central railway station or use one of the myriad local travel agents in Sofia.

Car

Bulgaria has more than 13,000 kilometres (8,000 miles) of roads linking its major centres. Road quality is variable, and some main roads have major potholes. Fuel costs around 70p a litre.

Your British driving licence is valid in Bulgaria. The minimum age for driving is 18. Speed limits are as follows: 60 kilometres (37 miles) per hour in built-up areas (50 kilometres per hour for motorcycles and for cars towing a trailer),

80 kilometres (50 miles) per hour outside built-up areas (70 kilometres per hour for motorcycles and for cars towing a trailer), and 120 kilometres (74 miles) per hour on motorways. Police are empowered to collect fines on the spot and should issue a receipt. Seat belts are compulsory for front-seat passengers. There is a zero blood alcohol limit. There is a priority-on-your-right rule, but trams always have priority. Pedestrians on marked cross-walks have priority when their pedestrian lights show green, but trams still have priority.

Rental cars are readily available in Bulgaria, but the international companies are relatively expensive. Expect to pay €60 a day for a small vehicle. A number of local car-rental companies offer two- or three-year-old vehicles at less than half that rate.

Car jacking is becoming more frequent in Bulgaria, usually occurring at night, and with some criminals even impersonating traffic police in the process. You're safest driving in daylight.

Bus

The country offers a good network of buses that are cheap and convenient – but with erratic timetables. Buses are often more comfortable and faster than the trains.

Buses also ply routes to Turkey, Greece, Romania, Macedonia, and Albania, but be prepared for long delays at border crossings, as officials examine visas and passports.

Buses are cheap (around £10 will get you from one end of the country to the other), plentiful, and run throughout the day and night. You can find the Web sites and phone numbers of all the major bus companies in Bulgaria on the Web site `http://get.info.bg/visit/Dir.asp?d=0-7-BusStations`.

Taxi

Taxis are available in all towns and also for intercity journeys, for which they are surprisingly cost-effective. Vehicles are metered but may not be in very good condition. Rates vary from 0.3 to 0.5 leva per kilometre (11–18p).

Urban

Bus, tramway, and trolleybus services operate in Sofia, where a single-line metro also runs. Flat fares are charged, and tickets must be pre-purchased. Plovdiv and Varna also offer trolleybuses. Usually a single ticket between any two stations on a network costs 0.5 leva (18p).

Chapter 13
Croatia

In This Chapter

- Understanding the potential in Croatia
- Discerning where you want to look
- Going through the purchase process
- Making your purchase work for you

At first glance, Croatia may not seem like a good place for purchasing property. Indeed, the nation has experienced much tumult – including over four decades of Communist rule, a bloody civil war, and ethnic cleansing.

The old order is now being quickly swept away, and foreigners are rushing to Croatia both for holidays and increasingly to snap up bargain properties. (Of course, Croatia's Dalmatian coast was a major tourist draw until a little more than a decade ago, pulling in more than 10 million visitors a year.) Travel to, from, and around the country is getting easier and is very affordable. Coastal towns from Pula in the north down to Split and to Dubrovnik on the Serbia–Montenegro border now play host to a fast-growing band of foreign property owners who have found the buying procedures user-friendly and the locals welcoming.

Property prices have been rising at more than 30 per cent a year, so bargains – though still around – are a little harder to find. Also, a combination of some dodgy ownership titles (though nothing like the situation in, say, Cyprus) and the possibility of Serbian landmines mean that buying property in Croatia is not without risk.

By taking the basic precautions I outline in this chapter, you can find and purchase Croatian property to provide you with both pleasure and profit for years to come.

Fast facts about Croatia

Area: 56,542 square kilometres, slightly larger than Belgium and Switzerland, and smaller than Ireland and Austria.

Population: 4.5 million.

Location: Southeastern Europe, sandwiched between the Adriatic Sea, Slovenia, Hungary, and Bosnia and Herzegovina. The whole coastline is 5,835 kilometres long but is largely made up of 1,185 islands, only 50 of which are inhabited. (You can investigate the inhabited islands by visiting `www.kroatien-online.com/en/tourism/islands`.) The River Danube, which runs through many other countries in the region, forms 100 kilometres of the border with Hungary.

Language: The official language is Croatian and 96 per cent of the population speak it. Before the break-up of Yugoslavia, this language was known as Serbo-Croatian (*Srpskohrvatski*) and was widely spoken throughout the region. Today few people call the language *Serbo-Croatian.* The Croatians call it Croatian, Bosnians call it Bosnian, the Serbs call it Serbian, and in Montenegro it is still called Serbian – though moves are afoot to change it to Montenegrin. While the standard language does differ in some ways, the differences are more symbolic than linguistic, and everyone can understand the others' 'languages' with little difficulty. The rest of the population speaks various languages, including Italian, Hungarian, Czech, Slovak, German, and increasingly English. You can find an online dictionary with all the words you are likely to need in Croatian at the Visit Croatia Web site (`www.visit-croatia.co.uk/croatianfortravellers`). The site includes online audio to aid in pronunciation.

Currency: The Croatian currency is the kuna (Kn), which is divided into 100 lipa (lp). The exchange rate is 7.3 Kn to €1 and 10.8 Kn to £1. The kuna is considered a reasonably stable currency.

Time zone: GMT +1.

European Union standing: Croatia started its European Union (EU) membership talks in October 2005. On 9 December 2005, the country received a boost in gaining membership when Ante Gotovina, Croatia's most wanted war-crimes suspect, was arrested in Spain and sent for trial to the war crimes tribunal in The Hague. Croatia hopes to conclude negotiations on EU membership in 2008 and enter the EU in 2009, aims which are widely considered ambitious.

Emergency services: Emergency switchboard staff rarely speak good English. If you need to call for assistance, do so through your local contacts or hotel receptionist. Emergency phone numbers:

Ambulance: 94

Fire service: 93

General information: 981

Police: 92

Road assistance: 987

Sea rescue: 9155

Visas: Citizens of EU countries, Switzerland, the USA, Australia, New Zealand, and Japan do not need a visa to visit Croatia for up to 90 days in any six-month period. Longer visits require a visa. You can find information about applying for a visa on the Croatian Embassy Web site (`http://croatia.embassyhomepage.com`). You can also get an application form by calling the Visa Form Request Line (0906-782-7674). British citizens can obtain temporary residence through the Croatian embassy in the UK or can apply locally at a police station in Croatia. Residence permits are valid for a maximum of one year and are renewable.

By air from the UK: Croatia has eight airports at Brac, Dubrovnik, Osijek, Pula, Rijeka, Split, Zadar, and Zagreb, which accept some international and national flights. For regular services, you are currently restricted to British Airways and Croatian Airlines (020-8563-0022; www.croatiaairlines.hr). Ryanair has regular flights to Trieste, an hour or so drive from Croatia's north Adriatic coast. The Visit Croatia Web site (www.visit-croatia.co.uk/gettingthere) has a useful guide to indirect routes to Croatia. Alitalia (0870-608-6003; www.alitalia.com) has flights from Heathrow to Zagreb and Split, with a change in Milan or Rome.

By train from the UK: You can travel by train to Zagreb, and then on to Pula, Rijeka, and Split. The route is fairly torturous, involving changes in Paris and either Munich or Venice. The trip takes the best part of two days to accomplish. You can book tickets in the UK through European Rail.

Other routes from the UK: The pan-European Eurolines bus network offers a no-frills option with its *ultra low-cost* European travel. The route from London to Rijeka, Split, Zadar, Zagreb, and a dozen other towns takes between 33 and 50 hours.

No direct sea route exists from the UK to Croatia, but ferries run from the Italian ports of Trieste, Venice, Chuggia, Ancona, and Pescara to a dozen ports along Croatia's coastline, with journey times of between 3 and 5 hours. Contact Cemar Ferries for fares and routes. (+39-010573-1800; www.cemar.it/dest/ferries_croatia.htm).

Accommodation: Most hotels in Croatia are slab block style, several storeys high, and functional rather than atmospheric. A handful of luxurious hotel buildings are left over from the days of the Habsburgs. A wholesale renovation process is going on, so if you want comfort and are willing to pay British-style prices, you can find a variety of lodging options. The Web sites Adriatica (+385-1241-5611; www.adriatica.net) and Find Croatia (www.findcroatia.com) have online booking to hundreds of hotels, apartments, villas, and rooms around the country, starting at £17 per day.

Private rooms (*privatne sobe*) come in three categories, ranging from basic at about 130 Kn (£12.28) per night to around 260 Kn (£24.46) for ensuite, which includes TV and smarter surroundings. Expect to pay a surcharge of around 50 per cent if you stay fewer than three nights, but you can usually negotiate a decent discount. You can find rooms by asking around, looking for signs that say *sobe* or the German phrase *Zimmer frei*, or talking with the landladies who frequently hang around bus and train stations.

Apartments *(apartmani)* come in much the same shapes and sizes as rooms, with prices starting at 300 Kn (£28.23) per night. The Web sites Apartments Croatia (www.apartments-croatia.com) and Dalmatia Tours (http://dalmatiatours.com/eng) list more than 17,000 rooms and apartments all over the country.

Getting to Know Croatia

Croatia has a lot to offer tourists and residents alike. The climate is more or less Mediterranean along the Adriatic coast, with warm welcoming waters and long sandy beaches. Cold winters around the capital Zagreb mean that the country also offers skiing in the Medvednica mountains.

Communications are good and getting better. Low-cost airlines are not around yet, but they are getting closer. Most major European airlines fly to Zagreb, Dubrovnik, Split, and Pula on a daily basis for less than £140, if you are prepared to change planes en route. Once in Croatia, internal travel options by plane, train, coastal ferry, or air-conditioned coach are plentiful and cheap.

Croatian culture

Located at what may well prove to be the centre of Europe after the Bulgarians, Romanians, and Turks join the EU, Croatia has much going for it.

Croatia declared its independence from the Federal Republic of Yugoslavia in 1991 and was recognised as an independent state the following year. A long history of war, invasion, and general unrest – from Roman conquests to mediaeval fortifications to recent bitter fighting with occupying Serb armies – has resulted in a nation with a rich cultural and architectural heritage. The area's houses, villas, castles, and public spaces offer great pleasure to tourists and new foreign residents alike. Additionally, the Adriatic coastline houses a treasure trove of antique ships and their cargoes, making the region one the world's best sub-aqua areas.

Landmines in Croatia

Some remote areas of Croatia, though welcoming and apparently safe, remain uncleared of landmines from the region's 1991–95 conflict with Serbian forces. Fourteen of the country's 21 counties (an area of 1,700 square kilometres) are still suspected to be contaminated with mines and unexploded weaponry; 270 square kilometres, mainly along the lines of demarcation of the conflict, are known with a fair degree of certainty to contain mines.

Under Article 5 of the Mine Ban Treaty, Croatia has until 1 March 2009 to complete the destruction of all antipersonnel mines. Unfortunately, various Serb military and paramilitary forces that operated in Croatia were less than scrupulous in recording exactly where they mined.

Only a handful of mine-related incidents occur in Croatia each year, and fatalities are in single figures. But much work is yet to be done to rid the country of this hazard. Check out the International Campaign to Ban Landmines Web site (`www.icbl.org`) to find out more about the situation generally and the Croatian Mine Action Site (`www.hcr.hr/index.php?link=minska-situacija&lang=en`) for county-specific details within Croatia.

Climate and weather

Croatia is an even distance between the North Pole and the Equator, but its climate is anything but even, as Table 13-1 shows.

- Northern Croatia has a continental climate, with a mean temperature in July of 22°C. Winter temperatures range from –1 to 30°C.
- Central Croatia has a semi-highland and highland climate; the mean temperature in the mountains in July can range between 10 °C in the highest areas and 18°C elsewhere. Winter temperatures range from –5 to 0°C.
- Coastal areas and the islands have a Mediterranean climate, with temperatures in July between 22 and 26°C. Winter temperatures range from 5 to 10°C.

The Velebit mountains, as well as the surroundings of Dubrovnik, have the heaviest rainfall and heaviest snowfall, while the eastern portion of the country experiences the lowest rainfall. Tables 13-2 and 13-3 list average number of days with precipitation for locations throughout the region.

Table 13-1 Average Daily Temperatures in Croatia

Location	*Jan–Mar*	*Apr–June*	*July–Sep*	*Oct–Dec*
Pula	7°C	16°C	23°C	10°C
Rijeka	8°C	18°C	24°C	11°C
Split	8°C	17°C	24°C	12°C
Zadar Puntamik	8°C	18°C	23°C	12°C
Zagreb	2°C	15°C	19°C	5°C

Table 13-2 Average Number of Rainy Days per Month in Croatia

Location	*Jan–Mar*	*Apr–June*	*July–Sep*	*Oct–Dec*
Pula	8	9	7	9
Rijeka	3	3	2	3
Split	10	8	6	9
Zadar Puntamik	3	2	1	3
Zagreb	8	13	11	10

Table 13-3 Average Number of Snowy Days per Month in Croatia

Location	*Jan–Mar*	*Apr–June*	*July–Sep*	*Oct–Dec*
Pula	0.5	0	0	0
Rijeka	0	0	0	0
Split	1	0	0	0
Zadar Puntamik	0	0	0	0
Zagreb	5	0	0	4

English-language media

Little English language media exists in Croatia yet. You will have trouble finding an English newspaper outside the major cities, and even then English papers arrive a day or two late and cost around 20 Kn (£2).

Two general online newspapers covering local and national news with a Croatian slant are Zagreb.com (`www.zagreb.com`) and Croatian News Online (`www.croatianewsonline.com`). Nacional (`www.nacional.hr/en`), another general online newspaper, has an extensive news archive database.

Started in 2005, Croatia Exclusive (0870-027-1902; `www.croatiaexclusive.com`) is a quarterly online magazine costing £12. It features articles on travel, property, events, festivals, and food and wine, with a regular property guide and advice on buying, owning, and maintaining a Croatian property.

You can receive the BBC World Service locally on FM and short wave at various times of the day. You can find details on frequencies on the BBC World Service Web site (`www.bbc.co.uk/worldservice`).

Tourism

Croatia, or at least the part of former Yugoslavia that is now Croatia, has a long history as a holiday destination. Seen as more exotic, private, and cheaper than the French Riviera, the region had great appeal to the Brits.

Before the Yugoslav wars broke out, more than 10 million overseas visitors arrived each year. By 1992, arrival numbers were in freefall as the world watched warships shelling once-bustling coastal towns, in places causing some significant damage (although Dubrovnik's old-town walls were so thick they survived the attacks.

Happily, tourism is growing fast again, with 8 million visitors arrive each year. Hundreds of cities, towns, and villages along the Adriatic coast, such as Porec, Rovinj, Korcula, Trogir, Hvar, and Dubrovnik, provide tourists with accommodation – fairly basic at present but improving fast – as well as basic sporting activities, entertainment, sightseeing, and shopping. Away from the coast Croatia has hundreds of villages, many largely untouched by recent conflicts, with their historical character and traditions preserved. Around the capital city of Zagreb, dozens of mediaeval fortresses, castles, and mansions appeal to visitors as well.

Croatia is almost totally dependent on getting its tourist industry back on track. Some 25 per cent of the country's wealth, 33 per cent of all employment, and 40 per cent of all foreign exchange is created by tourism. The country's government is working hard to create a tourist-friendly environment with world-class facilities.

Sports and leisure

Croatia is rich in water-centred activities:

- **Yachting and sailing:** The country has some great boating waters, easily comparable with the Greek islands. Croatia's 50 marinas with 18,000 berths are home to 140 charter companies with a combined fleet of 2,700 modern yachts.
- **Diving:** The Adriatic Sea is reasonably calm, with no high waves, few strong currents, and virtually no tide. Sea temperatures at average diving depth (20–30 metres) stay constant throughout the year, close to 17°C.
- **Canoeing and rafting:** You can paddle many inland rivers, including the Cetina Kupa, Gacka, Zrmanja, Mrežnica, and Trebižat. Most are exhilarating rather than challenging, with much of the real action on the river bank in the form of old castles such as that at Trakošćan, the massive fortress of Knin, and the remains of Roman Burnum. (But shooting down the 20-metre-high Štrbački buk waterfall on the River Una, the border between Croatia and Bosnia, should get most people's adrenalin flowing.)

Other popular activities include mountain biking, horse riding, ballooning, hunting, and fishing. The Medvednica mountains rising above Zagreb are accessible to even the most inexperienced hiker and climber, with no peaks higher than 2,000 metres. Caving is also popular in Istria, Papuk, and in the regions of Kordun, Lika, Dalmatia, and Zagora Gorski kotar.

Twenty minutes from Zagreb, Croatia offers a small ski resort on the slopes of the Medvednica mountains. With six runs and a single cross-country route amounting to less than 10 kilometres in all, the area warrants only a day or two of attention – though the £7 daily lift pass comes as a welcome surprise if you're accustomed to more typical £20 fees elsewhere.

Sailing away from VAT

EU residents who use or own yachts must have their value-added tax (VAT), which can run to £5,000–10,000, paid up before entering EU waters. Croatia is the most convenient place for EU owners to moor up, as you can stay indefinitely without paying Croatian import duties or VAT on the vessel, spare parts, or additional equipment.

To obtain a residence permit, you need only moor a yacht in a Croatian marina, where charges are lower than in the UK. With a Croatian residence permit (see the earlier sidebar 'Fast facts about Croatia'), you can venture into EU waters for up to 18 months during any two-year period before being liable to pay VAT on your yacht.

Croatia is not a country to head for if you're a golfing fanatic. The nation has only two golf courses, one in Pula and the other in Krasic. Visit `www.croatia-golf.hr` for more information.

The Croatian National Tourist Board has comprehensive information on all these activities discussed here and more. Visit its Web site at `www.croatia.hr`.

Talking Business

While the Communist era came to an end in 1990 when the Croats elected their first non-Communist government, it was not until 1995 when the war with the Serbs was concluded that normality returned to the country.

In February 2005, Croatia implemented the Stabilization and Association Agreement with the EU, giving the country tariff-free access to many EU markets and financial and technical assistance. While this move undoubtedly spurs the economy on, many problems still lie ahead. Croatia does not have major export industries and has considerable borrowings. But already some major trading companies have arrived to take advantage of the liberated market.

This section covers the most important business factors to bear in mind from a property-owning perspective.

Examining the cost of living

The cost of living in parts of Croatia is not particularly cheap compared with other *transitional countries*, nations that are changing from Communist to market economies. Mercers Cost of Living Survey (`www.mercerhr.com`)

ranks Zagreb at 85, with more expensive New York City being the anchor rating of 100. The survey puts Croatia's theoretical cost of living higher than that of Bulgaria, Turkey, Romania, Slovenia, Lithuanian, Estonia, Poland, and Cyprus.

Life outside Zagreb is still very inexpensive: £10 a day can cover food expenses when eating at home. Short journeys by ferry to neighbouring islands or by bus to nearby towns are less than a couple of pounds. Even longish journeys around the country are unlikely to cost more than £15 or so – all a far cry from costs in the UK.

Identifying areas of value

Croatia is still very much a niche market for foreign investors, with at most a few hundred Brits owning properties in the country. But this is changing fast.

The country is continuing its remarkable success by becoming more stable politically and economically. It has recovered quickly from the damage inflicted since the war with Serbia and looks set to turn into a good investment opportunity as the tourist industry revives.

The Croatian government has granted a number of new development licences on land that is free from contentious property ownership disputes. Several developers have plans in place, mostly for coastal resort properties on the Dalmatian coast.

Croatia is not a bargain-basement market. A refurbished two-bedroom apartment on the waterfront at Korcula, a popular island resort north of Dubrovnik, sells for around £75,000. On Bulgaria's Black Sea coast, similar property sells for around £55,000. However, the summer season in Croatia is longer than in Bulgaria, and travel time to from the UK to Croatia is an hour less than that to Cyprus, Greece, or Turkey. Also, Italy, a country with sophisticated health-care facilities and worldwide travel links, is very close to Croatia.

Assessing potential rental yields

Croatia currently has a serious shortage of good-quality hotels, apartments, and holiday villas, and pressure to find such accommodation is mounting as tourism picks up. You should have little difficulty finding renters during peak summer months.

Attracting renters in autumn and winter is far less certain. At present the country offers no obvious or compelling attractions, such as good skiing, great music festivals, fantastic museums, big business conference facilities, or amazing gastronomy. Several neighbouring countries enjoy all these competitive advantages.

Continuing questions about property appreciation rates

Although coastal studio apartments in need of substantial renovation can still be had for £35,000 and countryside houses in similar condition are available for less than £10,000, no one knows for sure what is happening to property prices in Croatia. The country does not have a central agency for gathering such statistics, and estate agents appear reluctant to share information except at an anecdotal level.

Property prices are reputed to be rising at 20 to 30 per cent per annum. In hotspots such as Dubrovnik, Hvar island (listed by Condé Nast as one the world's 10 most beautiful islands), and Korcula island (which locals claim to be Marco Polo's birthplace), prices are rising at twice that rate. But these rises are from a low baseline.

Some areas of Croatia are doing better than others at attracting visitors year round. For example, Istria, to the north, is described as 'Tuscany with sea views' and is situated close to the Italian border and about an hour from Trieste. The city is proving popular with Italians who want to motor to a holiday destination.

Outside of Zagreb, little potential for long-term rental income exists. Even in the capital, rental income opportunities are limited – some people may prefer renting to buying in the capital, but no obvious reason exists for a major influx of international business people. Of course, the situation may change.

Average rental yields are likely to be below 5 per cent, with most gain coming from capital growth. The key driver for buying in Croatia is because you love the country and want to spend time yourself enjoying your property, rather than in the expectation of benefiting from an amazing income.

Choosing Where to Buy

The Croatian property market has sprung into life with incredible vigour since the end of the war with Serbia and Bosnia. Some believe the market growth looks too good to be true, which means that it probably is.

A variety of problems linger: Proving title can be difficult, some areas are still strewn with mines, the country's capacity to meet the demands of more sophisticated tourists is still in question, and the amount of inward investment – and hence valuable Western business tenants – has been slow.

Prudence suggests confining your search to areas best served by airports and with strong leisure and business appeal. Limiting yourself in this way may rule out some of the greatest bargains, but you can be more certain of getting a good rental yield, if that is what you want, as well as somewhere interesting and enjoyable to stay when you are in Croatia. At the end of the day, you are more likely to achieve a decent return on your investment when you sell up.

I concentrate on only three areas in Croatia that make good sense according to the preceding criteria: Istria, Dalmatia, and Zagreb. Istria and Dalmatia have the greatest potential for attracting affluent tourists willing to pay the going rate for quality properties. Zagreb and the zone approximately 100 kilometres around the capital city offers beautiful countryside that's seriously underexploited from a property perspective.

No reliable national statistics (such as the UK's Halifax House Price Index) exist on property prices or rental yields in Croatia. While the actual figures when you research your own property will undoubtedly vary from those I list here, the relative costs in the various areas are probably similar. Table 13-4 lists some indicative prices and rents for the three areas I focus on in this chapter.

Table 13-4 Indicative Purchase Prices and Monthly Rents for Three-bedroom New Property in Croatia

Location	*Purchase Price*	*Weekly Rent (Low/ High Season)*
Dalmatia	£150,000	£600/800
Istria	£120,000	£400/600
Zagreb and inland (non-city centre)	£100,000	£300/750

Istria (Istra)

Istria is virtually a peninsula edged by Italy and Slovenia in the upper northwest of Croatia, between the gulfs of Trieste and Fiume.

Although Italy gave up claims to the area in 1975, Italian influences abound. The area is best reached by flying Ryanair (see the sidebar 'Fast facts about Croatia') to Trieste and then travelling via train. The Croatian Railways Web site (`www.hznet.hr/ENG/index.htm`) has a timetable in English with details. There is an airport at Pula that may well develop a range of international flights in time.

Several great coastal resorts – including Novigrad, Poreč, Vrsar, Rovinj, Labin, and the islands of Cres, Rab, and Krk – are all nearby. The only serious concern is that Istria's accessibility may lead to it being overdeveloped. (The area can be very crowded in the summer.) Still, while property may appear relatively expensive, the opportunity for rental income is good, with plenty of Italian, German, British, and Irish tourists frequenting the region.

New development apartments are on sale from as little as £33,000 off plan, but the range is more usually from £40,000 to £50,000. Properties featuring traditional Istrian stone houses and a couple of barns, in need of total renovation and about 15 minutes from the sea, begin selling from £55,000.

Away from the coast, the area is densely forested and is mainly rural, but with a couple of biggish coastal cities, including Pula and Rijeka. Pula is a little pricey, with small town-centre apartments fetching as much as £100,000.

Dalmatia (Dalmacija)

The Dalmatia region runs the whole length of Croatia's Adriatic coast, from Rijeka in the north to Dubrovnik and the Gulf of Kotor on the coast of Montenegro in the south. Away from the immediate coastal area, Dalmatia is by and large mountainous, with the Dinaric Alps running to the east.

Dalmatia is too long a strip of coast to take at one bite. When looking for property, divide the area into two sections, north and south, as I do in describing the region. And be forewarned: The mostly single-carriageway road that runs through the region gets seriously congested in summer, making journey times long.

Northern Dalmatia

Northern Dalmatia is loosely defined as the area between Zadar, the historic capital of the county country, and Split, the provincial capital. Both cities have airports, though only Split currently has international flights.

Zadar was occupied and developed in a manner similar to Istria – except by the Romans rather than the Italians. Austria, France, Hungary, and Turkey have all laid claim at one stage in the not too distant past and left their mark. Aqueducts, a forum, and an amphitheatre mark the Roman influence, and remnants of a Benedictine abbey and St Anastasia's (sv. Stošija) cathedral signal the influence of the Catholic Church.

The Krka national park embraces much of the region. Towns worth exploring for property include:

- **Šibenik**, famous for its three-aisled basilica, the Cathedral of Saint Jakov.
- **Trogir**, a near perfectly preserved Veneto-Dalmatian city from the Middle Ages, and now a UNESCO World Heritage Site.
- The inhabited islands of **Ugljan**, **Pašman**, and **Long Island (Dugi Otok)**, which can all be reached easily from Zadar.

Around Zadar, a six-room house 50 metres from the sea sells for around £85,000, while in more desirable Šibenik, a four-bedroom family house sells for about three times that sum.

Southern Dalmatia

Southern Dalmatia runs south from Split to Dubrovnik, with international airports in both cities.

Split is Croatia's second city, dominated by a busy port. Small apartments start from £80,000.

Split is also the jumping-off point for the islands of Vis, Brac, Hvar, Kercula, and Mijet. These islands tend to be pricey, with lots of big swish villas selling for between £500,000 and £1 million. However, you can still find reasonable deals:

- **Brac** still offers habitable old stone houses in need of some restoration, beginning at around £130,000.
- **Hvar** has newly converted apartments – a bit on the small side it must be said – from £50,000.
- **Vis**, the furthest island – as well as inland locations around **Klis** and **Imoski** in Biokovo nature park – feature lower housing prices (and poorer communications). Four-bedroom houses in these areas often sell for around £100,000, but you are unlikely to find many ready-built developments.

Dubrovnik, the jewel of the Dalmatian coast, is a walled city fortress built to protect the port from marauding Arabs, Venetians, Macedonians, and Serbs, among others. In 1991 and 1992, the Serbs shelled the city and inflicted more damage in a week than the city experienced in the preceding century or two. Thanks to international aid and spirited townsfolk, the city has been restored to its former splendour. Property in Dubrovnik is generally expensive, with apartments with sea views coming in at £100,000. However, a few miles out, in towns such as Pelješac and Slano, you can get a small house in need of a little TLC starting at £70,000.

Zagreb and inland

The principal attraction of Zagreb and the region roughly 100 kilometres around the capital is its rich mixture of different geographical features:

- The **Zagorje** region to the north has the feel of an Austrian country landscape with squat knolls, vineyards pumping out quality white wines such as Kraljevina, Mješavina, and Neuberger, picturesque villages, and even the odd ski slope.
- **Žumberak**, to the southwest of the capital towards the Slovenian border, lies in low mountains that blend in to the Plitvice lakes, an interconnected series of 16 lakes joined up by waterfalls. Deer, bears, wolves, and wild boar populate the wooded national park.
- **Podravina** to the east offers wide expanses of open farmland, irrigated by the Drava river. The popular local dish here is pork half shanks, Podravina style, which is served with boiled potatoes, sauerkraut, or sour turnip and accompanied by a glass of red wine – *vino vrhunske kakvoće*.

This is a region for country lovers, not sun worshippers. It can be cold and damp here, and the temperature is always a few degrees lower than further south on the coast.

Apartments close to the centre of Zagreb go for upwards of £90,000, and don't expect more than a couple of rooms. Something smart with two bedrooms and parking costs £250,000.

The city of Budinscina has its own railway station connecting to Zagreb and is approximately 45 minutes' driving time from the capital. Properties here typically cost about a quarter of what they do in Zagreb.

Go further afield in this region and properties in little towns and hamlets such as Breznièki Hum or Globocec go for less than £10,000 (in need of total renovation) or £20,000 (in reasonable repair).

Buying into Croatia

A few legal restrictions exist on foreign ownership of properties in Croatia. For example, some strategically sensitive areas are excluded, as is agricultural land, though precise definitions of what counts as agricultural land are often obscure.

The greatest concern, however, lies in finding a property with a clean ownership title. Ethnic cleansing and the emigration of many Croats to escape the troubles of the past 50 years have left tens of thousands of properties in legal limbo at worst and in some doubt as to ownership at best. Croatia's relaxed approach to registering property ownership has not made the situation any easier. Until recently, the accepted procedure was to pass down a family home to another generation simply by adding new names to title deeds. Consequently, lots of absent owners must often be rounded up to give their consent to a transaction they know nothing about. Of course, the whiff of cash can easily foster ill will between relatives, complicating the entire purchasing process.

You definitely need the services of a lawyer to purchase property in Croatia. You need to get all the documentation translated, and your application must be written in Croatian. The Minister of Foreign Affairs of the Republic of Croatia must approve all property purchases by foreigners.

Find a lawyer who has a good command of English and who is independent of the estate agent or developer that you are dealing with. Ideally, the lawyer should have offices near to where you are buying property, as they will have a good insight into local issues, such as new developments, road works, and any other factors that might detract from the value of your property. Look for lists of English-speaking lawyers via the Web site of the Foreign and Commonwealth Office (`www.fco.gov.uk`). Use their Quick Search to find lawyers. You can also find English-speaking lawyers at `www.helplinelaw.com/lawyers/Croatia`, the Martindale-Hubbell Lawyer Locator (`http://lawyers.martindale.com/marhub`), the International Law Office (`www.internationallawoffice.com/Directory`), and Legal500.com (`www.icclaw.com`).

The basic procedures in the buying process are:

1. **Research the market.**

   Chapter 3 explains how to find properties, but you can work with a number of English-speaking estate agents who specialise in Croatian property and who have offices in the country.

   The Croatian Real Estate Exchange, *Burza Nekretnina* (+385-1457-2492; `http://burza-nekretnina.com/partner_listEng.aspx`) provides a listing of its 36 members along with full contact details. The exchange was set up in 1996 as the region's trade association. Its estate agents specialise in the three geographical regions I focus on in this chapter.

   In Istria:

   - **Croatia Properties** (0783-440-8427; `www.croatiaproperties.biz`) is the UK arm of Giardini Real Estate, an agency established in 1995.
   - **Neu Blu** (+385-5244-1383; `www.nelblu.net`) is a Croatian real estate agency with more than 10 years' experience handling conveyancing for foreign buyers on the Istrian peninsula.

In Dalmatia:

- **Biliškov** (+385-2126-0792; www.biliskov.com), founded in 1993 by lawyer Jasmika Biliskov, claims to be one of the first real estate agencies in Croatia. With offices in Split and Munich, Germany, the agency has details on more than 2,000 properties, including family houses, weekend houses, apartments, hotels, marinas, agricultural land, and even whole islands (such as Srednji Jadran, a 5,000-square-metre mound close to the coast on offer for £750,000).

In Zagreb and inland:

- **Croatia Select** (01485-529-111; www.croatiaselect.co.uk) sells properties primarily in the Krapina–Zagorje area, between Zagreb and the border with Slovenia. Properties start at £7,000 and go up to £400,000, with the majority priced between £25,000 and £50,000.
- **Zagreb West** (+385-1481-1848; www.zagrebwest.hr), founded in 1995, has a range of apartments to rent and buy in and close to Zagreb city centre.

2. **Find a property and carry out a thorough inspection.**

   Generally buyers do not carry out building surveys in Croatia, and no professional association exists to carry out this work. A land surveyor (*geodet*) can check out the boundaries of a property, but generally architects do this work.

   The Royal Institute of Chartered Surveyors (www.ricsfirms.co.uk) and the Royal Institute of British Architects (www.ribafind.org) list members either working in or with extensive experience of domestic property work in Croatia. Your estate agent and lawyer can also put you in contact with a local architect.

   For a new building with no obvious signs such as cracking walls, a survey may not be essential. But you should get an older building surveyed. Expect survey prices of £500–1,000, depending on the property.

   It is best to find a professional through personal recommendation of someone whose judgement you respect and who is impartial. I cover this subject in Chapter 4.

3. **Negotiate and agree on the final price with the current owners.**

   After viewing a property, you can negotiate directly with the owners or through the estate agent, which may be more convenient if any language differences exist.

   Keep in mind that the total price you pay includes the following:

   - Actual c**ost of buying:** May vary slightly but usually works out to 8–11 per cent of the purchase price.

- **Property tax (equivalent of UK stamp duty):** 5 per cent payable on the land element of the transaction, unless the building was built before 31 December 1997. In that case, the tax applies to the whole transaction. (This is a simplified version of a complicated set of rules, which you can view in full on the Croatian Ministry of Finance Web site at `www.pu.mfin.hr/en`.)
- **Estate agency fees:** Usually around 5 per cent, with buyer and seller sharing the cost equally. A minimum of £1,600 is the going rate.
- Notary fees: £15. A public notary must witness all signatures. You can find a Croatian notary through their association, *Hrvatska Javnobilježnička komora* (+385-1455-6566, `www.hjk.hr`). Unfortunately, the Web site is not provided in English.
- **Translator fees:** Around £70. Even if you speak fluent Croatian, an official court translator must be present for all transactions involving foreigners.
- **Legal fees:** A customary charge is around 1.5 per cent of the selling price but is unlikely to be less than £1,500.

Lawyers are a law unto themselves in Croatia, with no set guidelines, so check out the fee before signing up. Legal services include searching the Land Registry, preparing the purchase contract, and submitting documentation to the Land Registrar, including paying the £60 Registry fee.

- **Application fees:** Permission to purchase from the Croatian Ministry of Foreign Affairs involves making an application (£3), getting it translated, which is obligatory (£40), and then paying to receive the decision (£8).

Getting consent granted by the Ministry of Foreign Affairs in Zagreb is a bureaucratic process that typically takes between 6 and 12 months. Your lawyer should ensure you have met all the required conditions before completing the purchase. Before the approval is given, you can move into your property or even let it out. But without the consent, you are not entitled to register the real estate in your name at the municipal court, so you may find difficulty with mortgage arrangements and you cannot resell easily. Find out how to get this permission on the Croatian Ministry of Foreign Affairs Web site (`www.mfa.hr`).

- **Property management charges:** £350–750 per year due on new properties in most holiday complexes. Charges vary depending on whether you simply want a key-holding service or a service dealing with utilities and so forth.

Dalmatian delight

Jan and Robert Brown had holidayed on the Dalmatian coast in the years before the Balkan war and had watched with horror the images of destruction of Dubrovnik, a UNESCO world heritage site, between October and December 1991. Many of the town's citizens were injured or died during the bombardment, which damaged or destroyed hundreds of the historical buildings in the city's medieval and 17th-century Old Town.

Jan and Robert were delighted to revisit in the winter of 2005 to find Dubrovnik largely restored to its former glory. They found three local property brokers on the Internet and followed that up with a visit to an international property exhibition in London. From their research before they returned to the country, they had a short list of six properties that met their criteria. After visiting all six, plus three more that they found when they arrived in Dubrovnik, they decided to put an offer on a fourth-floor, two-bedroom property with 87 square metres of living space and amazing views over the Old Town, which was on the market for €230.000. The Browns were confident that the asking price represented good value for money, as they had thoroughly researched the market both before going to Croatia and for a week in Dubrovnik and the surrounding areas. They were seeing the town in winter so were not seduced by the summer sun.

4. **Draw up and sign the initial contract.**

   After you and the seller agree to a price, have your lawyer draw up an *initial contract*, which outlines the details and any conditions that must be met before the sale completes (for example, repairs). After you and the seller sign the initial contract and you pay a 5–10 per cent deposit, the sale is legally binding.

5. **Carry out the last checks and sign the final contract.**

   After signing the initial contract, your lawyer carries out the necessary checks and searches and ensures that the vendor provides all the relevant title documents, permissions for use, and information on any mortgages and loans outstanding.

   The key task your lawyer must perform at this point is to ensure that the property you are buying comes with a *clean title*. In simple English, a clean title means that the person or developer who is selling you the property legally owns it. Don't just accept your estate agent's word for it. Often estate agents say in their advertisements that all their properties come with clean titles; however, few agents are qualified to do the necessary checks. See the sidebar 'Property title problems' for more information.

Your lawyer needs a certificate from the Land Registry with three sections to prove a clean title:

- Section A gives a description of the real estate.
- Section B states who owns the real estate.
- Section C lists any *burdens* on the real estate, such as mortgages.

Currently all title documentation is paper-based, but by 2010 documents will be electronic. The title-checking process, which currently takes a month or so, should then become faster and more reliable.

6. **Pay for your property.**

   You must pay for your property in Croatian currency. To do this, you can either instruct your bank or buy currency through a specialist company, which may offer more competitive rates (see Chapter 18). You can have the purchased currency sent directly to your own bank account in Croatia, or you can use your lawyer's *escrow account*, a client account in which your funds are kept separate and cannot be accessed without your permission.

   After you and the seller sign the sales contract, you have to register the purchase at the authorised tax authority within 30 days. The public notary handling your property transfer also submits one copy of the sales contract to the tax authorities.

   You must pay for the property tax within 15 days of receiving the demand for payment. If you don't, you are charged interest on a daily basis on arrears.

Forming a Croatian company

Unless you are investing a seven-figure sum in your property, forming a Croatian company may be more trouble than it is worth. However, Croatian companies don't need to get permission from the Ministry of Foreign Affairs to own property, so forming one can speed up the buying process.

You must open a company bank account and deposit £3,000 (which you can withdraw later so it is not a cost). A public notary then prepares company documentation, which an official court translator must translate – all at a cost of around £400. Additionally, complying with all Croatian company legislation, filing accounts, and so forth is time-consuming and costs around £100 a year.

If you operate through a company, you may enjoy some tax advantages when letting or selling your property, but you need to take professional advice (see Chapter 17 to determine what's best for you).

Property title problems

The problem with property title in Croatia came about for three principal reasons:

- In the past, properties were bought and sold without proper registration and documentation. Sometimes this was to avoid taxes, but more often in rural areas properties were inherited by siblings in equal shares but never registered as such.
- Under Communism, significant portions of land and property were confiscated from wealthy families, divided up into smaller lots, and handed out to the deserving poor or (more usually) Party hacks. Original owners are now beginning to reclaim their property rights.
- Conflict with the Serbs and others led to certain ethnic groups being evicted unlawfully from their properties, which were then seized, occupied, or sold.

7. **Transfer utilities.**

   After you become the owner of your Croatian property, or perhaps a little before, contact the following organisations to make arrangements for your supply:

   - **Electricity:** Electrical current is 220V/50Hz. Electric bills are issued monthly and can be paid at the local office of the electric utility company office. Contact the Croatia National Electric Company, *Hrvatska Elektroprivreda d.d.* (HEP), for details about opening an account and for office locations throughout the country (+385-1460-1111; `www.hep.hr/index.en.html`).
   - **Gas:** Natural gas is available in many districts of most cities and large towns. For connection fees and to establish an account, contact the main office of the Gas Distribution Company, *Montcogim-Plinara Ltd* (+385-1337-3745; `www.montcogim.hr/indexe.html`).

     Liquid petroleum gas (LPG) tanks are commonly used throughout Croatia for cooking and heating, especially on the islands. You can find LPG vendor outlets throughout the country.
   - **Water:** Tap water is generally considered safe to drink throughout Croatia, although some areas, especially in major cities, may have a high mineral content. Some of the islands may have only well water, spring water, or collected rainfall as a water source. For details on availability, cost, and setting up an account, contact the Water Management Directorate (+385-1630-7339; `www.mps.hr`) at its main office in Zagreb.

Your lawyer must make a properly conducted title search that involves dealing with the Land Registry and the Cadastral Registry. The Land Registry Office of the municipal court keeps records on real-estate ownership. The data are public and can be relied on legally to show true ownership. The Cadastral Registry Office maintains records of both real estate and property built on the real estate.

Getting Settled in Croatia

Buying a Croatian property can be pleasantly uncomplicated, and getting settled into the country is often quite easy. While you don't find armies of foreigners owning property, the number is growing steadily.

People involved in your purchase – estate agents, lawyers, and so forth – have something to gain by smoothing your path, so that is what they do. After your purchase is complete, you are to some extent on your own. While some matters, such as capital gains tax, may seem a distant concern, the actions you take early on can mitigate the pain later.

This section covers topics related to establishing yourself in Croatia after your purchase is finished.

Taxing matters

Croatian taxation related to property includes the following:

- **Business tax:** This is a flat-rate tax of 20 per cent on profits. In Croatia, profit is income minus allowable expenses, which in the case of property includes insurance, management fees, maintenance, and so forth.
- **Capital gains tax:** This is applied at the same rates as for income tax. However, a single property owned for at least three years is free of tax in Croatia, though not in your home country unless you move your domicile to Croatia. (See Chapter 17, where I deal with these and other tax matters.)
- **Double taxation treaties:** Croatia has assumed from the Socialist Federal Republic of Yugoslavia a double taxation treaty with the UK and with many other countries. This ensures that you don't end up paying tax twice on the same income or paying more tax than you should. (I cover double taxation treaties in Chapter 17.)

- **Individual tax:** The rate runs on a sliding scale, starting at 15 per cent on the first 36,000 kuna of annual income and rising to 45 per cent on income above 252,000 kuna. Foreigners are taxed only on their income in Croatia. For property rents, the taxable amount is 70 per cent of the income received. This rule eliminates the need for complicated accounting for expenses related to the property.
- **Other taxes:** A number of other taxes apply to holiday homes and undeveloped land and buildings. The rate varies between 5 and 15 kuna per square metre per year.
- **Value-added tax:** VAT is levied at three rates: 22 per cent, 10 per cent, and 0 per cent. The whole VAT code and rule book are currently being revised to harmonise with the EU. You can keep track of changes in VAT and tax rates on the worldwide wax Web site (www.worldwide-tax.com).

See the Ministry of Finance Web site (www.pu.mfin.hr/en) for more detailed information on tax in Croatia, as well as Chapter 17, where I cover foreign tax matters in general.

Find out more about the tax regime in Croatia by visiting the PricewaterhouseCoopers Web site (www.pwc.com/ua/eng/main/home/index.html) and following the Publications link.

Opening a bank account

Opening a personal or business account in either the local or a foreign currency such as euros or sterling is a very easy process in Croatia. The simplest way is to discuss your needs face to face, on the telephone, or by e-mail with one of the local banks.

Two banks with Web sites in English that provide all the information you need are Raiffeisenbank Austria d.d (+385-1 456-6466; www.rba.hr) and Zagrebačka banka d.d. (+385-1480-8222; www.zaba.hr).

When you open an account, bring a completed Croatian kuna non-resident account application form (which you can get from the bank), a photocopy of the first and second pages of your passport, and a letter explaining why you want to open an account.

Opening or closing an account costs nothing, but charges for handling foreign exchange – usually the most expensive part of banking for overseas property buyers – vary greatly. Check out these fees carefully before deciding on a bank.

You can do almost anything with a Croatian bank account that you can do with a British account. Chequebooks, credit and debit cards, direct debits, and telephone and Internet banking are all readily available.

No UK banks currently offer retail operations in Croatia, but you can find details on all the bank networks on the Croatian National Bank Web site (www.hnb.hr).

Bank hours are usually 8am to 5pm Monday to Friday, and 8am to noon or 1pm on Saturday. Automated teller machines (ATMs) are readily available in banks, supermarkets, and many other establishments in all resorts, towns, and cities. British pounds, US dollars, and euros are easily exchangeable throughout Croatia.

Credit cards can be used in some Croatian hotels, expensive restaurants, and some bigger shops, but they are not as popular as in Western Europe, and people generally pay with, and ask for, cash.

Staying healthy

The Croatians are starting to take health care more seriously. The country is attempting to modernise its health-care system and bring it closer to Western standards. The Croatian Institute of Health Insurance (HZZO) administers Croatia's health-care system. The system is publicly funded but has an increasing degree of private service provision.

Health facilities in Croatia, although generally similar to those in more developed economies, are seriously strapped for cash. Don't be surprised if doctors and dentists expect payment in folding notes on the spot.

The country has 65 public hospitals and two privately owned hospitals. Doctors and dentists are available in every town and city, and you can get minor complaints dealt with quickly at a pharmacy (*ilekarna*). Medical staff often speak some English. You can find contact details for English-speaking doctors and dentists on the Web site of the US Embassy in Croatia (www.usembassy.hr/consular/acs/services.htm#medical).

Some medicines are in short supply in public hospitals and clinics. As a British citizen you have to pay for all prescribed medicines, and as a result you should have little difficulty finding almost any medicines privately.

Getting Around the Country

You have several options for conducting daily business and travelling within Croatia. This section covers your major transportation options.

Train

Croatian Railways' (*Hrvatske Zeljeznice*) network is modest by any standards. Its 4,000 kilometres of track are largely based around Zagreb, which is the hub from which most trains leave.

Major cities such as Dubrovnik appear to have been left out of the network altogether. (This is because the system was designed in the 19th century when Croatia was simply a cog in the Austro-Hungarian Empire's machine.) The major cities are connected, but not necessarily in the most obvious way. To get to Dubrovnik from Zagreb, for example, you must travel through neighbouring Bosnia and Herzegovina, while Istria is only connected by rail using the Slovenian network.

Trains are slower and less frequent than buses, but trains are around 15 per cent cheaper and are a veritable bargain by British standards. For example, the 423-kilometre journey from Zagreb to Zadar costs about £14 second class or £20 for first class. You can choose from express and local (slower and cheaper) trains, as well as an overnight sleeper train between Zagreb and Split. Croatian Railways (+385-1457-7111; `www.hznet.hr`) has an online train timetable and fare calculator in English on its Web site.

Plane

If time is of the essence, getting around the country is best done by air. A journey you may do on an overnight sleeper train can take less than an hour by plane. You pay double the price, but double very little is still not a lot!

You have no choice at present but to use Croatian Airlines (+385-1487-2727; `www.croatiaairlines.hr`), which flies routes between Zagreb, Pula, Split, Zadar, Dubrovnik, and, periodically in the summer, Bol on the island of Braž.

Flights are cheap if you book them on the Internet. For example, you can get a return flight from Zagreb to Zadar for £52

Car

The roads in Croatia are poor – and that is being charitable. Aside from a 40-kilometre stretch of motorway from Zagreb to Karlovac, parts of a motorway between the Hungarian border and Zagreb, and a motorway near completion from Zagreb to Split, with spurs to Zadar and Sibenik, the road network has been neglected for years. But the situation is beginning to improve.

If you are not in a hurry, drive down the Adriatic road (*Jadranska magistrala*) that connects Rijeka to Dubrovnik, the most scenic route in Croatia. A new 'European' motorway is being constructed to join these cities to Greece through Montenegro and Albania by 2015.

Garages are quite common, and all grades of petrol and diesel are available. On-the-spot speeding fines are the norm, so stick to the limits: 50 kilometres per hour (31 miles per hour) in built-up areas, 80 kilometres per hour (49 miles per hour) on main highways, and 130 kilometres per hour (80 miles per hour) on motorways.

Croatian drivers are world class in tailgating and reckless overtaking, so be prepared for an interesting experience if you decide to drive. Always carry your vehicle registration documents and international Green Card insurance documents.

Bus

As with much of Eastern Europe, the Croatian bus service is better developed, with a wider range of routes, than the airways and the trains. Even the smallest villages have some sort of bus connection.

Express buses cover longer distances, can be very comfortable, and are inexpensive. Every larger town has a bus station (*Autobusna Stanica*) that sells tickets and displays timetables.

The following companies operate bus services throughout Croatia and have timetables and fares on their Web sites:

- Autoprometno Produzeće (+385-3427-3133; www.app.hr).
- Autotrans (+385-5121-3821; www.autotrans.hr)
- Croatia Bus (+385-1235-2333; www.croatiabus.hr)

Taxi

Taxis are usually safe but not always inexpensive. They are available in all main towns and cities, either from taxi stands or ordered by phone (970 in Zagreb).

Standard meter rates start from 25 kuna, with an additional 10 kuna per kilometre thereafter. Rates are higher after 10pm and at weekends.

By water

In high season, boats and ferries sail the Adriatic and connect all major ports on Croatia's coast, including Rijeka, Dubrovnik, Zadar, Split, Hvar, and Korcula – as well as almost all inhabited islands.

The Croatian ferry company Jadrolinija (+385-5166-6111; www.jadrolinija.hr) covers most ferry routes in Croatia. Losinjska Plovidba (+385-5131-9000; www.losinjska-plovidba.hr) covers the route north from Zadar virtually to Trieste.

Chapter 14

Romania

In This Chapter

- Understanding the potential in Romania
- Discerning where you want to look
- Going through the purchase process
- Making the purchase work for you

Romania is hopeful, at the time of writing, of becoming a full member of the European Union (EU) in 2007. At worst, its entry may be delayed until the following year. The country has more to gain from EU membership than almost any other that I cover in this book, save for Bulgaria and Turkey. Membership will unlock additional funds to help Romania modernise its infrastructure and spur other countries, including the USA, to increase involvement in investment projects.

A substantial portion of the Romanian property market is based in and around the capital, Bucharest, which has many of the nation's most alluring tourist attractions. However, there are compelling reasons for looking beyond Bucharest's boundary, including a lengthy strip of Black Sea coastline and the stunning Carpathian mountains.

Romania's brokers claim that the property market is on a roll. They are busy talking up the current circumstances to anyone who listens. While locals can only see their own country, you have at least a dozen others to compare it with. Use this advantage to sidestep the sales pressure and hunt out real value. Check up on the market yourself using the resources I describe in the later section 'Talking Business'.

Fast facts about Romania

Area: Total: 237,500 square kilometres, which is the same size as the UK.

Population: 22,303,000, which is around three times the population of Austria and a third of the population of the UK.

Location: Aside from a coastline of 225 kilometres on the Black Sea, Romania has 2,508 kilometres of borders with Bulgaria (608 kilometres) to the south, Moldova (450 kilometres) to the east, Hungary (443 kilometres) and Ukraine (531 kilometres) to the north, and Serbia and Montenegro (476 kilometres) to the west.

Language: The official language Romanian belongs to the Romance group of languages, which also includes French, Italian, Portuguese, and Spanish – all of which descend from Latin. About 22 million people in Romania speak Romanian, as do 3 million people in Moldova and more than 1 million more people in Bulgaria, Greece, Macedonia, Albania, Serbia and Montenegro, Hungary, Ukraine, and even countries further afield such as the USA and Canada.

Around 15 per cent of the population speak Hungarian and 1.5 per cent German. Given the country's connections to the former Soviet Empire, speaking Russian was important in Romania, but now even those who know Russian are reluctant to speak it. English, however, is definitely on the up, and many people in the towns and cities are in the process of learning English.

Currency: Romania's currency is the leu (plural lei), and each leu is subdivided into 100 bani (singular ban). To eliminate the impact of a long period of galloping inflation, on 1 July 2005 Romania dropped four zeros from its national currency. Today 50,805 old Romanian lei (ROL is the international designation for the old currency) per pound sterling now equal 5.08 new lei (RON is the international designation for the new currency) per pound sterling. Both old and new coins and banknotes are in circulation until 31 December 2006, when the old currency is scheduled to be withdrawn.

Time zone: GMT +3.

EU standing: Romania was the first Central and Eastern European country to establish official relations with the European Community. The bilateral agreement on Romania's inclusion in the European Community's Generalised System of Preferences dates back to 1974, but the country did not establish diplomatic ties with the EU until 1990. Romania formally applied for EU membership on 22 June 1995 and the Accession Treaty, the final stage in the process of applying for membership, was signed on 25 April 2005. At the time of writing, Romania appears to be on track to become a member of the EU on 1 January 2007, but a clause in the Accession Treaty allows for a delay of up to a year if the country fails to show signs of eliminating high-level corruption.

Emergency services: Staff at the main emergency number (112) usually speak English, but other switchboard personnel may not speak good English. Consider using your hotel operator for assistance. Important phone numbers include:

Ambulance: 961

Fire: 981

International emergency (usually speak English): 112

Police: 955

Visas: EU nationals and citizens of Iceland, Liechtenstein, Norway, Switzerland, the USA, and a number of other countries do not require a visa for stays of up to 90 days in any six-month period. You can extend your stay in Romania by submitting an application to the offices of the Authority for Aliens in your area of residence up to 30 days before your initial right to stay expires.

To check whether you need a visa or to find out how to stay for periods longer than 90 days, visit the Romanian embassy Web site (www.roemb.co.uk/Consular/romanianvisa.htm).

By air from the UK: Bucharest lies in the southeast part of Romania, close to the Bulgarian border, and provides the best gateway for most other destinations. You can reach Bucharest and other cities in Romania, including Arad, Bacau, Cluj, Oradea, Sibiu, and Timisoara, by direct flights from airports in Austria, Germany, Italy, Hungary, and Turkey. So far, the only direct flights from the UK to Romania are provided by Transporturile Aeriene Române, Tarom (+40-21-337-2037; www.tarom.ro) and British Airways. The cheapest non-direct flights are usually with Swiss Air (0845-601-0956; www.swiss.com) and Austrian Airlines (020-7766-0300; www.aua.com/uk/eng).

By train from the UK: Travelling by train from the UK means going first to Paris by Eurostar and then overnight to Vienna. From there, you take the 'Dacia Express' to Bucharest. The journey takes about 46 hours. The simplest way to book is by phone with either Deutsche Bahn's United Kingdom office or European Rail. The Man in Seat Sixty-One (www.seat61.com) provides an overview of the route.

Other routes from the UK: Eurolines runs between London and Bucharest as well as to Arad, Brasov, Deva, Fagaras, Lugoj, Nadlac, Ploiesti, Sebes, Sibiu, and Timisoara. The journey time is around 50 hours.

Accommodation: Accommodation in Romania is plentiful and relatively inexpensive, particularly outside of Bucharest and other key tourist areas. In Bucharest, you can find rooms for €120 (£84) per month and small apartments from around €350 (£250), but you have to look long and hard after reaching Romania, using the newspapers and Web sites that I list in the later section 'English-language media'.

Bucharest Romania Hotels (www.bucharest-romania-hotels.ro) has hotels in 41 towns and cities throughout the country. Hotels range from luxury to fairly basic, with prices to match. Expect to pay €22–180 (£15–126) a night. Hotels Romania (www.hotelsromania.com) covers 31 key cities and towns with a slightly more up-market range of hotels. Hostels.com (www.hostels.com/en/ro) lists accommodation around the country with nightly rates starting at €12 (£8) per night per person, with discounts for longer stays. East Comfort (0740-500-983; www.eastcomfort.com) has special rates for stays of a week or longer. Romanian Vision (+40-21-322-6533; www.romvision.ro) offers a smaller up-market range of apartments from around £42 (€60) a night. Expats Romania (www.expatsromania.com) has apartments, houses, and rooms for long-term let around the country.

Getting to Know Romania

Romania has more going for it now that at any stage in its history: The economy is growing fast, people have jobs, and wages are rising in line with increasing productivity. Companies, in particular from the USA, are rushing to set up factories and operations in the country and take advantage of its skilled labour force.

Romania is gradually adjusting its hotels and attractions to the needs of more affluent tourists, not just its Moldavian and Bulgarian neighbours. Romania has something to offer in every season. The skiing infrastructure is receiving new investment and although Romania can't compete with France or Italy in terms of quality, prices are low enough to appeal to families and novice skiers.

Romanian culture

The Romans knew a good thing when they took over the area of present-day Romania at the beginning of the 2nd century AD. They left a lasting legacy in the region's Latin-based language and bags of interesting architecture.

The outside world has long known Romania primarily as the home of Count Dracula, a mythological vampire loosely based on Vlad Ţepeş, a real-life count with a penchant for killing fellow nobles. (Vlad Ţepeş never owned Bran Castle, now known as Dracula's Castle. However, this fact hasn't got in the way of a good marketing wheeze.)

A ring of mountains, the Carpathians, almost completely surround the hilly and forested Transylvanian basin that covers much of central Romania. In the countryside, horse-drawn carts and steam trains are still fairly standard transportation between thousands of beautiful villages. Fortified churches, Gothic and Renaissance castles, and mediaeval towns such as Sighisoara vie with Byzantine paintings in Bukovina and lush vineyards for today's discerning tourists.

Property as a pension alternative

Anelia and Michael Waterside are buying an off-plan apartment that sleeps six near Mamaia, Romania's second-largest resort on the Black Sea coast. Situated just 10 kilometres northeast of the city of Constanţa, which has its own international airport, the apartment is in a condominium complex with a swimming pool and tennis court. Beaches, shops, bars, restaurants, and medical facilities are nearby. Anelia expects to rent out the unit for £200–400 a week.

The Watersides have invested €60,000 (£41,000) in this Romanian property instead of putting money into pensions or British property. 'Property prices in the UK are too high at the moment and the rental yield – the ratio between the purchase price and what you get in terms of rent – just isn't attractive,' the Watersides say.

Still, the couple planned meticulously for their purchase. They did a lot of research to gauge what to expect from a holiday home. They visited a large UK property exhibition and met representatives from a number of brokers before choosing an organisation they were comfortable dealing with. They conducted an inspection visit and intended to buy a property that was already completed. Instead, they decided to buy an off-plan property because it seemed superior to those that were already built. The developer took the Watersides around a number of other projects that he had completed and let them speak to other off-plan buyers. The deal came complete with a mortgage, which was the clinching factor.

The Danube is an exciting river to ride down (see Chapter 12 on Bulgaria for details on travelling this river). Romania also has a great stretch of the Black Sea coast, a summer favourite, as well as rapidly improving ski resorts.

The capital city of Bucharest offers wide, tree-lined boulevards built in the late 19th century by French and French-trained architects. The city hosts all the usual paraphernalia of urban leisure life: First-rate stage plays, opera performances, classical and jazz concerts, discos galore, art exhibitions, poetry readings, and more.

Bucharest is just a fraction of what Romania has to offer. Other temptations include the following:

- **Maramureș** is a region locked into a rural lifestyle, where time literally appears to have stood still. Hand-built wooden churches, traditional costumes, and festivals are all part of the lifestyle here.
- **Murfatlar**, a region lying around 12 kilometres to the west of the Black Sea coast, has around 300 days of sunshine each year, which makes it ideal for producing sweet dessert wines such as late-harvest Chardonnay, Muscat Ottonel, and Pinot Gris. The region also produces soft, rich red wines such as Cabernet Sauvignon, Pinot Noir, and Merlot.
- **Sinaia**, in Transylvania, known as the Pearl of the Carpathians, is famed for its skiing as well as the palace of King Carol I.
- **Transfăgărăşan highway:** At 2,000 metres, this is one of Europe's highest roads. It runs for 90 kilometres, taking in the Balea lake at its highest point and then snaking down to the Balea Cascada waterfall.
- **Wallachia**, a region in the south of the country, is home to some of Romania's most famous monasteries as well as Roma (Gypsy) culture.

Climate and weather

Romania's climate is somewhere between temperate and continental, resulting in some great seasonal variations in temperature and four distinct seasons. The Carpathian mountains play a major part in creating the confused weather pattern, as they serve as a barrier to Atlantic air masses while blocking the worst of the influences sweeping down the Russian plains.

Winter can be cold, with average temperatures of –1°C. Spring is pleasant, with warm days from the middle of the morning to early evening, and cool thereafter. Summer average temperatures are around 21°C, with a fair amount of sunshine. Autumn is dry and cool. See Table 14-1 for more information about typical temperatures throughout the country.

Regional climate differences throughout Romania are significant. For example, the average annual temperature is 11 °C in the south and 8 °C in the north; annual rainfall (usually falling as snow in the mountains in winter) averages about 635 millimetres in central Transylvania, 521 millimetres at Iasi in Moldavia, but only 381 millimetres at Constanţa on the Black Sea. See Tables 14-2 and 14-3 for precipitation information.

Table 14-1 Average Daily Temperatures in Romania

Location	*Jan–Mar*	*Apr–June*	*July–Sep*	*Oct–Dec*
Brasov (Transylvanian Alps)	–1°C	12°C	16°C	2°C
Bucharest	2°C	16°C	20°C	4°C
Constanţa (Black Sea coast)	3°C	16°C	21°C	7°C

Table 14-2 Average Number of Rainy Days per Month in Romania

Location	*Jan–Mar*	*Apr–June*	*July–Sep*	*Oct–Dec*
Brasov (Transylvanian Alps)	3	5	5	3
Bucharest	5	8	6	6
Constanţa (Black Sea coast)	5	6	3	5

Table 14-3 Average Number of Snowy Days per Month in Romania

Location	*Jan–Mar*	*Apr–June*	*July–Sep*	*Oct–Dec*
Brasov (Transylvanian Alps)	5	0	0	2
Bucharest	4	0	0	2
Constanţa (Black Sea coast)	2	0	0	1

English-language media

English newspapers are available primarily in Bucharest and in the main Black Sea resorts, but they arrive a day or two late and cost around 10 lei ($2). English-language print media are difficult to find elsewhere.

You can pick up the local and some of the international news in English on the following Web sites, some of which also provide print versions:

- **Bucharest Daily News** (www.daily-news.ro) is locally owned and claims to be a one-stop shop for business information about Romania. The publication is available on subscription for about 2.5 lei (50p) an issue and for around 30 per cent more from the newsstand.
- **Bucuresti What, Where, When** (www.bucurestiwww.ro) is a monthly magazine freely distributed in most major hotels and available online. It provides listings of activities in Bucharest and beyond, property information, and an expat community section.
- **Expat Focus** (www.expatfocus.com/expatriate-romania) keeps English-speaking foreigners informed of events and activities throughout Romania and provides information on renting and buying property.
- **Nine O'Clock** (www.nineoclock.ro) is a daily newssheet launched in 1991 by a group of enthusiastic Romanian journalists who borrowed the English concept of fair play to rule out bias in their reporting. Today, *Nine O'Clock* keeps you abreast of business, cultural, and financial affairs in Romania. The publication is distributed in all Romanian towns with more than 100,000 inhabitants by subscription or direct sales (€20 per month/€1 per issue at newsstands). In 1997, the journalists launched a Web edition of the publication.
- **Romanian Press Review** (www.pressreview.ro) is a general online newspaper with two sections aimed at keeping expats informed about local issues.

The BBC World Service is available locally on FM and short wave at various times of the day. Find details on the BBC World Service Web site (www.bbc.co.uk/worldservice).

Tourism

Romania is the world's fourth-fastest developing tourist market according to World Tourism Statistics. But before you get carried away, barely 6 million people arrive in the country each year (half the number that go to Hungary, for example). Overall, Romania ranks as the 65th most popular destination in the world. A quarter of the tourists come from Moldova, Bulgaria, and other nearby countries whose inhabitants can't afford to go on holiday anywhere else. However, the past three or four years have seen changes, and now around half a million tourists a year come to Romania from Germany, France, Austria, and the UK.

Romania needs a new vision for its tourist industry, but more important than its current tourist numbers are the prospects for even more affluent visitors in the future. The past year or two has seen growth in tourists of an annual average of 7.9 per cent, with a significant proportion of these coming from Western Europe and the USA. These tourists present a good opportunity for property buyers who want to enter the potentially lucrative holiday rental market.

Bucharest is not yet in the same league for partying as Prague and Budapest, due to a shortage of low-cost budget flights into the Romanian capital. But after the easyJets and Ryanairs of the world arrive, the city can doubtless soak up as many pleasure-seeking tourist as want to come.

Outside of the capital, only a couple of ski resorts and Black Sea coast resorts appeal to anyone other than true nature lovers seeking rural peace and quiet.

Sports and leisure

Within an hour or so's travel from Bucharest you can find almost any sporting activity you like.

The Lac de Verde golf club among the hills of the Prahova valley is an hour's drive from the capital. While Romania has only a couple of golf courses, keep track of new additions on the Golf in Europe Web site (`www.pmfgolfguide.com/romania/romania.htm`).

More adventurous tourists ride in the Carpathian mountains (`www.riding-holidays.ro`), raft down the rivers Cris and Olt, or ski, snowboard, or tube in mountain resorts such as Poiana Brasov, Sinaia, Predeal, Paltinis, and Runcu (`www.skiresorts.ro`). If that's not enough to whet your appetite, you can find opportunities for hunting, trekking, climbing, boating, diving, camping, mountaineering, and bird watching. The Romanian Travel (`www.rotravel.com/romania/info/mshfs.php`) and About Romania (`www.aboutromania.com/sport.html`) Web sites keep you posted on all these sporting activities and more.

The Romanian Tourist Board (`www.romaniatourism.com`) and Virtual Tourist (`www.virtualtourist.com/travel/Europe/Romania/TravelGuide-Romania.html`) provide tons of links to tourism and leisure facilities throughout every region and almost every town in the nation.

Talking Business

Romania has one of the fastest rates of economic growth of countries I cover in this book. At 8.5 per cent annual growth in gross domestic product (GDP), a reasonably reliable measure of wealth creation, Romania is well ahead of its neighbour Bulgaria (around 5 per cent) and old Europe's average of around 1.8 per cent. However, keep in mind that Romania's growth is coming from one of the lowest starting levels of any country in Europe.

Nevertheless, foreign companies are piling into Romania at an ever-increasing rate, creating new jobs, more local wealth, and a growing need for improved living accommodation. Levels of foreign direct investment (FDI) have risen to more than €4 billion a year, around a fifth of that going into all the former Soviet satellite countries. As of December 2005, 107,000 foreign firms had a total of $13.6 billion invested in Romania, according to the Ministry of Justice's National Trade Register Office (NTRO). About 4,200 US companies have invested in business in Romania. The Romanian Agency for Foreign Investment (`www.arisinvest.ro`) gives a sector-by-sector overview of foreign firms.

These economic factors bode well for the property sector of the economy for two reasons:

- Romanians are getting wealthier because the economy is fast becoming export-led, with the nation selling manufactured products, machinery, equipment, and food to other countries. Romania has even become a base for industries as diverse as motor manufacturing and film production. Romanians are beginning to enjoy their nation's prosperity and are forming a potential market of property renters and buyers.
- Strong business activity results in a high number of foreign executives visiting Romania to help establish local enterprises. These executives need somewhere to stay – often of higher quality and recently built – for the few years that they are in Romania.

Romania's greatest economic concern is inflation. At 9.6 per cent a year, its inflation is perhaps the highest in Europe. Inflation is a problem for property buyers as it changes prices without changing values. The concern is that local brokers report that property values are rising when in fact they may not be rising as much as they appear. For example, if property prices are rising at 10 per cent and inflation is running at 9 per cent, then the real rise in property prices is only 1 per cent.

Examining the cost of living

The cost of living across Romania is considerably lower than in the UK. For example, a three-course meal with wine for two people in a mid-range restaurant in Bucharest runs to an average of £18, while in the UK a similar meal costs more than three times that at £73. Table 14-4 offers a cross-section of prices.

Bucharest is very expensive compared with other cities in Romania, but by way of compensation you have the benefits of living in a cosmopolitan city with good amenities.

Romania ranks 65th out of the 177 countries listed in the United Nations' Human Development Index (`http://hdr.undp.org/reports/global/2005`), compared with Bulgaria (55th), Latvia (48th), and Cyprus (29th). So although Romania is inexpensive, it is not as good a place to live as any of the other countries I cover in this book, save for Ukraine and Turkey.

Identifying areas of value

Romania is perhaps the best value in Europe for property. The prospect of hefty price hikes in the years following the country's entry to the EU makes buying Romanian property even more appealing. Local brokers reckon that you need flared trousers in your wardrobe and to remember beehive hairstyles to have experienced comparable prices in the UK. For example:

- A two-room apartment in Blvd Tineretului, located near Unirii with a front view on the top floor sells for €59,000 (£40,320). Such apartments are fully fitted with wall and floor tiles, wooden floors, double-glazing, air-conditioning, satellite dish, and Internet, and you can use them for either commercial or residential purposes.
- Newly built villas in Bisericii Street, Pipera – one of the more attractive areas in Bucharest – sell for €149,500 (£102,167). 170-square-metre villas built on three floors have large reception rooms, two double and two king-size bedrooms, three bathrooms, dressing rooms, storage areas, gardens, parking for two cars, and private security. The area is close to shops and schools, a 10-minute drive to Bucharest city centre and five minutes to the main international airport. Think of this area as London's Hampstead, but with £500,000 still in your bank account.
- A second-floor apartment in Stefan cel Mare Street, Constanţa, located just 500 metres from a Black Sea beach, sells for €59,000 (£40,320). The area is near to Tomis Mall, so shopping day or night is easy. If you tire of the local beaches, you can truck out to Mamaia, the most famous summer resort in Romania, just 10 minutes' drive away.
- In Brasov, a town in Romania's longest-established ski area, new three-room apartments on the second floor sell for €78,400 (£53,565). The location offers good mountain views and nearby shopping, skiing, and restaurants. Larger apartments and penthouses are available with prices ranging up to €250,000 (£170,808) for massive 200–300-square-metre properties. Brasov also has bags of entertainment off season, including an opera house, museums, and its own beer festival.

Assessing potential rental yields

According to Investment Romania (`www.investmentromania.com`), a property agency run by a British-Irish lawyer working in Romania since 2003, rental yields have risen from 6.5 per cent gross in 2004 to 7.5 per cent gross in 2006, and the market gives all the appearance of strengthening further. (Investment Romania often joins with investors in paying a share of the purchase price or takes a share of profit on sale instead of commission – and anyone prepared to put their money where their mouth is deserves to be taken seriously.)

Actual yields depend a lot on a unit's location, appeal, and furnishings. Also, any estimates of potential yield may be seriously adrift if you have to carry out extensive refurbishment or wait several months to find a tenant.

From a gross rent, you have to deduct running costs such as agents' fees, repairs, renewals, and taxes (see 'Taxing matters' later in this chapter), which can eat up between a fifth and a quarter of the gross rent.

Unless you are going to let the property yourself, you must also budget for an agency fee of one month's rent plus 19 per cent VAT and management fees of up to 12 per cent plus 19 per cent VAT on the annual rental income. Whatever way you choose to rent out your property, you need to expect to pay tax of 16 per cent on profits.

Away from Bucharest, no one is venturing even tentative figures for rental yield. Bearing in mind that most tourism and business opportunities are in and around Bucharest, budget for a figure between a half to two-thirds of the yield that you can obtain on property within the capital.

Occasionally, local government officials receive side money to reclassify agricultural land to more valuable building land, often by means of dubious titles. For this reason, you really need a lawyer to keep you safe from title problems; see the later section 'Buying into Romania' for more on this topic.

Choosing Where to Buy

Romania is a large country, and Bucharest – currently the nation's most viable international airport and preferred entry point – is stuck in the south-eastern corner, miles from anywhere. Anywhere that is except the three most attractive places for overseas property buyers to hunt out value: The Black Sea coast and Brasov, Romania's most popular ski area, are only a couple of hours' drive from Bucharest.

I divide Romania's property market options into three buying zones: Bucharest, which is the safest (and usually most expensive) region; the areas around Constanţa on the Black Sea coast, which has the most developed tourist infrastructure after the capital; and Brasov, for ski and mountain lovers. Table 14-5 lists some example prices and rents for these three regions.

If rental income and capital appreciation are not so important to you, the rest of Romania is a rich opportunity for purchasing seriously low-cost property. The Virtual Tourist Web site (`www.virtualtourist.com/travel/Europe/Romania/TravelGuide-Romania.html`) has a comprehensive guide to every district, city, and town in the country. I cover research methods in Chapter 3.

Table 14-5 Indicative Purchase Prices and Monthly Rents for a Three-bedroom Property in Romania

Location	*Purchase Price*	*Weekly Rent (Low/High Season)*
Brasov	€100,000 (£70,000)	€300/600 (£206/412)
Bucharest	€160,000 (£112,000)	€300/600 (£206/412)
Constanţa/Black Sea coast	€70,000 (£48,000)	€150/400 (£103/275)

Bucharest

Bucharest (*Bucureşt*) is the capital and the largest city of Romania, with a population of 2.5 million. Founded in the late 14th century as *Cetatea Dambovitei*, or Dambovita citadel, Bucharest was a military fortress and an important commercial town straddling the trade routes to Constantinople.

The city's early sophistication led to the nicknames 'Paris of the East' and 'Little Paris' (*Micul Paris*). A Triumphal Arch on the Soseaua Kiseleff, a boulevard bigger and better than Paris's renowned Champs-Elysées, harkens to the city's French influences.

During the 1980s, Romanian president Nicolae Ceauçescu had a shot at transforming Bucharest into a model Soviet city replete with massive new state buildings, such as the Museum of Romanian History. He even had the Dimboviţa river re-routed through southern Bucharest to fit his vision. His former residence, now known as the Palace of Parliament, is a truly staggering building with 1,000 rooms. Many old churches and the French style villas were demolished to create this building. Fortunately, both Ceauçescu's money and time in power expired before he could do any more damage.

Bucharest has a thriving cultural scene and regularly hosts world-class concerts. Its National Opera House, National Theatre, and a host of smaller theatres, such as the Comedy Theatre, the Nottara Theatre, and the Odeon Theatre, ensure that virtually every taste is catered to. The city has an extensive transport system including a metro with four lines and 45 stations, as well as 30 tram lines, 3 light metro lines, and 20 trolleybus lines.

Bucharest meets the demands of all but the most discerning dwellers. It is on a par with cities such as Bristol, Birmingham, and Glasgow in terms of general facilities. Although public transport systems can be congested at peak times, the city is easy to get to and around.

Constanţa

Constanţa, population 356,000, is Romania's main Black Sea port and naval base and a major seaside resort. Its airport, Mihail Kogalniceanu, is just over 20 kilometres from the city centre, has regular connecting flights to Bucharest. The A2 motorway, nicknamed the 'Sun's Motorway' (Autostrada Soarelui), is scheduled for completion in late 2006, linking Constan$a and Bucharest with a 255-kilometre freeway. But don't hold your breath: These forecasts have a habit of being overly optimistic.

Constanţa is steeped in history, having started out in the 7th century BC as the Greek colony of Tomi. A host of smaller coastal resorts surround Constanţa, including Mamaia, Eforie Nord, Eforie Sud, Olimp, Costinesti, Mangalia, Techirghiol, and the exotically named Neptun, Jupiter, and Venus. You find the usual paraphernalia of seaside life, including sailing, wind surfing, camping grounds, restaurants, bars, nightclubs, and cinemas, and a fair amount of warm mud, as the region's waters are renowned for their healing properties.

Brasov

Brasov is 100 kilometres from Bucharest and reachable in a couple of hours by train, car, or coach. English skiers travelling with major tour operators rate Brasov as top value for money. A week's hire of skis and boots, a lift pass, and four hours of lessons a day costs £104 for an adult and £85 for a child.

The Carpathian mountains are beautiful, as are the pine forests. But *Poiana Brasov*, the resort's full name, is a purpose-built resort, so don't expect Swiss-style chalets. The ski area is compact, with just a score of runs. Few – save the 3-kilometre Lupului ('Wolf') black run – are particularly challenging. In the evenings a lively après-ski life is on hand, or you can while away the time listening to gypsy musicians. Check out the Romanian Federation of Skiing Web site (`www.skiresorts.ro`) for more information.

Other possibilities

Romania contains many other beautiful and ancient cities. Cluj-Napoca is the capital city of Transylvania and is the home of Babes-Bolyai University, with over 43,000 students, the largest university in Romania. There are also old

German cities, such as Oradea, with the lowest unemployement rate in Romania (2.2%), Sighisoara, with its medieval citadel, and Sibiu, which is to be the 2007 European City of Culture. Further west lies the city of Timisoara, sometimes referred to as 'Little Vienna' because of its beautiful architecture.

Buying into Romania

Foreigners can buy a residential property in Romania in a personal capacity, but they cannot own the land on which it stands – or indeed any land for that matter. This, however, is little more than a technicality, as foreigners can own land through a company, which you can set up easily at a minimal cost of around £300 along with a similar charge each year for filing relevant documents. Your lawyer can make the necessary arrangements. With Romania's entry to the EU, the government is expected to lift this restriction in so far as it applies to citizens of other EU states.

Find a lawyer who has a good command of both Romanian and English and who works close to where you are buying the property, so that he or she knows the local conditions. Don't just take a lawyer recommended by an estate agent or broker, as they are unlikely to be unbiased. You can find lists of English-speaking lawyers at the Martindale-Hubbell Lawyer Locator (`http://lawyers.martindale.com/marhub`), the International Law Office (`www.internationallawoffice.com/Directory`), the Web site of the British embassy in Bucharest (`www.britishembassy.gov.uk/servlet/Front?pagename=OpenMarket/Xcelerate/ShowPage&c=Page&cid=1048078508528`).

Signing a pre-agreement is binding on both seller and buyer, and any breach of such an agreement can be a costly affair. Disputes concerning pre-agreements are decided under contract law, and the Romanian courts are slow, costly, and stressful. Consider this approach only if you are certain that you want the property and definitely have the necessary funds.

Notaries in Romania perform a neutral role. Their job is to satisfy the state that the buyer and seller are who they claim to be and that the property being sold belongs to the vendor. Notaries are also responsible for collecting any taxes due to the Romanian government that arise from the transaction. Notaries are not there to give advice in any respect, so get your own lawyer to look after your interests. Proceedings in front of a notary are conducted in Romanian with a certified translator present, at your expense, so that the notary can satisfy him- or herself that you understand the proceedings. (See Chapter 4 for more information on hiring a translator.)

The basic procedures for purchasing property in Romania are:

1. **Research the market.**

   Chapter 3 explains how to find properties, but many Romanian estate agents have someone in their offices who speaks English. Start by asking 'Vorbeşte cineva aici engleză?' to see who can translate for you. Using a bit of Romanian should make a favourable first impression, as Romanians, like most people, prefer it if you show some commitment to their country.

   Agents with an extensive range of properties both for sale and to let include the following:

   - **Anglo-Romanian Development** (0870-145-3853; www.anglo-romaniandevelopment.co.uk) has offices in London and Cluj-Napoca in Romania. The business is currently based around finding properties to meet clients' specifications. The site includes bags of information on the property market, but no property database as yet.
   - **Homes in Romania** (+40-723-774-738; www.homesinromania.co.uk), run by Edward Russell, has a database of properties around the country starting from €65,000 (£46,000). The site offers plenty of information on the Romanian property scene, but to view the property database you have to register (free) and get a password.
   - **Nick Intermed** (+40-21-252-2540; www.eimobiliare.ro/en) was founded in 2001. The site features a comprehensive listing of properties for sale and to rent, mostly in and around Bucharest.
   - **Romanian Business Connection** (020-8748-5868; www.romanianhomes.com) has a small selection of properties for sale with prices starting from €10,000 (£6,800), all in the countryside.
   - **Romanian Properties** (0870-224-2942; www.romanianpropertiesltd.co.uk), lists properties for sale throughout Romania, starting from €16,000 (£11,200). Its Web site also has a comprehensive FAQ section that explains in detail the ramifications of buying property in Romania, forming a company, and adhering to local property tax regulations.

Confirm that any estate agent you deal with is a member of a professional association, such as the Federation of Overseas Property Developers, Agents and Consultants (www.fopdac.com) or the National Association of Estate Agents, UK (www.naea.co.uk). The ARAI, the Romanian Association of Real Estate Agencies (+40-21-637-2178; www.arai.ro), has a membership list, code of ethics, and Web site details in English.

2. **Find a property and carry out a thorough inspection.**

   Generally in Romania, buyers do not carry out building surveys on new developments as these properties come with guarantees of quality. Survey old buildings, buildings that you want a mortgage on, and buildings that you have any concerns about. Your estate agent, lawyer, or mortgage provider can put you in touch with a local surveyor. The National Association of Licensed Valuers (Asociatia Nationala a Evaluatorilor Din Romania or ANEVAR) (+40-021-315-6564; `www.anevar.ro`) can put you in contact with a surveyor. You can also search the Royal Institute of Chartered Surveyors' online database (0870-333-1600; `www.rics.org`).

   Alternatively, you can search the Romanian Yellow Pages (`www.yellowpages.ro`), where you can find almost every type of service provider in the property field throughout the country. You can also find furniture suppliers, translators, tax consultants, and more. Of course, you are usually best off finding a professional through the personal recommendation of someone whose judgement you respect. I cover this subject in Chapter 4.

3. **Negotiate and agree on the final price with the current owners.**

   After viewing a property, you can negotiate directly with the owners or through the estate agent. Keep in mind that the total price you pay also includes the following:

   - **Actual cost of buying:** May vary slightly but usually works out to 3–4 per cent of the purchase price (selling costs 8–10 per cent). When VAT is due on new-build properties, buying costs can be significantly higher.
   - **Purchase tax (equivalent of stamp duty):** 2 per cent of the market value, paid through the notary.
   - **Estate agency fees:** Usually 2–6 per cent. Typically the seller pays these fees, but if you employ a local broker to search out properties for you, you may face a bill for 1–3 per cent of the purchase price.
   - **Fees related to forming a company:** Around €360 (£250), including lawyer fees, notary fees, stamp duty, and bank charges.
   - **Notary fees:** €285 (£200).
   - **Legal fees:** Around €1,000–1,500 (£680–1,360).
   - **Annual property taxes:** These are low and unlikely to exceed €200 (£136) a year.
   - **Property management charges:** €300–700 (£206–480) due on new properties in most holiday complexes and apartment blocks, depending on the services you select.

All property transactions have to go through the Romanian land registry and be duly recorded. But the mere registration document is not a guarantee that all is in order and the property is free to be sold. A registered title under the Romanian land registration system comes with a 'health warning': The buyer is responsible for ensuring that the property is not mortgaged, that the current owner has not granted a lease on the property to someone else, and that no other undesirable claims are outstanding. This, in a nutshell, is why you need a lawyer.

4. **Draw up and sign the initial contract.**

   After you and the seller agree to the price, your lawyer draws up an initial sale and purchase contract, which outlines the details and any conditions that must be met before the sale completes (for example, repairs).

   After you and the seller sign the initial contract and you pay a deposit of 10 per cent, the sale is legally binding. You normally have up to three months for your lawyer to complete the property checks with the land registry. Should you fail to go ahead with the purchase for any reason other than that allowed by law, you forfeit your deposit. If you are not going to be in Romania when this contract has to be signed, you need to give your lawyer power of attorney, which I cover in Chapter 4.

5. **Carry out the last checks and sign the final contract.**

   After the initial contract, your lawyer carries out the necessary checks/searches and ensures that the vendor provides all the relevant title documents, permissions for use, and information on any mortgages and loans outstanding.

   Your lawyer needs to see your permission from the local authorities or company registration documents before you sign the final deed of transfer of the property.

   On 4 March 1977, an earthquake registering 7.4 on the Richter scale struck near Vrancea in the eastern Carpathians. Some 35,000 buildings were damaged and more than 1,500 people died. Most of the damage was concentrated in Bucharest, where about 33 large buildings collapsed. Since then, the Romanian government has imposed higher standards for building construction. Your lawyer should check the register made after the earthquake that lists buildings that are considered to be at significant risk.

6. **Pay for your property.**

   You need to pay for your property in Romanian currency. To do this you can either instruct you own bank or buy currency through a specialist company, which may offer more competitive rates (see Chapter 18). You can send your purchased currency directly to your own bank account in Romania or you can use your lawyer's escrow account, a client account in which your funds are kept separate and cannot be accessed without your permission.

7. **Transfer utilities.**

   Registering for electricity, gas, water, telephone, and refuse collection is time-consuming and involves lots of paperwork and many issues. The process can last several days and, in some cases, weeks. Before moving in, deal with everything well in advance, or take into account that for some days you may be in your new home without electricity and gas.

After you register the change of ownership at the land registry, you receive a printout identifying you as the new owner. You can't transfer the utilities until you have this documentation. Also, unless you are fluent in Romanian, transferring utilities is definitely not something to tackle on your own. Your broker can, if asked, arrange for all utility meters to be read and recorded and then transferred to your name. Most brokers expect to do this as part of their general service, but you may still need to ask them to do so.

Getting Settled in Romania

Romania is not too difficult to settle into. The internal transport systems are reliable, inexpensive, and nicely interconnected. While there is no single coordinating body, a handful of Web sites with good information and booking systems in English are available.

Banking is user-friendly, and finding a branch with English-speaking staff, in the cities at least, is not difficult. Health care is poor, even by Eastern European standards, and you need to hunt out English-speaking medics.

In the following sections, I cover all the little details to make your new residence in Romania feel like home.

Taxing matters

Romanian taxes related to property include the following:

- **Capital gains tax:** 16 per cent when selling a property, except if you have owned the property for more than two years – then the rate drops to 10 per cent.
- **Death duties:** The rates of inheritance tax and gift tax range from 0.5 to 20 per cent, depending on the relation between inheritor/donor and acquirer/heir/donee.

- **Double taxation treaties:** Romania has a double taxation treaty with the UK and many other countries, which ensures that you don't pay tax twice on the same income or pay more tax than you should.
- **Individual and business tax:** Since January 2005 Romania has had a flat rate of tax on both personal and business income of 16 per cent – one of the lowest rates and simplest tax systems in Europe.
- **Local taxes:** Several administrative and local taxes cover other matters, such as environmental fees for air and water pollution and waste-deposit fees. These sums are small, and the factor to keep in mind with all such local taxes is that the average monthly wage in Romania is 983 lei (€319.55 or £220).
- **Tax on rental income:** Companies pay tax at a rate of 16 per cent on profit – that is, rent minus expenses including depreciation. Individuals pay tax at 16 per cent on the full rental income but can deduct 25 per cent of rent by way of expenses.
- **Value-added tax:** VAT is charged at 19 per cent, and the registration threshold is 200,000 lei (approximately €57,000 or £39,000).

To find out more about the tax regime in Romania, visit the PricewaterhouseCoopers Web site (`www.pwc.com/ua/eng/main/home/index.html`) and follow the Publications link. You can find a comprehensive and up-to-date guide to tax and much else besides.

Opening a bank account

Opening a current bank account (*Conturi Curente*) requires nothing more complicated than turning up at a bank branch with an identification document such as your passport. You can open accounts in Romanian currency, British pounds, or euros with little or no difficulty. The bank usually expects you to hold a minimum of £35 to keep the account open.

The following banks have full information in English as well as details of their branch networks and opening hours. The Romanian Banking Association (`www.arb.ro`) has an online membership directory listing all the major banks in the country. Additionally, check out Chapter 18, where I cover the whole subject of financing offshore.

- **Alpha Bank** (`www.alphabank.ro`) has a network of 36 branches strategically placed around Romania.
- **Banca Comerciala Romana** (`www.bcr.ro`), one of the country's largest banks, has 411 branches.
- **City Bank Romania** (`www.citibank.com/romania`) has only a handful of branches in Romania, but they are in Bucharest, Constanţa, and Brasov.

- **HVB Bank Romania** (www.hvb.ro) has a private banking facility aimed at high-net-worth individuals. The bank is a bit coy on defining high net worth, but you can be sure it is well below the threshold of £100,000 liquid assets used by some British banks. HVB offers about 40 branches in all the places that matter to property seekers.
- **Raiffeisen Bank** (www.raiffeisen.ro) has 220 branches covering the whole country.

Credit-card fraud is rife in Romania. Never give your card over to anyone such as a waiter or receptionist in a hotel to pay a bill. Keep the card in your sight all the time.

Staying healthy

Medical treatment available in Romania is far from adequate. Expenditure per head on health care is one-twelfth of the EU average and barely half that spent by neighbouring Bulgaria, not exactly the greatest place to get ill in either. Life expectancy in Romania is five years lower than in Western Europe, infant mortality is three times higher, and communicable diseases such as tuberculosis and AIDS, particularly among children, are still a major problem.

Although doctors in Romania are well trained, emergency services are barely adequate and a language barrier can exist if you don't speak Romanian. Health services are currently stretched because everyone in Romania is entitled to full health care. Private facilities, except for foreigners, are virtually unheard of.

You may find that doctors, dentists, hospitals, and ambulances often expect cash payment for their services, so be sure to get receipts. The US embassy in Bucharest (www.bucharest.usembassy.gov) offers information on health-care services in Romania.

If you do not speak Romanian and experience sudden illness or serious injury, call the emergency services on the central number, 112. Operators on this line speak English and, after establishing your problem, they contact appropriate emergency services on your behalf, staying in contact with you to interpret where necessary.

Getting around the country

Romania is a large country, and you have a variety of options to get from town to town and to explore the larger cities. This section covers your travel options within Romania.

Plane

Romania, unlike many Eastern European countries, has two airlines serving most cities with at least a daily service. If time is scarce and money tight, plan your longer internal travel between major cities using one of these airlines.

Tarom (020-7224-3693; `www.tarom.ro`) operates domestic flights between Bucharest and several cities in Romania. CarpatAir (020-8602-7077; `www.carpatair.com`), started up in 1999, has hubs in Timisoara in the far southwest of the country and Cluj in the northwest, and flies to most major Romanian cities and to a few neighbouring countries.

Bus

Buses are usually a fast and comfortable way to get around the country. Autogari (`www.autogari.ro`) operates buses within Romania and to international destinations. It operates hundreds of coaches and travels to 55 cities and towns throughout Romania daily. Its English-language Web site offers timetables, information, fares, and online booking services.

Car

Your British driving licence is valid in Romania, but it must have a photo, otherwise you also need an International Driving Permit. Vehicles in Romania drive on the right. Speed limits are 50 kilometres (31 miles) per hour in built-up areas, 90 kilometres (56 miles) per hour outside built-up areas, and 120 kilometres (74 miles) per hour on motorways. Wearing seatbelts is compulsory, and drinking before driving is absolutely prohibited.

Romanian traffic laws are very strict, and the police can confiscate driving licences for between one and three months and impose on-the-spot fines for a whole range of traffic offences. The Romanian Automobile Association, *Automobil Clubul Roman* (ACR) (+40-1-222-2222 or +40-1-222-1552) offers 24-hour roadside assistance.

Romania's one fully functional motorway, Piteşti–Bucharest, is generally good, as are major urban roads. In the countryside, the roads are often narrow, poorly maintained, and heavily used by agricultural machinery, animals, and pedestrians. Take care driving in Romania and expect to be stopped frequently by police checking documents while hunting for illegal aliens.

Taxi

Taxis are plentiful and usually cheap throughout Romania. However, many Romanian taxi drivers, particularly in Bucharest, are often dishonest and try to take advantage of foreigners. To avoid overcharging, try when possible to book a radio taxi from a reputable firm, such as *Cobălcescu* (Tel: +40 723 009451) or *Cristaxi* (http://www.cristaxi.ro/, tel: (40) 444.15.15) , and pre-negotiate the fare. If you have no choice but to use a taxi in the street, make sure that it is visibly marked with a company or commercial name and has an identification number. Keep a careful eye on the meter to make sure that it isn't set to 'fast forward'.

Taxi fares are rising with the increase in general wages and fuel, but most city trips should still cost no more than 5–10 lei (£1–2). Keep some small notes to pay the fare and don't expect to get any change back.

Info taxi (`www.infotaxi.org`) is an online resource for information on reputable taxi companies. The site offers contact information for services in major Romanian cities.

Train

The Romanian rail network is comprehensive, going to even the most remote locations. InterCity trains, which connect the hubs in Cluj-Napoca, Sibiu, and Bucharest to other major cities, are fast, clean, and reliable. Rapid and Accelerat trains are slower, covering more remote areas. Romanian railways, known as CFR (Societatea Nationale a Cailor Ferate Române), has a timetable and booking system on its Web site (`www.cfr.ro`), which, although far from user-friendly, works if you persevere. Fares are very inexpensive by British standards, with journeys typically costing less than £12 to cross the entire country.

Check the weather forecast before travelling by train. In winter snow storms often cause long delays, and in summer the trains may be forced to run slower as heat deforms the rails.

Metro and tram

Buses, trolleybuses, and trams run in Bucharest and several other major cities and towns.

Bucharest's system is the most comprehensive, with a wide range of options connecting the city's districts and suburbs. Within Bucharest, RATB (`www.ratb.ro`) is the surface transport operator. On its Web site you can find information, timetables, and fares for the city's metros and bus routes.

Chapter 15

Turkey

In This Chapter

- Finding out what Turkey has to offer
- Deciding where to buy
- Ensuring a smooth purchase
- Living comfortably in Turkey

Europe's gateway to Asia is increasingly popular with British house buyers. House prices in Turkey are still as low as they were in Spain 20 years ago, but in some areas they're rising as fast as 30 per cent per year – so it's no wonder that many brokers are touting Turkey as the next property hot spot.

While the promise of a smart investment may lure so many UK tourists and buyers to this huge country, the glorious summers, mild winters, world-class food, and amazing historical sights all combine to make Turkey a gem for sun seekers and house hunters. And when Turkey eventually joins the European Union (EU), tourism is sure to experience a bigger boom than ever, providing additional economic growth for the entire country.

Table 15-1 Turkey's Inflationary Record

Year	*Inflation (%)*
1997	85.7
1998	84.6
1999	64.9
2000	54.9
2001	54.4
2002	45.0
2003	25.3
2004	17.5
2005	11 (estimate)

Fast facts about Turkey

Area: 779,452 square kilometres – three times the size of England and roughly the size of Texas.

Population: 69 million, a quarter of whom are under the age of 14. Over-65s account for 6 per cent, or one in 17 people.

Location: Turkey straddles two continents. Its main borders are on the south of Eastern Europe, making it the final frontier between Europe and Asia. Turkey has land borders with Armenia, Azerbaijan, Bulgaria, Georgia, Greece, Iran, Iraq, and Syria. Its 7,200-kilometre coastline passes through four seas: the Black Sea, the Aegean, the Mediterranean, and the tiny Sea of Marmara.

Language: The official language is Turkish, but significant minorities also speak Kurdish, Arabic, Armenian, and Greek. English is widely spoken around the coast and in the major tourist resorts, as is German and, to a lesser extent, French.

Currency: The Turkish YTL (Yeni Turk lirasi) replaced the old Turkish lira (TL) on 1 January 2005. One YTL, divided into 100 kurus, is equivalent to 1 million lira. One British pound is worth around 2.5 YTL.

Time zone: GMT +2 hours.

European Union membership: Turkey is actively seeking to join the EU and, in the summer of 2005, was given a timetable for achieving membership. The UK is championing the Turkish application, but many other EU members are less enthusiastic. Turkish EU membership is now thought unlikely to happen before 2015.

Emergency services: Emergency switchboard staff rarely speak good English. If you need to ring for help, ask your local contacts or your hotel receptionist to make the call. Emergency phone numbers:

Directory assistance: 118

Fire: 110

Medical aid: 112

Police: 155

Traffic: 154

Visas: If you're a British national staying in Turkey for less then 90 days, you can get a tourist visa by taking your valid British passport to any of Turkey's ports of entry and paying a £10 visa fee in cash. If you plan to stay in Turkey for more than 90 days, you must obtain the appropriate visa beforehand. The Turkish Embassy Web site (`www.turkishconsulate.org.uk`) has all you need to know about the visa process, and an online application process now exists to speed things up.

By air from the UK: British Airways and Turkish Airlines (020-7930-4581, `www.thy,com`) fly direct from London to Istanbul. To fly to Ankara, you need to change at Istanbul. Try also Cyprus Turkish Airlines (020-7930-4581, `www.kthy.net`), Excel Airways (0870-169-0169, `www.xl.com`), and Thomsonfly.

Most of Britain's best-known budget airlines don't fly to Turkey. Until they do, one way to cheat the pricey flights system is to get a cheap flight to Germany's Cologne-Bonn Airport and fly from there to Istanbul or Izmir. Budget airlines flying from the UK to Cologne-Bonn include Germanwings (`www.germanwings.com`), Hapag-Lloyd Express (`www.hlx.com`), and easyJet. From Cologne-Bonn, fly to Istanbul or Izmir with Germanwings, or to Antalya, Dalaman, and Samos with Air Berlin (`www.airberlin.com`).

By train from the UK: From London to Istanbul takes more than 70 hours by train. Contact European Rail for information.

Other routes from the UK: Eurolines runs coach services to Ankara, Istanbul, Izmir, and Kayseri. Alternatively, get a coach or train to Venice and catch a ferry from Venice to Izmir, which takes 63 hours.

Something you'd better know: Turkey, unlike most other countries reviewed in this book, is still struggling to get inflation under control (see Table 15-1). When inflation is rampant, investing in assets such as property becomes more risky. Inflation doesn't directly affect your property after you buy it, but people coming into the market after you may get even more for their money.

Getting to Know Turkey

Turkey has been hitting the headlines lately thanks to the ongoing debate about EU membership. All the political wrangling can make you forget that this country, the biggest economy in Eastern Europe, continues to be a spectacular tourist destination.

In Turkey you find two of the seven wonders of the ancient world: The Temple of Artemis at Ephesus near Izmir, and the Mausoleum of Halicarnassus in Bodrum. The 3000-year-old former capital, Istanbul (once Constantinople), is a vibrant seat of history and culture, full of mosques, churches, and palaces. The ruins of ancient Troy are on the outskirts of Canakkale, and you can explore more recent history on the Gallipolli battlefields.

Beach lovers can also find much to enjoy on Turkey's vast coastline, and nothing is quite as relaxing as a day at one of Turkey's baths or spas.

The Özal government of the 1980s made a huge effort to promote the tourism industry, and it seems to have worked. Visitor numbers have grown year on year, and in 2005 more than 20.5 million tourists flocked to Turkey to see the beautiful ancient ruins and keep the local economy in good shape.

Turkish culture

Living or visiting Turkey today offers an unbelievable variety of attractions:

- **Local treasures:** Museums are something of a new invention in Turkey. Until the 20th century, the only museum in Turkey was the Archaeology Museum, established by a Turkish Sultan to house his own archaeological finds. Even today, tourists used to the museums of London, Paris, and Rome are surprised to find museums thin on the ground in Turkey. Fortunately, plenty of places embody the history and culture of the country as well as any museum: Topkapi Palace, St Sophia, Sultan Ahmed Mosque, the Grand Bazaar, and the Chora Church are all well worth a look.

- **Open-air attractions:** Turkey is full of permanent open-air sites to rival Italy's Pompeii. Gems include the temple and shrines at Ephesus, the exhibition of underwater archaeological finds at Bodrum, and the Ottoman fortress of Rumeli Hisar in Istanbul, which is used as an open-air theatre in the summer.
- **Shopping:** Turkish carpets and kilims (rugs) are known (and bought) around the world, but copperware, textiles, and ceramic tiles are also much in evidence at the vibrant street bazaars. Also head for an auction to snap up old paintings or Ottoman treasures such as silver-worked candelabra and traditional Turkish coffee sets.
- **Entertainment:** The Istanbul music festival and jazz festivals provide weeks of music. Beyond the summer months, there are film festivals and plays to attend.

Climate, weather, and more

Blissful sunshine and an amazingly low cost of living – no wonder so many British people want to buy a place in Turkey. But the sun doesn't always shine here. Turkey is a vast country, so the climate differs depending on where you are. It's possible to be blocked in by winter snow or locked indoors to escape the unbearable summer heat.

Following are some quick insights into the climates of different Turkish regions:

- **Istanbul, the Aegean, and the Mediterranean and coastal regions** are what climate buffs call 'temperate humid'. The weather is similar to that of southern Greece and Italy – long, hot summers and mild, rainy winters, with an average temperature range in January of 3–9°C and in July of 19–28°C. Rainfall averages 700 millimetres annually and is heaviest between October and March. In between, there may be only three or four rainy days each month. In these regions, you should be able to bathe in the sea from April through to mid-October. As a rule of thumb, the further south you go down the coast, the warmer the weather and the longer the sea holds its temperature.
- **Ankara**, Turkey's capital, is located on the central Anatolian plateau (known as 'inland Turkey'). This area has a continental climate, with hot summers and colder winters than the coast or Istanbul. Average temperature ranges from –3 to 4°C in January and from 15 to 30°C in July. Average annual rainfall is 410 millimetres. The Black Sea coast is about 10°C cooler than the Mediterranean and Aegean coasts and experiences more rain. July and August are reliably hot and dry, but other than that the weather is a bit hit and miss. The mountains inland from the Black Sea are snowbound in the winter and all but inaccessible.

Find out more about the climate on the Turkish state meteorological Web site, available in English at www.meteor.gov.tr/indexmaster_eng.htm.

If you feel the ground shaking under your feet in Turkey, head for the nearest wide-open space. The country lies on a boundary of tectonic plates, and it suffered the third-largest loss of life in an earthquake in the past 30 years in September 1999.

About 90 per cent of the country lies within an earthquake zone, so you need to take this into account when looking for property. Your insurance company can give you a clear idea of the risks in your chosen area. Insurers ask whether you want to include earthquake cover in your buildings and contents insurance – expect to pay around double if you want earthquake cover. You also need to think about earthquake risk when weighing the merits of high-rise flats versus villas and older properties versus newer buildings that have been built specially to withstand the shock.

English-language media

English papers are widely available in Istanbul, Ankara, and other Turkish cities served by flights from the UK. Papers tend to arrive up to a couple of days late and cost around 6 YTL (about £2.50). In general, English papers are harder to find during the winter because fewer tourists are around to buy them.

The *Turkish Daily News*, Turkey's first and largest English-language daily, is available year-round in major cities and resort areas. You can read the electronic edition at www.turkishdailynews.com.tr. *Zaman*, a national daily paper similar to the *Daily Mail*, has an English-language Web version at www.zaman.com. Also worth a read for Turkish-related news in English is Dünya Online at www.dunyagazetesi.com.tr (follow the links for the English version).

A number of smaller local English-language papers are springing up in the main tourist areas, such as *Land of Lights* (www.landoflights.net), which serves the British community in and around Fethlye, Marmaris, and Bodrum, on the popular Mediterranean coast. Annual subscription costs £25.

The Directorate General of Press and Information (www.byegm.gov.tr) has summaries of news stories in English as well as links to all the Turkish newspapers, periodicals, television, and radio stations.

You can receive the BBC World Service locally on FM and short wave at various times of the day. Find details on frequencies on the BBC World Service Web site (www.bbc.co.uk/worldservice).

Is Turkey safe for women?

Most women think nothing of going on their own to view property in the UK. But in Turkey, viewing flats and houses is not something that women should do alone.

In some respects, Turkey is a thoroughly modern country. Religious and state affairs have been legally separate for almost 100 years, and women have long been allowed to vote and stand for election.

However, only a quarter of Turkish women go out to work, and most of those are in the agricultural sector. This situation seems reflected in the attitude of many Turkish men towards women. Western women, even when accompanied by men, often receive unwelcome attention. If attention ever goes beyond staring, you can try shouting *utanmaz* ('you shameless'), but you're probably safer to avoid acknowledging strange men or being alone with a man you don't know, particularly in a car.

Tourism

Turkey's tourism industry has been a slow burner. Few Western tourists visited Turkey until the 1980s, when the industry began to take off slowly. The 1990s saw a faster rise in visitor numbers, and now the industry is seeing something of a boom.

Some 20.5 million tourists visited Turkey in 2005, over a million of whom were British. They spent around £6 billion during their stays, so it's no surprise that the Turkish government sees the tourist industry as an important source of income. Hotel, restaurant, and other tourist infrastructures are still largely in local hands, though international property development companies and hotel chains are making an appearance.

Sports

Turkish sporting life is an exciting mixture of old and new:

- **Football:** The Turks are great footballers. The country has hosted some stunning international matches and seen its fair share of British fans.
- **Tennis:** The Istanbul Tennis Cup attracts world-class players.
- **Wrestling:** Fans can watch ancient and modern versions of the sport. Look out for the greased wrestling matches held in early summer near Edirne.

- **Yachting:** The Turkish coast has dozens of marinas with yachts for hire. International yacht races and regattas have become fashionable in recent years.
- **Other sports:** You can enjoy water sports inland as well as on the coast. The lakes at Ataturk Dam at Sanliurfa and Keban Dam at Elazig are used for water sports of all varieties. Also inland you can find trekking, rafting, horseback riding, climbing, and, in the winter months, skiing. Basketball, though in its infancy here, is fast growing – and horse-racing fans can get their fix too.

Talking Business

Turkey is a fast-developing economy. The growth rate of 4.5–6 per cent a year is higher than that of many other Eastern European countries. Turkey can thank its fast-flowing rivers for much of its recent economic success. The rivers power a sizeable hydroelectricity industry and irrigate the land.

Just under half the workforce is in agriculture, but that's changing quickly as Turkey makes the move from agriculture to industry. Industrialisation and privatisation efforts may help Turkey secure membership of the EU. Turkey was the second country to sign a European Community Association Agreement as long ago as 1963, but since then negotiations have moved slowly. In December 2004 the European Council decided that Turkey met the set of basic standards covering democracy, human rights, and respect for minorities, and that it was a suitable candidate to join the EU. The UK is championing Turkey's application, but resistance is coming from other EU members, notably France.

Turkey is a major trading partner of the UK, with bilateral trade running at around £4.5 billion. The UK is the fifth largest investor in Turkey, with over 41 British companies such as BP, Tesco, and Shell established there.

Examining the cost of living

If you want an inexpensive place to live, go for Turkey. Local professional salaries average between £2,000 and £5,000 a year, and the cost of living is appropriately low – so you can potentially get by on a basic British state pension. Unemployment is high and state benefits low, so the cost of living looks set to remain low until EU entry takes place, when things may well change.

Having fun and making money

Judith (28), a Manchester-based representative for a multinational pharmaceutical company, and her partner Thomas (29) recently bought a two-bedroom flat with roof terrace and a large balcony that faces the sea in Bodrum, a pretty town that, despite new development, has kept its original character. They paid £58,000 for their apartment and intend to rent it out during the summer tourist season. They will use it themselves off season during slightly cooler weather and then take time to visit nearby ancient historical sites – such as the ruins of the ancient city of Halicarnassus and the castle built by the Knights of St John of Jerusalem – while renters are staying at their apartment.

Judith and Thomas looked around Spain but could find nothing comparable – even for double what they paid in Turkey. They also looked in on Bulgaria's Black Sea coast (see Chapter 12), where prices were comparable but the summer season about five weeks shorter. Bulgaria and its almost certain entry to the EU still tempted them, but the ease of air travel from and to the UK ultimately swung their decision in Turkey's favour.

Letting out your property

Many people who own property in Turkey choose to rent out their homes to travellers during the high tourist season (see the sidebar 'Having fun and making money in Turkey' for an example).

Many factors drive the amount of money you can make from letting out a property. Some are within your control, such as the decor, fixtures, and extras – swimming pool or air-conditioning – that you include. Some are outside your control but are even more important. Factors working in Turkey's favour include the following:

- **Overseas influences:** The influx of overseas businesses to Turkey is bringing a flood of executives who are accustomed to higher standards of accommodation than is currently available in the country. The Turkish government offers many incentives to foreign companies setting up in Turkey, such as investment allowances and tax exemptions. Istanbul recently beat Moscow, Milan, Paris, Barcelona, and other international cities by being named the best city for development prospects by the Urban Land Institute/PricewaterhouseCoopers. These executives need somewhere in Turkey to stay for the few months or years they are in the country, and only the newer developments are of a satisfactory standard to meet the needs of these clients.
- **Standard of living:** The Turks are getting wealthier and can afford a better grade of property, such as those that were originally built for and sold to UK buyers.

- **Tourism:** Turkey's tourism market is growing fast, and an increasing number of destinations within the country are being served by more airports abroad. This in turn brings in more people searching for more accommodation, leading to opportunities for property owners to rent out their homes to holiday makers.

Renting

Renting in Turkey is not like renting in the UK. Turkish rental properties are usually unfurnished, especially if you're renting for a year or more. And when they say unfurnished, they mean unfurnished – you probably get no light fixtures, curtains, cooker, fridge, carpets, or even a kitchen sink.

To avoid what may be a disappointing trip to your new rented accommodation, always find out in advance exactly what fixtures are included. Landlords expect you to haggle over the rent, much as you do a rug in a bazaar, so get an idea of local rental rates before going into a negotiation. In general, landlords offset your rent against the cost of repairs and basic improvements.

If something looks too good to be true, it usually is

Andrea and David Bishop had hoped to move to Turkey long before their planned retirement dates. Unfortunately, they didn't bargain for the local bureaucratic web they encountered.

In 1995 they bought a small plot of land in an area close to the Aegean coast at a price they thought was an absolute bargain. They made their purchase using correct procedures and with the assistance of a local Turkish lawyer. When they attempted to collect their title deeds, they were advised first that foreigners were not allowed to own land in the region. When they pressed for clarification, they were advised that the law was in fact intended to prevent Greeks who had been expelled from the region from returning to claim their land. Their lawyer advised them to transfer ownership to a Turkish national, whom they knew and trusted, which they did and were duly granted title.

By 2000, after much hard work and £30,000 spent on materials, they finished building a house. But then a year later, the Bishops were taken to court and advised that the land belonged to the Turkish state and their title deed had been cancelled. The new claimant to the land was the Turkish forestry commission. The Bishops have been advised that the Turkish forestry commission is unlikely to claim their title, but they feel highly vulnerable and have a virtually unsellable property on their hands. They have been assured by their lawyer that the situation will eventually be resolved in their favour, but at ages 59 and 63, time is not exactly on their side.

The moral here is that there is no way to eliminate every danger in buying a property anywhere, either at home or overseas. The further a country is from the customs and laws that you are used to, the greater the potential risk. In Chapter 4, I cover the practical steps you can take to minimise both risks and their consequences.

English-speaking estate agents advertise in the *Turkish Daily News* (www.turkishdailynews.com.tr). Also look out for signs saying *Kiralik Ev* (house for rent) or *Kiralik Daire* (apartment for rent).

Weighing pros and cons

Holiday home property prices, according to Turkish estate agents' estimates, are increasing by between 20 and 40 per cent a year, depending on location, facilities, and type of property.

Fortunately, Turkey's property market has low entry costs. You can still locate perfectly habitable homes for as little as £10,000. Low entry costs have opened up the market to many more potential buyers who are unable to invest in mature overseas property markets where costs run to £100,000 and up. Additionally, the costs of owning and running property in Turkey are low, as is the tax on any gain you make.

However, Turkey is also a market with risks. In addition to natural hazards such as earthquakes (see the section earlier in this chapter, 'Climate, weather, and more'), you need to consider the following:

- **EU membership.** If progress towards Turkey's full membership of the E slows down or even stops, the effect in confidence may hurt the property market.
- **Neighbouring nations.** With Iraq, Iran, and Syria on one side (offering the possibility of unrest and terrorism) and the former Soviet Union satellites to the north (polluting the Black Sea and increasing the potential for oil and gas spills), Turkey's economic health may fluctuate greatly over the next several decades.
- **Pollution.** Istanbul, Ankara, Erzurum, and Bursa are all currently dealing with air-pollution problems due to increased fuel consumption for heating and transportation. Public transport is underdeveloped, and a transition to unleaded fuel only began in 2005. Because Turkey has not signed the United Nations Framework Convention on Climate Change or the Kyoto Protocol, it has little international obligation to address air pollution. No tourists like to come to a highly polluted country, so unless Turkey addresses these problems tourism could be adversely affected.

Choosing Where to Buy

Turkey is an absolute giant of a country, and you can easily spend fruitless days and weeks running all over the place investigating remote properties and lots that sound like incredible bargains. However, without a nearby airport or some tourist infrastructure in place, many of these 'bargains' offer little opportunity of producing decent rental yield or property-value growth.

Think about the situation for a minute. You have a lot at stake when buying a property and are probably prepared to hunt high and low for a good deal. By contrast, a potential renter looking to book a couple of weeks' holiday almost certainly doesn't share your sense of adventure. Most tourists stick to places they can get to easily and cheaply. If you're planning to let your property – or just want a better chance for your property to increase in value – investigate established, tourist-friendly destinations first.

In this section, I divide Turkey up into five big chunks. Each area has a mixture of airports with good UK and international connections and can serve as a good hub for local travel. These areas offer the greatest potential for both profit and enjoyment and have an excellent selection of properties across price ranges. Table 15-2 gives an indication of the average prices for two popular property types. Bear in mind that the listed prices are averages, and even within each region prices can vary greatly.

Table 15-2 Average Property Prices Across Regions in Turkey

Region	*Average Price Range for 2-Bedroom Apartment*	*Average Price Range for 3-Bedroom Villa*
Aegean coast (Izmir, Bodrum)	£40,000–65,000	£70,000–100,000
Black Sea coast (Sinot, Trabzon)	£30,000–55,000	£55,000–85,000
Interior (Ankara, Kayseri)	£60,000–110,000	£100,000–150,000
Istanbul	£80,000–130,000	£130,000–220,000
Mediterranean coast (Antalya, Antakya)	£45,000–80,000	£80,000–120,000

Istanbul

If you're in search of city life, Istanbul has instant appeal. As well as being a great place to live, the city's property market is buoyant. Once nearly impregnable due to the surrounding Black, Mediterranean, and Aegean seas, Istanbul now welcomes business investors and pleasure seekers from throughout the globe via aeroplane. With good communication systems internally and externally, great cultural life, fantastic restaurants, and beautiful architecture, the city is, not surprisingly, a major tourist attraction as well as home to 11 million people.

Today, tree-lined boulevards and modern shopping centres give parts of Istanbul a distinctly European feel. By contrast, the Asian-influenced side of Istanbul, with its skyline of domes, minarets, 2,562 mosques, and hectic traffic, exudes the Orient. Yet even in these ancient neighbourhoods, westernisation is encroaching with newly developed office centres in areas such as Altunizade and Kozyatagi springing up to house developing businesses.

New construction is abundant throughout the city. New manufacturing and warehouse facilities have been set up in Tekirdag to the west of Istanbul, Hadimkoy on the European side of Istanbul, and Gebze on the Asian side. The Istanbul Metropolitan Authority has built 16,000 new housing units in the past four years in satellite towns around Istanbul for workers. And according to a report by international property company CB Richard Ellis, the private sector has completed some 1,500 up-market villas on the European side of the city, selling at prices of between $500 and $4,000 per square metre, depending on quality and location.

Istanbul offers cultural opportunities to suit nearly every taste. Cinemas generally have the latest films in their original languages with Turkish subtitles and the city has its own international film festival in April each year. Thanks to government subsidies, attending theatre, opera, and ballet is not a wallet-busting experience compared with London. Check out the Istanbul Festival Web site (`www.istfest.org`) to keep tabs on such events as the international theatre festival and various classical music, arts, and jazz festivals.

If you plan to spend some time in the city and want a good snapshot of the rental market, visit Time Out Istanbul (`www.timeoutistanbul.com`), which offers an invaluable listing of events and activities in the city. Also, Istanbul Life (`www.istanbullife.org`) is packed with details about city life as well as information on property. Istanbul has a bi-monthly publication known as *The Guide*, published in English and available in many hotels throughout the city.

The Black Sea coast

Jason is said to have led his Argonauts along the Black Sea coast on his quest for the Golden Fleece. Today, the 1,500-kilometre stretch of land is ripe for a quest of a different kind – property development.

As yet the region is seriously underexplored and underrated. True, it is not so easy to get to as the flashier Aegean and Mediterranean coasts, but that is set to change. The Turkish government is investing serious money in expanding and improving the main highway to and through this region, making travel easier for tourists and business people. Although Istanbul is the closest direct air link to the UK at present, a new airport at Samsun (halfway along the coast) can handle larger planes, and the regional airport at Trabzon provides flight support at the Georgian end of the coast. The Black Sea has also taken on new strategic importance as an energy lifeline for the West with Turkey offering alternative routes for the oil and gas resources of the Caspian Sea basin to reach Western Europe.

The culture, cuisine, and dialect along the Black Sea are different from the rest of Turkey – and so is the climate. If you're interested in something other than baking in the hot sun, this region has masses to offer. The region is cooler and wetter than the other coasts, and the sea is cooler too. The sky is often overcast, but the land is green and fertile most of the year and the climate is warm enough for tea, hazelnuts, tobacco, and corn plantations to flourish.

If you have a more adventurous nature, the mountains parallel to the coast offer thrilling climbing. Winter sports enthusiasts enjoy skiing in the Bolu mountains, 250 kilometres from Istanbul, in a resort designed by an Austrian ski expert. The nearby Bolu-Seven lakes and the Artvin-Tortum waterfall are ideal for hiking. The Coruh river, one of the fastest flowing in the world, provides challenging rafting along its 466-kilometre route from the Mescit mountains (3,225 metres) to the Black Sea.

Start your property search start in Trabzon, on the western edge of the Kackar mountain range and at the far end of the Black Sea coast. Trabzon has dozens of churches, mosques, old houses, and cobble-stoned streets, as well as an airport with connections from Istanbul.

Work your way westwards along the coast, and visit Samsun. With a population of about 350,000, this regional capital features a good airport, old Greek houses and villas, and acres of flowers and fruit trees. The fortified town of Sinop is about 50 kilometres away.

Amasra, built on a peninsula with two prominent bays and within five hills, boasts a dramatic fortress. The coastal roads to the east and west are, to say the least, indifferent, so Amasra gets only a moderate number of summer visitors, making it ideal if you like peace and quiet.

Other towns worth a look include Ordu, Giresun, Rize, and Bartin with its traditional wooden Turkish houses. Another 80 kilometres west is Zonguldak, with beautiful beaches in Kopuz and Uzunkum.

The Aegean coast

The Aegean coast of Turkey runs from Marmaris in the south to the opening of the Dardanelles at Canakkale, close to Truva (also known as Troy, which was immortalised in Homer's *The Iliad*).

From a property-hunting perspective, the region can be divided into three sectors: The northern Aegean, the Aegean interior, and the southern Aegean.

Northern Aegean

The northern Aegean remains Turkey's secret paradise – full of sandy beaches, historic towns, clear Aegean seas, mountains, and olive groves, and reflecting thousands of years of civilisation. It has some of the cheapest property for sale in Turkey, with prices in this area two or three years behind those in the more developed areas.

What has held the region back is the limited number of direct air links with the UK. But if you don't mind travelling via Istanbul, this lack of air-travel options need not be a problem. Izmir has direct flights to the UK and is only 45 minutes from Istanbul by air. Additionally, the Canakkale coastal highway carries regular overnight buses from Istanbul and features a good train service. The Bandirma ferry provides a five-hour ride across the Marmara sea, and Turkish Maritime Lines operates overnight car ferries from Istanbul to Izmir several times a week, as well as a crossing from Venice in the summer and autumn months.

The northern region has much the same climate as the southern areas, with hot summers (frequently around 28–30 °C), little rain, and a gentle breeze (*Meltem*) which blows in from the forested Kaz mountains national park. The region's geography and history are every bit as appealing too.

Towns to explore for property include Foca, a picturesque seaside town set around two arching bays, known locally as Big Sea and Little Sea. The Siren Rocks made famous in Homer's *Odyssey* can be seen across the bay, and the area features some excellent restaurants and uncrowded beaches. Bergama, one of Turkey's finest archaeological sites, Dikili, a regular stop for cruise liners, and Ayvalik, a small, delightful port, are all worthy of exploration, as is the Gulf of Edremit, referred to locally as the Olive Riviera. The gulf, which is reputed to have been home to the world's first beauty contest, is dotted with small seaside resorts such as Kucukkuyu, Altinoluk, Akcay (with thermal springs), Edremit, and Oren. All feature beautiful beaches.

The Aegean interior

If you are less interested in the beach life, the Aegean interior may appeal to you. The region's numerous hot springs, which claim medicinal proprieties as well as relaxation, now feature luxury spas and resorts and vineyards.

Towns to investigate here include Manisa, with well-preserved examples of Seljuk and Ottoman architecture, Gordes and Usak, particularly known for fine carpets, and Kutahya, which produces exquisite ceramics.

Although property here is even cheaper than on the northern coast, keep in mind that it may not appeal as much to the rental market as it does to you. For the time being, your rental income may be much lower.

The southern Aegean

The southern Aegean is the region's tourist honey pot. Served by airports at Izmir, Bodrum, and Dalaman, all the coastal towns are within a handful of travelling hours from the UK. Weekending in your property here is not out of the question.

However, the region is already beginning to show some signs of being overexploited by less than scrupulous property developers. High-rise apartment blocks of limited appeal and low build quality have been encouraged by notoriously lax planning laws.

Start your research at Kusadasi, once a small fishing village and now one of the busiest resort towns on the southern Aegean coast. Aside from its splendid coastal scenery, it is next door to the ruins of Ephesus, the biggest and best-preserved ancient city in Turkey and considered to be one of the Seven Wonders of the Ancient World.

Marmaris, your next port of call, is either the end of the Aegean coast or the start of the Mediterranean, depending largely on what the local estate agents believe will have the greatest appeal. Marmaris vies with Bodrum in the nightlife stakes but wins by a mile in terms of its marinas. The town has a friendly almost Bohemian feel when packed with summer tourists. It somehow balances its ancient character – exotic bazaars and the wailing cry of the muezzin – with thoroughly modern pleasures such as scantily clad sunbathers, yachting, nightclubs, and discos. As arguably the country's premier yachting centre, the city is a good jumping-off point for the Greek island of Rhodes, where ferries and hydrofoils call several times a day.

Altinkum, meaning appropriately enough 'golden sand' in Turkish, is another busy town fast becoming a British 'colony', with restaurants and bars to cater for tourists' needs.

If Kusadasi, Bodrum, Marmaris, and Altinkum all sound too busy for your tastes – and they can definitely be near nightmares in the summer – consider visiting Içmeler, Bozburun, Datça, Golenye Icmeleri, and Yenihisar, which are all less touristy and much smaller. Inland small cities and towns such as Mugla and Denizli, which has an airport with a daily flight to Istanbul, offer some of the delights of the Aegean but with a more commercial leaning. Denizli, for example, has a number of spectacular towns nearby, including Pamukkale, a UNESCO World Heritage Site with an open-air amphitheatre dating from the 2nd century BC.

Unfortunately, the southern Aegean has more risks than being overdeveloped. In January 2005, a moderate earthquake (5.1 on the Richter scale) struck Turkey's southern Aegean coast. The only reported casualty was a man taken to hospital in Marmaris with minor injuries after jumping from a balcony in panic. The event was a reminder that quakes are frequent in Turkey, much of which lies atop the active North Anatolian fault.

The Mediterranean coast

In Turkish, the Mediterranean is called Akdeniz, or 'white sea'. Its 1,600-kilometre coastline is stunningly beautiful for much of its length. With the Taurus mountains as a backcloth, the region has a rugged feel outside of the main towns. The weather is reliably excellent, but high-rise hotels line most of the beaches on the coast. The airport at Antalya is now busier in the summer months than either Istanbul or Ankara. Airports at Dalaman, Antalya, and Izmir also provide good direct links with the UK.

From a property-hunting prospective, confine your search to the first couple of hundred miles, which is both the most developed and the most accessible. This short stretch of the Mediterranean neighbouring the Aegean is referred to as the Turquoise Coast (after the colour of the sea) and the Turkish Riviera.

Fethiye

Start looking for property in and around Fethiye. The old town was mostly destroyed in an earthquake in 1957, but a newer and still reasonably attractive town has replaced it. The houses of the old town look down on the little port from a hill crowned with a fortress built by the Knights of Rhodes. You can find dozens of local estate agents and hundreds – if not thousands – of properties for sale. While locals have begun to call this highly developed area 'the concrete coast', the views out to sea are still gorgeous. Many of the popular beaches are standing room only in the peak months, so ask locals to find the less crowded areas.

Ölüdeniz and surrounding areas

Ölüdeniz, reputed to be the most famous beach in Turkey, is near the hilltop towns of Ovacik, Hisarönü, and the suburbs of Karagoz and Çalis. This incredibly attractive area is reputed to have nearly 3,000 British property owners and more than 15,000 additional foreign owners, so you certainly won't be alone. The area is awash with historic sites and all the usual seaside attractions. Nearby Baba Dag is among the top five destinations in the world to paraglide, while Turkey's first long-distance footpath, the Lycian Way, offers spectacular scenery between Fethiye and Antalya.

Antalya

Antalya, a city with palm-lined boulevards, an internationally acclaimed marina, and more than 1 million people is a – some say *the* – major tourist centre in Turkey. The city offers dozens of hotels, restaurants, bars, nightclubs, shops, museums, and cinemas showing films in English, and hosts sporting events such as international beach volleyball, triathlons, golf tournaments, archery, tennis, and canoeing competitions. Two of the country's best ancient sites, the city of Perge and the acropolis at Termessos, are nearby, as is the sunken city of Simena. For those less culturally inclined and who want a day off the beach, the Aqualand water park near Konyaalti offers family-friendly excitement.

Alanya

Alanya, 130 kilometres further round the coast, is also worth your attention. Serviced by the airport at Antalya, the city has a population of around 300,000, which doubles in the summer as tourists flood in to bask on its two long sandy beaches. Aside from droves of attractions such as fortresses, caves, and some unspoilt villages in the nearby Taurus mountains, the city hosts a number of alternative international sports events, such as swimming marathons, mountain cycling, beach volleyball, and beach football.

The country between Fethiye and Alanya is accessible, well populated by tourists, and experiencing considerable business expansion. The prospects for discerning property buyers are as good as anywhere in Turkey. Having said that, the area is closer to saturation than anywhere else in Turkey, so you must do your research on the ground thoroughly and negotiate the best price you can. (I cover these topics in Chapters 3 and 4.)

Other cities worth considering

If you're more adventurous – or prepared to take more of a gamble – take your research as far on as Silifke, Mersin, and Tarsus. None of these towns has an airport, but all are within an hour or so of Adana, Turkey's fourth largest city and reputedly a boom town. The Adana Sakirpasa international airport has some direct flights to the UK in the peak summer months, but for the rest of the year plan to fly through Istanbul to Adana. Although the beaches and countryside are every bit as attractive and interesting as the rest of the Mediterranean coast, the region is less accessible from the UK, offers fewer properties, is less well known to tourists, and is near the Syrian border.

Northern Cyprus is only 150 kilometres away. Fast ferries and planes fly there daily, so also consider Cyprus as an option after you get this far down the coast.

Inner Turkey

A vast swathe of Turkey, stretching from Ankara to and around Kayseri, is virtually unknown to property hunters. This inner region is home to several ancient capital cities, including the following:

- **Gordion**, the Phrigian capital 100 kilometres west of Ankara. Gordion is where Alexander the Great is reputed to have cut the Gordion knot, as well as where the legendary King Midas worked his magic with gold.
- **Hattusas**, home to the Hittites, two hundred kilometres north east of Ankara based around the village of Bogazkale. The Hittites were a superpower of the Ancient World, along with the Egyptians and Babylonians.
- **Konya**, the capital of the Selcuk Empire and 260 kilometres from Ankara, is where the Sufi order known as the Whirling Dervishes began.

While the region is strong in history, it is short on beaches and access points. The Black Sea coast is 3–5 hours away, and the Mediterranean 5–11 hours away. The two largest airports, in Ankara and Kayseri, have good connections with Istanbul, and a sleeper train runs from Istanbul to Ankara. But after that, you must resort to buses, taxis, or hired cars to drive the often four- to six-hour hauls in and around the region.

Ankara

Ankara, Turkey's second largest city and its capital, is the best place to start your property hunting in inner Turkey. Famous for its long-haired goats that produce Angora wool, the city offers a variety of opportunities for buying properties due to its location as a jumping-off point for regional tourist activities, its large student population, and its numerous governmental and civil service activities.

With a population of more than 5 million – equivalent to Manchester, Birmingham, Glasgow, and Edinburgh combined – Ankara is a thoroughly modern European city with tinges of the Orient thrown in for good measure. Ankara's old quarter, erected around the ruins of an ancient citadel, has narrow twisting streets and is crammed full of buildings. The new city, laid out in 1928, is spacious and well planned, with broad boulevards, reminiscent of Paris.

The streets of Kizilay and the bars of Sakarya are packed with university students most of the year. All arms of the military are based here, and Saturday afternoon sees Genclik Park full of uniformed troops promenading alongside droves of language school students. Ankara's thriving expat population is made up largely of the commercial and diplomatic communities. The city's range of cultural activities – cinema, theatre, music, and so forth – is similar to Istanbul but on a more modest scale.

Cappadocia

If you are looking for something with more in-your-face tourist appeal, head for Cappadocia, located in central Anatolia between the cities of Nevsehir, Nigde, and Kayseri.

Millions of years ago, violent eruptions of the volcanoes Mt Erciyes and Mt Hasan covered the surrounding plateau with soft volcanic rock. Over the centuries, wind and rain have moulded the rock into hundreds of bizarrely shaped pillars, cones, and 'fairy chimneys' in a kaleidoscope of colours. These unusual natural structures, which have been made into cave churches, monasteries, and even private dwellings, are popular tourist destinations. Sightseers traipse around the area in their hundreds of thousands, trekking, bird watching, shopping, and visiting unique sites such as the underground cities of Kaymakli, Derinkuyu, Mazi, and Ozkaynak.

Increasingly, these tourists are staying in holiday houses and rental apartments owned by German, American, French, and now a few British investors. But don't fool yourself into thinking that Cappodocia has the family appeal of the coastal resorts. Although you should be able to net a modest rental return on a property here, the demand is still low. However, the potential exists for some serious capital growth over the long term.

Other towns

Other inner Turkey locations to research include the following:

- **Göreme**, home of the main cave-dwelling population. Citizens in this town, despite bureaucratic pressure, are sticking with their thermally efficient homes.
- **Nevşehir**, a good transport hub but otherwise dull.
- **Uçhisar, Ürgüp, and Ihlara**, and the other towns along the old *Silk Road* – the route that has taken exotic Asian products to Europe for centuries – are all worth a look.

Get a bird's-eye view of the region and combine the business of house hunting with the pleasure of sightseeing by taking a hot-air balloon ride in and around any of these locations.

Skiing areas

Turkey may not immediately come to mind when you think of skiing but there are places where you can go to ski:

- **Ilgaz** (2000 metres), 250 kilometres north of Ankara in Kastamonu province, features a popular ski centre.
- **Kartalkaya** (1800–2210 metres), about 80 kilometres from Ankara off the main Istanbul–Ankara highway, is a busy weekend ski destination.

Elmadag, just 23 kilometres from Ankara, also has a small ski area but is not worth a special trip unless you are staying in the capital.

- **Sarikamis and Palandöken** (2200–3100 metres) offer some of the longest and most difficult courses and best snow conditions in Turkey. You can reach both cities from Istanbul and Ankara by flying to either Erzurum or Kars and then taking a short drive. Kars has the distinction of being Turkey's coldest town, where temperatures have been known to plunge to –30 °C.
- **Uludag** (1750–2547 metres), a few hours from Istanbul, is known in mythology as the place from which the gods watched the Trojan War. Uludag can be reached by cable car from Bursa and provides around 120 days' skiing a year. It gets very busy at the weekends with city dwellers heading out for a few days' exercise.

Buying into Turkey

Foreigners must navigate numerous restrictions when buying property in Turkey. At first sight the regulations may seem onerous, but in practice they are not that much of a problem.

Foreigners cannot buy or rent properties in Military Forbidden Zones and Safety Regions. These restrictions apply to a fairly small area, mainly on Turkey's borders where disputes are likely to flare up.

Despite a Turkish government in July 2005 ruling that the restrictions that prohibit foreign nationals from buying in some parts of the country were unconstitutional, the law remains unchanged. The areas most likely to be prohibited cover properties within the boundaries of a village with more than 2,000 registered inhabitants, and land or farms larger than 74 acres. If you are looking at such properties, until a new law is ratified and approved by the parliament to remove the prohibition, any applications made by foreigners to the Turkish land registry office cannot be processed. No timescale has been given for resolving the matter, but the Web site of the British embassy in Turkey (`www.britishembassy.org.tr`) keeps a watching brief on the subject.

As long as you work with a reputable lawyer, you can minimise your chances of falling foul of these modest restrictions on foreign ownership. However, you must remember that Turkey is not free from corruption or bureaucratic muddle. While this state of affairs is frustrating, it is also part of what is keeping down property prices.

Find a lawyer who has a good command of both Turkish and English and who is independent of the estate agent or developer that you are dealing with. Ideally, the lawyer should be based somewhere near the property you are investigating. This ensures that the lawyer is well versed in local matters such as prospective building activities that could interfere or even enhance the value of the property, for example new developments planned or roads to be built. You need to find the lawyer before you make an offer on a property so that they can be involved in every stage of the transaction. Check out lists of English-speaking lawyers at the Martindale-Hubbell Lawyer Locator (`http://lawyers.martindale.com/marhub`), the International Law Office (`www.internationallawoffice.com/Directory`), or Legal500.com (`www.icclaw.com`).

You can also find lawyers on the Web site of the British embassy in Ankara (`www.britishembassy.org.tr`) by selecting 'Services' and then searching for English-speaking lawyers. I also cover finding a lawyer in Chapter 4.

The basic steps in the property-purchasing process are:

1. **Research the market.**

   Chapter 3 explains general strategies to locate properties. You can find a number of English-speaking estate agents who have offices in Turkey, including the following:

   - **Ayvalik Property** (01622-764200; `www.ayvalikproperty.com`) has offices in Ayvalik, on the Aegean coast, and in the UK.
   - **Tapu** (the Turkish word for a property deed) (+90-252-618-0236; `www.tapu.co.uk`) is run by Jonathan Bowker. The site includes links to a database of 25,000 properties all over Turkey.
   - **Turkish Holiday Homes** (020-8509-3691; `www.turkishholidayhomes.com`) has a helpful Web site and frequently runs inspection tours and exhibitions in the UK.

2. **Find a property and carry out a thorough inspection.**

   If you are buying a new property, you can expect to see a *habitation certificate* that certifies that the property complies with the local regulations. Properties are not sold subject to survey, and you are unlikely to persuade a vendor to accept any such get-out clause. For resale purposes, have a survey carried out. The survey can take between 7 and 10 days and costs between £350 and £1,000, depending on the size of the building.

   In Chapter 4 I cover finding a surveyor and describe the sort of preliminary work you can carry out yourself to ensure that you are satisfied with the property before spending a lot of money on professional advisers.

3. **Negotiate and agree the price.**

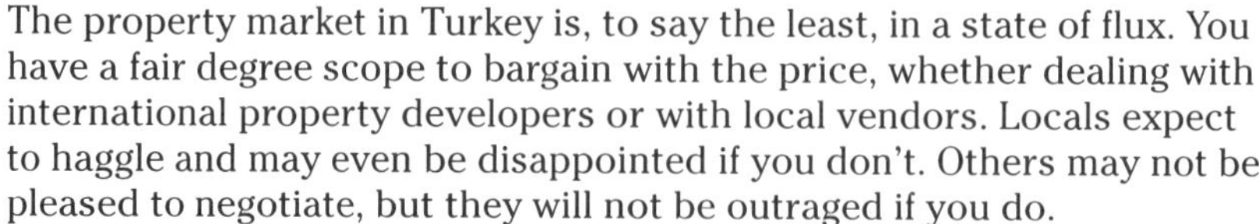

The property market in Turkey is, to say the least, in a state of flux. You have a fair degree scope to bargain with the price, whether dealing with international property developers or with local vendors. Locals expect to haggle and may even be disappointed if you don't. Others may not be pleased to negotiate, but they will not be outraged if you do.

Keep in mind that the total price you pay needs to include the following:

- **Annual property taxes:** 0.1 per cent for buildings and 3 per cent for land developments. New properties are exempt from the annual property tax for five years.
- **Earthquake insurance (compulsory on taking title deed):** Approximately £70.
- **Estate agency commission:** The standard rate charged to the buyer is 3 per cent.
- **Land registration, including maps:** Approximately £550.
- **Legal costs:** Around 0.5 per cent, subject to a minimum charge of about £750.
- **Notary charges:** £100–250.
- **Photographs:** Approximately £20.
- **Purchase tax (stamp duty):** 0.3 per cent.
- **Sworn translator:** Approximately £50.

You may also incur some minor administration charges for various items of paperwork.

4. **Draw up the contract and pay the deposit.**

After you agree the price, the purchase can proceed in one of two ways: In Turkey you can sign the contract in front of a notary public or in the land registry office (*Tapu Dairesi*). Both are perfectly legal ways to proceed. While the latter is more common for Turkish buyers, as a foreign buyer you should follow the advice of your lawyer.

Along with signing a preliminary contract that binds both parties to the deal, you pay a deposit at this stage, usually around 10 per cent of the purchase price. The deposit should be paid through your lawyer, who can hold the money until he or she is satisfied that it is safe to proceed. After your deposit is paid to the seller, the *ownership document* is sent to the city council, which in turn sends it to the Army Office. In Turkey, you must acquire the army's permission before the purchase can be completed. This entire process can take five to eight weeks, and sometimes a little longer when a backlog of applications exists.

During the purchasing process, you must provide the local Title Deeds Registry Office (*Tapu Sicil Mudurlugu*) with the following documents:

- Title deed or a document indicating the property's exact location (plot or parcel number).
- Your passport and/or ID card.
- Two recent passport (4 x 6 centimetres) photos of you.
- Power of attorney giving your lawyer authority to act for you. (For more on power of attorney, see Chapter 4.)
- Passport and/or ID card of your agent if power of attorney is in effect.
- Two recent passport photos of your agent if power of attorney is to be used.

5. **Complete the purchase and pay for your property.**

   After military clearance is received and – if the property is being built – after the construction is completed, you can complete the purchase and have the deed registered in your name. To do this, you or your professional adviser need to do the following:

   - Register in the Turkish tax office and receive a Turkish tax number. This requires only proof of identity. Your lawyer can do this on your behalf with very little pain.
   - Have the transfer of title made in the Land Registry Office.
   - Register as new owners of the property in the municipality.
   - Prepare and submit your estate tax statement to the Turkish tax office.
   - Have all utilities (electricity, water, telephone) registered in your name after you take over the property.

Getting Settled in Turkey

Plenty of people, including your estate agent and lawyer, have something to gain by smoothing your path when buying your property, but they may not have *only* your interests at heart. Although some matters, for example capital gains tax, may seem a distant concern, the actions you take early on can significantly mitigate future pain. This section covers several of the most important matters to address as you establish yourself in Turkey.

Taxing matters

Turkish taxes that you should consider while owning a property and or living in Turkey include the following:

- **Business tax:** This is at a flat rate of 35 per cent of profits, such as the profit from renting out your property. This profit is the rental income minus any expenses incurred in keeping the property in a rentable condition.
- **Capital gains tax:** Capital gains made from the sale of a property are taxable in Turkey if the owner is a company. For individuals, the tax, after charging for renovation and the like, is at your individual income-based rate, unless you have owned the property for at least one year. After that, there is no capital gains liability in Turkey. If you are a UK resident (see Chapter 17 for more on residency), you may be liable for capital gains tax in the UK.
- **Individual tax:** If you earn money in Turkey – whether from employed or self-employed activities or from renting out property – you are liable to pay tax in Turkey. If you are resident in Turkey for tax purposes, you must also pay Turkish taxes on your worldwide income. (In Chapter 17, I explain the rules on residency.) Non-residents are liable to pay tax on earned income at rates starting at 15 per cent on sums up to 6,600 YTL, progressively rising to 35 per cent on sums of 78,001 YTL and over. (The top rate rises to 40 per cent if the income comes not from employment but from investments or property rents.)
- **Value-added tax:** The general rate of VAT is 18 per cent, but it varies for some items.

Turkey has a double taxation treaty with the UK and with many other countries, which ensures that you don't end up paying tax twice on the same income – or pay more tax than you should. I cover double taxation treaties in Chapter 16.

To find out more about the tax regime in Turkey, visit the World Wide Tax Web site (`www.worldwide-tax.com/turkey/indexturkey.asp`), which provides a comprehensive up-to-date guide.

I cover finding tax advisers in chapter 17.

Opening a bank account

Opening a personal bank account in Turkey is essential for all property-related activities. You can open accounts in both Turkish currency and a foreign currency such as euros or sterling. Most likely, you need a current account (*vadesiz*) for regular local transactions and a sterling account for transferring larger sums for buying property. Formalities are fairly simple and the costs negligible.

To open an account, you need your passport, proof of a local address, and a tax identification number, which you or your lawyer can obtain on presentation on proof of identity. Some UK and international banks have branches in most of the key cities in Turkey. English-speaking staff are typically available.

Banks are open from 8.30am until 12 noon and from 1.30pm until 5pm, Monday to Friday. Some banks are open during lunch hours. Exchange offices are usually open longer. Automated teller machines (ATMs) are almost everywhere in Turkey, so day-to-day access to cash is generally not a problem.

Credit cards can be used with relative ease in Turkey for major purchases, but smaller shops and most traders still deal only in cash. Fraud is fairly rampant, so keep a close watch on your credit-card statements.

Staying healthy

Turkey's health-care system is, in the main, not as advanced as those in Western European countries. Although the situation is improving, the funds allotted for medical and health-care resources are insufficient. The quality of Turkish hospitals varies tremendously, and good medical care may be difficult to find anywhere outside the major cities. Even if you have health insurance – and here you certainly should – many doctors and hospitals expect payment in cash.

Istanbul and Ankara have newer, private facilities with fairly modern equipment and training programmes, including the International Hospital (82 Yesilkoy 34800, Istanbul; +90-212-663-3000). However, these facilities may still not be able to address all serious medical conditions. For life-threatening medical problems, you should consider getting to a country with state-of-the art medical facilities.

If you are on medication, keep a six-month supply on hand as local pharmacies may not be able to fill certain prescriptions reliably.

For a list of hospitals, doctors, and dentists in Istanbul, Ankara, Adana, and Izmir, visit the Web site of the US embassy (`turkey.usembassy.gov`). The Web site of the British embassy in Turkey, which you can access through the Foreign and Colonial Office site (`www.fco.gov.uk`), has a more extensive list of hospitals around the major tourist areas. I cover health-care choices in detail in Chapter 19.

Getting around

Turkey is a large country that requires residents to use a variety of transportation methods to tour the region and conduct daily business. This section covers your major transportation options.

You can find out more about travelling around Turkey on the Turkish Ministry of Culture and Tourism Web site or through its UK office (020-7629-7771; www.tourismturkey.org).

Plane

Onur Air (+90-212-663-9176; www.onurair.com.tr), the local budget airline, flies between Istanbul and Antalya, Bodrum, Diyarbakir, Erzurum, Gaziantep, Izmir, Kars, Kayseri, Malatya, Samsun, and Trabzon.

Turkish Airlines (020-7766-9300 in the UK, +90-212-663-6300 in Istanbul; www.turkishairlines.com) provides regular domestic service within Turkey from Istanbul, Izmir, Ankara, Dalaman, Antakya, Adana, Bursa, Denizli, Kayseri, Samsun, Erzurum, Erzican, Mayatya, Diyarbakir, Urfa, Elazıg, Kars, and Van.

Walk-on flights can be problematic during peak tourist periods and *bayrams* (religious holidays), so book at least a couple of weeks ahead where possible.

Train

Turkey has 6,340 miles of rail track, much of which was built by the Germans during a long period of mutual cooperation. The routes between the main cities can be reasonably quick and comfortable, but off those routes buses are generally considered more comfortable, faster, and cheaper.

The Istanbul–Ankara sleeper rail service is a good alternative to flying. A single-cabin sleeper costs around £20, and a three-course meal in the dinning car with wine adds another £5 to the cost.

Turkish Railways, Türkiye Cumhuryeti Devlet Demiryollan (TCDD), offers routes within the country. Its Web site (www.tcdd.gov.tr) provides train times and fares, but only in Turkish. For English-based help, visit www.turkeytravelplanner.com, where you can find a helpful dictionary of key words and phrases needed to interrogate the timetable and booking service, along with direct links to the key parts of the TCDD Web site. The Man in Seat Sixty One (www.seat61.com/Turkey2.htm) also provides a good overview of the whole rail network and the trains and facilities on offer.

Bus

Buses are the transport method of choice for most people because they are extremely economical. Expect to pay between £1 and £2 per journey hour as a rough rule of thumb. The major regional transport hubs are all connected with regular day or night services from which you get on to smaller buses until you get to your destination.

While Turkey has around 12 bus companies, the following offer the most comprehensive services and have minibuses at major destinations to collect and deliver passengers to outlying regions. They also have English-language Web sites. These companies and most others have counters at local bus stations (*otogar*) and offices around towns and cities.

- **Dolmus** is a minibus company running set routes within cities and towns, and between cities and nearby towns and villages. The fares are very cheap – 50p or so – and the minibuses are plentiful. Dozens of routes are covered all over cities and big towns. The minibuses have their destinations written on the front of the vehicle. Dolmus means 'filled', which is what it needs to be before it departs on its route. They pack as many people in as they can, so don't expect much comfort.
- **Ulusoy** (+90-212-444-1888; `www.ulusoy.com.tr/eng`) runs buses from Istanbul.
- **Varan** (+90-212-444-8999; `www.varan.com.tr/english/default.asp`) runs buses from Istanbul.

An oddball worth considering if money is tight and you want to scoot around as much of the country as possible is the Fez (+90-212-516-9024; `www.feztravel.com`). These hop-on, hop-off buses, pitched at budget travellers and backpackers, cover virtually the whole country every second day in an anticlockwise direction from Istanbul. You buy a pass that is valid from 25 April until 27 October for around £129. You can start anywhere you like around the circuit. Just let the service know where you want to start your travel. Fez buses are fully air-conditioned, non-smoking, 15- to 46-seater coaches with onboard public address systems and stereos. There is an English-speaking guide on each coach who can fill you in on information as you go along. Booking accommodation along the way is down to you.

Taxi

Using Turkish taxis can be a challenging experience. You can be certain of being taken for a ride in every sense of the word, as many taxi drivers rely on your ignorance of the geography to clock up a few extra miles. Make sure that the meter is running. If you are travelling between 7am and midnight, check that the less expensive day rate (*gunduz*) is alternately flashing with the metered fare – less scrupulous drivers push the night-rate (*gece*) button to increase the fare. The fares are not very expensive – in fact they are positively parsimonious by UK standards.

Boat

Car ferries can save you days of driving, and some throw in a virtual mini-cruise along the Turkish coasts into the bargain. Ferries operate from Istanbul to

Izmir and from Istanbul to Trabzon. You can also take a hydrofoil from Istanbul to Yalova, for Bursa.

You can go further afield if you feel like exploring more while you are in the region. Frequent ferries go to Turkish Cyprus from lots of ports on the Mediterranean coast. A weekly ferry runs from Istanbul to Odessa in Ukraine and to Venice and Brindisi in Italy. For online timetables, prices, and reservations go to www.ido.com.tr or www.tdi.com.tr.

Chapter 16

Ukraine

In This Chapter

- Understanding the potential in Ukraine
- Discerning where you want to look
- Going through the purchase process
- Making the purchase work for you

Ukraine is changing fast. Since 2000, the country has made rapid strides to get closer to the European Union (EU):

- In September 2005, the visa restrictions that made travel difficult were swept away, and EU citizens can now stay for up to 90 days without restriction.
- The economy, after decades of stagnation, is now growing at 12 per cent, six times faster than the economies of the other big countries of Europe and faster even than that of China.
- Travel to, from, and around the country is easy, accessible, and affordable.
- New property laws that ensure security of title and make transactions more transparent have been brought into force.

All these factors make Ukraine more appealing to property hunters and tourists than ever before.

Of course, parts of the country have long appealed to visitors: Kiev, Odessa, and Crimea have thriving tourist markets, and their property sectors have been showing signs of life for a few years, thanks in the main to Russian roubles.

Fast facts about the Ukraine

Area: 603,700 square kilometres, slightly larger than France and about twice the size of the UK.

Population: 47.43 million.

Location: The second largest country in Europe after Russia. Ukraine borders Belarus, Hungary, Moldova, Poland, Romania, Russia, and Slovakia. It has a coastline of 2,782 kilometres divided between the Baltic and the Sea of Azov. The Dnieper river, the third-longest river in Europe, flows through the whole length of the country from southwest of Moscow to the Black Sea, near the Ukrainian city of Kherson. The river is entirely navigable and is ice-free for eight months a year.

Language: Ukrainian is the official language and 67 per cent of the population speak it. Russian is the native tongue of 24 per cent of the country, and you can find small Romanian-, Polish-, and Hungarian-speaking minorities. A significant majority of the population are bilingual, speaking Russian and Ukrainian. During the *perestroika* liberalisation of the late 1980s, public signs became bilingual. In the early 1990s, signs were changed from bilingual to Ukrainian only during the Ukrainianisation campaign that followed the country's independence. The preferred language in most cities of southern, eastern, and northern Ukraine is Russian, while official documents are in Ukrainian. However, business people e-mail each other in English, and many natives speak with each other primarily in Russian.

Currency: The hryvnia (UHA, sometimes hry), which is divided into 100 kopecks and converts at the rate of 10 UHA to £1.

Time zone: GMT +2.

EU standing: In 2005, Ukraine signed an EU action plan detailing how the country can converge with EU law, comply with human rights legislation, create a market economy, and provide for stable development. Ukraine hopes to be part of an EU free-trade regime by 2006, in an association agreement by 2008, and negotiating for full EU membership by 2010–12.

Emergency services: Emergency switchboard staff rarely speak good English. If you need to call for assistance, use your local contacts or hotel receptionist. Emergency phone numbers:

Ambulance: 03

Fire: 01

Police: 02

Visas: Citizens of EU countries, Switzerland, the USA, and Japan do not need visas for visits of up to 90 days. If you are visiting for longer, you do need a visa. You can find information about applying for a visa and an application form on the Ukrainian Embassy Web site (`www.ukremb.org.uk/eng/cvs`). If you plan to stay in the country for more than six months, you must register with the Ministry of Internal Affairs when you arrive in Ukraine. Your passport must be valid for at least one month after your planned date of departure from Ukraine.

By air from the UK: British Airways and Ukraine International Airlines (+380-44-461-5050; `www.ukraine-international.com/eng`) have daily flights between the UK and Ukraine. Try also AeroSvit (+380-44-490-3490; `www.aerosvit.ca`) and Estonian Air (+372-6401-163; `www.estonian-air.ee`).

By train from the UK: You can travel from London to Kiev, Odessa, and Lviv by train (via Brussels or Paris, and onward through Berlin, Prague, or Vienna) using Eurostar. The journey is safe, comfortable, and easy to book in the UK with one phone call: Contact European Rail (020-7387-0444; `www.europeanrail.com`). The journey takes around two days.

Other routes from the UK: Eurolines bus network is playing the no-frills game with a concept termed *ultra low-cost* European travel. You can reach Kiev, Lutsk, Lvov, Rivne, and Zytomir from London in about 50 hours with a flexible return ticket costing £159.

No direct sea route exists from the UK to Ukraine, but ferries run from Odessa, Sevastopol (also known as Sebastapol), and Yalta to Istanbul in Turkey. The Ukr Ferry Shipping Company (+380-482-344-059; www.ukrferry.com) runs ferries on this route and throughout the Black Sea. (See Chapter 15 for more about ferry routes to mainland Europe.)

Accommodation: Hotels in Ukraine range between a handful with excellent five-star rating and a vast swathe of indifferent budget hotels with basic facilities. Radisson SAS Hotel (+800-3333-3333; www.radissonsas.com), which opened in September 2005, is one of the first Western hotel chains in Kiev. A reasonable-quality three-star hotel in Kiev or Odessa costs around £60 a night for two, but you can search out adequate hotels for half that figure. Unipress (www.travel-2-ukraine.com) runs a Web-based hotel reservation system covering 23 Ukrainian cities. Hotel rooms start at £20 per day; apartments for four start at £40 per day. The site also offers loads of useful information for travelling in and around Ukraine. Hotels Ukraine (www.hotelsukraine.com) has wider coverage of more expensive hotels, but without the helpful map. If you are operating on a tight budget, visit any railway station and look for older ladies offering rooms in private houses for 45 hty (£7) per person per day, including meals. Also, ask your estate agent for recommendations, checking first that he or she has actually stayed there.

Although you can still make money in Ukrainian property – as well as have loads of fun visiting the southern beaches, the Carpathian mountain ski resorts, and the burgeoning city nightlife – the country is definitely one of the riskier sectors in Eastern Europe. Property prices that rise more than 35 per cent in a year, as some have in parts of Ukraine, always carry commensurate risk. Additionally, the language and Cyrillic alphabet are all but unintelligible unless you know the lingo, corruption is rife, and property title is still problematic. Fortunately, English-speaking estate agents, some firms partly owned by British nationals, are appearing in the region, and English-speaking lawyers are fairly easy to find. You can even take steps to insure against potential deficiencies in property law.

Getting to Know Ukraine

Ukraine has a lot to offer tourists and residents alike. While the climate is not exactly Mediterranean, it is continental, which usually means that cold winter weather is compensated for by some good warm spells. The country has a bit of everything to offer – from ski slopes in the Carpathian mountains in the north to long sandy beaches on the Black Sea coast in the south.

Communications are good and getting better. You can reach Kiev by most major European airlines on a daily basis for less than £180 if you're prepared to change planes en route. (Low-cost airlines are not around yet, but they are getting closer.) Once in Ukraine, internal travel options by plane, train, river, and air-conditioned coach are plentiful and cheap.

Ukrainian culture

Ukraine has culturally and historically always lain somewhere between Asia and Europe. As a result, Ukrainians have a strong mixture of Asiatic and Arabic heritage. Additionally, Ukraine has long been coveted and conquered by neighbouring countries. These various visitations have added to an already diverse wealth of attractions. For example:

- **Dance:** Folk dancing is strong in Ukraine, with many dances tracing their roots to the drunken celebrations that followed Cossack military victories. In a departure from this tradition, Ukraine hosted the 2005 Eurovision Song Contest, in which its entrant ended up trailing the field.
- **Education:** The population is well educated, despite having only seven universities (courtesy of years of Soviet domination). While Ukraine has less than 1 per cent of the world's population, it has 6 per cent of the world's physicists, chemists, mathematicians, biologists, computer programmers, and other highly trained professionals.
- **Food:** Peasant dishes form the heart of local cuisine, based largely on grains, potatoes, cabbage, beetroot, and mushrooms with boiled, fried, or stewed meat thrown in for good measure. Desserts are usually laden with honey and fruit such as cherries and plums. Small dumplings known as *varenyky* are a popular Ukrainian snack. Ukrainians enjoy the centuries-old dish of *salo*, or pig fat, in much the same way as the English love roast beef. The only Ukrainian dish to have global recognition is borscht, a beetroot and mixed-vegetable soup usually served with cream.

Unfortunately, good Ukrainian food is now hard to find in Ukraine, as most restaurants – in a mistaken effort to attract tourists – serve French and Italian cuisine. Wait for an invitation to someone's house for a taste of authentic Ukrainian cooking.

Climate and weather

Ukraine generally has a temperate continental climate, with warm summers across the greater part of the country, as Table 16-1 suggests. Rainfall is highest in the west and north around Lviv. Snowfall follows similar patterns, with areas in the Carpathian mountains getting snow one out of three days during winter months. (See Tables 16-2 and 16-3 for more precipitation information.) The southern Crimean coast from Odessa to Yalta has a near-Mediterranean climate, with temperatures regularly hitting 30°C. Winters vary from cool along the Black Sea to cold farther inland to very cold in the mountains, where temperatures of –10°C are quite usual.

Table 16-1 Average Daily Temperatures in Ukraine

Location	*Jan–Mar*	*Apr–June*	*July–Sep*	*Oct–Dec*
Kiev	–2°C	14°C	17°C	2°C
Lviv	–1°C	12°C	17°C	2°C
Odessa	1°C	15°C	21°C	5°C

Table 16-2 Average Number of Rainy Days per Month in Ukraine

Location	*Jan–Mar*	*Apr–June*	*July–Sep*	*Oct–Dec*
Kiev	4	8	6	6
Lviv	7	9	8	7
Odessa	6	7	5	6

Table 16-3 Average Number of Snowy Days per Month in Ukraine

Location	*Jan–Mar*	*Apr–June*	*July–Sep*	*Oct–Dec*
Kiev	8	0	0	0
Lviv	10	1	0	5
Odessa	6	0	0	3

English-language media

Finding an English newspaper outside of the major Ukrainian cities is difficult. Even within the cities, papers arrive a day or two late and cost around

20 UHA (£2). You can pick up all the local and some international news in English on the following Web sites:

- **BRAMA** (`www.brama.com`) is a Ukrainian Web portal with links to news and general information Web sites. The classified ads section includes listings for apartment rentals, translation services, and tourist guides.
- **Forum** (`http://eng.for-ua.com`) claims to provide objective news about Ukrainian events, free of commercial interests and political bias.
- **Mirror-Weekly** (`www.mirror-weekly.com`) is a Kiev-based English-language online political and social affairs newspaper. The publication was launched in 2002 by a team of professional reporters and editors with experience working in some of the world's prime news organisations.
- **Ukrainian Journal** (`www.ukrainianjournal.com`) is one the leading English-language daily newsletters. Like its print counterpoint, the Web site covers breaking political and business news from Ukraine.
- **Ukrainian Observer** (`www.ukraine-observer.com`) is an online subscription-based English-language magazine about general business, politics, and culture in Ukraine. The news section is open to non-subscribers.
- **Ukrainian Weekly** (`www.ukrweekly.com`) was founded initially to serve the Ukrainian-American community. It publishes worldwide news about Ukraine and Ukrainians. Issue summaries are available online.

You can receive the BBC World Service locally on FM and short wave at various times of the day. Find details on frequencies on the BBC World Service Web site (`www.bbc.co.uk/worldservice`).

Tourism

Ukraine joined the World Tourist Organization (WTO) in 1997 and has since begun establishing a serious tourist industry. Around 12 million visitors come to the county each year, but total spending is only £3 billion. (In Spain, for example, 52 million visitors spend £30 billion each year.)

Ukraine shows signs of taking tourism seriously. Much-needed investment in the hotel sector is under way, and many of the country's 1,500 hotels are being upgraded. The 5,000 or so businesses in the tourist sector have shrunk to around 2,500, which may appear on the face of it to be a setback. However, new requirements for sound financing and a demand for greater professionalism should ensure that the remaining organisations are more successful in dealing with the demands of more sophisticated tourists.

Chernobyl

On 26 April 1986, a reactor at Chernobyl nuclear power station, 100 kilometres north of Kiev, exploded and unleashed 90 times more radioactive material than the bomb at Hiroshima. The irony is that the explosion was the result of a safety test that went wrong. Nearly 5 million people were affected, with many still paying the price for inexpensive nuclear power.

Proof that nothing is too bizarre to attract a crowd, Chernobyl now has a ghoulish tourist trade. Tour guides say that they take people only to 'safe' areas. But considering that plutonium has a half-life of 20,000 years, these claims probably aren't true and the click of a Geiger counter only serves to confirm the danger. Spend £160 on a tour if you like, but a better way to find out about the world's worst peacetime nuclear disaster – and perhaps help out – is to visit `www.childrenofchornobyl.org` and see what can be done to ease some of the suffering.

Sports and leisure

Ukraine shares the former Soviet Union's mania for sports, with hundreds of stadiums, swimming pools, gymnasiums, and other athletic facilities. Unfortunately, few of these are in great shape. The country's most popular sports include track and field, football, volleyball, shooting, basketball, swimming, and gymnastics. Other popular leisure activities include mountain biking, quad biking, and strategic paintballing. Several national parks, such as the Carpathian national park and the Shatskyy national park, offer picnicking, swimming, and hiking.

Ukraine's skiing industry, while surprisingly prolific, is poorly equipped by Western standards. The best ski resorts are in the Carpathian mountains and have, at present, only limited appeal for foreigners. You can find a variety of runs and decent infrastructure, though nothing yet near the level of Western European resorts. Bukovel, 130 kilometres from Lviv, which has an English-language Web site (`www.bukovel.com`), is one of the best ski resorts with a full range of support services including equipment hire, instructors, and hotels. Prices remain low by European standards for both lift tickets and rental equipment.

The Black Sea coast, especially the areas around Sevastopol and Yalta, features many harbours and small marinas for yachting, boating, and sailing. Also, diving schools are beginning to prosper in the region.

Talking Business

Since 2000, Ukraine has taken some drastic steps to transform its economy by pursuing a policy of economic liberalisation. As the second largest European country after Russia and with a population of 47.2 million, the country has experienced rapid economic growth.

Foreign direct investment is accelerating fast, currently running at £1.6 billion a year, with approximately £10 billion invested since 1999. The UK is the third most important investor in Ukraine, after the USA and Cyprus.

High taxes, corruption, shortages of hard currency, and frequent and abrupt changes in legislation all make doing business in Ukraine difficult. However, a glimmer of light is on the horizon: Taxes are being lowered and regulations are lightening. The nation is determined to make the business environment in which both Ukrainian and foreign companies operate less burdensome.

This section covers the most important economic factors to bear in mind from a property-owning perspective.

Examining the cost of living

In Ukraine's major cities, you can enjoy a standard of living comparable to that of many more developed economies by EU standards, and often for considerably less cost. For example, according to human resources consultants Mercer, living in Kiev is 42 per cent cheaper than living in London. Mercer ranks Kiev 52nd in its list of the most expensive places to live, putting the city on a par with Birmingham.

Benefits of the Orange Revolution

From 1990 to 2000, Ukraine suffered a decade of economic decline. High inflation, unemployment, and debt re-payments, coupled with stifling state interference, kept the country in the economic basket-case category.

Since the Orange Revolution in 2004 led by Viktor Yushchenko, Ukraine has implemented a whole raft of economic and legal reforms that have pushed the economy to a growth rate faster than China's and four times faster than old Europe's. Although growth was occurring pre-Yushchenko, as a direct consequence of Yushchenko-led policies, foreign investors are increasingly venturing into Ukraine. The appearance of these investors brings a requirement for property to rent and buy.

Outside of the major cities, the cost of living and the quality of life drop sharply. A three-room apartment in Krivoy Rog, about 400 kilometres from Kiev, costs £40 per month; a similar property in Kiev runs to £400. Away from the cities you will find no English-language cinemas and few theatres or cultural activities, and restaurant menus won't be in English either. This is definitely only an option for truly self-reliant people or people who speak (or are prepared to learn) the language.

Basic meals out are very cheap – a couple of pounds covers most occasions. You can cross the country by train or bus for the price of a few London Tube fares.

Estimating value and potential yield

Even in Kiev and the other major Ukrainian cities, properties are still relatively cheap by UK standards. Across the country as a whole, the average cost of purchasing residential property is around £250 per square metre. Prices vary greatly – and sometimes for little apparent reason. For example:

- Kiev apartments can range from £4,100 per square metre for a luxury three-bedroom property in Shevchenka T. Blv. down to £800 per square metre in Shovkovychna Str., both reputedly attractive areas in the capital.
- You can still buy a two-bedroom property within a couple of hours' drive of Kiev city centre for £6,000.

Rental yields throughout the more developed areas in Ukraine are very high and likely to remain so for some time. Real-estate advisory firm Jones Lang LaSalle in Moscow claims yields of around 13 per cent for all types of property in the areas around Kiev, Odessa, and Lviv. The reason is simple: Good-quality property is scarce, and demand outstrips supply. Nowhere in old Europe offers yields anywhere near 13 per cent, so despite the greater risks, Ukraine still looks like a market with a head of steam.

According to a study published in the *Banker Magazine* (`www.thebanker.com`) in October 2005, property prices in Kiev have risen by 35–37 per cent in the past six months and 250 per cent in the past three years. However, Ukraine remains somewhat behind its Eastern European peers such as Bulgaria in terms of economics. View any property investments as long term, rather than expecting a fast gain.

Choosing Where to Buy

With the Ukrainian property market still struggling to its feet after seven decades of Soviet discouragement, prudent overseas buyers should confine property searches to the centres best served by airports and with strong leisure or business appeal. While limiting yourself in this way may eliminate some of the greatest bargains Ukraine offers, you can be more certain of enjoying good rental yields if you choose to let out your property, an interesting location to stay, and a decent return on your investment when you sell up.

I concentrate on only three areas in Ukraine that make good sense according to the preceding criteria. For the next few years, the best places to look for property in Ukraine are around the major cities of Kiev, Lviv, and Odessa. These areas all have the greatest potential for attracting inward investment, as well as Western executives in search of quality properties to rent. Lviv and Odessa are also near the country's fast-expanding tourist markets around the Carpathian mountains and the Black Sea coastal area, respectively.

The prices and rental yields that I list in the following sections are indicative only. Currently, Ukraine does not have reliable national statistics on property prices or rental yields, such as British-based information available through the Halifax House Price Index. While the actual figures you may encounter when researching property in Ukraine will undoubtedly vary from the prices I list, the relative costs in the various areas will probably be similar.

Kiev

Kiev (or Kyiv), the capital of Ukraine, is a city of close to 3 million people situated on the Dnipro river. The local football team is Dynamo, which could well describe the city itself.

Kiev is the easiest Ukrainian city to travel to, with a dozen flights in and out each day connecting to most European capitals. Borispol (KBP), the international airport, and Zhulyany-Kiev, which handles domestic flights, are 12 and 7 kilometres from the centre, respectively. Taxi rides to the airports cost £20–30, while buses (a 25- to 35-minute trek) cost a more modest £3.

Once in Kiev, getting around is easy and the city is well worth exploring. The three-line underground covers much of the city and is clean and reliable, running from 6am to midnight. Other public-transit options include buses, trolleybuses, trams, and the *marshrutky*, which are small, privately run minivans/buses that cruise around the city and suburbs. *Marshrutky* do not have any fixed stops or timetables, but their services are relatively cheap, fast, and efficient: 50–60 kopecks (around 10p) can get you round much of the city's public transportation system.

Kiev has museums, churches, cathedrals, an opera house, and a couple of English-language cinemas. Westernisation is under way throughout the city, with O'Briens Irish Pub and TGI Friday's recently arriving to provide places for foreign visitors to meet up.

From a property-investing perspective, Kiev is the most liquid sector of the Ukrainian market, with thousands of buyers and sellers. See Table 16-4 for indicative prices. One of Ukraine's largest property developers, XXI Century, floated on the London Stock Exchange in 2006, only the second-ever Ukrainian firm to get a London listing. Founded by Ukrainian-born Georgian Lev Partskhaladze and advised by Dutch bank ING, XXI Century has seen the value of its properties, much of them high-end apartment blocks in Kiev, expand eightfold in five years.

Table 16-4 Purchase Prices and Monthly Rents for Good-Quality Apartments in Kiev

Apartment Size	*Purchase Price*	*Monthly Rent*
2 bedrooms	£155,000	£800–1,500
3 bedrooms	£270,000	£900–2,000
4 bedrooms	£310,000	£1,500–2,500

Carpathian mountains

The Carpathian mountains spread across six countries of Eastern and Central Europe: The Czech Republic, Hungary, Poland, Romania, the Slovak Republic, and Ukraine. Within the Ukrainian Carpathian region, the area of greatest interest from a property-investment perspective lies roughly between Lviv (also known as L'vov) and Ivano-Frankivsk. Table 16-5 lists some indicative property and rental prices.

The Carpathians at their highest altitude are only as high as the Middle Region of the Alps, so the mountains here are not covered in snow year round and glaciers do not exist. These warmer conditions make multi-season occupancy possible, with skiing in the winter and walking, hiking, and cycling for the rest of the year.

The region is currently enjoying a tourism boom, but so far not enough to threaten the 50,000-hectare Carpathian National Reserve (CNR) or to scare off local mammals such as lynx, wolves, and bears. Most new developments are fairly basic by Western European standards. You won't find equipped camp-sites, hikers' refuges, groomed hiking trails, or many signs. Hikers have to make do with logging roads and improvised trails. But you can find plenty of small, modest-scale ski resorts.

The road access to and around the region is adequate, but getting there involves an overnight train journey from Kiev or a minibus from Lviv or Uzhhorod if you take a local flight into one of those cities.

Table 16-5 Purchase Prices and Monthly Rents for Good-Quality Apartments in the Carpathian Region

Apartment Size	*Purchase Price*	*Monthly Rent (All-Seasons Average)*
2 bedrooms	£35,000	£350–750
3 bedrooms	£60,000	£500–1,000
4 bedrooms	£80,000	£1,100–1,800

Odessa to Yalta and Sevastopol: the Crimean coast

The beautiful coastline of Crimea with its fine resorts, beaches, cliffs, and hotels has been a favourite destination for Russia's rulers since the days of the tsars, the last of whom had Livadia Palace near Yalta as a summer home.

Crimea is on the same latitude as Venice, and its summer temperatures are similar to those on the southern Mediterranean coast. Crimea is virtually an island in the Black Sea, protected by mountains from the winter north winds and the fresh sea breezes, which keep summer temperatures bearable. Scuba diving, sailing, visiting the Byzantine ruins of Khersoness, or just lazing on a beach is what summers are all about here.

The key cities are:

- **Odessa**, a boomtown that attracted immigrants from all over Europe in the years before the Soviet empire.
- **Sevastopol**, a coastal community – and until 1996 the home of Russia's Black Sea fleet – with whitewashed neoclassical buildings and stone forts.
- **Yalta**, a 19th-century bolt-hole where Russian aristocrats came to cure their tuberculosis among the palm trees.

Throughout the region, and particularly around Yalta, vineyards are in abundance. The first of these planted Semillon, Aligote, Pedro Ximenez, and Pinot grape varieties imported in the early 19th century by Prince Lev Golitsyn and Count Mikhail Vorontsov.

Along the Crimean coast, luxurious palaces, run-down sanatoriums, failing hotels, brand-new apartment complexes, and country villas are all for sale, at a wide range of prices. Table 16-6 offers some indicative prices. You can still find bargains, but the desirability of the area, the prospects of a growing tourist market, and the influx of the Russian mafia all serve to keep prices up.

Table 16-6 Average Purchase Prices and Weekly Rents for Apartments in the Crimean Region

Apartment Size	*Purchase Price*	*Weekly Rent (Low/ High Season)*
2 bedrooms	£100,000	£280/420
3 bedrooms	£170,000	£630/840
4 bedrooms	£350,000	£700/1,750

Buying into Ukraine

While foreign ownership of Ukrainian properties is permitted, the procedure for buying and selling is fraught with dangers – especially in rural areas where homes are rarely registered and ownership is doubtful.

You definitely need the services of a lawyer to purchase property in Ukraine. You can find Ukrainian lawyers at the Martindale-Hubbell Lawyer Locator (`http://lawyers.martindale.com/marhub`) or the International Law Office (`www.internationallawoffice.com/Directory`). You must have all the documentation translated from Ukrainian or Russian into English. Be sure to have a current passport to conclude any property transaction, as well as a tax number, which your lawyer can obtain from the offices of the regional tax administrator. Find a lawyer who has a good command of English and who is independent of the estate agent or developer that you are dealing with. Ideally, your lawyer should have offices near to the property you are buying, as they will have a good insight into local issues, such as new developments, road works, and any other factors that might detract from the value of your property. I discuss the intricacies of hiring a lawyer in Chapter 4.

Mortgages in Ukraine

As of October 2001, changes in the Ukrainian Land Code allow private ownership of land and the sale of land. Since this point, landowners have been able to obtain credit on the security of land and property in the form of mortgage (*zastava*) loans. In 2002, only ten banks operated in the mortgage market, but now most major banks are in the game.

The typical terms are 30–50 per cent downpayments, a maximum loan period of 5 years, and annual interest rates of 14 per cent or more for loans tied to foreign currencies (primarily the euro) and 20 per cent or more for local-currency loans (because the inflation risk is higher). Standard agreements prevent the borrower from selling, leasing, or in any other way transferring the use of the property during the life of the mortgage. Banks typically charge loan-arrangement fees of £500–1,000.

Only Oschadbank (www.oschadnybank.com), the country's state-owned savings bank, offers 100 per cent mortgage financing, but terms are for two years or less and in hryvnias only.

Following are the basic procedures for purchasing property in Ukraine:

1. **Research the market.**

   Chapter 3 explains how to find properties, but you can find a number of English-speaking estate agents who specialise in Ukranian property and who have offices in the Ukraine, including the following:

   - **Real Estate & Service** (RES) (+380-44-279-7092; www.res.com.ua/eng), set up by Andre Petrovitsky in 1992, has the goal of locating the perfect home away from home for foreigners. It has an extensive range of properties for rent as well as for sale.
   - **Teren Plus** (+380-44-428-1010; www.teren.kiev.ua), established by Sergiy Shevchuk, is an estate agency successfully working in Kiev since 1996.
   - **Uaproperty.com** (+380-44-278-2473, 01205-35583; www.uaproperty.com), founded by Alexander Abramovych and Englishman Jeremy Cornah, covers property in all parts of the country.

2. **Find a property and carry out a thorough inspection.**

   Generally buyers do not carry out building surveys in Ukraine. You can see from the deeds when the house was built and examine what state it is in at present. If a lot of renovation work needs to be done, ask a building company to inspect the property and quote for any repairs/renovations before you make an offer. Inspection fees are modest, perhaps £50 for a two-page report on a small property. The builder or owner is more likely to speculate on getting the renovation work done themselves before sale.

3. **Negotiate and agree on the final price with the current owners.**

   After viewing a property, you can negotiate directly with the owners or through the estate agent, which may be more convenient if language differences exist.

   Keep in mind that the total price you pay also includes the following:

   - **Actual cost of buying:** 7–10 per cent of the purchase price, but may vary slightly.
   - **Property tax (equivalent of UK stamp duty):** 1 per cent, which the notary is responsible for paying on your behalf to the tax authorities.
   - **Estate agency fees:** 3–5 per cent. With little competition at present, expect to pay towards the higher end. You may be able to be negotiate on larger purchases and where fees are quoted above 3 per cent.
   - **Notary fee:** Approximately 1.5 per cent.
   - **Insurance:** In Ukraine, you have the option of insuring the contract for 1 per cent of the purchase price, which offers a bit of protection against the uncertainty of title to the property (see Step 5 later).
   - **Special pension fund charges:** 1 per cent charge on the acquisition of real estate payable by individuals and companies that purchase real estate. The tax base is the contractual value of the real estate.
   - **Property management charges:** £200–700 per annum at most holiday complexes, depending on the level of service you select.

4. **Draw up and sign the initial contract.**

   After you and the seller agree a price, you have to see a notary (*notarius*) and draw up an *initial contract*, which outlines the details and any conditions that must be met before the sale completes (for example, repairs). After you and the seller sign the initial contract and you put down 5 per cent of the price, the sale is legally binding.

   The initial contract includes a date by which the final contract (completion) must take place.

   Both buyer and seller commonly use the same notary, and meetings are generally held with all parties present, which makes sorting out any queries or problems much easier, faster, and cheaper than in the British conveyancing system. However, using the same notary does mean that you are not receiving independent legal advice, so have your personal lawyer present at this point to provide independent legal advice.

5. **Carry out final checks and sign the final contract.**

   After the initial contract, the notary carries out the necessary checks and searches and ensures that the vendor provides all the relevant title documents, permissions for use, and information on any mortgages and loans outstanding.

As of 1 January 2004, Ukrainian property rights laws aim to make foreign ownership rights more transparent and secure. As of July 2004, an additional law is supposed to consolidate all information on real-estate encumbrances, but a comprehensive database has not been created yet. The new laws establish that all property rights must be registered with the All-Ukrainian Real Estate Ownership Rights Register. Despite this impressive-sounding name, proving the true title to property in Ukraine can be uncertain. Even when title is certain, properties are still sometimes sold with an undisclosed liability, such as a mortgage.

When you and the seller sign the final contract, you must also pay over the remaining 95 per cent of the money due. In Ukraine, loans secured on a property remain attached to the property and not the owner, so you must ensure that the vendor provides a document from the council offices on the day of signing that confirms that the property has no outstanding loans secured on it.

6. **Pay for your property.**

   You must pay for your property in Ukrainian currency. To do this, you can either instruct your own bank or buy currency through a specialist company, which may offer more competitive rates. See the section 'Opening a bank account' later in this chapter and Chapter 18 for more information.

   You can either have the purchased currency sent directly to your own bank account in Ukraine, or you can use your notary's *escrow account*, a client account in which your funds are kept separate and cannot be accessed without your permission.

7. **Transfer utilities.**

   After you become the owner of your Ukrainian property, expect to spend the rest of the day with the old owner trailing round the electricity, telephone, and water provider offices to put the utilities in your name. Unfortunately, you can rarely transfer utilities by telephone or letter – and bank standing orders are not completely reliable.

   Ideally, you need someone in the country to help with these matters. If you are letting the property, then you can expect your local letting agent to handle all these matters within its fee. Otherwise, speak to your estate agent, notary, or – better still – neighbours and come to some equitable arrangement.

Getting Settled in Ukraine

Buying a property is in many respects the easy part of getting into Ukrainian life. The language is difficult, made even more so because you need to know both Russian and Ukrainian to really fit in well. The immense friendliness of the people – many of whom will gladly welcome you into their homes – somewhat compensates for this difference.

Plenty of people, such as estate agents and lawyers, have something to gain by smoothing your path during the purchase process, so that is what they will do. After that, you are to some extent on your own. Although some matters, for example capital gains tax, may seem a distant concern, the actions you take early on can mitigate pain later.

In this section, I cover the day-to-day matters for establishing yourself in Ukraine.

Taxing matters

Ukrainian taxes to consider in relation to property include the following:

- **Business tax:** If you work on your own or employ no more than ten people, you're taxed under a *single (unified) tax regime*, as long as the annual proceeds from the sale of goods or services do not exceed 500,000 UAH ($95,000). This tax is paid monthly in a range fixed by local authorities and varies between 20 UAH and 200 UAH (approximately $4–38), depending on the type of activity.

  Payment of single (unified) tax relieves a private entrepreneur from all other taxes.

- **Capital gains tax:** Until 2005, those disposing of property in Ukraine escaped capital gains tax. As property prices had barely stirred for 70 years, the Ukrainian treasury wasn't missing out on much income. Now that property prices are rising, the taxman has got his trowel out. As of 1 January 2006, income from disposal of real estate is taxed as follows:

  - Sale of one property bought before 1 January 2004 is taxed at the rate of 1 per cent for the first 100 square metres of premises and 5 per cent thereafter, based on the property value.
  - Second and subsequent properties sold in any one year that were bought before 1 January 2004 are taxed at 5 per cent of the property value.
  - Property bought after 1 January 2004 is taxed at the standard rate of income tax (see the first bullet in this list), based on gain realised from the sale.

  For the sale of one property each year, the taxable gain can be reduced by 10 per cent for each calendar year of ownership following the year the property was bought.

- **Double taxation treaties:** Ukraine has a double taxation treaty with the UK and with many other countries, which should ensure that you don't end up paying tax twice on the same income – or paying more tax than you should. (I cover double taxation treaties in Chapter 16.)
- **Income tax:** For 2004–2006, thc standard tax rate for those resident for tax purposes is 13 per cent, and from 1 January 2007 a standard rate of 15 per cent applies. (See Chapter 16 for details of residency rules.) The standard rate is applicable to most types of income, including salary income, dividends, royalties, and investment income. Income received by non-residents is subject to tax at the double standard tax rate of 26 per cent. (See 17 for more on double taxation treaties.)
- **Local taxes:** 14 different local taxes can be levied at the discretion of the local authorities. Follow advice from your estate agent or lawyer as to how to handle these taxes.
- **Value-added tax:** Ukraine introduced VAT in 1992 and altered the legislation in 1997 to model it more closely on general EU VAT rules. VAT is levied at two rates: 20 per cent on domestic supplies of goods and services and imports of goods; and 0 per cent on export of goods, supply of processing and repair services to non-residents, and international transport services.

To find out more about the tax regime in Ukraine, visit the PriceWaterhouseCoopers Web site (`www.pwc.com/ua/eng/main/home/index.html`) and follow the Publications thread for a comprehensive and up to-date guide to tax and much else besides.

Opening a bank account

Opening a personal bank account in Ukraine is both advisable and essential for all property-related activities. You can open accounts in both Ukrainian currency and a foreign currency such as euros or sterling. You probably need a Ukrainian currency account for regular local transactions and a sterling account for transferring larger sums for buying property.

Credit cards can be used in some Ukrainian hotels, expensive restaurants, and some bigger shops. However, credit cards are not as popular as in Western Europe and people generally pay with, and ask for, cash.

In May 2005, a resolution of the board of the National Bank of Ukraine sought to simplify regulations on opening, using, and closing bank accounts in domestic currency and foreign exchange. Bank accounts are usually opened in person in Ukraine. You must present a valid passport (some banks require an additional document with a photo, such as a driving licence). You may need to take with you an interpreter or someone who knows the language to help you communicate with bank staff, who seldom speak fluent English.

The National Bank of Ukraine (`www.bank.gov.ua/ENGL`) has useful information on the country's banking system and regulations. Ukraine Today (`www.ukraine-today.com`) has a directory of all the banks in Kiev.

Staying healthy

Ukraine spends £250 per person per year on health care – barely 10 per cent of what the UK spends, half what Bulgaria spends, and less than either Albania or Kazakhstan. Ukraine's lack of health-care spending shows: A version of the British National Health Service started as an experiment in 1987, but Ukraine didn't start training family doctors until 1995. Ukrainian medical facilities are adequate only for very basic services. If you are hospitalised, you are responsible for your own supply of bandages, medication, and food.Bring an adequate supply of any prescription medicines you have.

Sexually transmitted diseases are rampant in Ukraine, and HIV is widespread, with eight people a day dying of AIDS-related diseases.

Don't drink Ukrainian tap water without boiling it.

The risk of radioactive contamination from the 1986 accident at Chernobyl is insignificant, other than within the exclusion zone immediately around the accident site.

Ukraine and the UK have a bilateral agreement on emergency medical treatment. However, if you have a serious illness, consider returning to the UK for treatment. I cover medical concerns in Chapter 20.

For health-care-related questions and information about air ambulance companies, visit the medical/health information page of the Web site of the US embassy in Ukraine (`http://kiev.usembassy.gov/amcit_medical_eng.html`), which includes contact details for medical services throughout Ukraine and fact sheets on health matters.

Getting around the country

Ukraine is a large country with a variety of transportation options available to help you tour the region and conduct daily business.

Train

Ukraine has an extensive, 22,800-kilometre rail network that connects most cities, towns, and villages throughout the country. Trains are a reliable and safe way to travel within Ukraine, especially in the winter when road travel is curtailed and many domestic flights are cancelled or delayed due to poor weather conditions. Trains in Ukraine are frequent and usually punctual, if slow. They are also cheap: Taking both berths in a first-class sleeper compartment for the 12–14-hour trek between Kiev and Odessa costs less than £50 for the round trip. If you are prepared to share a compartment, the cost is a quarter of that figure.

For detailed information about rail travel in Ukraine, visit Travel-2-Ukraine (`www.travel-2-ukraine.com`). For travel between Ukraine and neighbouring Commonwealth of Independent States (CIS) see the Poezda Web site (`http://www.poezda.net/en/index`).

Plane

Domestic air travel is the fastest and easiest way to get around the country, except perhaps in the winter months when the weather is poor. 14 Ukrainian cities operate internal flights: Kiev, Odessa, Kharkov, Simferopol, Dnepropetrovsk, Lviv, Donetsk, Ivano-Frankivsk, Uzhgorod, Lugansk, Mariupol, Chernivtsi, Kerch, and Khmelnitsky.

Most flights within Ukraine are either not available from travel agents abroad or are very expensive. You can check out timetables and costs and book tickets online with UkraineFare (`www.ukrainefare.com`). Fares are £35–50 each way on most routes.

Alternatively you can book direct through AeroSvit Airlines (+380-44-490-3490; `www.aerosvit.ca/eng`), which was among the first Ukrainian airlines to offer flights on modern Boeing 737 and 767 aircraft. The AeroSvit network covers 11 Ukrainian cities and 40 destinations in 23 countries.

Car

Speed limits are 60 kilometres (37 miles) per hour in built-up areas, 90 kilometres (55 miles) per hour outside of built-up areas, and 110 kilometres (69 miles) per hour on motorways. Traffic drives on the right; right-hand-drive cars are prohibited. Drinking and driving is strictly prohibited, with heavy fines being imposed if traffic police smell alcohol on a driver's breath. An International Driving Permit and Green Card insurance are necessary. The roads are generally poor, even in many cities, and driving standards are low. Taking a car into the country is complex and expensive and probably pointless: Taxis are inexpensive and hiring a car with a local driver costs only slightly more than hiring a taxi (see later for information on taxis).

Bus, tram, rapid tram, and metro

Bus services between towns and cities are generally antiquated, slow, and uncomfortable. Buses are gradually being phased out in favour of trains and planes as the distances are great.

One company offering a satisfactory frequent bus service around the country is Autolux (+380-652-632-057; www.autolux.com.ua). This runs four buses a day between 7.30am and 10pm from Kiev to Odessa, with fares around £7 each way.

Trams and trolleybuses operate in many of the larger urban areas, usually for a flat fare of 50 kopecks (£0.03). You can pre-purchase tickets and passes. Once on board the bus or tram, punch your ticket in one of the special machines located on posts throughout the bus. Kiev, Dnepropetrovsk, Kharkiv, and Kryvy Rih all have metros or rapid tram routes. Visit www.urbanrail.net for detailed maps of the routes covered.

Taxi

Taxis are available in all main towns. You can usually find them at ranks or order one by phone. The current rate is around 5 UHA (£0.50) for the first three kilometres and 1.5 UHA (£0.15) thereafter. State-owned taxis have yellow-and-black signs on the roof and are metered. Negotiate fares in advance for private taxis.

River

Cruising down the river is a lazy but pleasant way to get from Kiev in the north to Odessa and Sevastopol in the south. You can book a trip through a tour operator. For example, a 14-day holiday cruise costs from £1000 to £2000 a person, depending on season. These cruises are made by comfortable modern vessels of roughly three- or four-star hotel standard. Blue Water Holidays river cruises (+44 1756 693609; www.rivercruises.info) and Choosing Cruising (www.choosingcruising.co.uk) are two companies that market these river trips.

Part IV
Getting Comfortable

"You'll find living here very quiet & peaceful, the people in the flat above work nights, so they sleep during the day."

In this part . . .

Buying a property abroad opens up lots of new and exciting opportunities including the possibility of moving to a more favourable tax regime and raising finance offshore. You also have the opportunity to rent out your property. As a landlord you have a lot to plan and do before the rent cheques start to appear. You need to find good tenants, be they for long or short terms, you need to furnish and equip the property, and deal with tax and the occasional problems that turn up from time to time. In this part the information you need to review these options and the potential risks and rewards are covered so that you can make the best decision for your circumstances.

Chapter 17

Becoming a Tax Exile

In This Chapter

- Choosing where to have your tax base
- Checking up on tax rates
- Minimising your tax bill
- Avoiding double taxation
- Deciding when to take advice

Buying a property abroad is, in many ways, the relatively easy part of living in another country. More complex problems to tussle with include what happens to your tax position if you start to spend more time in your new property and how you should deal with any profit you make on your property if and when you sell up.

The answers to these questions depend *entirely* on your personal circumstances. Few if any universal guiding rules exist. Always seek professional advice on tax matters to be sure that your personal position is properly taken into account.

Also, the way in which you deal with and attempt to minimise tax depends greatly on your appetite for risk and complexity. If you prefer less paperwork and fewer dealings with lawyers and accountants, you may elect for a path that can end up giving a greater share of income and gain to the tax authorities or some other third party. But that may matter less to you than enjoying a peaceful life. By contrast, you may be the type of person who crosses hot coals to keep money out of the hands of the tax authorities – within the bounds of the law, of course.

The following sections offer a brief guide to tax and legal issues that may impinge on your decisions related to purchasing an overseas property, be it a temporary or more permanent arrangement.

Understanding Residence Rules

Where you have your tax residence is the deciding factor on where you pay your taxes and how much you pay.

Unfortunately, deciding your tax residence is not totally within your gift because you have to follow certain rules and procedures, which in some circumstances can be determined by factors other than tax considerations. For example, if you have elderly relatives or other pressing issues that require you to be in the UK for more than 90 days a year, you may have little choice but to keep your tax affairs in the UK because staying away for that period is an essential precondition of overseas residence.

Domicile and residence made simple

You can't avoid paying taxes somewhere, but you do have some choice as to *where* you end up paying them.

The governing rule regarding to whom you pay your taxes is not so much about where you live, nor necessarily where your income comes from, as it is about where you are resident. The word *resident* has a particular meaning in regard to taxation and is not necessarily the same as having a residence card (which some countries require before you buy property there) or living in the country. Nor is residence the same as *domicile*, which is the place where you have your roots, where your family comes from, and usually where you where born.

If you have been living and paying taxes in the UK, simply going overseas does not change the fact that you are *ordinarily resident* in the UK. If you leave the UK to take up permanent residence abroad and so inform the Inland Revenue, they normally accept this at face value and treat you as ceasing to be resident on the day following your departure. Usually becoming resident for tax purposes in another country you will need to demonstrate that you spend at least 186 days a year in that country.

If you spend an average of 91 days or more per year in the UK over any four-year period, you will be swept back into the British tax net. The days of arrival and departure are not normally counted, so in theory you can spend an awful lot of long weekends in the UK before you use up your allowed days. You are, since a rule change in 1993, even allowed to have accommodation available for your use in the UK. You can see the British government's take on residence at `www.hmrc.gov.uk/pdfs/ir20.htm#residence`.

For most people, the arcane rules of tax residence are largely irrelevant. Generally, you are not expected to prove how long you have spent out of the UK to be able to qualify as being resident for tax purposes in your chosen country. However, where a large sum of tax, say from selling up your British business or dealing with the capital gain on your British house, is at stake, HM Revenue & Customs may become a bit more rigid about applying residence rules. You may have to take steps to prove your movements, using travel and hotel receipts. Also, you may be wise to have no accommodation available to you in the UK and sign up to pay taxes in your chosen country as quickly as you can.

In matters of grave importance, of which health and tax are two, conduct any discussions in a language with which you have more than a nodding acquaintance.

Deciding whether to change your residence

Eastern and Central European countries are intent on building an investor-friendly climate. A central plank in achieving that goal has been to simplify and reduce taxes. In recent years, British tax has become more complex, with many more taxpayers moving into the higher tax brackets. Several countries that feature in this guide have been moving sharply in the *opposite* direction. Latvia, for example, swept away 21 categories of personal income taxes, five tax brackets, and scores of exemptions and deductions, replacing them with a single flat rate of 19 per cent. This rate applies irrespective of the level of income earned, which is the direct opposite of the progressive taxation applied in the UK. In *progressive taxation*, the more you earn, the higher the rate at which you are taxed.

Countries that adopt flat personal income tax claim that the system makes it more attractive for high-earning expatriates to relocate tax affairs to their countries. If you are in the 40 per cent bracket and want to pay only 19p in the pound, you should certainly at least consider your options when deciding on tax residence. Even a basic 26 per cent taxpayer can enjoy a tax rate that is 7 per cent lower in a low-tax country. I cover the actual tax rates that apply within each country in each chapter of Parts II and III.

The only reason for changing your tax residence is to move into a more favourable tax regime – one in which the local tax authorities are entitled to a smaller slice of your cake. But you do need to look carefully across all the different types of tax for which you may be liable in order to make sure that your *total* tax bill – not just one particular tax – is lower. For example, a seemingly advantageous foreign country with a low income tax rate may become very unappealing when you also consider a high capital gains tax (CGT) on property sales.

Determining when to change

The main purpose of changing your tax residence is to lower your *overall* tax bill, not just the bill you may get by moving your tax affairs to another country. So you need to make sure that you don't end up paying unnecessary taxes in the UK *before* you switch over regimes. In order to get the biggest benefit from changing your tax residence, you have to manage the effective dates carefully.

Consider the following areas carefully:

- If you do intend to sell your principal British residence on moving abroad, you can do that without being liable to pay any CGT, as this is an exempt asset for British tax purposes. But if you sell the property after taking up residence in your new country, any capital gains you make may be subject to taxation in your new country. (See the tax rules in each country-specific chapter for more information.)
- If you plan to sell, say, a British holiday home, perhaps to raise funds to buy abroad, then you may be liable for CGT on that property in the UK. You may be able to escape or at least lower this tax if you sell the property *after* you move to your new tax residence – if that country has a more favourable tax regime than Britain has.
- This information on its own may suggest that the best plan is to change over your tax residence quickly. If only the situation were that simple. British tax residents can invest in a self-invested pension plan (SIPP), which allows you to invest a substantial sum of money into a pension in any year and so reduce, and perhaps even eliminate, your entire tax liability. (I cover SIPPs in Chapter 22.) You have little reason to leave the UK at a point when you can arrange your affairs in such a way as to have no tax bill, just to move to a country where you may have to pay a nominally low one. Of course, this is a complex subject – one on which you should certainly take professional advice.

If you run into unexpected personal problem soon after deciding to move tax residence, HM Revenue & Customs can make exceptions to the previously discussed rules. You can return to the UK for *compassionate reasons* – the death or serious illness of a relative or loved one, for example – within a tax year, and HM Revenue and Customs does not sting you if you just exceed the limit of days allowed in the UK.

Watch out for the five-year rule: If you do sell a second home or other assets and by changing your tax domicile to another country escape the clutches of British tax, you must not become resident in the UK for at least five years. If you do, you are liable for the tax that you thought you had escaped.

You also need to consider timing implications of changing tax residence on other investment assets such as investment savings accounts (ISAs) that are exempted from tax only while you are resident in the UK. You cannot make further investments into an ISA after you leave the UK, and such investments may attract tax in your new country of residence.

Choosing a new tax residence

You can find no shortage of countries happy to sign you up for tax domicile, including every country I cover in this book. These countries are also happy to sign up your spouse, as he or she may also, by a concession known as *trailing spouse*, be treated as not resident in the UK from the day after your departure to the day before your return.

However, having your spouse domiciled in the UK while you are domiciled abroad may be to your advantage from a taxation point of view. You may be able to overcome some potential timing problems that I discuss in the preceding section by picking and mixing the best tax rules in both the UK and your chosen country abroad. Always work with a tax or financial professional to determine the approach that is best for you.

Generally, you cannot be in two places at once. For taxation, however, you may qualify for an exception if you spend, say, 250 days abroad and 100 days in the UK. In this scenario, you may end up being liable for tax on the same activities in *both* countries. In a surprising fit of generosity, the tax authorities have decided that this type of situation is unfair and have drawn up *double-taxation agreements* to eliminate this danger. (See the section 'Double-taxation agreements' later in this chapter for more information.)

Considering All Your Tax Obligations

Several different types of tax affect your decision to change your tax residence. Some of these taxes carry major advantages, others less so.

Most people buying properties abroad, regardless of whether they live in their properties full time and move their tax residence, still end up with taxable events in both countries.

Even after you decide to move your tax residence overseas, you still need to consider when the best time is to make the transfer. Your timing can adversely affect your final tax bill in the UK. And of course, you must also consider the matter of what happens if and when you come back to the UK. Little point exists in expending hours of time and hundreds – perhaps even thousands – of pounds rearranging your tax affairs, only to end up with a hefty tax bill on your return.

This section covers the most common types of tax that can influence your tax residence decisions.

Employment and income taxes

Generally, irrespective of the country you choose for tax residence purposes, the country in which you earn money – whether from employment, self-employment, or renting out a property – grabs back a slice of that income by way of tax.

Exactly how much the tax authorities grab varies from country to country and according to the legal structure that you use for buying the property. If you use a company to purchase a property, for example, the tax rates are usually lower. I cover the tax structure in each country-specific chapter and the general principles of using a company to hold property assets in Chapter 4.

Similar tax implications apply to any income you earn from employment or rent generated in the UK. British employers deduct tax at from your pay. If you let out your British property (see Chapter 19 for more on renting out your home), HM Revenue & Customs requires a managing agent (or the tenant if no agent is used) to withhold a portion of the rental income (representing the basic tax rate) before passing the balance to a landlord resident abroad. Although overseas landlords can get permission from HM Revenue & Customs to receive the rent free of tax, the income is not necessarily free from eventual British tax liability.

The onus is on you and your tax adviser to make sure that you pay the right amount of tax in the appropriate country and that you recover any tax overpaid by using the relevant conditions of any double-taxation agreement (see 'Double-taxation agreements' later in this chapter).

Capital gains taxes: At home and abroad

One of your goals in buying a property is probably to sell the property some day for a bit more money than you paid for it. Nothing wrong in that.

However, you do need to take into account a few factors before you can pocket your gain:

- **Selling expenses:** Although buying property can cost as little as 3 or 4 per cent, selling involves rather more costs. (See each country chapter for specific buying costs.) Estate agents take 4–5 per cent, and property taxes can eat up another couple of per cent. Combined with legal fees, selling expenses can consume up to 10 per cent of your selling price. This means that if the value of your property rises by 30 per cent, selling costs consume a third of that gain.
- **Paying for gains:** In many countries in this book, local capital gains tax rates are either low (around 10 per cent) or non-existent if you own a single property for between three and five years. However, unless you are *domiciled* for tax purposes in the overseas country, you are still liable for capital gains tax in the UK, at a rate of 25–40 per cent, depending on your tax code.
- **Currency costs:** Unless you plan to keep the proceeds of any sale in the country concerned, you have to transfer funds back to the UK. If the exchange rate has moved against sterling, you may potentially have costs for changing the currency as well as losing out on the exchange rate (see Chapter 4). In recent years, the pound has moved adversely by as much as 10 per cent against the euro, the principal currency used for buying property in many of the countries I cover in this book.

Inheritance tax

They say that death and taxes are the two events you can be sure will hit you. When they come together – in the form of inheritance taxes – take the time to be well prepared.

Recent research from the Halifax bank shows that almost two-thirds of people living in the UK owning a detached house now fall into the inheritance tax trap – they would pay a 40 per cent higher tax rate when they die, even though they may never have been a high-rate taxpayer in life. This fact alone may encourage you to consider inheritance as part of your tax residence plan because almost any country, in this book at least, is an infinitely cheaper place to die than the UK.

While you may escape UK inheritance taxes by moving your tax base abroad, you may have a different problem to face.

Always consider who inherits when you or any joint owner of your property dies. Express your decisions in a will; if you don't, the death in question is dealt with under the intestacy laws. These regulations are a nightmare to deal with, especially if anyone questions whether matters should be dealt with under British law or the law of the overseas country in which you are tax resident.

Unlike under British law, under some foreign laws certain family members have automatic inheritance rights. For example, spouses and children, even illegitimate ones, sometimes cannot be cut out of a will. However, if you are still a British citizen, irrespective of your tax residence arrangements, your will, as long as you make one, is dealt with under English law.

In whichever country you are domiciled, the local authorities are interested in the disposal of any assets on death. Have your overseas will drawn up in the local language and signed in whatever legal manner is prescribed in that country, usually in front of a notary.

While an English will is valid under any foreign law, take the time to draw up a will in the country where the property to be inherited is located. Doing so saves time distributing the estate and any administrative costs. Making a will in that country smoothes the process and ensures that the deceased's wishes are faithfully carried out.

Your overseas and English wills must not conflict in any way; discrepancies provide opportunity for interminable disputes, time delays, and additional costs.

You need an executor for your foreign will. While in the UK lay people often act as executors, validating a will abroad, especially for a foreigner, can be complex. Appoint a lawyer to steer the inheritors in the best direction.

Double-taxation agreements

At first sight, the tax regime in your new country may look more attractive than British regulations. The situation, however, is rarely a matter of either/or, as many investors who buy property or move abroad soon find out.

You can potentially be tax resident in both countries if you meet residence rules in both nations. For example, if you spend 200 days in a foreign country, 100 days in the UK, and the remaining days elsewhere, both the foreign and British tax authorities can reasonably lay claim to you.

Most countries, including the UK and all the nations that this book covers, have *double-taxation agreements* designed to settle the argument. *Tie breakers*, as the relevant clauses in double-taxation agreements are known, deal with cases where people have homes, assets, and income in both countries. In these circumstances, you are deemed normally to be a resident of the country of which you are a national. (The word 'normally' should be a sign to the wary that this is not an area to tread without taking timely advice.)

The aim of double-taxation agreements is to help make sure that you don't pay tax on the same taxable event twice – once in the overseas country where your new property is and again in the UK.

However, you may still end up paying different taxes in each country. Just a few examples include:

- You pay capital gains tax overseas on personal property owned in that country.
- You do not normally pay capital gains tax in the UK after you settle abroad, except for property in the UK.
- If you are taxed on a gift or income made in the UK, the tax paid is offset against any tax liability accruing overseas.
- Income from British property rent is normally taxed at source in the UK.
- British non-government pensions are taxed in the country you live in, if that is where you receive the money. Government pensions are taxed in the UK.

If you spend more than 183 days in one foreign country during one calendar year, you may become liable for taxes in that country regardless of whether you take out a formal residence permit. The days you spend do not have to be consecutive, and you become resident for tax purposes on the morning of the 184th day. Temporary absences from the foreign country are ignored for the purpose of the 183-day rule, unless you can prove that you were resident in another country for more than 183 days in a calendar year.

Coming Home

If you decide that living overseas is not for you and return to the UK (as around 100,000 people a year do), you have a number of important tax matters to consider. If you kept your tax residence in the UK, then from a tax point of view you have never left, so you can relax. You will be neither worse off nor better off tax-wise when you return.

For those who do elect to change their tax residence to another country, the following section covers the main factors to consider.

Selling up abroad

If you do not intend to keep your overseas home, selling it before you move your tax base back to the UK probably makes the most sense. This decision probably applies to you if the tax rules are more favourable in the overseas country (for example, if the rates are lower) or if your period of ownership has been very brief. I cover the capital gains regime on selling property in each country-specific chapter.

If you are considering keeping your property abroad, perhaps letting it out or expecting it to increase in value over time, allow for the extra tax you may incur later when you finally sell up.

Selling up at home

Hold on a minute. I know this section is supposed to cover returning to the UK, not getting rid of a British home. But tax is something you have to take the long view on.

One day in the future, you probably will sell your British home after you return to the UK, and this action can cause an extra tax to kick in. If you have kept on your British property and not let it out while you were away, coming home and living in that house may not upset your tax apple cart. The issue is whether the British tax authorities treat your home as your principal private residence while you did not live in it. British tax authorities make this decision depending on your chosen place of tax residence. If you decided to reside abroad for tax purposes, your British home is no longer your principal residence. If you have let the property out while you were abroad, regardless of whether you elected for tax residence abroad, the property is no longer considered as your principal residence.

In these circumstances, your property is not considered your principal private residence for a period of time. You are then allowed to have a proportion of British tax relief when you sell up, based on how long the property was your principal residence. Say you owned the property for 10 years before you moved abroad, let it out for five years, and then sold it on your return. In this case, you are liable to pay tax on five-fifteenths (or one-third) of the gain made when the property is sold. This is the portion of time that the property was not your principal residence.

You also have a tax-free allowance that can be offset against any gain. And another measure can further reduce the tax: If you were to return to the UK and live in the property as your main residence for a period of time (informally, six months is the accepted minimum), your last three years of ownership qualify for principal private residence (PPR) relief, which reduces your capital gain. Using the example I outline in the preceding paragraph, if you stay in the property for six months on your return, you can gain three extra years of principal residence tax rights. So from a tax perspective, you end up owning the property for 18 years rather than 15. Now the proportion on which you can be taxed drops to five-eighteenths, rather than five-fifteenths.

Using Tax Advisers

If you don't currently have an adviser, consider locating one now. Becoming a tax exile is a complex decision, and professional assistance is incredibly helpful. Exactly how much advice you need is based on how complicated your tax affairs are, how much you know about tax, how much tax you pay, and what your objectives are in buying a property overseas.

If your primary goal is investment, tax is almost always the single biggest expense that can eat into your profits; professional tax advice can be critical to meeting your financial goals. Also, serious consequences apply to getting things wrong tax-wise. You may incur penalties many times larger than the tax that would have been paid in the first place.

Unless you are expert yourself, always take some tax advice when buying a property overseas, particularly if you are considering moving to a country on a long-term basis.

This section covers the ins and outs of finding high-quality tax advice.

Be wary of tax claims

Web sites and literature from some brokers who deal in overseas properties suggest a passing recognition of the tax issues you should be aware of. Most brokers, however, dwell only on the potential for lowering your tax bill, without offering any serious advice as to how you can do so legally.

Some brokers even go so far as to suggest that if the sums of money are small, to you that is, you can consider dispensing with *all* professional advice from lawyers, accountants, and surveyors.

This is patent nonsense, as the amount of money involved in an overseas property purchase is only one of many factors to be taken into consideration. You can, if you get things wrong, end up with a British tax bill on the sale of your UK home that dwarfs the entire purchase price of your property overseas. (See the section 'Selling up at home' for more information.)

Seeking out free advice

You can find out a substantial amount about the tax implications of buying a property abroad and moving tax residence by doing some diligent research. Indeed, by doing your own preliminary research, you put yourself in a much better position to decide what help you need with your tax affairs and to make best use of an adviser's services.

Most professional advisers charge on an hourly rate, so anything you can do to cut down on the amount of their time you use is money in the bank for you.

The following Web sites contain much of the background information you need to make a good decision about what type of tax adviser you require:

- **HM Revenue & Customs** (www.hmrc.gov.uk/menus/links.htm) has links to the bodies responsible for tax collection around the world. It also publishes a series of online leaflets at www.hmrc.gov.uk/leaflets/c9.htm, including information on residence, British tax liability, UK pensions, overseas income, non-resident landlords, and double-taxation treaties.
- **The Property Tax Portal** (www.property-tax-portal.co.uk) carries a selection of information tables as well as specific tax rates for some countries. The site also has a useful Frequently Asked Questions section covering the whole topic of becoming a tax exile.
- **Worldwide-Tax.com** (www.worldwide-tax.com) has key data on taxes around the globe, including taxes on income, capital gains, inheritance, and rent. Comparison tables enable you to easily see differences between countries.

You may very well have someone in your network of business associates, friends, and other advisers who has been along this road before. One of these individuals may be able to offer some useful tips on taxation. I cover working up your network in Chapter 3.

Finding tax advisers

Anyone can call themselves a tax adviser, accountant, or bookkeeper – even if they have no professional qualifications or even much expertise.

If any tax laws are broken, you – not your adviser – pick up the tab. This is the case regardless of whether the adviser is qualified and competent. But if he or she is a member of one of the major accountancy or related bodies in the UK (or of a professional body in an overseas country), you at least have the comfort of knowing that he or she almost certainly carries professional indemnity insurance against which you can claim for wrong advice.

Locating an adviser

Professional associations for accountants are a good place to start your search for a tax adviser.

The main accountancy bodies in the UK are the Institute of Chartered Accountants in England & Wales (www.icaew.co.uk), the largest professional accountancy body in Europe, with more than 127,000 members, and the Association of Certified and Chartered Accountants (www.accaglobal.com). Both organisations have directories of members and offer advice on how to choose the right adviser for you.

If you think that your tax affairs are likely to be very complex, consider members of the Chartered Institute of Taxation (www.tax.org.uk). This is the leading professional body in the UK concerned solely with taxation with a large international membership. The Web site has a comprehensive directory of members.

You can also consider using tax experts in the country you are going to buy a property in. After all, if anyone knows about tax affairs in their country, they should. However, you also need to be sure that they know enough about the British tax system. Worldwide-Tax.com (www.worldwide-tax.com) has a directory of accounting and tax advisers in each country.

Choosing an adviser

To get the best advice, choose someone who already deals with tax affairs in the country in which you are going to buy a property. This way you know that your adviser probably has experience dealing with the problems that you are likely to face as well as claiming any tax breaks that may be available.

If you already use an accountant, don't overlook this individual. He or she may have sufficient expertise to deal with your new tax issues – and if he or she doesn't, ask. Your current professional almost invariable knows someone who can help.

Tax advisers and accountants usually charge by the hour. The rates vary between £50 and £250 an hour, depending on the complexity of the work. A top tax lawyer used for handling serious company legal issues can charge £650 an hour. The potential for tax savings can give you a pointer as to what fees are worth incurring.

Chapter 18

Financing Offshore

In This Chapter

- Checking out the mortgage world
- Sorting out your banking needs
- Moving money around
- Keeping up with international banking

Finding your dream property may be the first bit of research you have to do, but it isn't the last. Getting the money together to make the purchase go smoothly is every bit as vital as finding the house. Money may make the world go round, but when you are buying a property abroad your main concern is to make your money go round the world, or part way round at any rate.

You need your money to move safely, quickly, and without losing too much value on its travels. I explain how in this chapter.

The cost-of-living calculator available through the National Association of Realtors (`move.realtor.com/move/tools/SalaryCalcInt.asp?gate=realtor&poe=realtor`) – an American lobbying association working to advance home ownership, real-estate investment, and private property rights. This website will show you what you need to earn in the country of your choice to have the same standard of living as you have in the UK.

Moving Money Around

Having money is clearly essential if you are hoping to play any part in the property game – but you also need to have enough of it in the right place at the right time. You have lots of ways to get your money from A to B, but all involve costs and the possibility of the sum shrinking as it travels. In fact, some methods are not only unnecessarily costly – they expose your hard-earned cash to greater dangers than are necessary. This section explores your money-transfer and exchange options.

Stage payments can be expensive

In January 2003, €200,000 converted to £129,900. By May 2003, the euro had gained approximately 10 per cent in value against sterling. If you had agreed to buy a brand new property under construction in January 2003, making just one stage payment of €25,000, you would still owe €175,000 plus an additional €17,500 to pay the differential in the exchange rate. Obviously currency volatility can work both for and against you, but buying a currency in advance at a fixed price takes some risk out of the equation. (See the section 'Employing specialist currency dealers' later in this chapter.)

Understanding exchange rate risks

Any property purchase takes time. The longer a purchase takes, the longer you are exposed to currency market forces that can make your payments unpredictable. Many of the countries I examine in this book try to ensure that their local currencies move within a narrow band of the euro. (The pound sterling also moves, informally, in some harmony with the euro.)

But none of these rules ensures that the value of any currency is stable over time. During my first spell of living abroad, which amounted to five years, sterling depreciated by 20 per cent against the currency I paid my bills in. That is like having a fifth sliced out of your monthly pension or pay packet – a very serious sum of money.

Using credit or debit cards

Using a British credit or debit card is probably the easiest and simplest way of moving money from the UK to another country for day-to-day expenses, food, fuel, meals out, and hotel bills. However, you may find in some countries – Bulgaria, Ukraine, and to a lesser extent Poland – that your card is less than welcome, as the credit card charge may eat up around half the profit the retailer expects to make on a transaction. (Of course, you can usually find one of Europe's many hole-in-the-wall locations with an automated teller machine (ATM) and draw out up to about €300 each day without too much trouble.)

If you do plan to use your card extensively abroad, let your card supplier know in advance. Otherwise your card may be rejected, as banking software is now programmed to rapidly detect any potentially abnormal purchases.

Credit and debit card companies often make a *foreign currency conversion charge* of around 1 per cent on all overseas transactions. Some actually charge as much as 2.75 per cent, though the figures are fairly hard to spot in the currency conversion process. Always build this cost into your thinking when paying for a purchase by card. Remember that you are also dealing in real time, so fluctuations of the euro or the local currency against sterling, or whatever currency your credit card operates in, are reflected immediately in your credit card purchases.

If you have an offshore euro account with a credit card, currency exchange isn't an issue when you make purchases in euros. Of course, you still have the problem of putting money into your offshore account in your domestic currency.

While credit and debit cards are helpful to move small sums around, they are not much use for paying regular utility bills or moving the larger sums needed to buy your property.

Paying with personal cheques

You can potentially receive personal or business cheques, say for interest and dividends, and arrange to have them paid direct into your overseas bank account. Likewise, you may be able to find a creditor abroad brave enough to take a personal cheque. However such transactions can take a while to clear, involve some additional charges, and expose you to the vagaries of the bank's rate of exchange for the currencies in question.

A banker's draft is another option – this is a bit like a cheque but as it is drawn by the bank itself, anyone receiving a banker's draft can usually rely on it as being as good as money after it's in their hands. The problems with banker's drafts are much the same as with personal cheques – they can be slow and costly tools for getting money from A to B.

Trying traveller's cheques

Traveller's cheques are a secure means of moving money, but they're more appropriate while you are visiting overseas rather than living there.

Traveller's cheques are an expensive way to move money. Charges can be as high as 13 per cent, with a small amount of government tax added on. You also still have the worry of exchange rate fluctuations, unless you take euro traveller's cheques to a country in which the euro is a standard local currency.

You must complete a bit of paperwork to acquire traveller's cheques. You also need to have your passport handy when you use them and you must keep a record of their numbers in order to report them as stolen or lost if necessary. Receiving replacement cheques can take some time, though American Express offers a three-hour replacement service at its offices.

Transferring between banks

Having your British bank transfer funds electronically to your bank overseas is fairly quick. The entire process can be done with relative ease in 24 hours (in theory at least). If you give your British bank instructions before noon, the money will appear in your overseas bank by close of business the following day. In practice though, allow three full working days for the money to clear.

As a property owner in Eastern Europe, exchange rates and money-transfer changes may be leading factors in your choice of British banks. You need to check exactly what your bank charges for its transfer service and what rate of exchange it uses. Banks have a great deal of leeway regarding rates of exchange. The tourist rate is the least advantageous to you – and naturally is the one banks favour. You need to insist on the commercial rate of exchange and push for as low a charge as you can secure.

Telegraphic transfers

If you really are in a hurry to get funds abroad, telegraphic transfer is the probably the answer, but it comes at a cost. A change from 5 to 10 per cent on transactions is not unheard of – but if it's that or lose a property or forfeit a deposit, a transfer can be a life saver.

Lots of companies are in the telegraphic transfer game, which is hardly surprising as it is so lucrative. For example, Western Union (`www.westernunion.co.uk`) operates a Money in Minutes service in which approved transactions are generally available for pick-up right away, subject only to the hours of operation at the receiving agent location. Citibank (`www.citibank.com/uk`) allows you to transfer up to £10,000 in sterling or in the currency of the recipient account every day. The service also allows you to view the exchange rate before you complete the transaction.

Carrying cash

Having oodles of readies is definitely a bad idea in any of the countries I cover in this book. Most of the time you need carry no more than £100 of currency on you.

You do, however, need to carry a lot of currency when you are obliged to buy a property where the price declared is less than that actually paid (I cover this in Chapter 4). In this cirumstance, you may be required to withraw up to half the real property purchase price in cash from a bank and take it round to the lawyer's office where the transaction is being executed. In most Eastern European countries I cover in this book, strict rules govern how such cash is to be moved from A to B, and you usually need to be accompanied throughout the process by a guard, often armed.

Employing specialist currency dealers

A new breed of firm has spring up that deals almost exclusively in helping you move currency around the world, either to buy property or complete other business-related transactions. Such firms aim to reduce the cost to you of moving money around, while making good margins themselves.

Currency specialists offer most of the following financial options. You can use one or more of these options, at a per-service cost, to give yourself certainty and security.

- **Spot contract:** Use this option when you need currency now at today's rate. The money is available within two working days of the agreement and can be telegraphically transferred immediately or held on account, pending your instructions. Whatever you do with the funds, the exchange rate is final.
- **Fixed-term forward contract:** Use this option when you have a future commitment to pay monies at a fixed date in the future, for example a stage payment on the purchase of a house under construction or for serious renovation work. The rate is fixed at the time of the agreement and remains constant irrespective of fluctuating exchange rates, for up to two years in advance.
- **Forward time option contract:** Use this option if some aspects of your costs have a variable date assigned to them. For example, the final payment on a property being constructed is bound to have a degree of uncertainty about it. Using this contract, you can elect to collect your currency at any time between two predetermined dates, usually with flexibility of 90 days between the two dates. The advantage of a forward contract is that you only need to put down a deposit of 10 per cent of the contract value. This means that you have the comfort of knowing that you have fixed the cost of your future commitment and yet you keep the use of your capital until the stage payments are due.
- **Limit order:** Placing a limit order enables you to specify a defined better rate of exchange that you want to buy at. Use this option if you believe that, for example, the euro is going to weaken against the pound. (Say the euro is currently trading at €1.50 to the pound – you can place a limit order to buy euros if and when they reach €1.52 to the pound.)

Limit orders remain valid until they are either executed or cancelled. They can be cancelled at any time.

- **Stop loss order:** This option enables you to set a lower level of exchange rate that you are prepared to buy at – in other words, a worse rate than that currently available. For example, if the market is trading at €1.50 to the pound and you think that you may get a better rate by waiting, you can still protect yourself in case the market moves against you by placing a stop loss order at €1.49. If the market improves to, say, €1.52 and you hope for further gains, you can move your stop loss order to €1.51 and thus protect the gains already made. Stop loss orders remain valid until they are either executed or cancelled. They can be cancelled at any time.

Some useful currency dealer Web sites include:

- `www.currenciesdirect.com`
- `www.currencies4less.com`
- `www.interchangefx.co.uk`
- `www.4xuk.co.uk`

Getting a Mortgage

Borrowing money is never a great idea – it's the surest way known to humankind to lose friends and alienate relatives. One exception to the maxim, however, is that borrowing can be useful if the money is used to buy an asset, such as property, rather than a consumable item or experience, such as a luxury holiday. I cover the benefits of borrowing to buy property in Chapter 1.

Even though borrowing to buy property is in principle a good idea, you still have to be able to afford the repayments in practice. Be sure to balance the following two factors:

- **How much do you need to fund the purchase of the property and carry out any repairs and modifications?** I cover this in Chapter 3.
- **Can you afford the repayments, bearing in mind that interest rates may change over time?** To work this out, you need to calculate your free income – the money you have that is not earmarked for living expenses and other fixed commitments. To this, you can add any income you expect to get from renting out your home in the UK or your new property. I cover estimating rental income in Chapter 19.

Table 17-1 shows how much to allow in mortgage costs to cover each €100,000 (£70,000) you borrow, for a range of time periods and at different interest rates.

Table 17-1 Interest and Repayment Expenses per €100,000 (£70,000) Borrowed at Various Rates and Terms

Interest Rate	*10-Year Mortgage*	*15-Year Mortgage*	*20-Year Mortgage*
4%	€12,329	€8,994	€7,358
5%	€12,950	€9,634	€8,024
6%	€13,587	€10,296	€8,718
7%	€14,237	€10,979	€9,439
8%	€14,903	€11,683	€10,185

A number of mortgage options are available today, many of which I explore in the following sections. However, as far as your budget is concerned, depending on time and interest rates you need to budget for between €7,358 and €14,903 in mortgage costs per €100,000 borrowed.

Remortgaging at home

Remortgaging is by far and away the easiest and maybe even the cheapest option for raising funds. You get to keep your house in the UK and, lender permitting, you can even let out your house (see Chapter 19) to help cover some or all the mortgage repayments for your property overseas.

All you really need to remortgage your home is a fairly substantial slice of unencumbered equity in the property; that is, the difference between what the property is worth and what you still owe the mortgagor. You don't even need to demonstrate an income in the UK, as you can go through a buy-to-let type scheme. You also want to avoid any exchange risk exposure after you complete the deal on your home. (See the earlier section 'Understanding exchange rate risks' for information on dealing with exchange rate issues.)

You can typically borrow up to 80 per cent of the value of your property, with an interest rate about 1 per cent or so more than a conventional mortgage (currently around 6 per cent total), depending on the lock-in term you select. Arrangement fees vary depending on your circumstances but are likely to be a few hundred pounds. The entire process takes a few weeks at the most, often much less. You may even be able to get an agreement in principle in a day or so, which at least gives you the comfort to get on with making an offer on a property.

Talk to your current mortgage provider and also see what brokers such as Charcol Online (0800-358-5560; `http://mortgages.charcolonline.co.uk`) can provide. Also check out the UK Mortgage Brokers Directory (0845-061-4282; `www.mortgages.co.uk/brokers`), which describes the services of more than 50 mortgage providers.

You don't need to go it alone

Investing as a group, Andrew George and his wife Martina, after careful research, narrowed down their choice of properties to Odessa in the Ukraine and a site on Turkey's Black Sea coast near a new airport at Samsun. Both properties have their appeal. Odessa is a city that (in Martina's opinion) has the potential to return to its former glory. Her grandfather lives in Deribasovka, not far from Odessa, and he has convinced the couple that the region is improving rapidly. The Black Sea coast appeals to them as they have spent many holidays there over the years.

After numerous discussions with colleagues at work, Andrew found two individuals who are prepared to co-invest, enabling him and Martina to buy both properties. Andrew's colleagues know little about the property market in either country but have been persuaded by both the Georges and what they have read in the press to take the plunge. All three investors are putting up £10,000 in cash each and remortgaging their homes to provide a total fund of £150,000. They all have the same objectives: They see their investments as having a five- to seven-year life. By then, they expect the prices to have risen substantially as both countries move towards European Union membership. If their investment works out and they can generate a reasonable rental income, they may increase the investment in time.

Mortgaging through a British or international bank

If putting your British home on the line with a remortgage appears too risky, consider looking to either British or international banks to put up the readies. Several British banks and building societies lend on homes abroad. But not every lender arranges loans on every type of property, lends the same proportion of the purchase price, or lends in both sterling and euros.

Banks to try for a mortgage include:

- **Newcastle Building Society** (0845-606-4488; www.newcastle.co.uk)
- **Norwich & Peterborough Building Society** (0845-300-6727; www.npbs.co.uk)
- **Lloyds Bank** (020-7374-6900; www.lloydstsb.com/mortgages/own_overseas).

All British banks impose conditions on loans, such as lending only on amounts above £60,000, advancing no more than 75 per cent, lending for no more than 20 years, or restricting use to owner occupation only. They also restrict themselves to places where they have reliable local partners, which does not always follow the same patterns as, say, the coverage of estate agents working in

English. For example, it is currently not possible to find any of the major UK banks offering a mortgage for a property in Hungary, even though Budapest has a very strong and growing property market.

International banks also offer mortage finance for overseas properties. See the later section 'Banking offshore with a multinational' for more information.

World Wide Tax.com (`www.worldwide-tax.com`) has a country-by-country database of all banks with their Web addresses. Visit the Web site and then select the country you want. Most of these Web sites have information in English as well as application forms for opening an account online.

Trying the locals

Banking services are evolving quickly in Eastern Europe, especially as the banking sectors are privatised and new owners from Austria, Germany, and other countries breathe fresh life into the sector. Many banks in the countries I cover in this book provide mortgages, though some are very new to the game. In at least one case, Bulgaria, the country's banks have been offering mortgage finance since only 2003, and by 2006 demand was so great that the brakes had to be slammed on, severely restricting supply.

UK-based mortgages still offer loans on a larger proportion of the purchase price, interest rates closer to the prevailing bank rate, and a faster service than the loans you can obtain from any of the countries I cover in this book. But the big plus of having a mortgage in a local currency is that you don't have to worry about exchange rates. The money you borrow in this way will be a set sterling amount, sufficient to cover the purchase price of your property whatever currency the property is being sold in. Your liability remains to repay a sterling amount, which if your income is also in sterling eliminates the currency risk.

Shop around for a mortgage abroad; interest rates and terms vary considerably depending on the bank, the amount, and the period of time. Mortgages are generally available in the countries I cover for up to 70 or 80 per cent of the mortgage valuation, repayable over up to 20 years, with interest rates 2–3 per cent above the local base rate.

Opening a Bank Account

Banking in Eastern and Central Europe has come a long way in the past two decades. The two factors that have had the greatest influence are the collapse of the Iron Curtain and the entry, or prospect of entry, to the European Union (EU). EU rules require that a member country must have a *functioning market economy*, which means banks that provide a comprehensive range of services to a wide cross-section of the country's populace.

Changes in banking are a healthy development from the property buyer's perspective, because having a banking facility in local currency in the country you plan to buy in is essential to get the buying process underway. You not only need to be able to put down a deposit quickly to secure a property, but also after you purchase the property you need to pay utility bills and other local expenses. You can set up many regular payments conveniently by means of standing orders with your Eastern European bank.

This section covers the nitty-gritty on getting your foreign financial accounts in good working order.

Heeding money-laundering rules

Money laundering is the process of moving money through various transactions to distance the funds from their original (typically criminal) source. For example, the money may start its life as a backhander to an official for awarding a contract. This money may then be put into a property development project, which is then sold to foreigners showing just half the value on the title, with the balance being passed under the table. After a few more transactions, perhaps also asking customers to pay their deposits into offshore banks, the exact source of the cash becomes more and more difficult to trace.

If you last opened a bank account in the UK a decade or more ago, you may be in for a shock when you try to do so now. In the past, banks were most concerned to see you thump some money on the table; until you needed an overdraft, they asked few questions about you or where your money came from.

Nowadays, in an effort to prevent criminals from moving money around banks, British banks must be much more circumspect in who they grant permission to open accounts. When opening an account, you need to prove who you are and where you live. The bank is also required to alert the authorities if it notices suspiciously large transactions going through your account. These regulations, in theory, give the government information as to possible criminal activity.

In many parts of Eastern and Central Europe, money laundering is still very much in full swing. If you are asked to under-declare the purchase price of a property (I cover this situation in Chapter 4) and pay the difference in cash, at best you are probably becoming party to tax avoidance and at worst money laundering.

The rules on opening bank accounts in Eastern and Central Europe and on monitoring for suspicious transactions are tightening up, but you still need to be on your guard to see that you are not drawn unwittingly into money laundering.

Banking with the locals

Most of the countries I cover in this book still have at least one locally owned bank, with a wide network of branches. For the most part, these banks are soundly based and seem unlikely to go to the wall in the foreseeable future. For the most part, the requirements for opening an account in an overseas bank are little more than a formality; usually presenting your passport suffices. (I cover the rules and the key local banks in each country-specific chapter.)

Most local banks are quite secure for transferring money through in order to pay for a property and for handling small sums on an ongoing basis. Leaving large sums either on deposit or even in the bank's vaults, however, may not be prudent. Unlike in the UK, most Eastern European governments do not currently protect bank holdings. Also, bank robberies are more frequent in certain countries, and unless you can prove the amount of cash held in a bank safe, you have little chance of recovering your money after a break-in. One developer I know left €250,000 in cash in a major Bulgarian bank in order to protect it from currency fluctuations. After the bank was robbed and his money taken, the developer spent 18 months of hard legal threats to recover just a portion of his funds.

When selecting an overseas bank, remember the following tips:

- Check out all charges and fees, especially those for using ATM machines, which can be up to £4 per transaction.
- Make sure someone in the branch can speak and read English.
- See that the bank has the ability to send and receive money from overseas and that the costs are competitive.
- Choose a bank with a convenient branch, as you spend a lot of time there while arranging to buy a property.
- Note the bank's hours of operation, which often vary from bank to bank.
- Make sure that the bank can pay standing orders and ideally offers Internet banking capabilities.

Banking offshore with a multinational

Banking with a multinational, often based in one of the world's 50 or so offshore tax havens such as the Channel Islands, Gibraltar, or the Isle of Man, may sound like quite a smart thing to do. A lot of mystique – or perhaps, more accurately, misinformation – surrounds such banks. Some attractions of offshore banking are quite legitimate, such as its relative secrecy, the ease of depositing funds in a variety of currencies, and the fact that interest can be paid without any withholding tax being deducted. On the UK Net Guide Web site (`www.uknetguide.co.uk/Finance/Banks_and_Banking/Offshore_Banking.html`), you will find links to information on offshore banking.

However, the advantages are not usually all they are cracked up to be. In Europe at least, the secrecy is being eroded by anti-money-laundering legislation. And the tax advantages are really only a smoke-and-mirrors illusion: Just because the bank doesn't deduct tax doesn't mean that you are not liable for tax. In whichever country you are domiciled, you are still liable for tax on your worldwide income, wherever and however it is earned. With an offshore account, you get to declare the income yourself rather than the bank doing it for you.

If you decide you need an offshore bank, look for these attributes:

- **High credit rating:** Some offshore banks, and indeed some tax havens themselves, look decidedly shaky. You need a safe home for your money, one with a credit rating close to AAA, the highest standard given by agencies such as Standard & Poor's. You may be wise to stick to offshore operations of British and American banks whose names you recognise and trust.
- **Minimum deposit levels:** Many offshore banks are really only looking for high-net-worth clients. They set their minimum deposit levels high with that in mind, some as high as €150,000 (£103,000) and many above €15,000 (£10,300). For your first exposure to this type of bank, you may prefer to put a toe in the water rather than jump straight in at the deep end.
- **Credit card services:** Does the bank offer international credit card capabilities?
- **Access to funds:** How long do you have to tie up your money for, and what are the penalties for early withdrawal? You may have to commit your capital for upwards of three months to get the best interest rates, but that can be too long if your property search moves quickly.
- **Costs and fees:** How much does the bank charge for each and every service?
- **Internet and telephone banking:** Are either of these facilities on offer by the bank? Do additional fees or restrictions apply?

Banking Online

You can find scores of online retail banking services based in the UK, most of which are full-service operations offering inter-account transfers, bill payments, and automated transactions for direct debits and standing orders. You still need a physical location where you can pay in or withdraw cash, but otherwise virtually anything goes. In the UK online bankers require you to be over 18 (some ask you to be over 21) and a resident in the UK. (See Chapter 16 for more on residency rules.)

Check out all the online banks on Find UK's Web site (`www.find.co.uk`). The site claims, with some justification, to be the UK's leading directory for financial Web sites.

Taking precautions

Online banks advise the following precautions (these safety tips apply to any Internet-based financial transaction as well):

- Ignore all e-mails that appear to come from your bank and ask for account details or passwords.
- Always enter the bank's Web address directly in your Web browser, rather than following a hyperlink in text or an e-mail message.
- Do not disclose your personal access data to anyone online.
- Always log out using the bank's log-off icon.
- Check your accounts regularly and report any suspicious transactions immediately.
- Install anti-virus and firewall software on your computer and update it regularly.
- Use a post-2001 operating system and browser, as these incorporate higher levels of security.
- Use public access points such as Internet cafés sparingly for conducting banking, because these facilities are rarely completely secure.
- Avoid using wi-fi connections when conducting online banking: Hackers can position themselves within 'digital earshot', gaining access to your private account details.

Many of the local Eastern European banks also offer online banking. See the country-specific chapters for more details.

Buy Off Plan

Buying off plan is a strategy to make your money go further in situations where your research convinces you that the property market is a sure-fire winner. (Refer to Chapters 3 and 4 for more information on researching the market and weighing up the risks.)

Buying off plan, in essence, is simple. A developer normally has a long lead time between buying the land, getting planning permission, building the property, and finally getting it sold. The time between shelling out initial cash and getting it all back (plus a bit more) can be years. In the meantime, the developer has to find new sites to develop, which in turn requires more money. If a developer waits for a development to sell out before buying another, he or she has workers hanging around doing nothing, and in the process misses out on some potentially good opportunities through lack of cash. (Sure, a developer can go to a bank, but that means paying interest every month.)

The alternative to bank financing is to use a property buyer as a bank of sorts by offering the buyer some inducement to break a cardinal rule of investing: Never give a builder money up front. In return for up-front money, the builder typically discounts the final purchase price by up to 20 per cent and perhaps throws in some furnishings for good measure.

Off-plan buyers can typically stage payments over the building process, which helps with cash flow. For a two-year building project, expect to pay out around 20 per cent in the first year, another 20 per cent halfway through the second year, and the remaining 60 per cent on completion. This formula is not hard and fast – but it is a reasonable rule of thumb with which to work.

The real attraction of buying off plan is the ability to make your money go further. For example, say you have a kitty of £100,000: Rather than buy just one apartment for that sum, you can put the same money towards buying five apartments off plan. By the end of year one (halfway through the building process), you have paid out just 20 per cent of the total asking price of £500,000 (5 units x £100,000). And you still have six months to sell, say, four of the apartments before the next payment is due. If your market estimates are correct, your properties may now be worth 5–25 per cent more than you paid a year earlier. If you factor in the 20 per cent discount you received for taking the risk in the first place, you may have sufficient profit to end up with one apartment that costs you absolutely nothing.

Buying off plan is not without risks, for various reasons:

- First and foremost, prices may not rise as you hope.
- When you buy off plan, all you have to go on is an architectural drawing, which shows the layout from above but doesn't tell you important features such as how high above the floor the windows are, for example. (If windows end up being above 1.2 metres in a sitting room, you can't see out of them when sitting down; below 1.2 metres in a bedroom, and you lose privacy.)
- No matter how realistic the computer image of a proposed site may look, it cannot tell you about the environment *around* the proposed property – for example, the refuse tip, quarry, scrap-metal yard, or building site next door or just down the street.
- The project may not be completed (or it may be shelved for years) if the developer goes bust or if insufficient interest exists for the project. In such circumstances, your chances of recovering any deposits and stage payments are slim. Even should another developer take over the project at a later date, you have no guarantee that the new developer will take on the liabilities of the bankrupt developer.

Many off-plan developments are offered by companies with little experience of this type of project. Check out companies offering off-plan deals carefully. Ask to see details of previous projects, and try to talk to a number of their clients who have bought through them. Ask several estate agents for their opinions of the company.

Chapter 19

Renting and Renting Out Your Property

In This Chapter

- Investigating temporary accommodation
- House swapping and house sitting while you search for property
- Preparing your property for rent
- Deciding on long- or short-term rentals
- Finding tenants at home and abroad

Buying a property anywhere can be a time-consuming business, and buying abroad often adds a further layer of complexity with almost inevitable additional delays. You may not know exactly where in your chosen country you want to buy, or you may even be less than certain about the country itself.

Renting – or finding some other way to stay in a country for a few weeks or months – is one option that can enable you to make informed purchasing choices. However, renting carries some notable risks and complexities. For example, renting almost always has tax and legal implications. In this chapter, I review the pros and cons of renting in your chosen country so that you can decide whether it is the right course of action for your needs.

I also look at the profit potential and possible pitfalls of renting out both your new property and the one you are leaving behind. Both are ways to generate some valuable cash, but finding good tenants and maintaining a rental property from a distance can be daunting endeavours. This chapter offers tips and solutions for becoming a successful landlord.

Renting before Buying

The most compelling reason for renting before purchasing property in Eastern Europe is that you can try before you buy. If, even after careful research, you find that the region, country, or even the type of property you thought was right for you is less than ideal, you can move out of temporary rented accommodation with relatively little pain or cost.

Taking short-term or holiday rentals in several countries that are on your short list of desirable locations gives you a chance to compare and contrast. Renting enables you to be more certain that the area you choose to buy in is a good long-term bet for you.

An effective way to use renting to refine your property research process is to return to the same area at different times of the year, perhaps renting different types of property. A highly desirable country location that is bustling with people in the summer may turn into a very lonely place in winter when the visitors have gone and the restaurants and bars have shut down.

Another big advantage of living in an area temporarily while looking for a property to buy is that you have a better chance of widening your network of contacts in the housing market. Spread the word that you are looking for a particular type of property, and in no time the owner of your favourite restaurant may introduce you to properties that his friends and relatives are thinking of putting on the market and so give you a slight lead before they come on to general release.

For more information on rental contracts, see the section 'Checking the agreement' later in this chapter.

The principal disadvantage of renting really only comes into play if you are investing in property in a sharply rising market or one with a great scarcity of the type of property you are looking for. In these markets, you may miss out on the type of property you're most interested in purchasing, or maybe the type of property you're seeking just doesn't exist yet.

The following sections offer advice for locating rentals – as well as non-traditional ideas for temporarily locating to an area in which you're interested in purchasing property.

Searching for rental properties

Throughout Eastern Europe, properties for rent are advertised in the local papers and in estate agents' windows. Also check out small ads in shop windows and notice boards in supermarkets, colleges, and universities for desirable proprieties.

Of course, you don't have to wait until you get to your chosen country to hunt out a place to rent short or long term. Look at any of the newspapers, magazines, and Web sites you're using to find properties to buy for help in identifying potential rentals. (I describe these publications in general in Chapter 3 and offer country-specific recommendations throughout Parts II and III.)

When I bought my first overseas property, I asked a local estate agent to find me a house to rent while I looked around the region. The agent appreciated my request because he was able to do one of his clients a favour by finding them a temporary tenant. And he eventually did himself a favour by selling me a house. So consider pumping your lawyer, estate agent, or anyone else you are going to use as part of your house-search team to help you locate rental properties. (I describe each of these contacts in greater detail in Chapter 3.)

If you think you may need months rather than weeks to find a property to buy, consider your creature comforts carefully. You don't want your first experience of living in a new country to be soured by renting unseen a place that turns out to be a disaster. Consider taking a room at a reliable hotel or renting a holiday apartment for a week or two while you look around for somewhere to rent longer term.

Exploring other temporary residence options

If renting a home or flat doesn't make sense for your circumstances – perhaps you plan to move around a country frequently – you can consider other ways to find short- to longer-term lodgings in Eastern Europe by living in a hotel, agreeing to house sit, or participating in a house-swap programme.

Living in a hotel

If you want to see and experience a number of different areas of a country or countries before you settle down to the serious business of buying a property, you can always stay in hotels. All the countries I cover in this book are awash with inexpensive places to stay for a few days, weeks, or months – without having to commit yourself to renting an apartment or villa for months at a time.

At the lower end of the scale, staying in a room in a private house can cost as little as €5 (£3.5) a night, while a two-star hotel with half board runs to €15–€35

(£10–24) a night. You can knock off as much as 40 per cent of these costs by staying for a week or more outside of high season.

I give country-specific hotel resources throughout Parts II and III. You can also check for bargain hotel breaks on Web sites such as the following:

- www.expedia.com
- www.lastminute.com
- www.travelocity.com

Some new search engines – operating on the principle of 'search with us, book with them' – claim to be even more efficient at sniffing out bargain hotel rooms. These sites include:

- www.kayak.com
- www.mobisso.com
- www.sidestep.com

House sitting for someone else

House sitting is an arrangement in which you live in a home while the owners are away. In exchange for free accommodation, house sitters typically perform specified duties to care for the home, garden, pool, and pets. The homeowner gets the benefits of having an occupied and hence safer home, while enjoying consistent maintenance of their property.

Homeowners typically expect house sitters to:

- Accept total responsibility of caring for their homes, including pets, gardens, and pool areas.
- Maintain the same standard of care for their homes and pets as house sitters would for themselves.
- Take all reasonable steps to ensure the safety and security of their homes, premises, and contents at all times.

House sitters can usually expect to pay for the utilities they use (electricity, gas, phone, and so on). Other recurring bills such as local or property taxes usually remain the responsibility of the owner. For more information on house-sitting agreements, see the section 'Checking the agreement' later in this chapter.

Useful Web sites of organisations that arrange suitable matches between homeowners and house sitters include the following:

- www.caretaker.org
- www.housesitworld.com
- www.housecarers.com

House-sitting organisations offer various levels of service to put you in contact with property owners looking for house sitters. Most are subscription-based services, so take care to establish that the service has clients in the country you are interested in before you sign up and commit any money. Fees are usually fairly modest, with €50–100 (£34–69) being the norm.

Rather than working with an organisation, you can also plug away at your network of contacts in the area where you're interested in staying. Your estate agent, lawyer, or translator may want a house sitter for his or her house or know someone else who does. (See Chapter 3, where I cover various people to include in your property-hunting network.)

You may also want to advertise that you're interesting in serving as a house sitter in one of the many English-language newspapers or Web sites in the country of your choice. I cover these media in each country-specific chapter.

House swapping

The idea of home-exchange holidays was developed in the 1950s when Dutch and Swiss teachers began to exchange homes during the long summer holidays, although an American firm, Intervac, lays claim to starting the idea as a business in 1953. The Internet has given the concept an enormous boost, and now you can find literally hundreds of house-swapping businesses. Worldwide, an estimated 100,000 house swaps are orchestrated each year – a figure that is growing exponentially.

Home exchanges generally operate as membership clubs run by agencies with a network of properties around the world. Some, such as Intervac, have staff in more than 30 countries that assist clients over the telephone, in person, or online.

To participate in a home-exchange programme, members submit brief descriptions and photographs of their house, as well as information about locations they are interested in visiting and dates they'd like to travel. Lengths of stay range from a few weeks to several months, but some listings are for a year or more. These details are then placed on a Web site that anyone can view for free, but only subscribing members can actually contact other homeowners.

Rather like a dating agency, the success of these schemes is based on having a very large database of people with homes to swap. In theory, by charging a membership fee, usually somewhere between €50 and €100 (£34–69), only reasonably serious people sign up.

The effectiveness of house swapping depends on the area you're interested in exchanging your UK home for. For example, a month in your British home may be appealing to a homeowner in Cyprus or Malta, but you may find fewer takers from, say, Ukraine or Croatia, nations that have some visa restrictions on inward travel to the UK. Having a single end destination in mind probably means you need to join several networks in order to find a suitable range of properties from which to choose.

After you find a suitable partner with a house to exchange, follow up with e-mails or phone calls, sharing sufficient information for both sides feel to feel happy. When both parties are ready, exchange a formal signed agreement, usually on a standard form that the agency supplies.

House swappers usually pay domestic bills on a reciprocal basis, though you should confirm this agreement in writing, as well as insurance cover. Inform your household insurers before swapping, but generally they accept that a home is at less risk of burglary when occupied and do not charge extra. For more information on house-swapping agreements, see the section 'Checking the agreement' later in this chapter.

You are unlikely to want to swap cars, as motor insurance is a very personal matter, but this too is a possibility in the house-swap arena.

Useful Web sites for more information about house swapping include:

- `www.dialanechange.com`
- `www.escapeartist.com`
- `www.swaphouse.org/eng`
- `www.exchangehomes.com`
- `www.intervac.co.uk`

Consider tapping into your network for prospective swappers. (See Chapter 3 for more information on developing your property-searching network.) You can also advertise in English-language papers or Web sites in the country of your choice. I cover media resources in each country-specific chapter.

Checking the agreement

Rental agreements for private properties vary from country to country, but for the most part they are standardised legal documents. The sidebar 'Rental contracts 101' covers basic language for most rental agreements.

If you are uncertain about any terms in a contract, have the document checked out by a lawyer before signing it. I cover how to find a lawyer in each country-specific chapter.

The agreements for house swapping and house sitting are more akin to a holiday let agreement. (See the later section 'Understanding the holiday market'.) You can also find guidelines and standard agreements for these transactions on any of the Web sites that facilitate house swaps or house sitting.

Taking inventory

Whether swapping, sitting, or renting, take a full inventory of the property and all its fixtures and furnishings, noting the condition of key items. Renters are typically expected to put up a deposit as a guarantee against damages, so taking a thorough inventory is in the interests of both landlord and tenant. Get the inventory signed and dated by both parties and keep it safe along with the rental contract.

Most estate agents involved in a rental transaction are responsible for taking the inventory as part of their usual services. They often make a small charge for the work, usually around €40–60 (£28–41), both on moving in and moving out.

Lawpack (`www.lawpack.co.uk`) sells downloadable inventory templates, and Macleod-Lorway, an insurance company, has a free inventory template on its Web site (`www.macleod-lorway.com/inventory.htm`).

Going into the Rental Business

If you decide to keep your house in the UK after you buy a property abroad, you may not need to have it available to you all the time. After all, you can hardly live in two places at once! This simple fact of life presents you with an opportunity to generate an income to contribute something towards the cost of running two homes – no doubt a welcome proposition.

You may also have in mind renting out your new property abroad as part of your investment strategy. If so, you have a number of additional factors to consider.

- Get to grips with local tenancy law. For holiday lets, laws are usually fairly simple, but still take legal advice, unless you intend to use a managing agency that handles all these matters for you.
- Notify the local tourist office and authorities of your intention to rent out your overseas propriety.

- Ensure that your gas, heating, and electrical systems meet all safety regulations. You may also need to install fire extinguishers, take out public liability insurance, and provide emergency care items such as blankets and a first-aid kit.

Property, as everyone who is in the game can tell you, is a long-haul business. Everything about it – from finding a place to purchasing it to readying it for occupancy – takes time. If you harbour dreams of a quick buck, go to the races or buy a lottery ticket, because the rental market is not for you. You may wait three to five years before you break even on your initial investment in purchase expenses and furnishing. Only property price inflation makes short-term financial gains economically viable.

If, however, you're patient and interested in having your homes in the UK and abroad help generate income, read on.

Examining the prospects of longer-term rentals

The local population in most Eastern European countries is rarely able, at present anyhow, to pay rents for properties that have good investment prospects. Therefore, most countries really offer only two prospective sources of longer-term, higher-quality rental clients – incoming business executives (whose numbers and quality are closely linked to the amount of inward investment a country receives) and members of the diplomatic community. Fortunately, both these groups continue to swell as trade and wealth expand in most countries in the region. To these categories you can also add exchange students, TEFL (Teaching English as a Foreign Language) teachers, and foreign students doing degrees. The number of multinational companies looking for more junior entry level staff to have work or living experience abroad is increasing too.

When a company chooses to set up operations, facilities, or a factory in another country, it usually sends a senior-level skilled team to get the activity under way. These executives, in the case of inward investment throughout Eastern and Central Europe, usually come from the USA, Germany, Austria, Italy, France, and the UK. They expect to live in accommodation of at least the same standard as they enjoy at home. For the most part, Eastern Europe has a shortage of property of this quality, and the property that is available is often highly desirable and expensive.

These visiting executives usually stay only a year or two in a country before moving on. Their primary role is to establish a venture and train locals to run it to the standards laid down by the parent business. Consequently, these executives rarely buy property in the countries they are working in because they don't know how long they will be staying and their companies often pay or contribute to the cost of rent. (A further reason these executives are discouraged from buying is that doing so eats into valuable time that they need to spend developing their businesses.)

You can attract prospective long-term tenants from the diplomatic community and incoming executives by doing the following:

- **Advertise in the relevant local media.** I give details of these in each country-specific chapter.
- **Contact relocation companies.** ROI Corporation (`www.roirelocation.com`) and The Move Centre (`www.movecentre.com`) specialise in helping companies establish their staff quickly in foreign countries.
- **Contact the human resources departments of international companies.** You can identify such companies by reading international financial publications as well as business-related publications within the overseas country you have chosen.
- **Contact the embassies of major countries.** The embassies in the overseas country in which you buy a property will be on the lookout for places to rent. The staff concerned may not always be senior and looking for 'luxurious' accomodation, so don't be deterred if the property you are buying is rather modest.

To quickly locate financial information, type a country's name and the term 'inward investment' into an Internet search engine, such as Google.

Understanding the holiday market

Being a successful landlord is much like running any business well: Find out what the customers want and give it to them at a reasonable price. Good marketing and tenant selection go some way towards achieving this goal, but the safest way is to have satisfied rather than disgruntled tenants.

The surest way to make a decent return on your property is to have it occupied for every available day – that's where the holiday market comes into play.

People coming on holiday have much the same expectations the world over: They hope to find something closely resembling the advertised description when they turn up at the door. A glowing description that is miles from the reality may lure a few customers but is unlikely to foster much repeat business – either from them or the agents they came through. Overpromised accomodation also hurts your reputation when word spreads throughout a client's network of friends and contacts.

Being a good landlord

Fortunately, working out what tenants want is not too difficult because they are all looking for much the same payback. As a landlord, try to do the following:

- **Offer reasonable value for the money paid.** Of course this seems logical, but some landlords believe – often incorrectly – that they can trade off bad service or poor conditions for a lower rent.
- **Respect your tenants' privacy.** While you have the right to visit or inspect a property, giving tenants plenty of warning and making sure that the time of your visit suits them are common courtesies. You need to create the illusion that a property is your tenants' home, so that they, in turn, treat it with respect and feel at ease.
- **Communicate all vital information all the time.** For holiday and short-term rentals, people don't have long to get to know the property and the area. Provide a property handbook – a few pages will do – explaining how everything inside the property works, who to contact if anything goes wrong, and what the house rule are. Also give details of doctors, good restaurants, supermarkets, taxi services, and any other useful tips that can make people's stay better. Longer-term tenants need to be kept informed about anything that may affect their stay, such as the common parts being painted or seasonal changes in utilities.
- **Respond quickly to complaints, enquiries, and requests from your tenants.** You don't have to give in to unreasonable wishes, but you do have to acknowledge all requests, explain what you can do to resolve the problem, and do whatever is needed quickly.
- **Go the extra mile (or, rather, kilometre).** This may be as minor as including a welcoming bottle of wine or bunch of flowers on arrival. Or you can upgrade some aspect of the property that was not included in the original contract – for example, adding an espresso coffee maker, a second television, or some new linen. Tenants' number-one complaint is that landlords don't show they care, and these are all ways to show that you do.
- **Keep everything up to scratch.** Have a maintenance plan to make sure that both the inside and outside of the property meet the best standards.

Fitting out a property

To compete in the market, you need to up your game. While you may be happy to sleep on a sagging mattress, cook on an ancient temperamental stove, and leave your clothes in suitcases, paying tenants are rarely so accommodating. Things don't have to be to designer standards, but the property does have to be clean, functional, and complete. So even if you don't personally use a microwave, have satellite television, or require an in-home washer/dryer, appealing rental properties do.

All essential furnishing should be in place before prospective tenants view the property. Tenants can only buy into what they can see, unlike prospective owners, who can indulge their imagination and see how things could be.

Using an agent

Rather than doing everything yourself when renting out your property in Central or Eastern Europe, another option is to use the management services of a local estate agent. Until you have some experience letting properties in your new country, working with a professional is almost always your best option. An agent can help you gain a thorough grounding in the intricacies of the rental market and the surrounding bureaucracy. Having a professional barrier between landlord and tenant can also help diffuse potentially contentious situations.

You can expect the local managing agent to market your property, arrange a cleaning service, deal with repairs, report breakages and damage, make sure that services and rent are paid for, and deposit your rental income (less the agent's commission) into your bank.

If you own a property with reasonable letting prospects, you may have several managing agencies to choose from. As with nearly everything, a personal recommendation from an informed and unbiased person is the most desirable way forward. Refer to Chapter 3 for advice on how to get recommendations from various individuals and organisations. If you still need help selecting an agent, start with an agency that you believe is trustworthy, check out other properties it handles, and ask to speak to two or three of its clients.

Agents typically charge between 15 and 30 per cent for their services. However, by keeping your property fully occupied, handling bureaucracy, and dealing with problem tenants, a good agent is often worth the considerable cost involved.

Confirm exactly what your managing agency does and does not do in terms of marketing and managing the property for you. Be sure that you completely understand all charges, how long the agreement between you and the agent lasts, and what notice is required to terminate the agreement. Keep a close watch on how the agency performs and, if you can, drop into the area unannounced to see how the property looks.

Doing it yourself

Becoming a landlord may sound like an elevation to the peerage, but it is a whole lot less exciting than that. Think of the prospect more as having another child – a teenager at that – and you may start to get the picture.

If you don't use an agent, you have to find clients yourself, arrange to get the property cleaned and serviced between lettings, and handle any problems that arise while the property is let. You must accomplish all these at a distance and in a foreign language.

To find clients, you can:

- Advertise in the appropriate British papers, such as *The Times*, the *Daily Telegraph*, or the *Daily Mail*. This is an expensive and risky route because you may end up with a big bill and no takers.
- Build or buy a Web site and promote your property on that. This too can be a costly and uncertain way to attract customers. You must pay for the site up front *and* keep it visible on the Internet.
- Promote the property to your family, friends, and business network via e-mail with an attached brochure file. This can actually be a pretty effective technique, capitalising on the power of viral marketing to spread your message quickly.
- List your property on someone else's holiday-letting Web site. Posting your home on a site such as World Holiday Rentals (`www.holiday-rentals.uk/com`) or Owners Direct (`www.ownersdirect.co.uk`) is paid-for advertising, but you can at least be reasonably confident that the Web site is visible and user-friendly, and it may even have online booking systems to clinch the deal on the spot.

After you have a client, you still need to find a cleaner or cleaning service and someone to maintain the property. Probably your best bet is to enlist the services of the broker from whom you bought your property. He or she may even be able to help with finding both short- and long-term tenants.

Handling the paperwork

You need to keep full accounts of income and expenditure and retain all the relevant paperwork. In practice, property rentals should require no more than dozen or so entry lines on a spreadsheet, from rental income down to profit before tax. Table 18-1 lists possible profit and loss scenarios for rental property owners.

Calculating how much you can actually make

Aside from the potential for capital gain, the two financial levers that determine how much money you can make are *rent*, which should be enough to make you a profit if all goes to plan, and *deposits* from tenants to cover you against damage if things go awry.

Rent

Deciding the rent is perhaps the most important decision that a landlord has to make. Set the rent too high and you may find great difficulty getting tenants; set it too low and you can't make a decent profit.

You need to do your research thoroughly to get the price right. Just looking at the adverts in the press or on Web sites is not enough. You must get out and see comparable properties in your area and check out their facilities. You can be sure that your prospective clients will have done so.

The two main mistakes that new landlords make are setting the rental price too high and overestimating the number of weeks each year that a property will be let for. Beginning landlords typically set the rent 20 per cent above what the market can bear and expect an occupancy rate of 90 per cent of the available weeks (75 per cent is a more likely figure).

Deposits

The *deposit* is normally about a month's rent and is intended to protect the landlord in case of damage or loss over the period of the tenancy. Unlike in many continental countries, the law in the UK is a bit vague as to how large deposits should be and when they should be returned. Irrespective of this lack of clarity, the market expects deposits to be equivalent to one month's rent and to be returned within two to three weeks of the lease's expiration.

Only deduct from the deposit against specific items listed in the inventory. The deposit is not intended to cover any third-party fees such as electricity or telephone services. Utility companies have to look after their own interests separately.

Renting Out Your Home Residence

If you decide to keep your house in the UK after you buy a property abroad, it may not need to be available to you all the time. After all, you can hardly live in two places at once. This presents you with an opportunity to generate an income to contribute something towards the cost of running two homes. Renting out your home certainly produces problems, but it also offers a potential reward, as I explain in this section.

Before you can even consider letting your property, make sure that it is a good letting prospect. Melanie Bien and Robert Griswold have included everything you need to know in their great book, *Renting Out Your Property For Dummies*.

Maintaining your property

To ensure that your home remains in top shape while you're away, create a maintenance plan that covers all of the following areas:

- **Emergency repairs.** Build a good relationship with some local tradespeople and make sure that they understand you are in business too. Your tenants do not want to wait days for the air conditioner's fuse to be replaced or for the fridge or washing machine to be repaired. Paying promptly for work done is one sure-fire way to get to the top of any supplier's work sheet.
- **Preventive maintenance.** This type of maintenance is about sorting things out *before* they happen. Heating systems, air conditioning, and swimming pools all need regular servicing to keep them in good repair. Carrying out this work extends an item's life and reduces the occurrence of emergency repairs. If a refrigerator is 200 years old, it's a dead cert for going wrong. If the fridge suddenly fails, you may have to take whatever appliance you can find on the day, which can be expensive and even result in your choosing an unsuitable appliance. The best strategy is to shop around for replacements before disaster strikes and get the right product at a good price. (You have the added bonus of giving your tenant a pleasant surprise when you turn up, announced in advance of course, with a shiny new appliance.)
- **Cosmetic maintenance.** This type of service concerns such items as paintwork, woodwork, work surfaces, pathways, curtains, blinds, wallpaper, carpets, and flooring. These visible areas hit the eye first and require regular attention and quick touch-ups.
- **Cleaning maintenance.** This service is absolutely vital for all holiday and short-term lets as well as between longer-term tenancies. The person or service you select has to be able to handle the changeover between lets on their own and, if necessary, replace light bulbs, top up the fridge, and handle basic problems. Remember that you won't be

> there; you may not even be in the country. When you find the right cleaning person, pay them 10 per cent over the local rate and give them a paid holiday too. Small presents when you come back and lots of thank-yous and praise are always appreciated too.

Carry out a full inspection of the property every year and after each change of tenant. In the inventory, note the condition of every item, as well as when you think the item will need servicing, painting, or replacing. Doing so ensures that short-term tenants don't escape paying for damage and long-term tenants see that you are interested in their well-being.

Finding tenants

After you make the big decision to let out your British home, you next need to find some willing clients.

Do you want long- or short-term tenants? The big attraction of letting long term is that you, as landlord, have much less to do after a tenant is installed. Unlike holiday and short-term lets, where people come and go virtually every week, you may not have any change of tenants for one or more years. Of course, the weekly rent for long-term properties is lower than for short-term, but this is almost certainly compensated for by a higher occupancy rate. Still, the biggest drawback with long-term rentals is that you can't carve out a few weeks to enjoy the property yourself while you're staying in the UK.

Shorthold: The long-term option in the UK

Unless you plan to charge an annual rent of less than £250 (£1,000 in London) or more than £25,000, or let to a company or other corporate body, you must use a rental agreement known as the Assured Shorthold Tenancy (AST). The Housing Act 1988 introduced this new class of tenancies and with effect from 28 February 1997, the AST is the default or automatic tenancy. The purpose of this tenancy agreement is to return sufficient power to landlords to make renting out their empty properties worthwhile. The agreement also encourages landlords to keep properties in good repair and to invest in bringing new properties onto the market. The £5 billion or so invested in the buy-to-let market is proof of the success of ASTs.

The initial period for an AST is six months. So unless the tenant breaks the terms of the agreement – for example, by not paying rent, by causing damage, or with some other disturbance – you can't get your property back for that period. As long as you don't need to return to living in your home for that period, an AST is an option worth exploring. After the initial six months, you can renew the AST for another fixed period or allow it to continue on a month-by-month basis indefinitely.

The agreement also stipulates that you, the landlord, need to give two months' notice and the tenant one month's notice to end the tenancy. You don't have to give any reason for wanting to repossess your property and you have an absolute right to do so.

You can't occupy a part of your property while an AST is in force unless you have a self-contained area with its own entrance.

You don't need a solicitor to draw up an AST. You can buy one off the shelf from a stationer for a few pounds or one of the many Web sites advertising the service, including `www.oyezformslink.co.uk/landlords` and `www.lawpack.co.uk/landlord`.

Holiday rentals

If you want to have the use of your home for any part of the year, you can consider opening your home to holiday renters (as well as students, which I cover in the following section).

Most second homers utilise holiday rentals to generate extra cash to cover some of the costs of having a holiday home abroad. Holiday lettings can range in type and duration, from as short as a weekend to as long as several months. A holiday letting agreement operates fundamentally under contract law, and so the tenant of a holiday letting has few rights of tenure and the repossession procedure is much simpler than for a standard residential tenancy. All that is necessary for the law to apply is that the landlord is satisfied that the purpose of the letting is genuinely for the purpose of a holiday.

You can find holiday-let tenants yourself by advertising in the press or on the Internet. Alternatively, you can use one of the many companies that specialise in holiday lets. As well as taking most of the workload off your shoulders, these services confirm that the tenant is coming on holiday only, the tenant has the appropriate agreement in place, and the tenant is able to deal with problems in your absence.

Useful British holiday rental Web sites include the following:

- `www.british-holidays.com`
- `www.cottageonline.co.uk`
- `www.cottages4you.co.uk`
- `www.country-holidays.co.uk`

- www.english-country-cottages.co.uk
- www.holidayrentalsuk.com
- www.houseweb.co.uk/prop/search/holrent.htm
- www.saga.co.uk
- www.theholidayplace.co.uk

Students

Students can also serve as convenient shorter-term renters. In general, students rent properties for the academic year and may or may not be staying over the vacations. In practice and in law, you are safest insisting that student renters take a long-term lease (shorthold), with the rent guaranteed by one or more of their parents.

If you are leasing to multiple students, get the lease signed by all the parties, pointing out to them that they are jointly and severally liable for the rent and any repairs. That means that if one defaults, the others have to cough up. This usually focuses the mind wonderfully, with a resultant quick reshuffle of prospective tenants.

Students are by nature prone to be noisy, accident-prone when it comes to furniture, and dilatory with the rent. Take two months' rent as deposit, insist on setting up direct debits for rent, and make the students sign a copy of the house rules. Draw their attention to the clause in the lease saying that they can be evicted if they cause a nuisance to the neighbours.

Taxing matters

You are liable for tax on any profit made from rental income in the country in which the profit is made. Most of the countries I cover in this book have a lower tax rate for rental income than that prevailing in the UK.

But before you jump for joy, paying less tax is not always as easy to achieve as it sounds. Although tax authorities in the country your property is in may be content with as little as 15 per cent of your profits, exactly how much tax you end up paying, to whom you pay it, and when you must pay are all issues that your residency and domicile influence. I cover these issues in Chapter 16.

Chapter 20

Settling into Your New Country

In This Chapter

- Speaking a new language
- Orchestrating the moving process
- Getting to know the locals
- Staying in contact with the outside world
- Making sure of health care

Researching, finding, financing, and purchasing your new house abroad may seem like hard and yet enjoyable work at times. However, establishing yourself in a new community, plugging into the health-care and education systems, and keeping current with taxes and pension contributions demands – and deserves – your attention.

Much is at stake, and getting these factors right can make all the difference in ensuring that your stay in your new home is enjoyable rather than unnerving. This chapter covers all the major topics and issues you need to address as you establish yourself in your home in Central or Eastern Europe.

Grasping the Language

In some countries, Malta and Cyprus in particular, people speak English widely. But in most of the other countries I cover in this book, few people outside of the cities and main tourist areas speak much English. From buying your property (where being able to negotiate or at least follow a discussion is an added advantage) through to making new friends, knowing at the very least the basics of the language of your chosen country can be immensely rewarding.

Aside from the language of the country you are considering buying a property in the most useful foreign language to consider studying is Russian. Some 300 million people in 18 countries, including Ukraine, Belarus, Poland, Czech, Bulgaria, and Serbia, all have languages that are similar to Russian. Of course, knowing the local language is best!

Getting up to speed before you go

No one institution in the UK offers tutoring, teaching resources, and aids in *all* the languages of Eastern and Central Europe. However, the following commercial resources are good places to start:

- **Grant and Cutler** (020-7734-2012; `www.grantandcutler.com`) offers the widest selection of books, CDs, films, and other foreign-language learning material in the country.
- **How to Learn Any Language** (`http://how-to-learn-any-language.com`) is a quirky Web site from Swiss entrepreneur Francois Micheloud. The site offers an introduction to most languages in the world and provides links to various resources for further study.
- **Transparent Language** (`www.transparent.com`) provides language-learning materials for more than 100 languages, available directly from the Web site or through Amazon.com. Self-study programmes start from as little as £8 for a basic book up to £200 or so for a complete set of CDs or DVDs.

You can also find a number of language-teaching institutions with centres around the country, including:

- **Cactus Language** (01273-775-868; `www.cactuslanguage.com`), which offers assistance with about 15 languages.
- **Inlingua** (01242-250-493; `www.inlingua-cheltenham.co.uk`), which offers help with more than 30 languages.

Language centre programmes are not cheap. A one-week crash course costs around €2,500 (£1,730), and a total-immersion week costs about €3,800 (£2,630).

You may strike lucky and find a local college offering the language you are interested in, in which case costs are around a tenth of those associated with a language centre. However, teaching materials and support in a college course are unlikely to be of a similar standard to those in a language centre course.

The tools for the job

The following Web sites provide links to dozens of online foreign dictionaries as well as information on books, videos, CDs, DVDs, and language-translation software:

- www.englishpage.com
- www.foreignword.com
- www.lingvosoft.com
- www.tranexp.com
- www.word2word.com
- www.yourdictionary.com

Gaining language skills in your chosen country

You are likely to find plenty of language schools after you get to your new country, though usually in the major cities. These language schools generally offer a range of classes at various hours of the day and evening, catering to absolute beginners and beyond. The most popular courses run for 20 hours a week for one to four weeks at a cost of around €100–300 (£69–208) a week.

Language Learning (www.language-learning.net) and Language Course (www.languagecourse.net) are online databases listing 10,000 language schools covering 88 languages in 115 countries. You can search the sites on more than 80 criteria, including length of course, location, accommodation, age group, and the additional leisure, cultural, and social activities on offer.

Private lessons are another option to consider – both in the UK before you go and after you're established abroad. Private lessons can be relatively expensive: Expect to pay around €10 (£7) an hour. Hunt for language tutors in local papers and on notice boards in shopping centres, supermarkets, and language colleges. Visit the local town hall, which usually has contact information for a number of tutors on file. Finally, talk with anyone you come across who has learnt the language recently; they probably know a good teacher.

You can save money and get the one-on-one attention of private lessons by finding someone who wants to do a *language exchange*. Essentially, you give your teacher English lessons or just conversation practice, and they teach you their language.

Managing Moving Day

Aside from drugs and guns, you can take just about anything with you to your new life. However, the big questions are: Do you *want* to take everything with you? And if you do, what is the best (and cheapest) way to get the job done? This section delves into all the details of packing up and establishing yourself in a new country.

The little things often cause big problems when you move. For example, bring spare light bulbs along with any appliances or lamps you take to your new home.

You have a few options when fitting out your new property, each with its own attractions and drawbacks:

- **Buy a furniture package.** If you are buying into a new development and intend to let the property out (or think you may do so in the not too distant future), this is a good route to go. Packages typically include everything in terms of furniture, linen, cutlery, and so on that holiday rental companies require before they represent a property. Your developer or estate agent can put you in contact with a supplier and discuss any options or upgrades to the furniture package. Expect to pay from around €6,000 ($4,150) to fully equip a studio to around €12,000 ($8,300) to outfit a two-bedroom apartment, including fitting out a kitchen.
- **Buy locally.** Many countries that this book covers have their own indigenous furniture makers as well as thriving second-hand markets. Though you can expect to make a substantial saving over the cost of buying a furniture package, the quality and design are usually not acceptable to renters. Still, you can often find one-of-a-kind furniture that meets your needs.
- **Ship out your own furniture.** Packing up your British belongings and shipping them offers the advantage of being able to surround yourself with familiar items in a new place. However, the drawbacks are many. Shipping costs can be extremely high, and British-style furniture may not be ideal for your new country's climate. Also, electrical fittings may not work – except in Malta and Cyprus, which use British-style three-pin plugs. Most importantly, shipping your furniture to your new home makes renting out your British home more challenging. The following section covers the pros and cons of shipping out items in greater detail.

Shipping out fixtures

You can find dozens of reliable firms that can move your furniture from Aberdeen to Budapest – that is A to B, in case you were paying more attention to the prospects of leaving home than to the realities of getting your belongings to their destination.

Selling everything and starting over

Beth and Alan Collins, at 58 and 61 respectively, decided to sell up their home in North Yorkshire and move lock, stock, and barrel to Malta, one of the sunniest and hottest parts of the Mediterranean. Their new home country has a large British population, a few of whom they have made friends with over the years while taking holidays there.

The Collinses decided that their furniture, while suitable for a house in a cold wet climate, was completely out of place in an apartment in a hot dry one. Also their refrigerator, washing machine, dishwasher, and cooker were already 10 years old. They chose to sell their Yorkshire house with contents included and auctioned off what their buyer didn't require. A year later they know they made the right decision in not taking their furniture with them to Malta.

You have enormous flexibility as to exactly how much you take to your new home. You go for a full load of your belongings or save some money with a part load. A part load can be quite substantial, and unless you are planning to sell up and move out permanently this may suffice. Shipping fees are calculated in cubic metres, so taking the Aga is not as much of a problem as you may think, even if it proves less useful than in the UK.

Moving the contents of the average family home to most of the countries this book covers costs €6,000–12,000 (£4,150–8,300), depending on where exactly you are coming from and going to.

Making your list

To begin planning your shipment, go through the following process:

1. **Go though your home and write an inventory of all the items that you are thinking of taking with you.**
2. **Review the list and eliminate items that may be valuable but virtually useless.**

   Carpets and heavy rugs, for example, are totally redundant in warmer climates.
3. **Carefully consider all bulky items on your list, determining whether they're truly worth shipping.**

   Because you pay for shipping by the cubic metre, remove from your list items that may be cheaper to simply replace. Wardrobes and chests of drawers fit into this category, and many new properties have these items fitted as standard.

4. **Investigate thoroughly before shipping any electronics or appliances.**

   Some items that you consider essential may turn out to be totally useless abroad. For example, British televisions operate on a system called PAL-1, while many countries in Europe are on PAL B/G. Unless you have a multi-standard television, it will not work in your new country. European washing machines are mostly cold-fill only, so check whether yours can work satisfactorily before shipping it.

5. **Review your list again. If you have not cut it in half, go through the process again until you have.**

Finding a remover

The *Yellow Pages* are stacked full of removal companies, so begin your search for a remover here. The property press, where many of these firms advertise, is also worth a look.

The most experienced and trustworthy removal firms are members of a trade association such as the British Association of Removers (`www.bar.co.uk`), the International Federation of Furniture Removers (`www.fidi.com`), or the Overseas Moving Network International (`www.omnimoving.com`). Companies in these associations carry bonds that give you a reasonable chance of redress if the removal firm fails to carry out the move on the terms agreed or if your belongings get lost or damaged.

Check that a remover's bond also covers you for hotel accommodation if the remover fails to turn up on time with your belongings.

Get at least three written quotations from reputable removal firms, and make sure that you compare like with like. Ensure that all quotes include specific estimates for packing, moving, unpacking, and reassembling furniture in the right rooms, as well as insuring and delivering to your schedule.

A few additional things to keep in mind as you compare and select removers:

- If you are happy with two or more of your researched firms, try to negotiate for the best deal. Aim to get between 5 and 10 per cent off the lowest quote.
- Going for a part load saves you money, but you have less flexibility over when your belongings are shipped over and eventually delivered. Larger firms have set days for delivering part loads to different parts of Europe. Check out these days thoroughly before hiring a remover.
- If you are doing your own packing, check the insurance cover in case of damage in transit because the remover may not accept liability. Also estimate the weight and value of every box you pack, or you will have to pay the removal company's driver to wait while you do it when they arrive.

Mad dogs and Englishmen?

Andrew Smith, a former prison officer, had an idyllic cottage in Galway, in the Irish Republic, which he bought with his wife Jean three years ago when he took early retirement. (Hey, I can hear you cry, I thought this book was about Eastern and Central Europe! Before you rush to the complaints department, allow me to finish . . .) The Smiths had one compelling reason for choosing Ireland as their second home. It certainly wasn't the weather, which competes with their native Scotland for rain and mist. No: They chose Galway simply because they couldn't bear to be parted from their precious dogs. But on 28 February 2000, the Smiths' world changed with the adoption of the Pet Travel Scheme, which allows animals to travel abroad. Within weeks the Smiths sold up in Ireland and acquired a bar on the sun-drenched Turkish Aegean coast (see Chapter 15).

- If you rent a self-drive truck, you almost certainly have to return it to where it was hired. Some of the large international hire companies may do a deal whereby you swap your vehicle in Calais for a left-hand drive one that they can rehire themselves after you finish.
- Say you will load the lorry yourself. This means that they will only bring a driver, which cuts down on the cost.

Moving your pets

The Pet Travel Scheme (PETS) allows cats and dogs – and an increasing array of other animals, including rabbits, ferrets, and reptiles – to visit certain other countries and return to their home country without the pain of sitting in quarantine for six months. PETS, in effect, eliminates the need to quarantine animals to prevent the transmission of disease, provided that certain conditions are met.

To use PETS, you need to comply strictly with the letter of the law. This is not as easy as it may sound, as the law's letter keeps changing. The underlying regulations have been updated and extended every year since 2000, sometimes more frequently. Countries have been added and conditions altered in line with developments in technology. For the latest information on PETS, visit the Department for Food and Rural Affairs Web site at `www.defra.gov.uk/animalh/quarantine/index.htm`.

1. **Establish a good bill of health for your pet.**

   Dogs, cats, and ferrets under three months of age must stay at home until the powers that be consider them old enough to travel. Check with your vet for details for your specific situation.

   Your pet must have an official veterinary certificate dated within four months of travel or up to the vaccine's expiry date, whichever comes sooner. Each certificate includes the following information:

   - Identification of the owner or person responsible for the animal.
   - Description and origin of the animal.
   - Microchip or tattoo number, location, and date of insertion.
   - Information on the rabies vaccine (the vaccine type must be inactive and must comply with the standards of the OIE (World Organisation for Animal Health)).

2. **Have your pet identified with a microchip or tattoo.**

   As of 1 October 2004, all animals in the European Union (EU) Pet Travel Scheme must be identified with either a tattoo or a microchip compatible with standards ISO-11784 or ISO-11785. Check with your vet that your identification device complies. If an animal is identified with a non-compatible microchip, you must supply the appropriate reading equipment and be prepared for a bureaucratic nightmare at customs.

3. **Prepare the transporting cage or carrier for your pet's travels.**

   Label the cage or carrier with your name, your address in your new country, and your contact phone number or that of the representative acting for you.

If you want to take your pets back to Britain, you must comply with PETS as well as the EU regulations in order for your pet to enter the UK without going into quarantine. The Animal Health Divisional Office (0845-933-5577; `www.defra.gov.uk`) gives specific advice on how to comply and a full list of offices throughout the UK.

Getting your pet home again

If you want to take your pets back and forth to the UK, the rules are a little more complicated. You need the following documents to allow your pet to re-enter Britain without quarantine:

- **A PETS re-entry certificate.** Issued by a vet in the UK, this certificate states that your pet has been fitted with a microchip that meets an ISO specification, has been vaccinated against rabies with an approved vaccine, and has had booster vaccinations as recommended.
- **A certificate of treatment.** This document states that the animal is free of a potentially dangerous type of tapeworm and ticks. The treatment

must be carried out by a vet 24–48 hours before re-entering the UK and must be done each time you enter the UK.

- **A declaration of residence.** This document confirms that your pet has not been outside any of the qualifying countries in the six months before entering the UK. This form is available from the transport company or from the Department of Environment, Food and Rural Affairs.

Taking your car

If you like adventure, then driving your car to your new home makes sense. If you think like an economist, skip taking the car: You can hire cars in most countries fairly inexpensively. For example, in Malta a car hired long term costs around £8 a day. In Bulgaria, for little more, you get a driver thrown into the deal.

Bringing a motor vehicle from the UK to any European country is fairly easy, though keeping it there can prove more troublesome. In the first place, if you bring in a car you generally have to get used to driving on the right-hand side of the road, except in countries such as Malta and Cyprus. Right-hand and left-hand drive cars are often manufactured slightly differently, so you may have difficulty with servicing and spares. You also stand out as a target for thieves, as foreigners everywhere are seen as easy targets.

You can bring in any EU-registered vehicle into other EU member nations for a continuous period of up to 180 days without formalities. You need to be the registered keeper or have his or her written authorisation to use the vehicle. After 180 days, you must go through the formalities of importing the car, something you do from the outset in the non-EU countries. Aside from being a seriously time-consuming chore everywhere, you may be responsible for a substantial import duty in non-EU countries.

Getting your car to your chosen country can cost between a few hundred pounds and a couple of days to travel to Croatia, for example, to perhaps a thousand or so pounds and a week of driving to get to Ukraine or Turkey. You can in many cases cover part of the journey by sea, but this adds significantly to the expense. I cover sea routes to each country in the individual country chapters.

Making Personal Connections

After you unpack and situate yourself in your new home, you may want to start meeting new people. Essentially, you have a whole lot of locals and a small group of expatriates with whom you can forge new relationships.

Meeting the locals

If you want to integrate and spend more time with the locals, you need to learn at least the rudiments of the language in your new country. Consider joining some local associations or sports clubs, activities that ideally provide you with shared purpose and opportunities for regular local contact. Running a business – developing property or giving English conversation classes – enables you ample opportunities to meet local people and in time be invited into their homes.

Linking with expats

Keeping up with your fellow Brits shouldn't be too hard as there are hundreds of expat associations. Check out a few expat Web sites, such as `www.britishexpat.com`, `www.expatica.com`, `www.expatexchange.com`, and (`www.liveabroad.com`), where you find chat rooms, discussion boards, and hundreds of invitations to meet up with other expats and swap experiences and tips on how to deal with almost every aspect of life abroad. You can search the Internet using Google, for example, and soon track down such organisations as Expats Hungary (`www.expatshungary.com`) and Expats in Prague (`www.expats.cz`). The English-language media listed in the country-specific chapters are also good places to find details of meetings, clubs, and associations aimed at the British expat community.

Taking Out Health Insurance

I cover basic health issues in each country-specific chapter, giving information on local health-care options and how to find doctors, dentists, and other medical help. But you may well find that you need additional protection against unexpected serious illness or accidents. That's where health insurance comes into play.

Going to and fro

If you intend to use your new property as a holiday home, you are likely to make several trips a year to the country concerned. As long as none of these trips is longer than 90 days, annual multi-trip holiday insurance should meet all but the most extreme medical and health situations.

EU nationals are for the most part eligible to receive free emergency medical treatment from government-funded hospitals and clinics in the all the countries covered in this book.. The Web site of the UK Department of Health (www.dh.gov.uk) has information on health-care entitlements for British citizens on its Health Advice for Travellers page.

The World Health Organization (WHO) recommends all travellers to be vaccinated for diphtheria, tetanus, measles, mumps, rubella, and polio, regardless of their intended destinations. Always check with your GP or a travel clinic about required vaccinations before travelling.

Multi-trip holiday insurance policies exclude prevailing medical conditions, terrorist attacks, kidnapping, and bills over £2 million. More than 450 different holiday insurance policies are on offer in the UK. Fortunately, the Money Supermarket price comparison Web site (www.moneysupermarket.com/travelinsurance) can do most of the research legwork for you in choosing the best-value product.

For various special situations, consider the following insurance providers:

- **If you or your partner are over 65**, look to companies such as Age Concern (0845-601-2234; www.ageconcern.co.uk), Help the Aged (0808-800-6565; www,helptheaged.org.uk), Saga (0800-056-5464; www.saga.co.uk), and Churchill (0800-026-5050; www.churchill.com), which claim to offer policies for anyone up to 99 years of age.
- **If you have an existing medical condition**, try Free Spirit (0845-230-5000; www.free-spirit.com), MediCover (0870-735-3600; www.medi-cover.co.uk), and Marrs Insurance Brokers (0870-920-2222; www.marrs.co.uk).
- **If you intend to take part in some seriously dangerous sport**, investigate Insure and Go (0870-901-3674; www.insureandgo.com), which covers more than 40 adventure activities. You can also try Insure and Go and Columbus Direct (0870-033-9988; www.columbusdirect.com) if you want to take a break of over 90 days.

Taking longer-term insurance

If you want full private medical cover all year in your chosen country and anywhere else you may go, including the UK, expect to pay €2,500–5,000 (£1,730–3,460) a year for a family of four, depending on age, sex, and medical condition for full medical and dental insurance cover.

Brokers that provide online quotes for health-care insurance for expats and others include Preferred Medical (0800-018-3633; www.preferredmedical.

co.uk), Medibroker (0191-297-2411; www.medibroker.co.uk), and Private Medical & Health Insurance UK (0870-770-0942; www.phahealth.co.uk).

Premiums for elderly people are punitive, and it is virtually impossible to apply for private health insurance (PHI) for the first time if you are over 75.

Going home

While talking about going home may seem a bit churlish when you may hardly have your foot in the door of your new property, I have to do it. Few Brits relish the thought of spending years of declining health in a country that hasn't got to grips with the public provision of long-term care.

Going home may solve one problem, but it sure as heck causes lots more. In the short term, assuming that you have taken residence in your new country, you are considered a foreigner in the UK. If your new country is in the EU, you need a European Health Insurance card, or EHIC (the replacement for the E111) to receive emergency health care in the UK. After returning, you need to re-establish your credentials with Social Services. You can check out what you are entitled to as a visitor on the Department of Health Web site (www.dh.gov.uk).

Keeping Up with Financial Benefits and Responsibilities

Even if you decide to take up permanent residence in your new country, you still need to be able to maintain and take advantages of your UK-based financial benefits. This section covers the basics of these important benefits.

Drawing your British pension

You can draw your British state pension while abroad. For up-to-date info, contact the Department for Work and Pensions (0191-218-7777; www.dwp.gov.uk) and ask for a copy of *Going Abroad and Social Security Benefits*, a basic guide to the benefits that you're entitled to if you go abroad. The following Web link takes you directly to a downloadable version: www.dwp.gov.uk/publications/dwp/2003/gl29_dec.pdf.

The Department for Work and Pensions can pay your benefit into your bank account either abroad or in the UK. Or, if you plan to be away for less than two years, you can take your pension as a lump sum when you return to the UK. You have to live in the UK to qualify for pension credits, but they're still paid if you leave the UK for only short periods (four weeks at a time).

You can have your UK pension paid in sterling into the bank of your choice. However, remember that if you choose a local bank, you are likely to be charged for converting sterling into the local currency. To limit the damage, you can get the money paid into a British bank account and withdraw the money when you visit the UK, or arrange for the money to be paid into a bank in your chosen country on a 13-week cycle, which reduces the number of transactions each year from 12 to 4, with a corresponding reduction in fees.

Keeping your unemployment benefit

If you have been unemployed in the UK and drawing unemployment benefit, you may be able to have the same rate of benefit paid in any country with full EU membership for up to three months while you are looking for a job. You need to get a form E303 from the Department of Work and Pensions in the UK and take it to the equivalent service in the country you are in.

The sting in the tail here is that you need to be looking for a job to keep this benefit. Although the economies in Eastern and Central Europe are growing much faster than elsewhere in Europe, unemployment at 18 per cent is about double the old European average. Competition for jobs is high – even the locals find looking for work exasperating and arduous. The problem is made more complicated by the fact that about a fifth of the economy is submerged out of view of the authorities. This *black economy* is an enduring if not endearing feature of local life. Also lots of jobs are gained through connections and family relationships. (So if you know someone with strings, don't be shy about pulling on them; if you don't, someone else will.)

The fastest-growing route to finding employment is – surprise, surprise – via the Internet. Internet recruitment offers a fast, immediate, and cheap service compared with more traditional methods of recruitment. Sites that can help you get started include Stepstone (`www.stepstone.com`) and Jobline International (`www.jobline.net`).

The European Employment Service (EURES; `http://europa.eu.int/jobs/eures`) operates a database of jobs available throughout the EU. Job Centre Plus (`www.jobcentreplus.gov.uk`) also has a section dedicated to employment opportunities throughout Europe.

Part V

The Part of Tens

"You & your husband have never heard of defenestration? — it's an old Czech custom for dealing with people we don't like — Look, I'll show you."

In this part . . .

You probably have a file somewhere marked miscellaneous, which contains all the information that you know one day you will find really useful. You can think of the Part of Tens as being a collection of tips, cautions, and suggestions that will help you make the best of buying a property in Eastern and Central Europe. This part has a list of the important people you should talk to before you buy a property overseas and pointers as to how to find them.

I also look at making a living in the country rather than building a property empire, with ten ways to make anything from pin money to a very comfortable living.

Chapter 21

Ten Ways to Make a Living in Eastern and Central Europe

In This Chapter

- Making language skills pay
- Using local knowledge
- Getting into franchising
- Selling services

Not only is Central and Eastern Europe a whole lot less expensive to live in than the UK; in these countries, you also have a unique and potentially beneficial attribute: You come from the UK and have – or could rapidly acquire – a useful network of business contacts.

You have a wide range of income-generating businesses you can consider starting in your new home country, many of which need little or no investment or special skills. Some areas, such as offering financial advice, recruiting contacts, and dealing with languages, may call for some additional training, but for the most part, all that you require to make an income is bags of gumption.

Teaching English as a Foreign Language

Wherever you go in Europe, everyone is eager to learn, practise, or improve their English. Executives, students, government officials, and even estate agents and lawyers are all potential students. Their need is your business opportunity.

You don't necessarily need any qualifications to teach your own language – though people usually take your business proposition more seriously and may even pay you more if you are qualified.

The best-known teaching qualification in the field is TEFL (Teaching English as a Foreign Language). You can attend courses leading to a TEFL certificate throughout the UK for about £1000 for a one-month intensive training programme. Find details of where and when these courses are run and much more on the Guardian Education Web site (`http://education.guardian.co.uk/tefl`).

You don't have to deliver English-language tuition in a classroom. You can also offer one-to-one sessions or even tutor on the telephone (a favoured method for busy executives who want conversation practice from their office desk).

Market your services through the English-language media listed in each country-specific chapter in this book, or rely on word of mouth through the people you come into contact with while searching for and buying a property. You may also find people and organisations that teach the language of your new country and be able to work out a deal to exchange potential client information. I cover some of these types of organisations in Chapter 19.

You can also look on sites such as Teflnet (`www.tefl.net`) and Tefl.com (`www.tefl.com`), which alone carries details of 191,000 jobs in 185 countries. These sites also include details of how to prepare lesson plans and offer other teaching aids.

Taking Up a Franchise

Eastern and Central Europe has more than 200 franchise chains, operating through some 10,0000 outlets, generating sales in excess of £1 billion. *Franchising* is a marketing technique that improves and expands the distribution of a product or service. The *franchisor* supplies the product or teaches the service to the *franchisee*, who in turn sells it to the public. The franchisee pays a fee and a continuing royalty to the franchisor, based usually on turnover. Franchisees may also be required to buy materials or ingredients from the franchisor, giving the franchisor an additional income stream.

The advantage to franchisees is a relatively safe and quick way of getting into business, but with the support and advice of an experienced organisation close at hand. Franchisors can expand their distribution with the minimum strain on their own capital and have the services of a highly motivated team of owner-managers.

Franchising is not a path to great riches; nor is it for the truly independent spirit, as policy and profits still come from 'on high'. But franchising can be a good first step into self-employment if you have business knowledge but no actual experience of running a business – often the case for someone looking to do something after a corporate career.

However, while franchising eliminates some of the more costly and at times disastrous bumps in the learning curve of working for yourself, it is not without risks. Wild claims are made about how much safer a franchise is compared with a conventional start-up. While the long established big franchise chains are relatively safe, smaller and newer ones are as vulnerable as any other venture in its early formative years.

The British Franchise Association (01491-578-050; `www.british-franchise.org`) provides full information on British and international franchising associations.

Selling Franchises

A twist on the franchise route is to sell the idea to others. Selling franchises is easier if you have some experience with the franchise itself, but not having that experience may not be a barrier. The way franchise selling works is that you take out a *master franchise* for a company that wants to expand into the country you are in. You become the person on the ground who helps get the franchise started in the new country and has the exclusive right to sell the franchise in the area or country. You and the franchisor share royalties based on the sales made by your franchisees.

You can find franchisors who may be interested in hiring franchise salespeople through the British Franchising Association (01491-578-050; `www.british-franchise.org`).

Becoming a Tour Guide

After you master your way around parts of your new country, you have a marketable asset. You can show other people around, and as an English speaker you have a unique advantage as more than half of all tourists speak or at least understand English.

You don't need to attend any special classes or undertake training to become a guide, but you do need to know all the relevant facts and history of the main tourist sites and attractions in the region. In some countries you have to be licensed, much as black-cab drivers are licensed in London. You can find out more about becoming a tourist guide and whether a particular country has a tourist guide association by visiting the Web site of the World Federation of Tourist Guides Association (WFTGA; www.wftga.org). Organisations such as the WFTGA and Global Guides (www.globalguides.com) offer help with marketing your services.

Running an Expat News Sheet

One of the most useful organisations for foreigners trying to find their feet abroad is an expat network. Some countries have one or more well-developed networks, and online newsletters often hold together these groups. Newsletter quality varies from something similar to a competent parish newsletter to slick and professional magazines. Check out your competition thoroughly and figure out what you can do better or differently.

You need four components to make a news sheet operation work: Basic Internet and computer skills, content, readership, and a business model.

To generate readership, you first need a catchy and explicit title guaranteed to comes up high in search engine listings. Including the country name and the word 'expat' usually does the trick. Also you can start to build up your own e-mail database using techniques such as viral marketing in which you send out e-mails to your contacts with a compelling message that they just have to pass on to their network with information on your newsletter.

Coming up with a business model – how you make money – is the trickiest part. The usual way is by selling advertising space. A harder way to sell space is to approach lawyers, estate agents, translators, and others with an interest in promoting their wares to the expat community. An easier way is to carry small ads for apartments to rent, various services, jobs offered and wanted, and – the real money spinner – dating.

My Newsletter Builder (www.mynewsletterbuilder.com) and Constant Contact (http://search.constantcontact.com) provide software and support for online newsletter publishers. Both offer 60-day free trials.

Offering Translation Services

Theoretically, you need to be able to read and write a foreign language to a high degree of competence to get into the translation business. However, while your linguistic skills may be limited, as long as your entrepreneurial ones are not, you can find someone to do the language tasks while you sell the service and run the business.

Translating and *interpreting* are different skill sets: Translators typically work with written words, while interpreters work with spoken words. Translators translate documents, Web pages, e-mails, and other correspondence and usually work alone, at their own pace. Interpreters work with other people and always under time pressure.

You can assure your clients that they are getting a suitable translation by becoming or working with someone with formal qualifications such as a Diploma in Translation (DipTrans) issued by the Institute of Linguists. Highlight the translator's relevant experience and membership of a professional body.

Sell your translating services as you do language teaching services. See the section 'Teaching English as a Foreign Language' earlier in this chapter for details. For translating documents you can charge anything from €50 to €200 (£35–140) per 1,000 words, depending on such factors as the complexity of the work and where you must do the work.

Organisations that can help with qualifications and rates include:

- **Association of Translation Companies** (020-7930-2200; www.atc.org.uk)
- **Institute of Linguists** (020-7940-3113; www.iol.org.uk)
- **Institute of Translation & Interpreting** (www.iti.org.uk)
- **Language Services Ltd** (www.languageservicesltd.com)

Working as a UK Employment Agent

The number of Europeans arriving the UK and staying for one year has doubled in the past decade – rising from 265,000 to 512,000. Almost 150,000 of these individuals come from Poland, the Czech Republic, Slovakia, Hungary, Lithuania, Latvia, Estonia, Slovenia, Malta, and Cyprus (often referred to as the EU10); the other new European states account for a further 150,000 people. The British economy seems to be growing faster than the economies of France or Germany, which have restricted temporary immigration policies.

This trend presents an opportunity to smooth the flow of workers to the UK by carrying out some of the routine recruitment and selection processes in overseas countries prior to new workers coming to Britain. The work can range from formal (or informal) agreements with employment agencies in your new country to helping Central and Eastern Europeans find employment agencies in the UK to setting up your own employment agency.

In the UK, anyone operating in the recruitment field has to comply with the Employment Act, regulated by the Department of Trade and Industry (www.dti.gov.uk/er/agency/regs-p1971.htm).

The Recruitment and Employment Confederation (020-7462-3260; www.rec.uk.com) runs a course on starting your own recruitment agency. The training course equipping you to start up costs £985 plus VAT, lasts three days, and is run a dozen times each year.

Selling Financial Services

The UK has one of the most sophisticated financial services sectors in the world. Information on pensions, mortgages, insurance, and investment products, including stocks, shares, and bonds, and trusts, is widely available from a range of providers including banks and independent consultants.

None of the countries of Eastern and Central Europe has anything like the UK's extensive range of products and services. Your fellow new expats are undoubtedly on the lookout for such products. They, like you, must deal with a range of issues, including what to do with any British investments. (I cover these issues in Chapter 16.) And in the not too distant future, when the wealth of Eastern European citizens increases, locals will also need such services.

In the UK, you must be trained and licensed to give financial advice. While this is not always the case in Eastern European countries, you will be more successful and effective if you are trained and licensed. If selling British products, you must be qualified and licensed. The Financial Services Authority (www.fsa.gov.uk/consumer) has details of how to go about getting qualified and licensed. Minimum qualifications are the Financial Planning Certificate, which gives an all-round knowledge of personal finance or the Advanced Financial Planning Certificate (AFPC). The Chartered Insurance Institute (020-8989-8464; www.cii.co.uk) validates all certificates and provides details of courses and fees. Additionally, UBS (www.ubs.com) has a very comprehensive guide to what it expects of its advisers.

Going into Import/Export

The import/export business concentrates on products, such as wine and English-language books, that are desirable but less attainable in other countries.

For example, Alan started out by filling his car boot with wine for periodic trips back to the UK and bringing back books on his return trips to Croatia. He now has a thriving business and two fellow Brits working with him, shuttling back and forth each week.

Business Link (www.businesslink.gov.uk) has a section on international trade that gives basic details on how to find out about any export and import duties that may apply to various goods and on transportation and paperwork. You can also qualify for grants and support available for businesses exporting from the UK. Grants may also be available in the country you propose to sell products from into Britain; you can obtain details from the small firms advisory service in that country.

Doing What You Did at Home

However exciting business opportunities look in your new country, your best opportunities for success are probably more closely related to your line of work before your move.

The guiding principles for starting a business abroad are much the same as for anywhere. Do your homework, do something you enjoy and are good at, prepare a business plan, and risk only what you can afford to lose. Check out where the multinationals are expanding to by reading the business press and then look on their Web sites for vacancies.

Chapter 22

Ten People to Talk to Before You Go

In This Chapter

- Getting the financial facts
- Interviewing the experts
- Keeping the family on side

You don't have to wait until you travel to an Eastern or Central European country in which you are considering buying property to start your research and preparation. Plenty of people are close at hand who can contribute much to your decision.

While not *all* the people I discuss in this chapter have first-hand knowledge of Eastern or Central Europe, you may be pleasantly surprised that several do. Even those who have bought a property anywhere in Europe have something to bring to the party. You know what they say: In the land of the blind, the one-eyed man is king.

Your Partner

Buying a property overseas involves a lot of time, research, and probably cost. Much of your effort can be a whole lot more enjoyable if you and your partner agree on a few issues at the outset:

- **Have the same goal:** Work together to narrow down the places to look at based on country, city, or region, type of property, and budget. Chapter 3 offers tips to help sharpen your focus.
- **Figure out whether you're moving or just visiting:** Buying a holiday home or a property as an investment is less of an upheaval than moving

to live in another country permanently. If you plan to relocate, many other factors come into play. Spend time in and out of season in the area, and be confident that enough cultural and social activities exist to sustain you both. (I cover these aspects in each country-specific chapter.) Around 100,000 British citizens return home each year; avoid becoming part of this statistic by doing your research thoroughly.

- **Check out inheritance laws:** The UK has simple inheritance laws. You can leave what you like to whomever you like, and that almost invariably means your partner. Some foreign countries have different views on inheritance, granting rights in varying proportions to all and sundry.

If you or your partner is divorced or separated and is the *resident parent* of children (the parent who provides the main home for such children), you have some additional factors to consider if you intend to take your children abroad with you. An application to the courts for permission to take a child abroad is mandatory if the non-resident parent objects. You must satisfy the courts that your plans to move abroad are in the child's best interest; that you have thoroughly researched educational, housing, and other needs that affect the child; that you have made satisfactory arrangements for the child to maintain regular contact with the other parent, covering any additional costs yourself; and that you can maintain a suitable standard of living for the child. You may also be required to demonstrate that being refused the opportunity to move abroad has an important adverse impact on *your* life. The Web site of the Child Support Agency (`www.csa.gov.uk/new/contact/abroad.asp`) has more details.

A Tax Adviser

The opportunity to reduce tax is one of the top three reasons people give for buying a property overseas (after climate and affordability). Unfortunately, neither owning nor even living abroad is in itself sufficient to give you much of a tax advantage – even when the country you are moving to has lower taxes than in the UK or, in the case of capital gains tax and inheritance tax, none at all. (I cover the tax rates in each country-specific chapter.)

A British tax adviser can discuss with you the tax implications of any decisions regarding selling up or letting out your UK property. He or she also knows about any *double-taxation agreements*, agreements that ensure that the UK and the country concerned get the right split of any tax due and that you don't pay twice for the same taxable event (I cover this topic in Chapter 16). Your UK adviser may even have other clients who have bought property in the country in question and have some first-hand expertise to share.

A Lawyer

Lawyers are the experts for buying and selling property, so the fact that so few people buying abroad bother to talk to one, before or during the buying process, is staggering. A lawyer's expertise spreads across every aspect of the deal, including financing, proving title (making sure that the property is really owned by the seller), making a will, and gauging the impact of tax on your decisions.

Ideally, talk to a lawyer with knowledge of property law in your chosen country, but all lawyers through their professional network have access to the rudiments of the law in most countries (see also Chapter 4).

Your Bank

Banks are often international these days. Hong Kong and Shanghai Banking Corporation (`www.hsbc.com`), for example, likes to call itself 'the world's local bank' and has branches in many of the countries of Eastern and Central Europe, as does Citibank (`www.citibank.com`). Because these banks both have branches in the UK with international banking expertise, you don't have to wait until you arrive in a foreign country to get informed about the banking regime.

You definitely need a bank account in the country in which you buy a property almost from the outset of the process in order to pay a deposit on a property. After you purchase your property, you still need an account in your new country to pay utility bills and operating expenses and for cost-effective day-to-day transactions. (Using a British credit card is a costly way to operate for anything longer than a holiday.) See also Chapter 18.

Your Best Friend

One person who knows you well and has little or nothing to gain in your buying a property abroad is a close friend. He or she can bring an impartial opinion to bear on the whole project. For example, a good friend knows whether you are really the type of person who can undertake a major building project or who can settle down easily and enjoy life in a remote, albeit beautiful and inexpensive, village.

The greater the difference between the property you are considering buying and the one you live in now, the more valuable a friend's insights can be. In the excitement of considering a change, you may not really grasp what relocating to another country can mean in practice. A good friend can also shed some light on how your partner, children, and other important family members may react to your plans.

Your Neighbours

If you are going to be away for longer than a month at a time from your property either in the UK or abroad, consider involving your neighbours (so long as they are not likely to gossip). Their reward can be a bottle or two of the local alcoholic speciality or the prospects of a holiday in your property.

Your neighbours can help with the following:

- **Creating a feeling of occupancy**. This can include coming into your home, opening and closing different curtains, and turning on and off various lights.
- **Collecting and forwarding post**, especially in areas where the postal service does not offer do this. Post lying around under a letterbox is a welcome sign to burglars and squatters. In the UK, you can get post forwarded for any period from three months to two years, for about £40 a year.
- **Contacting you** or your plumber, electrician, or builder should an emergency occur.
- **Looking after your garden**. A neglected garden is an invitation to thieves and takes twice as long to get back into shape when you return. If you are going to be away often, consider changing your garden completely to a low-maintenance format.
- **Starting and running your car periodically**. If you are leaving a car behind, have someone move it so that it does not rest on the same part of the tyres. Your battery may go flat unless someone runs the car for fairly long periods, so be prepared to recharge it.

A Builder

Builders can help you with two important aspects of buying a new property – and they don't have to be in the country in question.

If you are keeping on your British property, talk with a builder about ways to put the property on a low-maintenance footing. For example, a 'frost' cut-in on your central heating boiler is an inexpensive addition that can prevent your pipes from bursting, which would cause untold damage, grief, and possible expense.

You can also use a builder in the UK to estimate renovation or repair costs for a property you are looking to buy.

Do some spadework yourself before any discussion with a builder so that you can get more out of your meeting. The What Price Web site (`www.whatprice.co.uk/buildings.html`) provides cost estimates for all kinds of building work, from general home improvement to completely building a new home. The cost estimates are for the UK, so expect to pay between a half and a third of those figures across Eastern and Central Europe. Alternatively you can check out books and software for estimating building costs at the Chartered Institute of Building online bookshop (`www.constructionbooksdirect.com`).

The Smartest Person You Know

Smart is a difficult term to define. Someone with a PhD or who is great at crosswords and pub quizzes is not enough. You need someone who is successful in some business sphere. After all, even if you're just purchasing one property to serve as a holiday home, one of your goals is still to make a profitable investment.

Dig around in your network of friends and contacts until you find someone who has made a pile of dough out of property. (I cover ways to work up a network in Chapter 3.) After you convince this person that you don't want a loan, try to have at least a telephone conversation and ideally a meeting with him or her. A drink or a meal usually lubricates the wheels here.

Before your meeting, arm yourself with a few questions, such as:

- How did you carry out your first successful property project?
- What were the biggest problems you encountered?
- What lessons would you pass on to a novice property tycoon?
- What people and organisations were of the greatest use to you?

Someone Who Already Owns Property in Eastern Europe

Finding someone who has done something similar to what you have in mind in the country of your choice can give you tons of useful information before you set off on your quest. Ideally, you want someone who is a lot further down the line and has gone through the whole purchase process.

Don't despair if no one in your network springs to mind. You are almost certain to meet someone while attending property exhibitions (see Chapter 3). While working with the brokers whose properties you are considering, ask if they can put you in contact with a British client who bought through them last year. If they don't have one, look for a broker who has – after all, you don't want to both be learning on the job.

Brokers may tell you that client contact details are confidential and they can't just give out information to anyone. That's fair enough, but you are not anyone. You are a prospective client, potentially worth a few thousand pounds in commission if you buy a property. At the very least, a broker should be willing to pass your contact details and information request on to his or her client. Keep approaching brokers until you find one who plays ball.

After you connect with a successful property purchaser, talk on the phone or e-mail him or her, starting with the questions I outline in the preceding section 'The Smartest Person You Know'.

A Financial Adviser

Back in 2004, self-invested pension schemes (SIPPs) were originally supposed to include overseas residential property in the allowable asset class. This allowance would have made buying overseas property very attractive indeed, effectively knocking off 26–40 per cent, depending on your tax rate. At the last gasp the Chancellor of the Exchequer backed away from allowing residential property to be held in individual SIPPs, though a more complex group investment is still on the cards.

The UK investment advice community was miffed to say the least as it was gearing up for a possible bonanza. Their loss is your gain. As part of getting prepared, a lot of financial advisers acquired the necessary knowledge on the investment aspects of overseas property deals. They became versed in such topics as potential profits, tax implications of letting and selling, disposing of British assets, and managing pensions and wills.

The Association of Investment and Financial Advisers (020-7628-1287; `www.aifa.net`) has a directory of members on its Web site from which you can locate advisers skilled in expatriate services. The Institute of Financial Planning (`www.financialplanning.org.uk`) has a directory of members on its Web site, including specialists in expatriate financial planning and offshore investment.

Index

• A •

• B •

• I •

• J •

• K •

• L •

• O •

• P •

• R •

• S •

• U •

FOR DUMMIES®

A world of resources to help you grow

HOBBIES

0-7645-5232-5

0-7645-6847-7

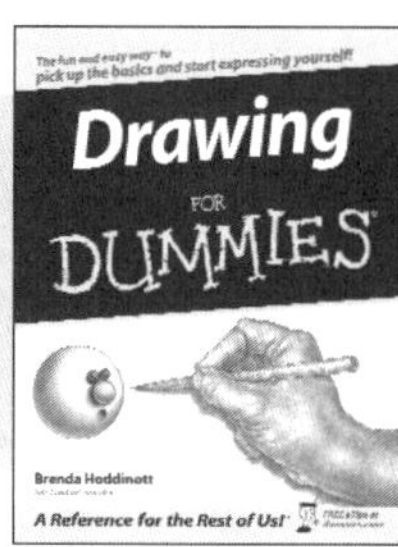

0-7645-5476-X

Also available:

Art For Dummies (0-7645-5104-3)
Aromatherapy For Dummies (0-7645-5171-X)
Bridge For Dummies (0-7645-5015-2)
Card Games For Dummies (0-7645-9910-0)
Chess For Dummies (0-7645-8404-9)
Crocheting For Dummies (0-7645-4151-X)
Improving Your Memory For Dummies (0-7645-5435-2)
Massage For Dummies (0-7645-5172-8)
Meditation For Dummies (0-471-77774-9)
Photography For Dummies (0-7645-4116-1)
Quilting For Dummies (0-7645-9799-X)
Woodworking For Dummies (0-7645-3977-9)

EDUCATION

0-7645-7206-7

0-7645-5581-2

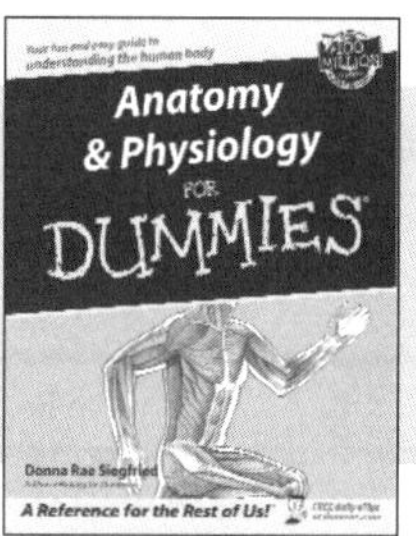

0-7645-5422-0

Also available:

Algebra For Dummies (0-7645-5325-9)
Algebra II For Dummies (0-471-77581-9)
Astronomy For Dummies (0-7645-8465-0)
Buddhism For Dummies (0-7645-5359-3)
Calculus For Dummies (0-7645-2498-4)
Christianity For Dummies (0-7645-4482-9)
Forensics For Dummies (0-7645-5580-4)
Islam For Dummies (0-7645-5503-0)
Philosophy For Dummies (0-7645-5153-1)
Religion For Dummies (0-7645-5264-3)
Trigonometry For Dummies (0-7645-6903-1)

PETS

0-7645-5255-4

0-7645-8418-9

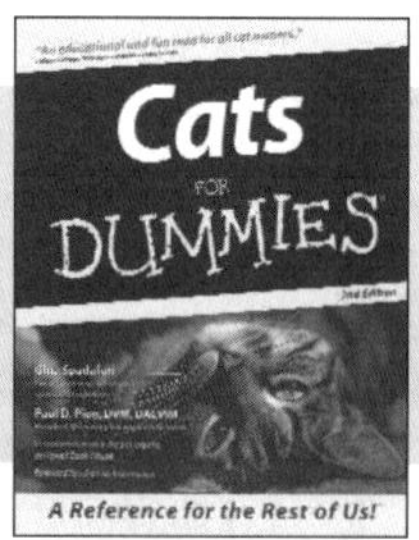

0-7645-5275-9

Also available:

Labrador Retrievers For Dummies (0-7645-5281-3)
Aquariums For Dummies (0-7645-5156-6)
Birds For Dummies (0-7645-5139-6)
Dogs For Dummies (0-7645-5274-0)
Ferrets For Dummies (0-7645-5259-7)
German Shepherds For Dummies (0-7645-5280-5)
Golden Retrievers For Dummies (0-7645-5267-8)
Horses For Dummies (0-7645-9797-3)
Jack Russell Terriers For Dummies (0-7645-5268-6)
Puppies Raising & Training Diary For Dummies (0-7645-0876-8)
Saltwater Aquariums For Dummies (0-7645-5340-2)

Available wherever books are sold. For more information or to order direct go to www.wileyeurope.com or call 0800 243407 (Non UK call +44 1243 843296)

9035_p2